Hossein Bidgoli
California State University, Bakersfield

Information Systems Literacy

Lotus 1-2-3 2.4

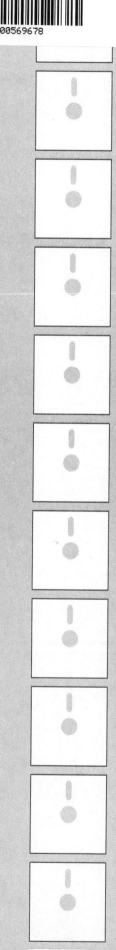

Macmillan College Publishing Company
New York
Maxwell Macmillan Canada
Toronto
Maxwell Macmillan International
New York Oxford Singapore Sydney

To so many fine memories of my brother, Mohsen, for his uncompromising belief in the power of education.

Cover photo: Copyright © Douglas E. Walker/Masterfile. Photo insets courtesy of International Business Machines Corp.
Editor: Charles Stewart
Production Editors: Colleen Brosnan, Mary Harlan
Photo Editor: Chris Migdol
Art Coordinator: Peter A. Robison
Cover Designer: Russ Maselli
Production Manager: Patricia A. Tonneman
Electronic Text Management: Marilyn Wilson Phelps, Matthew Williams, Jane Lopez, Karen L. Bretz
Illustrations: Precision Graphics

This book was set in Baskerville by Macmillan College Publishing Company and was printed and bound by Von Hoffmann Press, Inc. The cover was printed by Von Hoffmann Press, Inc.

Printed in the United States of America

The Publisher offers discounts on this book when ordered in bulk quantities. For more information, write to: Special Sales Department, Macmillan College Publishing Company, 445 Hutchinson Avenue, Columbus, OH 43235, or call 1-800-228-7854

Macmillan College Publishing Company
866 Third Avenue
New York, New York 10022

Macmillan College Publishing Company is part of the Maxwell Communication Group of Companies.

Maxwell Macmillan Canada, Inc.
1200 Eglinton Avenue East, Suite 200
Don Mills, Ontario M3C 3N1

Library of Congress Cataloging-in-Publication Data
Bidgoli, Hossein.
Information systems literacy. Lotus 1-2-3 (2.4) / Hossein Bidgoli.
p. cm.
Includes index.
ISBN 0-02-309514-8
1. Lotus 1-2-3 (Computer file). 2. Electronic spreadsheets—Computer-assisted instruction. 3. Computer software. 4. Microcomputers. I. Title.
HF5548.4.L67B5288 1994
650'.0285'5369—dc20 93-37690
CIP

Printing: 1 2 3 4 5 6 7 8 9 Year: 4 5 6 7

Preface

Lotus 1-2-3 Release 2.4 is a component of a modular series of textbooks developed for use in introductory computing coursework. This Lotus 1-2-3 text is written for first courses in spreadsheet design or for use in conjunction with texts in any course where a spreadsheet tutorial is required.

Chapter 1, "The World of Microcomputers," takes a comprehensive look at microcomputer hardware and software and their applications. This chapter provides a thorough discussion of the types of applications software used today and provides the foundation for the hands-on section of the text.

Chapter 2 provides a quick review of MS-DOS and PC-DOS. This presentation should help readers use their PC and Lotus 1-2-3 program more effectively.

The software tutorials in this book are designed to give the student comprehensive training and reference, all organized into manageably sized chapters. This approach gives the instructor a choice as to which and how many topics to cover, and gives the student a valuable reference to use long after the class is completed. Advanced topics not covered in many texts are included here, as a growing number of students are coming into introductory courses with some software literacy; this book allows students to go further in their studies.

The software chapters are pedagogically designed with the student in mind. Features include:

- Introductory sections that explain, in basic terms, what the software is, why it was developed, and how it is used. Too many books "jump right in" without giving the student a sense of context.
- Frequent use of computer screen illustrations to augment written instruction.
- Each chapter ends with 15 to 25 review questions, 5 to 8 hands-on experience assignments, and 10 multiple choice and 10 true/false questions.
- Each chapter includes a complete summary of key terms and key computer commands.
- When appropriate, chapters include a unique section entitled "Misconceptions and Solutions." Common errors, improper operating procedures, and how to avoid or solve them are highlighted for the student.
- The commonly used SmartIcons are introduced in Chapter 4. These icons can significantly simplify ordinary tasks in 1-2-3.

In any hands-on computer lab, having an accurate text makes managing the lab far easier. The best way to make a text accurate is to use it. In the seven years that I spent developing this text I have received corrections and suggestions that make this book one you should find both easy to use and reliable.

Appendix A includes command summaries and maps and, as an aid to students, answers to selected end-of-chapter review questions.

Appendix B provides comprehensive information about file transfer—how to export and import data files to and from the most popular software programs.

Appendix C explores Windows 3.1 as the most popular graphical environment for personal computers.

Ancillaries available to instructors are:

- Instructor's Manual, including Test Bank, Transparency Masters, and a data disk that enables students to access the programs and exercises included in the text. The manual also has lecture outlines, answers to review questions and exercises, and additional projects.
- Computerized Test Bank

ACKNOWLEDGMENTS

Several colleagues reviewed different versions of this manuscript and made constructive suggestions. Without their help the manuscript could not have been refined. The help and comments of the following reviewers are greatly appreciated: Kirk Arnett, Mississippi State University; Tom Berliner, University of Texas–Dallas; Glen Boswell, San Antonio College; Michael Davis, Texas Technical University; Steve Deam, Milwaukee Area Technical College; Beth Defoor, Eastern New Mexico University–Clovis; Richard Ernst, Sullivan Junior College; Barbara Felty, Harrisburg Area Community College; Pat Fenton, West Valley College; Phyllis Helms, Randolph Community College; Mehdi Khosrowpour, Pennsylvania State–Harrisburg; Candice Marble, Wentworth Military Academy; John Miller, Williamsport Area Community College; Charles McDonald, East Texas State University; Sylvia Meyer, Community College of Vermont; J. D. Oliver, Prairie View A&M University; Greg Pierce, Penn State University; Eugene Rathswohl, University of San Diego; Herbert Rebhun, University of Houston–Downtown; R. D. Shelton, Loyola College; Sandra Stalker, North Shore Community College; G. W. Willis, Baylor University; and Judy Yeager, Western Michigan University.

I thank Stephen Brown, Gannon University; Jerry Chin, Southwest Missouri State University; Don Harris, Lincoln Land Community College; Ray Knab, Central Connecticut State University; Mable Kung, California State University–Fullerton; and Sam Wiley, LaSalle University, for reviewing the corepack modules.

Many different groups assisted me in completing this project. I am grateful to over five thousand students who attended executive seminars and various classes in information systems and software productivity tools. They helped me fine-tune the manuscript during its various stages. My friend Bahram Ahanin helped me to improve many concepts of hardware/software and put them in a non-technical and easy-to-understand format. My colleague and friend Dr. Reza Azarmsa provided support and encouragement. I am grateful for all of his encouragement. My colleague Andrew Prestage assisted me in numerous trouble-spots by running and debugging many of the screens presented in the book.

I am indebted to Jacki Lawson, Denise Candia, Julie Gunn, and Vivian Cochneuer, who typed and retyped various versions of this manuscript. Their thoroughness and patience made it easier to complete this project. They deserve special recognition for all this work.

A team of professionals from Macmillan Publishing Company assisted me from the very beginning of this venture. Charles Stewart had faith in this project's potential from the onset, for which I thank him. Colleen Brosnan, Mary

Harlan, JoEllen Gohr, and Russ Maselli, all from Macmillan, assisted me in completing this project. I am grateful and appreciate their work.

Finally, I want to thank my family for their support and encouragement throughout my life. My two sisters, Azam and Akram, deserve my very special thanks and recognition. My wife, Nooshin, has been very supportive and patient. My little baby, Morvareed, has been very patient throughout this work. I extend my deepest love and appreciation to both.

Dr. Hossein Bidgoli is professor of management information systems at California State University, Bakersfield. He holds a Ph.D. degree in systems science from Portland State University with a specialization in design and implementation of MIS. His master's degree is in MIS from Colorado State University. Dr. Bidgoli's background includes experience as a systems analyst, information systems consultant, and financial analyst. He was the Director of the Microcomputer Center at Portland State University, where the first PC lab in the United States was established.

Dr. Bidgoli, a two-time winner of the MPPP (Meritorious Performance and Professional Promise) award for outstanding performance in teaching, research, and university/community service is the author of forty-two texts and numerous professional papers and articles presented and published throughout the United States on the topics of computers and MIS. Dr. Bidgoli has also designed and implemented more than twenty executive seminars on all aspects of information systems and decision support systems.

Contents

11
1-2-3 Macros 237

Appendix A
Lotus 1-2-3 257

The World of Microcomputers

1

1–1 INTRODUCTION

In this chapter we discuss microcomputer fundamentals. Hardware and software for micros are described. Different classes of application software are introduced. Guidelines for successful selection and maintenance of micros are highlighted. A brief explanation of the advantages of micros compared with mainframes is presented. The chapter also includes a hands-on session with a microcomputer. The chapter concludes by defining these important concepts: computer files; types of data, values, and formulas; and priority of arithmetic operations. The information in this chapter should help you to be a more effective microcomputer user.

1–2 WHAT IS A MICROCOMPUTER?

The terms **personal computer** (PC), **micro**, or **microcomputer** refer to the smallest type of computer when measured by such attributes as memory, cost, size, speed, and sophistication. Although small, these computers are so powerful that sometimes the difference between PCs and larger computers is blurred. The reason for such confusion is the ever-increasing power and capability of PCs.

Since the beginning of the microcomputer era in roughly 1975, the capability of these computers has improved beyond imagination. Still, some experts believe this is only the beginning—there is a lot more to be done by micros.

A microcomputer consists of input, output, and memory devices. Figure 1–1 illustrates a typical microcomputer system. The **input device** is usually a keyboard. A PC keyboard is similar to a typewriter but with some additional keys. Figure 1–2 displays an IBM enhanced keyboard and a standard keyboard. In the future, voice input devices may be part of the system. Other input devices include a mouse, touch technology, light pen, graphics tablet, optical character reader (OCR), magnetic ink character recognition (MICR), camera, sensor, and bar code readers.

The common output devices for microcomputers are a cathode-ray tube (CRT) monitor, sometimes called video display terminal (VDT), and the printer. The

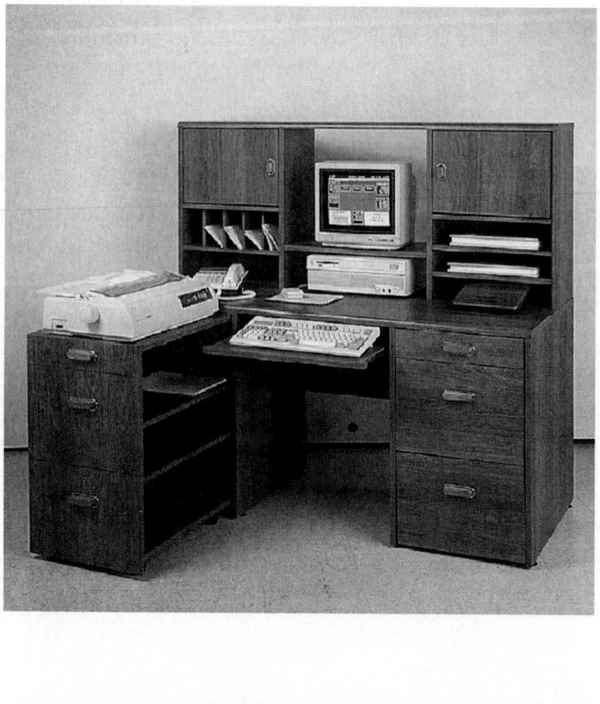

Figure 1–1
Typical microcomputer system (courtesy of Radio Shack, a division of Tandy Corp.).

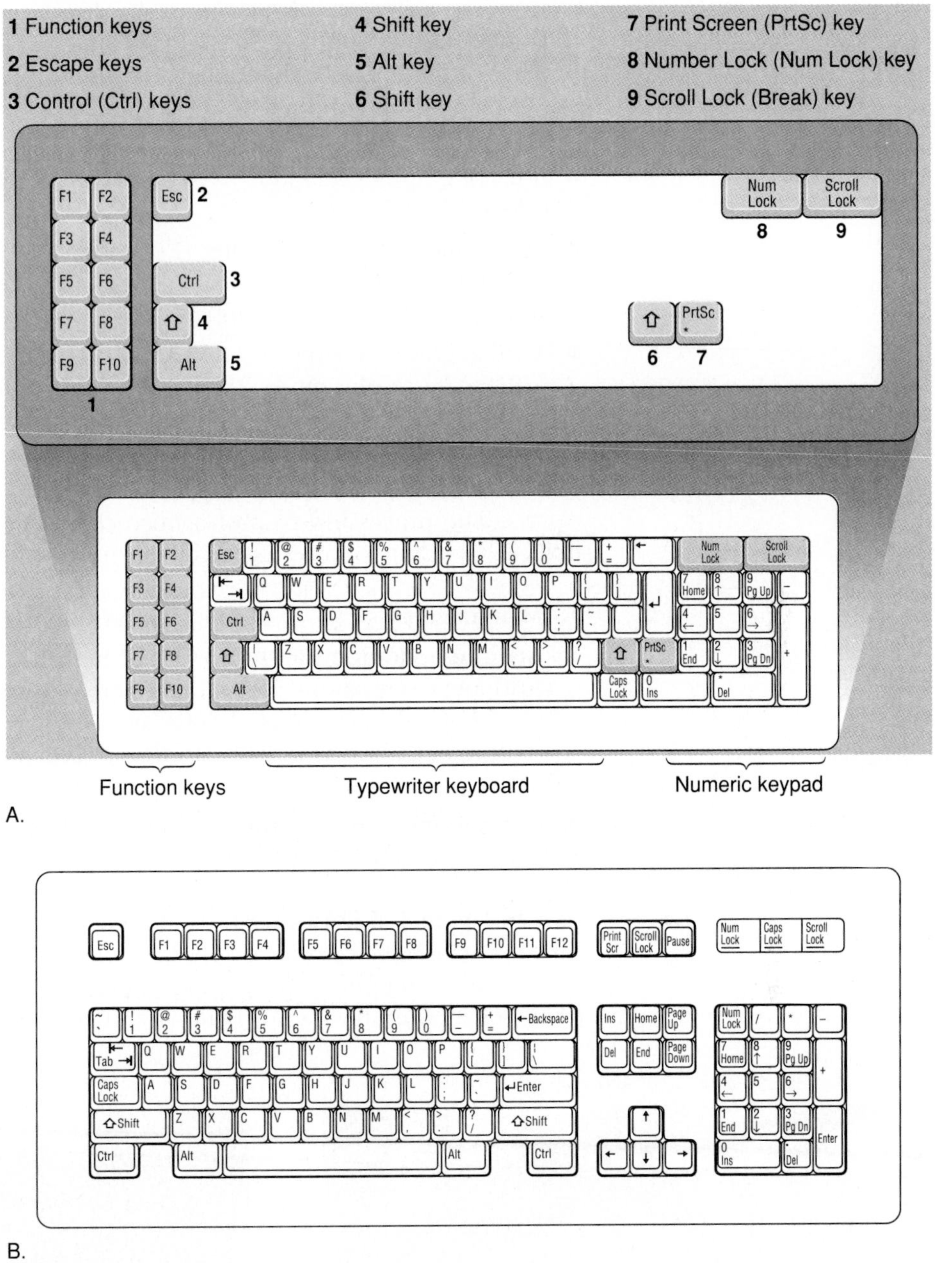

Figure 1–2
A. IBM standard keyboard. B. IBM enhanced keyboard (courtesy of International Business Machines Corp.).

output generated on the monitor is called soft copy and printed output is referred to as hard copy. Other output devices include cameras, floppy disks, and plotters.

Two types of monitors display output. Some microcomputers utilize a monochrome-type screen. As the name indicates, this type of screen generates one color, such as green, although some screens are amber (orange). Either type of monochrome monitor can generate graphic output if accompanied by a graphics card or graphics adapter. The other type of monitor is called a color monitor (sometimes referred to as an **RGB** monitor—red-green-blue monitor). It shows data in a color format.

The sharpness of images on the display monitor is referred to as resolution. The intersection of a row and a column is called a pixel. The higher the number of these pixels, the higher the resolution. Color monitors come in various levels of resolution such as CGA, EGA, VGA, super VGA, and XGA:

- A color graphics adapter (CGA) displays 320-by-200 (pixels) resolution in 4 colors
- An enhanced graphics adapter (EGA) displays 640-by-350 resolution in 16 colors. More advanced versions of EGA display 640-by-480 resolution in 16 colors and 320-by-200 resolution in 256 colors.
- A video graphics array (VGA) displays 640-by-480 resolution in 16 colors and 320-by-200 resolution in 256 colors. Super VGA and XGA monitors display more than 640-by-480 resolution in many different colors. The exact resolution depends on the specific type of the monitor.

The processing part of a microcomputer, that is its **central processing unit** (CPU) or microprocessor, includes three components:

1. **Main memory** stores data, information, and instructions.
2. **Arithmetic logic unit** (ALU) performs arithmetic and logical operations. Arithmetic operations include addition, subtraction, division, and multiplication. Logical operations include any types of comparisons, such as sorting (putting data into a particular order) or searching (choosing a particular data item).
3. **Control unit** serves as the commander of the system. It tells the microcomputer what to do and how to do it.

Figure 1–3 illustrates two different microprocessor chips, or microchips, which contain the electronic components necessary for processing.

Microcomputers are getting smaller but more powerful. Among the various types are portable (laptop) micros and notebook micros (see Figure 1–4).

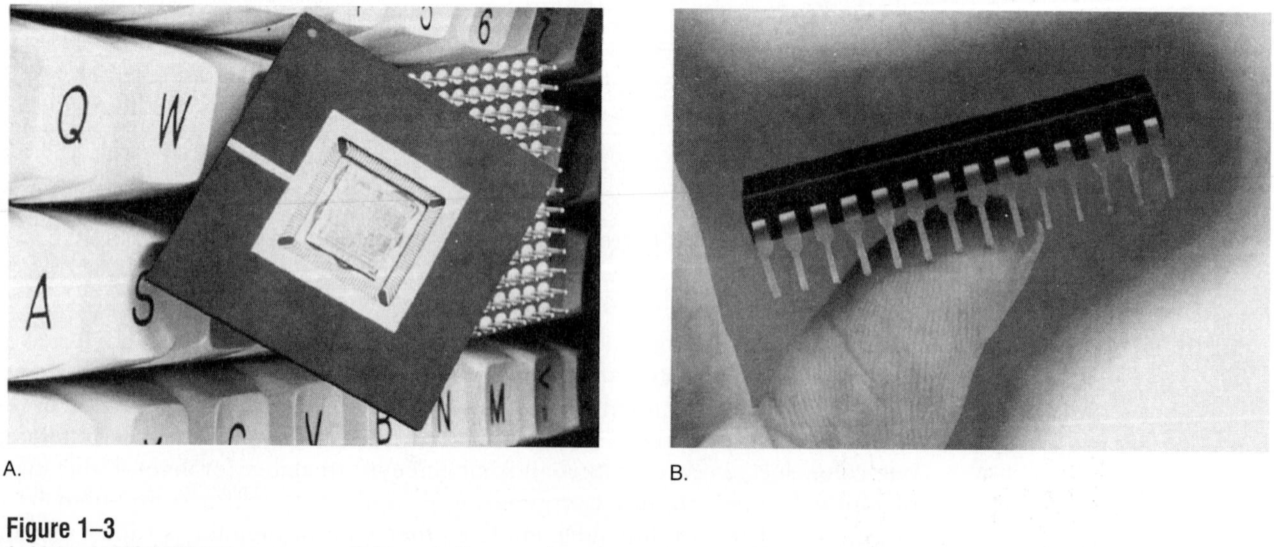

A. B.

Figure 1–3
A. Motorola MC 68020 microprocessor in its protective ceramic package (courtesy of Motorola, Inc.).
B. AT&T Bell Labs microprocessor (courtesy of Radio Shack, a division of Tandy Corp.).

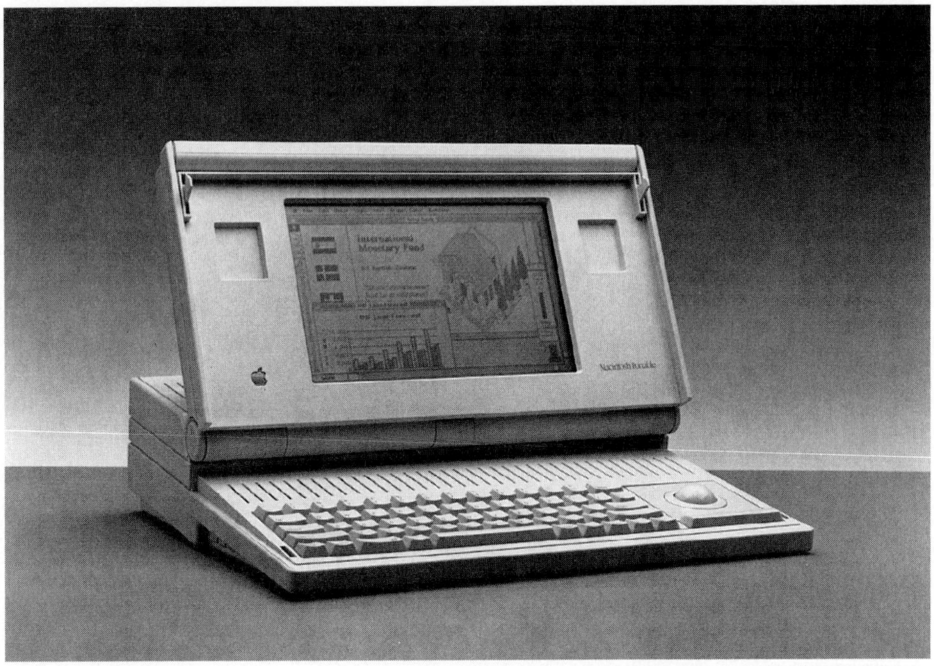

A.

B.

Figure 1–4
A. The all-in-one design of the Apple Macintosh Portable integrates the CPU, Active Matrix Liquid Crystal Display, keyboard, pointing device, battery and disk storage into a single easy-to-carry package. B. With the Macintosh PowerBook computer, customers can take advantage of notebook convenience and Macintosh power anywhere, whether at home, school or on the road for business (courtesy of Apple Computer, Inc.).

1–3 THE KEYBOARD

As you can see in Figure 1–2B, an enhanced keyboard is divided into three sections. On the top are 12 function keys. In a standard keyboard, there are only 10 function keys. Some keyboards have the function keys on the left (Figure 1–2A). With most application software, these keys perform special functions, or they can be programmed to perform a particular task. For example, Lotus 1-2-3, Quattro Pro, dBASE, and WordPerfect effectively use 12 keys (F1 through F12) for performing different tasks.

The middle part of the keyboard is similar to a typical typewriter. However, notice some special keys that a typewriter does not have (e.g., the Alt key).

The right section has a numeric key pad similar to that of an adding machine. It is used to facilitate numeric data entry (when the Num Lock key is pressed down) or for cursor movement.

The purpose of function keys and some of the special keys varies in different application programs. For example, F1 in WordPerfect 5.1 cancels a selection or performs "undelete" operations. In Lotus 1-2-3, Quattro Pro, or dBASE, it accesses the online help command.

1–4 IMPORTANT AUXILIARY DEVICES

Besides the obvious input/output devices, some additional devices are required for effective utilization of a microcomputer. Disk drives and adapter cards are two of the most important devices.

1–4–1 Disk Drives

Disk drives enable the microcomputer system to retrieve data from a disk into main memory and to store data from main memory to a disk. Disk drives come in various capacities. Your system may have one or more floppy disk drives. It may also have a hard disk drive. As you will see later, **hard disks** are capable of storing masses of information. The capacity of a hard disk is many times greater than that of a **floppy disk** (also called a diskette or just a floppy). A floppy disk can hold from 360 kilobytes (K) to 1.44 megabytes (MB) of data. Some new floppies are capable of storing 2.88 MB. The capacity of a hard disk varies from 5 to 600 MB or more.

The capacity of a storage device is measured in terms of bits or bytes of data stored on that device. Table 1–1 summarizes the memory equivalents.

1–4–2 Adapter Cards

Adapter cards are installed in expansion slots (channels) inside the computer (see Figure 1–5). These cards are used to attach a particular option to the system unit. Table 1–2 summarizes typical adapter cards.

Table 1–1
Memory Equivalents

0 or 1 is equal to one bit
8 bits is equal to one byte
1,024 (2^{10}) bytes is equal to one kilobyte
1,048,576 (2^{20}) bytes is equal to one megabyte
1,073,741,824 (2^{30}) bytes is equal to one gigabyte
10,995,627,776 (2^{40}) bytes is equal to one terabyte

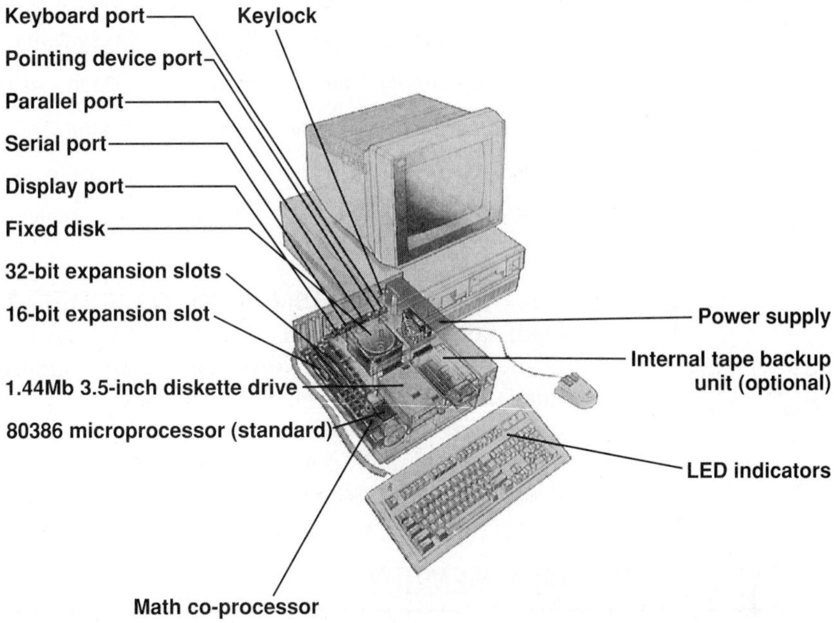

A.

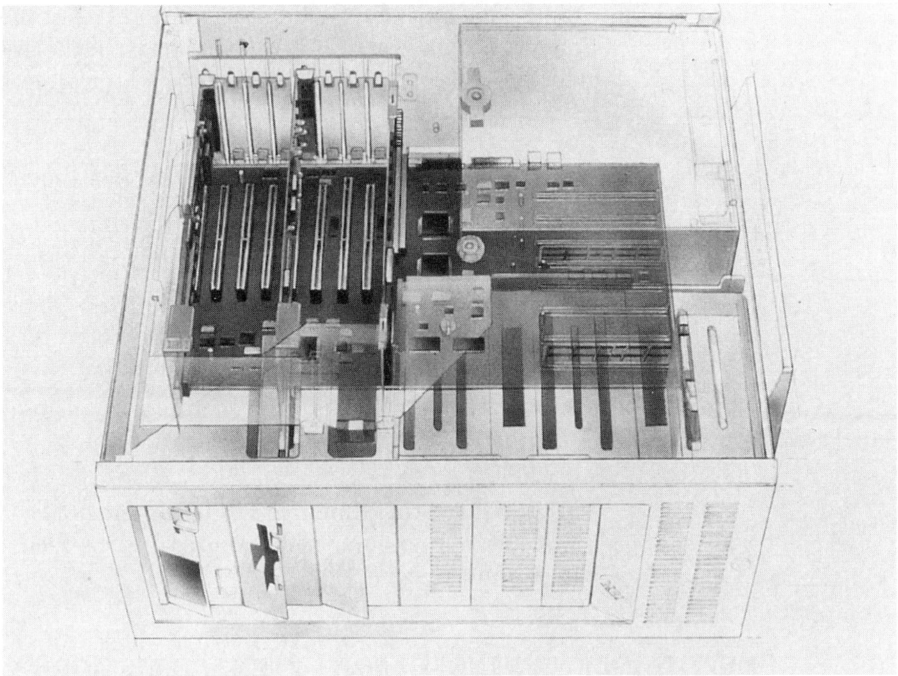

B.

Figure 1–5
Inside your PC. A. Port and expansion slots in a microcomputer (courtesy of International Business Machines Corp.). B. Inside a microcomputer. This model is IBM's PS/2 95XP 486 (courtesy of International Business Machines Corp.).

Table 1–2
Commonly Used Adapter Cards

- Disk drive card for connecting disk drives to the system unit
- Display card for connecting the CRT to the system unit
- Memory card for connecting additional RAM to existing memory
- Clock card for connecting a clock to the system unit
- Modem card for connecting the PC to the outside world
- Printer interface card for connecting a printer to the system unit

The original IBM PC has five expansion slots; the IBM XT and AT have eight slots. Adapter cards usually have outlet ports that are accessed at the back of the system unit. It is important to know that the newer PCs do not require as many adapter cards. Ports, which are either parallel or serial, connect devices to the system unit. You must connect a serial device to a serial port and a parallel device to a parallel port. Serial devices transfer one bit of data at a time; parallel devices transfer a series of bits of data at a time.

1–5 TYPES OF PRIMARY MEMORY

Computers store data in two kinds of memory: main, or primary memory, and auxiliary, or secondary memory. **Primary memory** is the heart of the microcomputer; it is usually referred to as **random-access memory** (RAM). This is a volatile memory. Data stored in RAM will be lost in the event of a power failure. To avoid this type of loss, always save your work on a permanent memory medium (i.e., secondary memory), such as a diskette.

Three other types of memory also can be referred to as main memory, but the user cannot have direct control over them:

1. **Read-only memory** (ROM): A prefabricated ROM chip is supplied by vendors. This memory stores some general-purpose instructions or programs. For example, some commands of the Disk Operating System (DOS) and some versions of the BASIC language are stored on ROM chips. DOS is the operating system for IBM microcomputers and compatible systems.
2. **Programmable read-only memory**: By using a special device, the user can program this memory. However, once programmed, the user cannot erase this type of memory.
3. **Erasable programmable read-only memory**: This type of read-only memory can be programmed by the user and, as the name indicates, erased and programmed again.

1–6 CONVENTIONAL, EXPANDED, AND EXTENDED MEMORIES

With the introduction of 386- and 486-based computers and the Pentium (the new high-powered microprocessor introduced by Intel), two new types of main memory have entered the market and have made the memory discussion even more confusing. The next few paragraphs briefly describe these two new memories and differentiate them from conventional memory.

Conventional memory, or RAM, is the first 640 K of the memory of your computer. The majority of XT-type machines come with 1 MB of memory; however, DOS can only directly reach the first 640 K of this memory. The other 384 K (1024 K–640 K) is used (as shown in Figure 1–6) by ROM BIOS (Basic Input Output System), adapter ROM, video memory, and the EMS (Expanded Memory Specification) window.

Expanded memory is located outside of the conventional memory and works based on a technique called bank switching. Lotus, Intel, and Microsoft (LIM) corporations devised the LIM Expanded Memory Specification (EMS) for expanded memory. This is like a memory storage area on an EMS-compatible expansion card inside your computer. To utilize expanded memory on your computer, you need both an EMS-compatible memory expansion card and a device driver known as Expanded Memory Manager (EMM). The EMM helps the microprocessor find a page(s) of data that your software is looking for and puts the data into a 64-K page frame as four 16-K pages. DOS can then locate the data, and your software program can use it. Expanded memory is useful for designing large spreadsheets.

Extended memory is also outside of conventional memory, but it functions basically as additional RAM and is accessible to your computer directly. No bank switching occurs with extended memory. This means that after DOS addresses the first 640 K of conventional memory, it then automatically accesses the next chunk of the memory, which is the extended memory (see Figure 1–6). A 286-based PC can access up to 16 MB of RAM, and 386- and 486-based PCs can access up to 4,096 MB of RAM.

Which memory should you get, expanded or extended? Well, the software in use dictates the type of memory. Earlier software requested expanded memory. Today's graphical environments, such as Windows, prefer extended memory. In fact, your additional memory can be configured either way using special software.

Figure 1–6
Conventional, extended, and expanded memories.

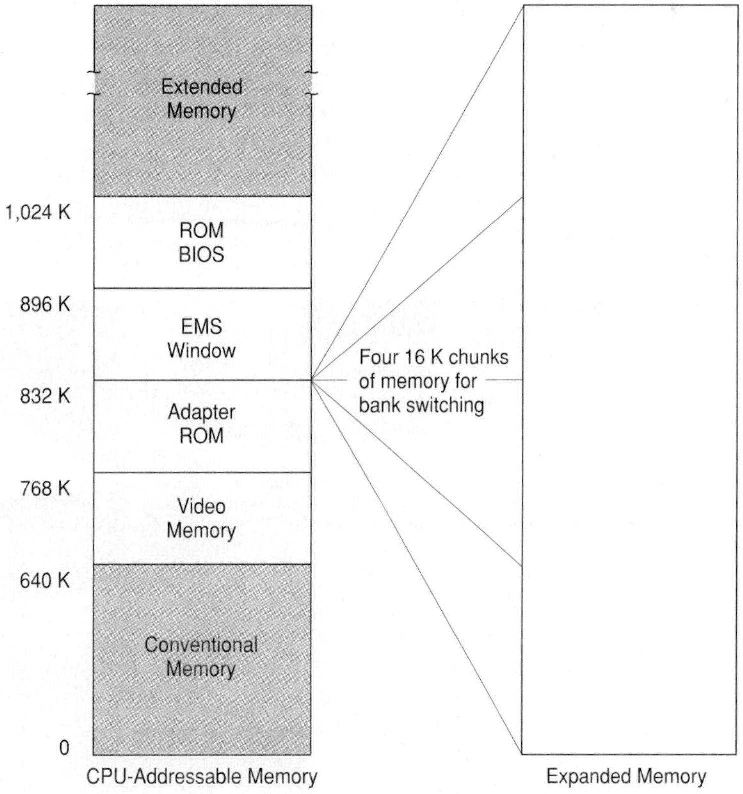

1–7 TYPES OF SECONDARY MEMORY

Since the main memory of a microcomputer is limited, expensive, and volatile, **secondary memory** storage devices are needed for mass data storage. Secondary storage is nonvolatile. Secondary storage devices are broadly classified into magnetic and optical. Let us briefly consider each group.

1–7–1 Magnetic Storage Devices

Magnetic storage devices include the diskette, mini floppy, hard disk, and Bernoulli box. The capacity of a diskette or a hard disk depends on its technical features.

There are three types of standard diskettes: 3½ inches, 5¼ inches, and 8 inches. The most recent floppy disk is a 2-inch floppy. Diskettes can be single density, double density, or high density. Density refers to the amount of information that can be stored on a disk. Diskettes can also be single sided or double sided. A 5¼-inch, single-sided, single-density floppy can hold roughly 125 K; a 5¼-inch, single-sided, double-density floppy can hold roughly 250 K; a 5¼-inch, double-sided, double-density floppy can hold roughly 360 K; a high-density (sometimes called quad-density) diskette can hold up to 1.2 MB. A 3½-inch, low-density floppy disk can store 720 K of data and a 3½-inch, high-density floppy can store 1.44 MB of data.

A hard disk (also called fixed disk or Winchester disk) can be 14, 8, 5¼ or less than 4 inches in diameter. The capacity of this device varies from 5 MB to 1 gigabyte.

A **Bernoulli box** is a removable medium. After finishing your computer work, you can pull this device out and store it in a safe location, which is not possible with a hard disk. A Bernoulli box uses high-capacity floppy disks to store 10 MB of data or more. Generally speaking, it is less prone to damage than a hard disk. This is true because the drive head of a Bernoulli box does not move as a hard disk head moves, often resulting in head crashes. In a Bernoulli box, the floppy disk moves toward the stationary read/write head through air currents. Figure 1–7 displays a Bernoulli box.

At the present time, the most commonly used secondary storage device is a 3½-inch floppy disk. However, at the beginning of the PC era, 5¼-inch floppy

Figure 1–7
A Bernoulli box.

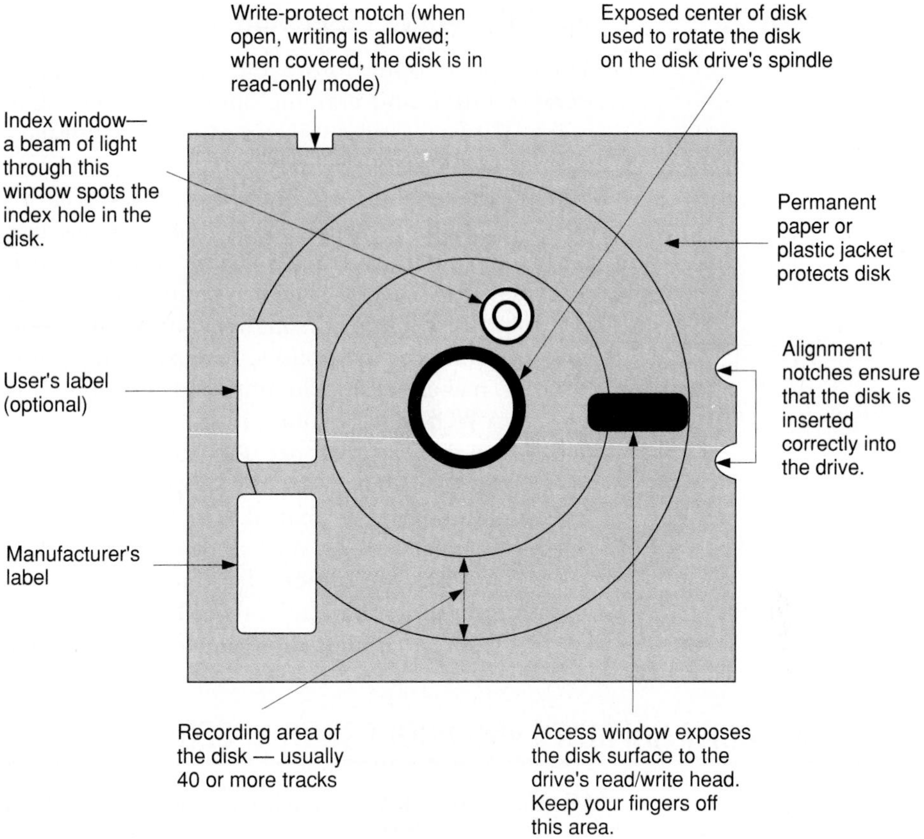

Figure 1–8
A 5¼-inch floppy disk.

disks were the most commonly used secondary storage devices. A floppy disk is made of plastic material coated with magnetic material. A 5¼-inch disk is enclosed in a permanent vinyl jacket to protect the disk. After using a floppy disk, you should put it back in its paper cover to protect it from dirt and dust. Do not touch exposed portions of the disk or data loss may result. Figure 1–8 highlights important areas of a 5¼-inch diskette. Figure 1–9 displays a 3½-inch diskette. The 3½-inch diskettes are more durable and easier to handle than the 5¼-inch disks. They also store more information.

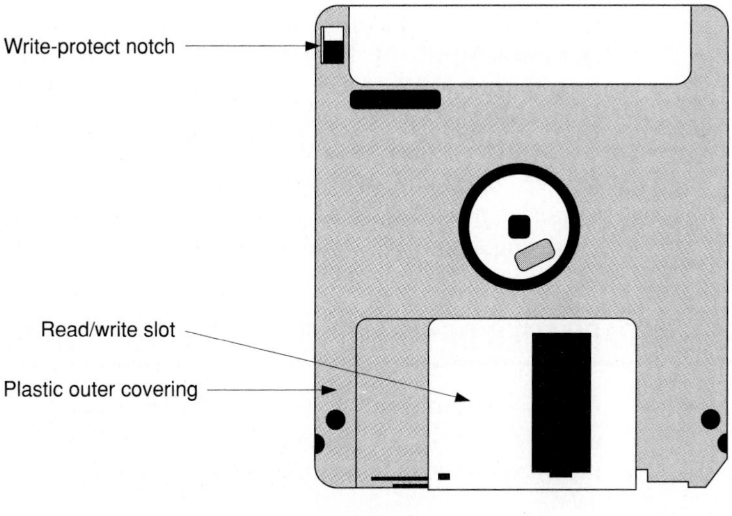

Figure 1–9
A 3½-inch floppy disk.

1–7–2 Optical Storage Technologies

Three types of optical storage have attracted much attention in recent years: CD-ROM, WORM, and erasable optical disk. The major advantages of optical technology devices are durability and massive storage capacity. The major drawback of optical technology is its slow speed; however, vendors are working rapidly to improve the technology. Let us briefly look at each type.

CD-ROM (compact disk, read-only memory), as the name indicates, is a permanent medium. In CD ROM, information is recorded by disk-mastering machines. A CD-ROM, which is similar to an audio compact disk, can be duplicated and distributed throughout an organization. Its major application is for large, permanent databases, for example, public domain databases such as libraries, real estate information, and corporate financial information.

A **WORM** (write once, read many) disk is also a permanent medium. Information can be recorded once and cannot be altered. A major drawback compared with CD-ROM is that you cannot duplicate a WORM disk. Its major application is for storing information that must be kept permanently, for example, information related to annual reports, nuclear power plants, airports, and railroads.

An **erasable optical disk** meets the needs of high-volume storage and updating. Information can be recorded and erased repeatedly.

Figure 1–10 illustrates each of the three types of optical storage.

1–8 MEMORY CAPACITY AND PROCESSOR SPEED

Microcomputer RAM capacity used to start at 512 or 640 K. Now PCs with capacities of 4 to 16 MB are becoming more common, and in the future, micros will approach minicomputer capacity.

For present and future planning, you should be able to calculate the memory requirements for your computing needs. For example, if you have a PC with 640 K of RAM, all of that memory may not be accessible to you. A large portion of that memory may be needed by software you use to carry out applications. As an example, Lotus Release 2.01 needs almost 200 K of RAM. So in your 640-K PC, you are left with only 440 K of memory to use (640 – 200 = 440).

Another consideration regarding memory is speed. The speed of the processor is measured in megahertz (MHz) and usually varies from 4 to 66. Vendors are rapidly extending this technology also. Soon, speeds of 100 MHz or more will be available. The higher the processor speed, the faster the computer.

Another factor that has direct impact on speed is the word size of the processor. Word size indicates the number of characters that can be processed simultaneously. Word size varies from 8 to 32 bits for microcomputers. The bigger the word size, the faster the computer.

The speed of your microcomputer may have a direct impact on your business operation. With a faster computer, you can process more information in a shorter period of time. However, always consider the additional cost incurred by buying a more powerful PC and the marginal benefit to be gained.

1–9 GENERAL CAPABILITIES OF MICROCOMPUTER SOFTWARE

A microcomputer can perform a variety of tasks by using either commercial software or software developed in-house. In-house developed software is usually more expensive than commercial software. However, software developed in-house

CD ROM

A.

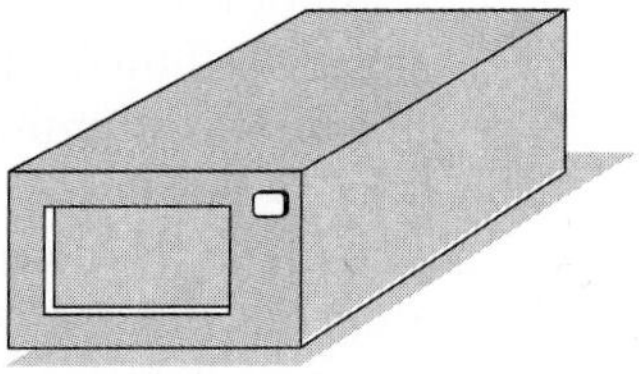

WORM disk

B.

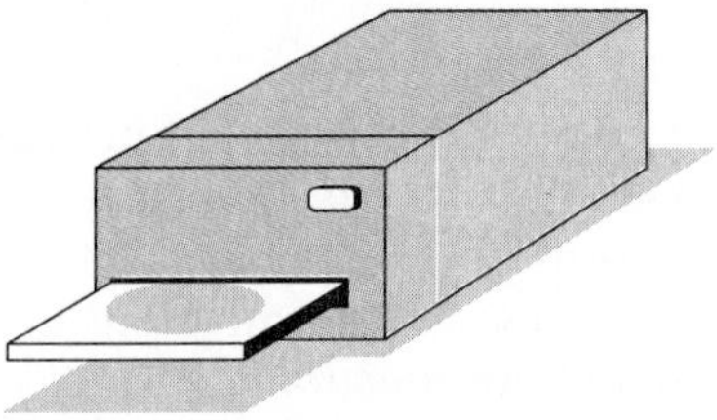

Erasable optical disk

C.

Figure 1–10
Optical storage devices for microcomputers. A. Close-up of CD-ROM (courtesy of Radio Shack, a division of Tandy Corp.). B. Disks and disk drive B (courtesy of NEC). C. Erasable optical disk.

is more customized and should better fit users' needs. Several thousands of software packages are available for PCs. For any task that can apply to several users, there is a software package on the market. The following are typical commercial packages and applications available for microcomputers.

1-9-1 Word Processing Software

A microcomputer that functions as a word processor is similar to a typewriter with a memory. With such a facility, you can generate documents, make deletions and insertions, and cut and paste. **Word processing software** is becoming more sophisticated. Some of the programs now provide limited graphics and data management features. Word processing programs allow users to save hundreds of hours by not typing the same document repeatedly. For example, organizations do not need to retype the letter that is sent to many of their customers. They need only change the names and addresses in the letters. Numerous word processing programs fill the marketplace. Some of the popular ones are WordPerfect (WordPerfect Corp.), Word (Microsoft Corporation), AmiPro (Lotus Development Corporation), and Wordstar (MicroPro International Corporation).

1-9-2 Grammar Checker Software

The ever-increasing speed and memory of microcomputers are promoting a new type of software. Most word processors now include spelling checkers, which are able to correct most of the typos in a document. The next challenge is the creation of documents that include correct verbs, subjects, adjectives, and a smooth style. Also, the creation of simple, easy-to-read, and simple sentences is of prime importance. **Grammar checker software** promotes good writing techniques.

Grammar checkers perform text analyses through linguistic analysis, parsing, and rule matching. Parsing means simply breaking long sentences into shorter ones. More sophisticated software includes more sophisticated parsers. Grammar checkers play an especially important role when multiple authors are involved in a project. In such cases, grammar checkers help create uniformity of tone, level, style, and usage. Grammar checkers are not 100 percent perfect yet, but they have come a long way. Among the more popular grammar checkers are Grammatik Windows and Grammatik IV (Reference Software International), PowerEdit (Artificial Linguistics, Inc.), and Correct Grammar for DOS (Writing Tools Group, Inc.).

1-9-3 Spreadsheet Software

A spreadsheet is a table of rows and columns. **Spreadsheet software** can be broadly classified into two types. One type is a dedicated spreadsheet; this means the program performs only spreadsheet functions. The other type of spreadsheet package can perform more than one type of function. Lotus 1-2-3, for example, is capable of performing spreadsheet functions as well as database and graphics functions. Other popular spreadsheet packages include Symphony (Lotus), Excel (Microsoft), SuperCalc (Computer Associates International, Inc.), and Quattro Pro (Borland International).

The number of jobs that can be performed by a spreadsheet program is unlimited. Generally speaking, any application suitable for analysis by row and column is a candidate for a typical spreadsheet. For example, say you decide to use a spreadsheet to prepare a budget. As soon as you have completed your budget, you can perform some impressive what-if analysis. This means you can manipulate variables on the spreadsheet. For example, reduce your income by 2 percent and direct the spreadsheet to calculate the effect of this change on other items in the spreadsheet.

1-9-4 Database Software

Database software is designed to perform database operations such as file creation, deletion, modification, search, sort, merge, and join (combining two files based on a common key). A file is a collection of a series of records. A record is a collection of a series of fields. A field is a collection of a series of characters. For example, the names, GPAs, and majors of all the students in our computer class constitute a student file. The name, GPA, and major of each student make up the record of each student. The name, GPA, or major is a field.

Popular database programs include dBASE III PLUS and IV (Borland), PC-File III (Buttonware, Inc.), Q&A (Symantec), Paradox (Borland), Omnis Quartz (Blyth Software), FoxBase and Fox Pro (Microsoft), and R-BASE (Microrim Corporation).

Think of a database as a table of rows and columns. The rows correspond to the occurrence of a record. The columns correspond to the fields within the record. Two common applications of database software are sorting and searching records. In sort operations, the user enters a series of records in any order, then asks the database program to sort the records in ascending or descending order based on the data in the fields. Search operations are even more interesting. You can search for data items that meet certain criteria, for example, all the MIS students who have GPAs greater than 3.60 and are younger than 20 years of age. Some databases (such as Q&A) allow you to search for key words within a text file.

1-9-5 Graphics Software

Graphics software has been designed to present data in graphic format. Data can be converted into a line graph to show a trend, to a pie chart to highlight the components of a data item, and to other types of graphs for various analyses. Masses of data can be converted to a graph and, in a glance, the reader can discover the general pattern of the data. Graphs can easily highlight patterns and the correlation of data items. They also make data presentation a more manageable job. Graphics can be done with integrated packages such as Lotus 1-2-3 or Quattro Pro or with dedicated graphics packages. Five popular graphics packages are Aldus Persuasion (Aldus Corporation), Hollywood Graphics (IBM Corporation), Harvard Graphics (Software Publishing Corporation), Freelance (Lotus), and Power Point (Microsoft Corporation).

1-9-6 Communications Software

Through a modem and **communications software**, your microcomputer can easily connect you to a wealth of information available in public and private databases. For example, several executives in different states or countries can work expeditiously on the same report by using communications software. The report is sent back and forth on computer to each location until it is completed. Communications software and a modem also make remote data entry an easy task. A modem converts computer signals (digital signals) to signals transferable on a telephone line (analog signals). Some software packages, such as Symphony by Lotus, include a communications program within the package itself. However, there are many communications software products on the market, among them Crosstalk

(Microstuf, Inc.), On-Line (Micro-Systems Software, Inc.), Pfs: Access (Software Publishing Corp.), and Smartcom II (Hayes Microcomputer Products, Inc.).

1–9–7 Desktop Publishing Software

Desktop publishing software allows you to produce professional-quality documents (with or without graphics) using relatively inexpensive hardware and software. All you need is a PC, a desktop publishing software package, and a laser or letter-quality printer. Desktop publishing has evolved as a result of three major factors: inexpensive PCs, inexpensive laser printers, and sophisticated and easy-to-use software.

With desktop publishing software, you can produce high-quality screen output and then transfer it to a printer—what you see is what you get (WYSIWYG). Today, newsletters, brochures, training manuals, transparencies, posters, and books are produced by means of desktop publishing.

Several desktop publishing software packages are available on the market. Pagemaker (Aldus) and Ventura Publisher (Xerox Corporation) are two popular ones. See Figure 1–11 for some of the output of desktop publishing software.

1–9–8 Financial Planning Software

Financial planning software works with large amounts of data and performs diverse financial analyses. These analyses include present value, future value, rate of return, cash flow analyses, depreciation analyses, and budgeting analyses. There are several packages for financial planning on the market. Among them are DTFPS (Desk Top Financial Solutions, Inc.), Excel (Microsoft), Finar (Finar Research Systems, Ltd.), Javelin (Javelin Software Corporation), Micro-DSS/Finance (Addison-Wesley Publishing Co.), Lotus 1-2-3 (Lotus), Quattro Pro (Borland), IFPS (Comshare), and Micro Plan (Chase Laboratories, Inc.).

Using these packages, you can plan and analyze your financial situation. For example, you can determine how much your $2,000 IRA will be worth at 5 percent interest in 30 years. Or, you can discount all future cash flows into today's dollars. You will know how much you have to deposit in the bank to have $90,000 in 10 years for your child's education.

1–9–9 Accounting Software

In addition to spreadsheet software which has widespread applications in the accounting field, there are dedicated **accounting software** packages that are able to perform many accounting tasks. The tasks performed by such software include general ledgers, account receivables, account payables, payrolls, balance sheets, and income statements. Depending on the price, these software packages vary in sophistication. Some of the popular accounting software packages are Business Works PC (Manzanita Software Systems), 4-in-1 Basic Accounting (Real World Corporation), Peachtree (Peachtree Software, Inc.), and DacEasy Accounting (Dac Software, Inc.).

1–9–10 Project Management Software

A project consists of a series of related activities. Building a house, designing an order entry system, or writing a thesis are examples of projects. The goal of **project management software** is to help decision makers keep time and budget under control by resolving scheduling problems. Project management software helps managers to plan and set achievable goals. Project management software highlights the bottlenecks and the relationships among different activities. This

A.

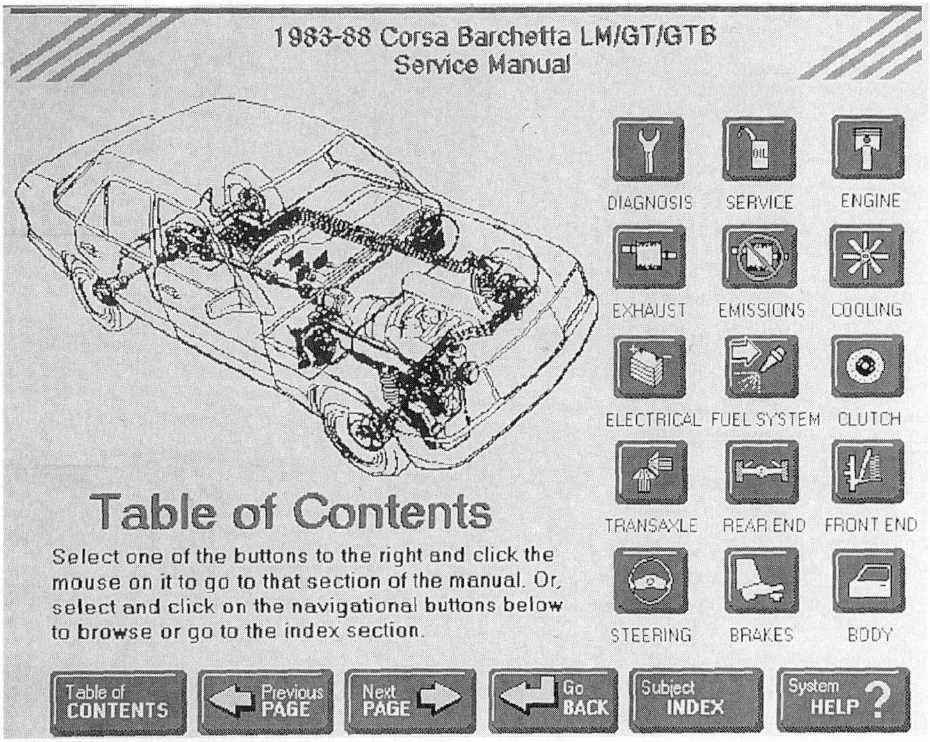

B.

Figure 1–11
Desktop publishing output. A. Desktop publishing combines text, graphics, and illustrations (courtesy of Aldus). B. With desktop publishing, business professionals can prepare high-quality documents on their own (courtesy of Ashton-Tate Corp.).

software allows the user to study the cost, time, and resource impacts of any change in the schedule. Several project management software packages are on the market: Harvard Total Project Manager (Software Publishing), Micro Planner 6 (Micro Planning International), Microsoft Project (Microsoft), Superproject Expert (Computer Associates) and Time Line (Symantec).

1–9–11 Computer-Aided Design (CAD) Software

Computer-aided design (CAD) software involves drafting and design. CAD software has replaced the traditional tools of drafting and design such as the T-square, triangle, and paper and pencil. It is used extensively in the architectural and engineering industries. CAD software no longer belongs only to large corporations. Because of the 386- and 486-based PCs and significant price reduction, small companies and individuals can afford this software. These new PCs have larger memory and are significantly faster than earlier PCs. With their enhanced power and sophistication, they are able to take advantage of most of the features offered by CAD programs. The home use of CAD software includes diverse architectural and engineering applications. There are several CAD programs on the market: AutoCAD (Autodesk), Cadkey (Cadkey), and VersaCAD (VersaCAD). See Figure 1–12 for some output from a CAD system.

A.

B.

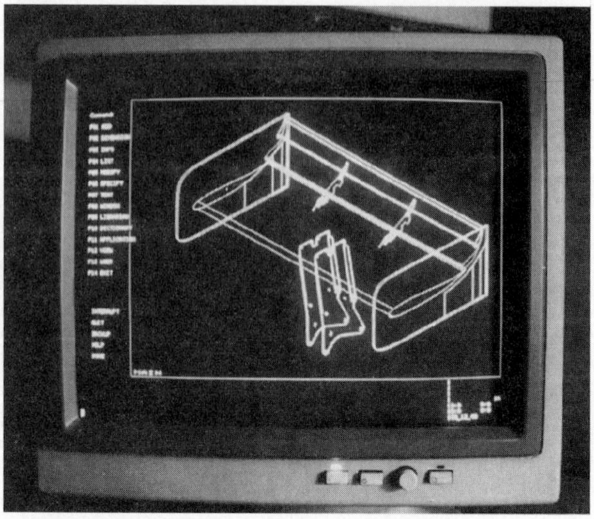

C.

Figure 1–12
A. CAD System for detailed architectural design (Larry Hamill/Macmillan). B. CAD system for design of a multicomponent product (courtesy of International Business Machines Corp.). C. CAD-supported design of aircraft landing gear (courtesy of International Business Machines Corp.).

1-9-12 Other Popular Software for Microcomputers

In addition to the 11 types of software just described, there are some others commonly used with microcomputers. Let us briefly consider them.

Utility software. These programs or utilities provide various DOS operations. Their goal is to simplify DOS operations for PC users. Depending on the sophistication of the program, various tasks are offered such as hard disk management, recovering a damaged disk or file, menu design, condensing a hard disk, and so forth.

Terminate & Stay Resident (TSR) Software. These programs are loaded when you start your PC and they stay in the background while other software applications are being used. TSR programs offer various features including screen printing, calendar, memo pad, and online calculator.

Investment Analysis Software. In addition to spreadsheet software, several other types of software are designed for investment analysis. By means of these programs, the user can track stocks, bonds, and other investment portfolios. Some of the programs are able to download financial data from public databases or stock exchanges. Others allow users to input their own financial data; then the programs perform financial analysis.

Tax Preparation software. This software assists a PC user in preparing taxes in a fairly straightforward manner. Some of the software packages enable the user to electronically download prepared tax forms to an IRS office.

Games software. Games probably form the oldest group of software for microcomputers, and they cover a broad range of activities. Although games are losing their popularity, they are still played by many PC users.

1-10 GUIDELINES FOR SUCCESSFUL SELECTION OF A MICROCOMPUTER

Because of the many microcomputers on the market, making a selection is a difficult task. The general guidelines provided here regarding the purchase and maintenance of a microcomputer may help you to choose a suitable computer and maintain it more easily.

Before you start the selection process, define your requirements. Sometimes this is called the "wish list" approach. You should have a clear idea of the type of microcomputer you *need* and the specific applications you want it to handle.

After you define your needs, think about software. Remember, if there is software on the market, there must be hardware to run it; but the reverse is not necessarily true. After defining the software and hardware you need and want, consider the technical support provided by vendors and reputation of vendors.

Important factors regarding selection and maintenance of a microcomputer are summarized next.

Software Selection

Good software should

- be easy to use
- be able to handle the business volume
- have good documentation
- have training available

- have updates available (free of charge or for a minimum charge)
- have local support
- come from a reputable vendor
- have a low cost

Hardware Selection (Processor and Keyboard)

Good hardware should

- have a comfortable keyboard
- have function keys
- have a general operating system (e.g., OS/2, MS-DOS, PC-DOS, Windows, or UNIX)
- have 16-bit or bigger processor (word) size
- have a high speed
- be expandable (memory and peripheral)
- have enough channel capacity or expansion slots (for attachment of peripherals)
- have a low cost

Hardware Selection (CRT)

A good monitor should

- have a separate CRT (not a built-in one)
- be easy to read (high resolution, super VGA or higher)
- have a standard number of characters per row and column

Hardware Selection (Disk Drive and Hard Disk)

A good disk drive should

- have a built-in, not separate, disk drive
- have adequate storage capacity (to load and run popular software)
- have a hard disk option

Hardware Selection (Printer)

A good printer should

- have a standard printer interface (without additional devices)
- produce high-quality output
- have high speed
- have a reasonable amount of noise suppression
- let you change tape, ribbons, or toner cartridge easily
- have a low cost

Vendor Selection

A good vendor should

- have a good reputation
- have a knowledgeable staff

- have training available for hardware and software
- have a hot line available
- support newsletters and user groups
- provide a "loaner" in case of breakdown
- provide updates (e.g., trade-in options)

Maintenance Contract Selection

A good contract should

- have a warranty period
- state a flexible time for repair
- limit downtime and inconvenience by providing flexible repair visits and timely repair of the computer
- have reasonable terms for contract renewal
- allow relocation and/or reassignment of the present contract
- observe confidentiality issues

1–11 TAKING CARE OF YOUR MICROCOMPUTER

To maintain the health of your microcomputer, consider the following factors:

- Protect your microcomputer against dirt, dust, and smoke.
- Make backup copies for security reasons and keep backups in different locations.
- Avoid any kind of liquid spills.
- Maintain steady power. Use surge protectors for power fluctuations and use lightning arresters in mountainous areas.
- Protect the system from static by using humidifiers or antistatic spray devices.
- Do not start your computer with a disk that you are not familiar with (avoid computer virus—the deadly program that erases and/or corrupts all your data).
- Do not download information to your computer from unknown bulletin boards. Downloading means importing information from other computers by using a modem and telephone line.
- Acquire insurance for your computer equipment.

1–12 ADVANTAGES OF MICROCOMPUTERS COMPARED WITH MAINFRAMES

Generally speaking, a microcomputer offers several advantages over a mainframe computer. Because of their extended memory and increased speed, microcomputers can perform many of the tasks performed by a mainframe but on a smaller scale. The advantages of microcomputers in comparison with mainframes follow:

- They are easier to use.
- They are less threatening to those who are not computer experts (e.g., they are smaller).
- They give the user more control.

- They are relatively inexpensive.
- They can be portable.

1–13 YOU AND YOUR PC: A HANDS-ON SESSION

If you place the DOS diskette or "boot disk" (disk that can be used to start the computer) in drive A, when you turn the computer on, your microcomputer will ask for the date. Remember, the majority of IBM or IBM-compatible systems come with a DOS disk. Either type the date in the desired format or press the Enter key to bypass the date. The computer then asks you for the time. Either type the time in the desired format or press the Enter key to bypass the time. Now you are at the A> prompt. This means your default drive is A.

If your computer has a hard disk, this start-up procedure is slightly different. You will get the system started from the hard disk and your prompt will be C> instead of A>. See Figure 1–13.

In any case, from this mode (the DOS mode), you can go to any application software.

For example, if the software (e.g., Lotus 1-2-3) is installed in the hard disk, use the DOS CD command to change to the directory that stores the software; then type *123* and press Enter. From the DOS mode, you can access any application software.

When you are at the C> prompt, you are in RAM. This area is called a working or temporary area. Any work you do in this area will disappear if you turn the computer off. To make your work permanent, you have to transfer it to a **permanent area**. The permanent area usually is either floppy disk or hard disk. Your work stays in the permanent area until you erase it.

While you are at the C> prompt, you can send any information to RAM by using the keyboard. This information can become permanent by saving it into a permanent medium. All application programs include a command for saving your work.

Beginning computer users are always worried about making mistakes! What happens if you make a mistake? Don't panic. Your mistake can be corrected easily. Some application programs have an UNDO command. If you realize you have made a mistake, you can recover from it by using the UNDO feature. All application programs include a feature for correcting mistakes. In the worst case, you can retype the correct statement over your previous material. Remember, any address (or cell) in the computer memory can hold only one value at a time. As soon as you type and enter a new value, the old one disappears.

1–14 WHAT IS A COMPUTER FILE?

A **computer file** is basically an electronic document. One way to create a document is to type and enter it using the keyboard. As soon as you save the document, you have generated a computer file.

To differentiate one file from another, you must save each file under a unique name—a file name. A file name is any combination of up to eight valid characters. Valid characters include letters of the alphabet (upper case or lower-

Figure 1–13
Getting the system started.

```
C>
```

case), digits 0 through 9, the underscore, and some special characters. If you provide a name longer than eight characters, some application programs give you an error message; others truncate the name and accept only the first eight characters.

In addition to a file name, a file is usually saved with a file extension. A file extension is similar to a file name but uses up to three characters. Some application programs automatically provide a file extension when you save the file. In other application programs, providing a file extension is the user's responsibility.

Several characters have special meanings in different application software. The asterisk (*) can represent any number of characters up to eight. The question mark (?) can represent any single character. These two characters are called wildcard characters. These **wildcards** can significantly improve your efficiency while you work with application programs. For example, all your Lotus 1-2-3 graphic files are identified by *.PIC. The * represents any file name and the PIC indicates that your file is a Lotus 1-2-3 graphic file. For example, if you want to copy all your Lotus 1-2-3 graphic files from the disk in drive A to the disk in drive B, type this DOS command at the A> prompt: *COPY *.PIC B:* (follow by pressing the Enter key). If you did not have this wildcard feature, you would have to repeat the COPY command as many times as the number of the graphic files. The file BRANCH?.* represents BRANCH1, BRANCH2, and so on. For example, in DOS if you type *DIR *.WK?* (and press Enter), your Lotus 1-2-3 files from version 1 and 1A (WKS) files, version 2 (WK1) files, version 3 (WK3) files, and student version (WKE) files will be displayed. The asterisk as the file extension indicates that the file can have any extension. Your entire disk can be identified by *.*. Using the COPY command, for example, at the A> prompt, to copy the entire disk in drive A to drive B, type *Copy *.* B:* (and press Enter).

1–15 TYPES OF DATA

Any application program or computer language accepts different types of data. The most commonly used data types are numeric and nonnumeric.

Numeric data include any combination of digits 0 through 9 and decimal points. Numeric data can be integer or real. Integer data include only whole numbers without any decimal points, for example, 656 or 986. Real data include digits and decimal points, for example, 696.25 or 729.793. Real data is sometimes called floating point data. Floating point means that the decimal point can move from right to left, for example, 222.2, 22.22, 2.222. Another type of real data is the fixed point, meaning that the decimal point is always fixed.

Nonnumeric data, or alphanumeric data, is sometimes called labels or strings. Any types of valid characters can be nonnumeric data, for example, Jackson or 123 Broadway Street. You cannot perform any arithmetic operations with nonnumeric data.

1–16 TYPES OF VALUES

Computers usually handle two types of values: variables and constants. **Variables** are valid computer addresses (locations) that hold different values at different times. For example, in A=65, A is the variable and 65 is the **constant.** B = "Brown": B is the variable and Brown is the constant. A variable holds a given value at any given time. As soon as you enter a new value into this variable, the old value disappears. The constant is always fixed. See Figure 1–14.

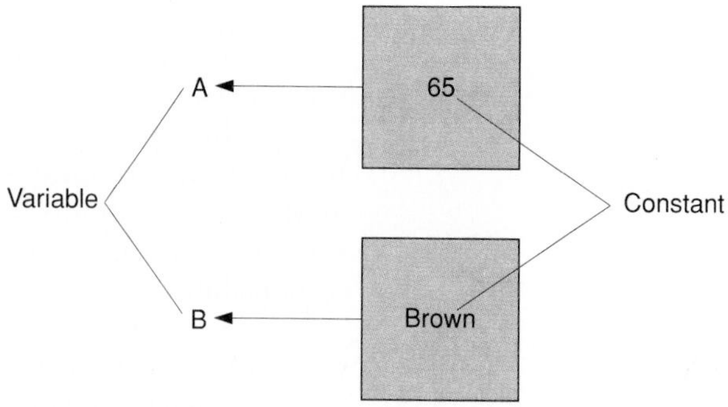

Figure 1–14
Example of a variable and a constant.

1–17 TYPES OF FORMULAS

Two types of formulas or functions are handled by computers: user-defined and built-in.

User-defined formulas or functions are a combination of computer addresses designed to perform a certain task. For example, the area of a triangle can be presented as A = B*H/2 (meaning base multiplied by height divided by 2). In this case, A is a formula or a function. When you enter different values for B and H, and a different value for A, the area of the triangle, will be calculated.

Built-in formulas or functions are already available within the application program or the computer language. As soon as the user provides values for a given variable or variables, the application program or the computer language dynamically calculates these formulas. For example, SQRT(X) is a function that calculates the square root of a variable, X. The X and any other information needed by these functions are called arguments. As soon as you provide a value for X, the square root is calculated; for example, SQRT(25) is equal to 5. The function FV(payment,interest rate,term) calculates the future value of a series of equal payments with a given interest rate over a period of time (term). This function can help you determine, for example, the future value of an IRA in which you plan to invest $2,000 for 30 years at a 10 percent interest rate.

1–18 PRIORITY OF ARITHMETIC OPERATIONS

When application programs perform arithmetic operations, they follow a series of rules. The rules for priority of arithmetic operations are as follows:

1. Expressions inside parentheses have the highest priority.
2. Exponentiation (raising to power) has the next highest priority.
3. Multiplication and division have the third highest priority.
4. Addition and subtraction have the fourth highest priority.
5. When there are two or more operations with the same priority, operations proceed from left to right.

The following examples should make the rules clear. First, an application program uses * (asterisk) for multiplication, ^ (caret) for exponentiation (raising the power), and / (slash) for division. If A=5, B=10, C=2, calculate the following:

A+B/C	=	10
(A+B)/C	=	7.5

A*B/C	=	25
(A*B)/C	=	25
A^C/2	=	12.50

SUMMARY

This chapter focused on microcomputers in general. Input, output, and primary and secondary memory devices for microcomputers were described. The general capabilities of microcomputers were introduced. The chapter presented a series of guidelines for successful selection and maintenance of a microcomputer. It also listed the advantages of micros over mainframes. A hands-on session included the basics for getting started as a computer user. The chapter concluded with a definition of computer files, types of data, types of values, types of formulas, and priority of arithmetic operations.

REVIEW QUESTIONS

*These questions are answered in Appendix A.

1. What is a microcomputer? What are some of the capabilities of a micro?
*2. What are some typical input devices for a micro?
3. What are some typical output devices for a micro?
4. Explain the difference between a primary memory device and a secondary memory device.
5. What is RAM? ROM? PROM? EPROM?
*6. What are the most commonly used secondary storage devices for a micro?
7. What is extended memory? What is expanded memory?
8. Describe optical technologies. What are their advantages and disadvantages?
9. How do you measure the memory capacity of a micro?
10. Besides memory, what other attributes are important when you buy a micro?
11. What is the difference between a floppy disk and a hard disk?
12. Give the speed range for a typical microcomputer.
*13. What is the memory size of a typical micro?
14. What is a good software?
15. What is a good hardware?
16. What is a good maintenance contract? Who are the good vendors?
*17. How should you care for your micro?
18. List some application programs for a micro.
19. What are some of the advantages of a micro compared with a mainframe?
20. What is permanent memory in a PC? What is temporary memory?
21. How do you send information from RAM to a floppy or hard disk?
*22. How do you correct your mistakes?
23. Define a computer file.
24. What is a wildcard character?
25. Describe different types of data.
26. What is a variable? What is a constant?
*27. What is the priority of arithmetic operations?
28. List the symbols used for arithmetic operations.
29. Turn on a PC. What do you see? Turn it off. Insert the DOS disk in drive A and turn the computer back on. What do you see this time?

30. Enter the correct date and time in your computer. What happens if you make a mistake?
31. Type *DIR* and press the Enter key. What is displayed at this time?
32. What types of PCs do you have on your campus? Describe different input/output devices used by the PCs in your school's micro lab. Do you have a Bernoulli box in the lab? What are some of the advantages of Bernoulli box over a hard disk?
33. What are the most commonly used disks on your campus—3½ or 5¼? Compare and contrast these two types of storage devices.
34. Consult computer magazines to find out which computers use optical disks.
35. Which of the types of software packages introduced in this chapter are available on your campus? What are the applications of each?
36. If you want to buy a PC for personal use, how should you start shopping? What attributes makes a PC attractive?

KEY TERMS

Accounting software
Arithmetic logic unit (ALU)
Bernoulli box
Built-in formulas or functions
Central processing unit (CPU)
CD-ROM
Communications software
Computer-aided design (CAD) software
Computer file
Constants
Control unit
Conventional memory
Database software
Desktop publishing software
EPROM
Erasable optical disk
Expanded memory
Extended memory
Financial planning software
Floppy disk
Grammar checker software
Graphics software
Hard disk
Input device
Main memory
Micro
Microcomputer
Nonnumeric data
Numeric data
Output device
Permanent area
Personal computer (PC)
Primary memory
Priority of arithmetic operations
Project management software
PROM
Random-access memory (RAM)
RGB monitor
Read-only memory (ROM)
Secondary memory
Spreadsheet software
User-defined formulas or functions
Variables
Wildcard
Word processing software
WORM disk

ARE YOU READY TO MOVE ON?

Multiple Choice

1. Choose the correct ranking of monitor display resolutions from lowest to highest.
   a. VGA, CGA, XGA
   b. EGA, VGA, CGA
   c. EGA, CGA, VGA
   d. CGA, EGA, XGA
   e. XGA, CGA, EGA
2. Which of the following is *not* a typical adapter card?
   a. printer interface card
   b. clock card

c. disk drive card
d. display card
e. punch card

3. Of the following types of main memory, which can the user control directly?
   a. ROM
   b. REM
   c. RAM
   d. PROM
   e. all of the above
4. What is now the most commonly used secondary storage device?
   a. 5¼ inch floppy disk and a hard disk
   b. 3½ inch floppy disk and a hard disk
   c. Bernoulli box and a hard disk
   d. hard disk with no floppy disk
   e. none of the above
5. What is the major advantage of optical storage technology?
   a. storage capacity
   b. cost
   c. durability
   d. both A and C
   e. all of the above
6. When we refer to memory and storage capacity sizes, we use kilobytes (as in 360 K). 1 K equals approximately
   a. 1 byte
   b. 1,000 bytes
   c. 1,000,000 bytes
   d. 1,048,576 bytes
   e. none of the above
7. Word size directly affects
   a. the speed of the computer
   b. the ability of the user to understand what is being said
   c. the maximum amount of data that can be displayed on the CRT
   d. the choice of which type of disk drive to use
   e. the meaning of the function keys on the keyboard
8. Which of the following are disadvantages of mainframes when compared with microcomputers?
   a. They are more difficult to use.
   b. They are more threatening to users who are not computer experts.
   c. The user has less control.
   d. They are relatively more expensive.
   e. All of the above are disadvantages.
9. After booting the computer with the DOS disk (loading DOS and entering the date and time), you are at
   a. the Lotus Access menu
   b. the DOS prompt (A> or C>)
   c. the parallel/serial interface
   d. the BASIC prompt
   e. none of the above
10. An example of alphanumeric data would be
    a. 123
    b. 123.25
    c. LOTUS-123
    d. A=(123-2)/4
    e. none of the above

True/False

1. The terms *personal computer,* PC, and *microcomputer* refer to different types of computers.
2. A typical microcomputer consists of input, output, and memory devices.
3. Monochrome CRTs cannot generate graphic output.
4. The purpose of function keys and special keys on a computer keyboard does not vary in different application programs.
5. The capacity of a hard disk is greater than the capacity of a floppy disk.
6. A WORM disk can be recorded and erased repeatedly when high-volume storage and updating are essential.
7. Typical microcomputer software packages and applications include spreadsheet, database, graphics, communications, and word processing.
8. The first step in selecting a microcomputer is to define your needs; then think about software.
9. The commands DIR *.* and DIR ????????.??? produce the same results.
10. Expressions inside parentheses have the lowest priority when it comes to performing arithmetic operations.

ANSWERS

Multiple Choice	True/False
1. d	1. F
2. e	2. T
3. c	3. F
4. b	4. F
5. d	5. T
6. b	6. F
7. a	7. T
8. e	8. T
9. b	9. T
10. c	10. F

A Quick Trip with MS-DOS and PC-DOS

2

2–1 INTRODUCTION

This chapter describes the basics of the Disk Operating System (DOS). The differences between internal and external DOS commands are explained as are the features of system date and time. After file specifications in the DOS environment are reviewed, the DIR command for generating a directory listing is discussed. Next, important keys in the DOS environment and the FORMAT command for creating a usable data disk are highlighted. Other DOS basics covered are the different versions of MS-DOS and PC-DOS, batch and AUTOEXEC files, the process of creating a directory, and commands for directories. Both DOS 5.0 and 6.0 are presented in general. A most useful feature of the chapter is a table summarizing important DOS commands.

2–2 TURNING ON YOUR PC

When you access a personal computer in a computer lab or any other location, the computer is either off or on. This text assumes that your computer has a hard disk and that the Disk Operating System (DOS) files are stored in drive C in the hard disk. DOS disks come with the computer when it is purchased.

Turn the computer on. This procedure is called a **cold boot**. Boot means getting the computer started. If the computer is already turned on, press the Ctrl, Alt, and Del keys simultaneously. This procedure is called **warm boot**. The warm boot is faster than the cold boot, because the computer does not check its memory in a warm boot as it does in a cold boot.

If your computer does not have a hard disk and you want to start it from a floppy disk, insert the boot disk in drive A and turn the computer on. When the computer is booted from the floppy disk, it asks you to enter the current date. Type the date in the format requested (mm-dd-yy). After typing the current date, press the Enter key. Your PC now asks for the current time. Type the current time in the format requested (hh:mm:ss). (Note that DOS operates on a 24-hour clock, 2:30 p.m. is 14:30, 9:15 p.m. is 21:15, etc.) After typing the time, press the Enter key. Now you should see the A> prompt. This means the necessary portions of DOS have been loaded into primary memory (RAM) and drive A is the default drive. Default drive means that from this point on this is the drive the computer accesses for executing commands. For example, if you decide to save a file, your file will be saved onto the disk in this drive. If you ask for a directory listing, the directory of the disk in this drive will be highlighted. At this point, you should be able to access any internal or external DOS commands.

If your DOS is installed on the hard disk (which is usually the C drive), your default drive will be the C drive. In a computer with hard disk, the date and time are maintained internally, so you do not need to enter them at boot-up time.

If you boot-up from the floppy disk and do not want to enter the date and time, you can bypass the prompts by pressing the Enter key twice. When the prompts are bypassed, the PC uses the default date and time when saving files. It is a good practice to enter both the correct date and time when you start the PC, so all your programs and data files are saved with this current information. The correct date and time can help you to determine the most or least recent versions of your files listed in the directory. A **directory** is the listing of all your files.

If you forget to enter the current date and time at the boot-up time, or if the date and time of your system are not correct, you can enter this information at any given time by using the DATE and TIME commands. At the DOS prompt, type *DATE* and press the Enter key. The computer will ask you to enter the current date in the format mm-dd-yy. Type the date and press the Enter key. Now type *TIME* and press the Enter key. The computer will ask you to enter the current time in the format hh:mm:ss. After typing the current time, press the Enter key. At this point the computer registers this information in its memory, where it will remain and be updated automatically until you turn the PC off. Computers with a hard disk have a battery-operated clock on their motherboard. The motherboard is where the computer's primary electronic circuitry resides. The date and time are maintained automatically, and user intervention is not required except for correcting the date or time.

Internal commands (sometimes called memory resident commands) are those commands that are loaded into the computer's memory at boot-up time. As soon as you see a DOS prompt such as A> or B> or C>, you can execute any internal command. Internal commands can be used without the DOS disk in any disk drive. CLS (clear screen) is an example of a DOS internal command. If at the DOS prompt you type *CLS* and press the Enter key, the screen will be erased.

External commands (sometimes called non-memory resident commands) are those commands that can only be executed by having the DOS disk in one of the drives. These commands are sometimes called DOS utilities. They are separate programs stored on the DOS disk. For example, DISKCOPY (generates a duplicate of a disk) is an external DOS command. A listing of most of these commands appears at the end of the chapter.

2–3 DIFFERENT DOS PROMPTS

Depending on how you get your PC started, you will see different prompts. If you have a hard disk in your system and you start the system from the hard disk, your prompt may be C>. The prompt indicates the current default drive. The default drive is the disk drive that the PC will access if no other disk drive is specified. If a file is located on a disk that is not in the default drive, the default must be changed or the disk drive containing the file must be specified. Changing the default is an easy task. At the C> prompt type *A:* (remember the colon) and press the Enter key. Now the prompt is A>. You can change this back to C> by typing *C:* and pressing the Enter key. The prompt can be customized by using the PROMPT PG command followed by pressing Enter. This command is useful when you use directories (discussed later in this chapter). By using this command, you know in which drive and/or directory you are at any given time.

2–4 DOS FILE SPECIFICATIONS

DOS files basically follow the same conventions that apply to other software. This means **file names** can be up to eight characters long. File names can contain digits 0 through 9 and some special characters such as underscore (_), pound sign (#), and so forth. To be on the safe side, limit the use of special characters in file names and do not use any space in a file name.

File extensions can be up to three characters long and contain the same characters used by file names. For example, TEST.TEX is a valid file name. Important file extensions in the DOS environment include these:

- BAK (backup): This extension indicates files generated by some word processing, spreadsheet, and database management programs; the files are backup copies of the original files.
- BAT (batch): This indicates a text file generated by the user. The file includes DOS commands and statements that are executed when the name of the file is typed.
- COM (command): This extension identifies files that can be executed by typing the name of the file.
- EXE (executable): Like COM files, files with this extension can be executed by typing the file name.
- SYS (system): This extension identifies files that can be used only by DOS.

2–5 DIR COMMAND

With DOS files installed in the hard disk, you can generate a listing of your current directory by using the DIR command. Type *DIR* and press the Enter key; information similar to Figure 2–1 will be presented to you. At the top of Figure 2–1, the listing indicates the volume in drive C is MS-DOS_6. This is the internal name for this disk. The LABEL command allows you to change this name. To do this, at the C> prompt type *LABEL* and press Enter. Specify the new label (name) of up to 11 characters and press Enter. From now on the internal name of this drive will be the name that you just specified.

The DIR command provides the name of each file, the file extension, the size of the file in bytes, and the date and time that the file was created or changed. At the end of the listing, the DIR command tells you the number of the files and the amount of bytes available on this particular disk. To erase the screen, type *CLS* and press the Enter key. To generate a listing for drive A, type *DIR A:* and press Enter. A listing of drive B can be created by typing *DIR B:* followed by pressing Enter.

The DIR command can be used with wildcard characters. Wildcard characters function as placeholders for other characters in the file name or file extension. The two valid DOS wildcards are the * (asterisk) and the ? (question mark). The asterisk replaces one or more characters in the file name or extension with any valid character. For example, *.COM refers to any file name with the extension COM. The question mark replaces only one character in the file name or extension with a valid character. For example, entering DIR *.COM displays all COM files. DIR *.PIC displays all Lotus 1-2-3 graphic files. DIR *.AB? displays any file that has AB as the first two letters of its extension, while the third character can be any valid character. DIR *.WK? displays Lotus WK1, WKS, WKE, or WK3 files. WKS are Lotus 1-2-3 files before Release 2.0, WK1 are Lotus release 2.0 and 2.01, 2.2, 2.3 and 2.4 files, WKE are Lotus 1-2-3 files in the student version of the software, and WK3 are Lotus 1-2-3 files in Release 3 or higher. It also displays Quattro Pro WKQ files.

2–6 DIR WITH DIFFERENT SWITCHES

The DIR command can be used with different switches (parameters) to provide different types of listings. DIR/W provides a wide directory; this means you get a horizontal listing of your directory. In this case, only file names and extensions

Figure 2–1
Directory listing of MS-DOS 6.

```
Volume in drive C is MS_DOS_6
Volume Serial Number is 1C22-913B
Directory of C:\DOS

.            <DIR>        06-06-92  12:24p
..           <DIR>        06-06-92  12:24p
DBLSPACE BIN       51214 03-10-93   6:00a
FORMAT   COM       22717 03-10-93   6:00a
NLSFUNC  EXE        7036 03-10-93   6:00a
COUNTRY  SYS       17066 03-10-93   6:00a
KEYB     COM       14983 03-10-93   6:00a
KEYBOARD SYS       34694 03-10-93   6:00a
SETUP    EXE       71974 03-10-93   6:00a
DOSSETUP INI        3735 03-10-93   6:00a
ANSI     SYS        9065 03-10-93   6:00a
ATTRIB   EXE       11165 03-10-93   6:00a
CHKDSK   EXE       12907 03-10-93   6:00a
EDIT     COM         413 03-10-93   6:00a
EXPAND   EXE       16129 03-10-93   6:00a
EDLIN    EXE       12642 06-13-91   5:00a
MORE     COM        2546 03-10-93   6:00a
MSD      EXE      158470 03-10-93   6:00a
QBASIC   EXE      194309 03-10-93   6:00a
RESTORE  EXE       38294 03-10-93   6:00a
MIRROR   COM       18169 06-13-91   5:00a
SYS      COM        9379 03-10-93   6:00a
UNFORMAT COM       12738 03-10-93   6:00a
SMARTDRV SYS        8335 06-13-91   5:00a
OS2      TXT        6358 03-10-93   6:00a
NETWORKS TXT       20463 03-10-93   6:00a
README   TXT       44990 03-10-93   6:00a
DEBUG    EXE       15715 03-10-93   6:00a
FDISK    EXE       29333 03-10-93   6:00a
DOSSHELL VID        9462 03-10-93   6:00a
19C1DOSC BAT          16 01-23-93   3:05p
DEFAULT  SET        4207 01-02-94  10:49a
DOSSHELL GRB        4421 03-10-93   6:00a
CHOICE   COM        1754 03-10-93   6:00a
DEFRAG   EXE       75033 03-10-93   6:00a
PACKING  LST        2507 06-13-91   5:00a
DEFRAG   HLP        9227 03-10-93   6:00a
DOSSWAP  EXE       18756 03-10-93   6:00a
EGA      CPI       58870 03-10-93   6:00a
RECOVER  EXE        9146 06-13-91   5:00a
EGA      SYS        4885 03-10-93   6:00a
HIMEM    SYS       14208 03-10-93   6:00a
MEM      EXE       32150 03-10-93   6:00a
XCOPY    EXE       15820 03-10-93   6:00a
MONEY    BAS       46225 06-13-91   5:00a
MSHERC   COM        6934 06-13-91   5:00a
DELTREE  EXE       11113 03-10-93   6:00a
GORILLA  BAS       29434 06-13-91   5:00a
4201     CPI        6404 06-13-91   5:00a
4208     CPI         720 06-13-91   5:00a
5202     CPI         395 06-13-91   5:00a
MOVE     EXE       17823 03-10-93   6:00a
ASSIGN   COM        6399 06-13-91   5:00a
RAMDRIVE SYS        5873 03-10-93   6:00a
BACKUP   EXE       36092 06-13-91   5:00a
SMARTDRV EXE       42073 03-10-93   6:00a
COMP     EXE       14282 06-13-91   5:00a
```

Figure 2–1
(continued)

```
DISPLAY  SYS     15789 03-10-93   6:00a
DOSHELP  HLP      5667 03-10-93   6:00a
DOSSHELL COM      4620 03-10-93   6:00a
DOSSHELL EXE    236378 03-10-93   6:00a
FASTHELP EXE     11481 03-10-93   6:00a
GRAFTABL COM     11205 06-13-91   5:00a
FASTOPEN EXE     12034 03-10-93   6:00a
HELP     HLP    294741 03-10-93   6:00a
HELP     COM       413 03-10-93   6:00a
NIBBLES  BAS     24103 06-13-91   5:00a
REMLINE  BAS     12314 06-13-91   5:00a
MODE     COM     23521 03-10-93   6:00a
POWER    EXE      8052 03-10-93   6:00a
EXE2BIN  EXE      8424 06-13-91   5:00a
PRINT    EXE     15640 03-10-93   6:00a
JOIN     EXE     17870 06-13-91   5:00a
LCD      CPI     10753 06-13-91   5:00a
QBASIC   HLP    130881 03-10-93   6:00a
PRINTER  SYS     18804 06-13-91   5:00a
SHARE    EXE     10912 03-10-93   6:00a
DELOLDOS EXE     17710 03-10-93   6:00a
SETVER   EXE     12015 03-10-93   6:00a
APPEND   EXE     10774 03-10-93   6:00a
APPNOTES TXT      8660 06-13-91   5:00a
KEYBHP   COM     15997 06-13-91   5:00a
MODEHP   COM     23232 06-13-91   5:00a
SSTOR    SYS     37260 06-13-91   5:00a
DISKCOMP COM     10620 03-10-93   6:00a
MOUSE    SYS     32730 06-13-91   5:00a
DISKCOPY COM     11879 03-10-93   6:00a
B        BAT        46 06-06-92   1:53p
589DOSCM BAT        16 01-23-93   3:01p
D5C0DOSC BAT        16 01-23-93   6:49p
2688DOSC BAT        16 01-23-93   3:08p
370CDOSC BAT        16 01-23-93   4:12p
D923DOSC BAT        16 01-23-93   5:50p
BA6EDOSC BAT        16 01-23-93   6:43p
D329DOSC BAT        16 01-23-93   6:49p
DRIVER   SYS      5406 03-10-93   6:00a
FC       EXE     18650 03-10-93   6:00a
FIND     EXE      6770 03-10-93   6:00a
GRAPHICS COM     19694 03-10-93   6:00a
GRAPHICS PRO     21232 03-10-93   6:00a
LABEL    EXE      9390 03-10-93   6:00a
SMARTMON EXE     28672 03-10-93   6:00a
SMARTMON HLP     10727 03-10-93   6:00a
SORT     EXE      6922 03-10-93   6:00a
LOADFIX  COM      1131 03-10-93   6:00a
MWBACKUP EXE    309696 03-10-93   6:00a
MWBACKUP HLP    400880 03-10-93   6:00a
REPLACE  EXE     20226 03-10-93   6:00a
SUBST    EXE     18478 03-10-93   6:00a
TREE     COM      6898 03-10-93   6:00a
DOSKEY   COM      5883 03-10-93   6:00a
VFINTD   386      5295 03-10-93   6:00a
MWBACKF  DLL     14560 03-10-93   6:00a
MWBACKR  DLL    111120 03-10-93   6:00a
MOUSE    COM     56408 03-10-93   6:00a
MSBACKUP EXE      5506 03-10-93   6:00a
MSBACKUP OVL    133952 03-10-93   6:00a
MSBACKFB OVL     69066 03-10-93   6:00a
```

Figure 2–1
(continued)

```
MSBACKFR OVL      72474 03-10-93    6:00a
CHKSTATE SYS      41600 03-10-93    6:00a
UNDELETE EXE      26420 03-10-93    6:00a
MWUNDEL  EXE     130496 03-10-93    6:00a
MWUNDEL  HLP      35741 03-10-93    6:00a
MWGRAFIC DLL      36944 03-10-93    6:00a
MSBACKUP HLP     314236 03-10-93    6:00a
WNTOOLS  GRP       2205 01-02-94    6:25p
MSBACKDB OVL      63098 03-10-93    6:00a
MSBACKDR OVL      66906 03-10-93    6:00a
MSBCONFG OVL      47210 03-10-93    6:00a
MSBCONFG HLP      45780 03-10-93    6:00a
DBLSPACE EXE     274388 03-10-93    6:00a
MEMMAKER INF       1652 03-10-93    6:00a
INTERLNK EXE      17197 03-10-93    6:00a
INTERSVR EXE      37314 03-10-93    6:00a
MSCDEX   EXE      25377 03-10-93    6:00a
DBLSPACE HLP      72169 03-10-93    6:00a
DBLSPACE INF       2178 03-10-93    6:00a
DBLSPACE SYS        339 03-10-93    6:00a
DBLWIN   HLP       8597 03-10-93    6:00a
DOSSHELL HLP     161323 03-10-93    6:00a
EMM386   EXE     115294 03-10-93    6:00a
MEMMAKER EXE     118660 03-10-93    6:00a
SIZER    EXE       7169 03-10-93    6:00a
MONOUMB  386       8783 03-10-93    6:00a
MSTOOLS  DLL      13424 03-10-93    6:00a
MSAV     EXE     172198 03-10-93    6:00a
MSAV     HLP      23891 03-10-93    6:00a
MSAVHELP OVL      29828 03-10-93    6:00a
MSAVIRUS LST      35520 03-10-93    6:00a
VSAFE    COM      62576 03-10-93    6:00a
MWAVDOSL DLL      44736 03-10-93    6:00a
MWAVDRVL DLL       7744 03-10-93    6:00a
AUTOEXEC UMB        703 01-01-94    5:34p
MOUSE    INI         28 01-01-94    5:34p
CONFIG   UMB        142 01-01-94    5:34p
MEMMAKER STS        851 01-01-94    5:40p
MWAVDLG  DLL      36368 03-10-93    6:00a
MSBACKUP INI         43 01-03-94    4:46p
MWAVSCAN DLL     151568 03-10-93    6:00a
MSBACKUP RST        608 04-13-92    7:07a
MSBACKUP TMP       5014 01-02-94   10:49a
MWAV     EXE     142640 03-10-93    6:00a
MWAVABSI DLL      54576 03-10-93    6:00a
MWAV     HLP      24619 03-10-93    6:00a
MWAVSOS  DLL       7888 03-10-93    6:00a
MWAVMGR  DLL      21712 03-10-93    6:00a
MWAVTSR  EXE      17328 03-10-93    6:00a
COMMAND  COM      52925 03-10-93    6:00a
MSAV     INI          0 01-01-94    3:01p
DEFAULT  BAK       4207 01-02-94    9:56a
MSBACKUP LOG     196811 01-02-94   10:54a
DEFAULT  SLT         64 01-02-94   10:49a
DEFAULT  SAV         64 01-02-94    9:56a
DOSSHELL INI      16424 01-02-94    1:02p
      176 file(s)      6563296 bytes
                     129966080 bytes free

C>
```

are listed. Figure 2–2 was generated by typing *DIR/W* at the C> prompt and pressing the Enter key. *DIR/P* gives you one screen of the file listing. At the bottom of the screen, a prompt tells you to strike a key to see another screen. Figure 2–3 was generated by typing *DIR/P* at the C> prompt and pressing the Enter key. (Notice that this is a partial listing.)

The DIR command enables you to get a listing of files in any drive by specifying the drive. For example, say the current drive is A; type *DIR B:/W* to display a wide directory of drive B. There must be at least one space between the DIR command and a drive name when you issue the command. Remember, to execute any DOS command, you must press Enter after typing the command.

```
C>DIR/W

 Volume in drive C is MS_DOS_6
 Volume Serial Number is 1C22-913B
 Directory of C:\DOS

[.]            [..]           DBLSPACE.BIN   FORMAT.COM     NLSFUNC.EXE
COUNTRY.SYS    KEYB.COM       KEYBOARD.SYS   SETUP.EXE      DOSSETUP.INI
ANSI.SYS       ATTRIB.EXE     CHKDSK.EXE     EDIT.COM       EXPAND.EXE
EDLIN.EXE      MORE.COM       MSD.EXE        QBASIC.EXE     RESTORE.EXE
MIRROR.COM     SYS.COM        UNFORMAT.COM   SMARTDRV.SYS   OS2.TXT
NETWORKS.TXT   README.TXT     DEBUG.EXE      FDISK.EXE      DOSSHELL.VID
19C1DOSC.BAT   DEFAULT.SET    DOSSHELL.GRB   CHOICE.COM     DEFRAG.EXE
PACKING.LST    DEFRAG.HLP     DOSSWAP.EXE    EGA.CPI        RECOVER.EXE
EGA.SYS        HIMEM.SYS      MEM.EXE        XCOPY.EXE      MONEY.BAS
MSHERC.COM     DELTREE.EXE    GORILLA.BAS    4201.CPI       4208.CPI
5202.CPI       MOVE.EXE       ASSIGN.COM     RAMDRIVE.SYS   BACKUP.EXE
SMARTDRV.EXE   COMP.EXE       DISPLAY.SYS    DOSHELP.HLP    DOSSHELL.COM
DOSSHELL.EXE   FASTHELP.EXE   GRAFTABL.COM   EDIT.HLP       FASTOPEN.EXE
HELP.HLP       HELP.COM       NIBBLES.BAS    REMLINE.BAS    MODE.COM
POWER.EXE      EXE2BIN.EXE    PRINT.EXE      JOIN.EXE       LCD.CPI
QBASIC.HLP     PRINTER.SYS    SHARE.EXE      DELOLDOS.EXE   SETVER.EXE
APPEND.EXE     APPNOTES.TXT   KEYBHP.COM     MODEHP.COM     SSTOR.SYS
DISKCOMP.COM   MOUSE.SYS      DISKCOPY.COM   B.BAT          589DOSCM.BAT
D5C0DOSC.BAT   2688DOSC.BAT   370CDOSC.BAT   D923DOSC.BAT   BA6EDOSC.BAT
D329DOSC.BAT   DRIVER.SYS     FC.EXE         FIND.EXE       GRAPHICS.COM
GRAPHICS.PRO   LABEL.EXE      SMARTMON.EXE   SMARTMON.HLP   SORT.EXE
LOADFIX.COM    MWBACKUP.EXE   MWBACKUP.HLP   REPLACE.EXE    SUBST.EXE
TREE.COM       DOSKEY.COM     VFINTD.386     MWBACKF.DLL    MWBACKR.DLL
MOUSE.COM      MSBACKUP.EXE   MSBACKUP.OVL   MSBACKFB.OVL   MSBACKFR.OVL
CHKSTATE.SYS   UNDELETE.EXE   MWUNDEL.EXE    MWUNDEL.HLP    MWGRAFIC.DLL
MSBACKUP.HLP   WNTOOLS.GRP    MSBACKDB.OVL   MSBACKDR.OVL   MSBCONFG.OVL
MSBCONFG.HLP   DBLSPACE.EXE   MEMMAKER.HLP   MEMMAKER.INF   INTERLNK.EXE
INTERSVR.EXE   MSCDEX.EXE     DBLSPACE.HLP   DBLSPACE.INF   DBLSPACE.SYS
DBLWIN.HLP     DOSSHELL.HLP   EMM386.EXE     MEMMAKER.EXE   SIZER.EXE
MONOUMB.386    MSTOOLS.DLL    MSAV.EXE       MSAV.HLP       MSAVHELP.OVL
MSAVIRUS.LST   VSAFE.COM      MWAVDOSL.DLL   MWAVDRVL.DLL   AUTOEXEC.UMB
MOUSE.INI      CONFIG.UMB     MEMMAKER.STS   MWAVDLG.DLL    MSBACKUP.INI
MWAVSCAN.DLL   MSBACKUP.RST   MSBACKUP.TMP   MWAV.EXE       MWAVABSI.DLL
MWAV.HLP       MWAVSOS.DLL    MWAVMGR.DLL    MWAVTSR.EXE    COMMAND.COM
MSAV.INI       DEFAULT.BAK    MSBACKUP.LOG   DEFAULT.SLT    DEFAULT.SAV
DOSSHELL.INI
      176 file(s)     6563296 bytes
                    129966080 bytes free

C>
```

Figure 2–2
Directory listing with DIR/W command.

Figure 2–3
Directory listing with DIR/P command.

```
C>DIR/P

 Volume in drive C is MS_DOS_6
 Volume Serial Number is 1C22-913B
 Directory of C:\DOS

.            <DIR>      06-06-92  12:24p
..           <DIR>      06-06-92  12:24p
DBLSPACE BIN     51214 03-10-93   6:00a
FORMAT   COM     22717 03-10-93   6:00a
NLSFUNC  EXE      7036 03-10-93   6:00a
COUNTRY  SYS     17066 03-10-93   6:00a
KEYB     COM     14983 03-10-93   6:00a
KEYBOARD SYS     34694 03-10-93   6:00a
SETUP    EXE     71974 03-10-93   6:00a
DOSSETUP INI      3735 03-10-93   6:00a
ANSI     SYS      9065 03-10-93   6:00a
ATTRIB   EXE     11165 03-10-93   6:00a
CHKDSK   EXE     12907 03-10-93   6:00a
EDIT     COM       413 03-10-93   6:00a
EXPAND   EXE     16129 03-10-93   6:00a
EDLIN    EXE     12642 06-13-91   5:00a
MORE     COM      2546 03-10-93   6:00a
MSD      EXE    158470 03-10-93   6:00a
QBASIC   EXE    194309 03-10-93   6:00a
Press any key to continue . . .

(continuing C:\DOS)
RESTORE  EXE     38294 03-10-93   6:00a
MIRROR   COM     18169 06-13-91   5:00a
SYS      COM      9379 03-10-93   6:00a
UNFORMAT COM     12738 03-10-93   6:00a
SMARTDRV SYS      8335 06-13-91   5:00a
OS2      TXT      6358 03-10-93   6:00a
NETWORKS TXT     20463 03-10-93   6:00a
README   TXT     44990 03-10-93   6:00a
DEBUG    EXE     15715 03-10-93   6:00a
FDISK    EXE     29333 03-10-93   6:00a
DOSSHELL VID      9462 03-10-93   6:00a
19C1DOSC BAT        16 01-23-93   3:05p
DEFAULT  SET      4207 01-02-94  10:49a
DOSSHELL GRB      4421 03-10-93   6:00a
CHOICE   COM      1754 03-10-93   6:00a
DEFRAG   EXE     75033 03-10-93   6:00a
PACKING  LST      2507 06-13-91   5:00a
DEFRAG   HLP      9227 03-10-93   6:00a
DOSSWAP  EXE     18756 03-10-93   6:00a
EGA      CPI     58870 03-10-93   6:00a
RECOVER  EXE      9146 06-13-91   5:00a
EGA      SYS      4885 03-10-93   6:00a
Press any key to continue . . .

(continuing C:\DOS)
HIMEM    SYS     14208 03-10-93   6:00a
MEM      EXE     32150 03-10-93   6:00a
XCOPY    EXE     15820 03-10-93   6:00a
MONEY    BAS     46225 06-13-91   5:00a
MSHERC   COM      6934 06-13-91   5:00a
DELTREE  EXE     11113 03-10-93   6:00a
GORILLA  BAS     29434 06-13-91   5:00a
4201     CPI      6404 06-13-91   5:00a
4208     CPI       720 06-13-91   5:00a
5202     CPI       395 06-13-91   5:00a
MOVE     EXE     17823 03-10-93   6:00a
ASSIGN   COM      6399 06-13-91   5:00a
RAMDRIVE SYS      5873 03-10-93   6:00a
BACKUP   EXE     36092 06-13-91   5:00a
```

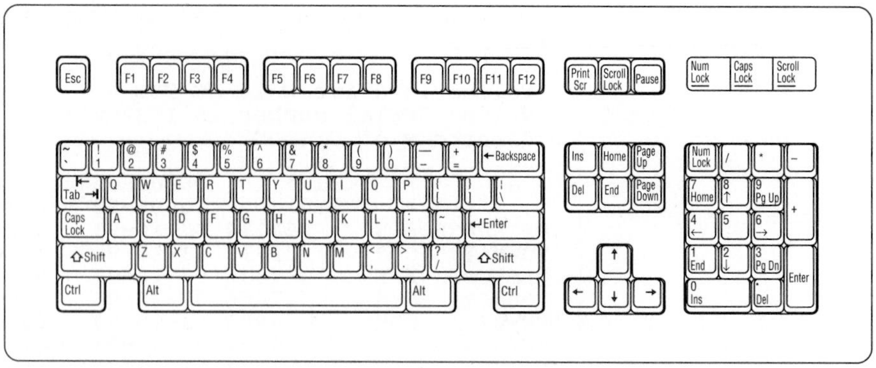

Figure 2–4
IBM enhanced keyboard (courtesy of International Business Machines Corp.).

2–7 IMPORTANT KEYS IN DOS ENVIRONMENT

Examine the picture of a typical keyboard in Figure 2–4. Several of the keys perform special tasks in the DOS environment. Table 2–1 briefly explains these keys.

2–8 CREATING YOUR OWN DATA DISK: THE FORMAT COMMAND

Before using a newly purchased floppy disk on your PC, you must format the disk. To format a disk at the C> prompt insert a blank disk in drive A; type *FORMAT A:* and press the Enter key. When the process is finished, DOS asks you if you would like to format another disk. If you answer Y (for yes), you will be prompted to insert a new disk. If you answer N (for no), the C> prompt will return. Various computers use different versions of the FORMAT command. Consult your DOS manual for the specific version of the FORMAT command for your computer.

When you format a disk, the operating system checks your entire disk for defective spots. It tells you if your disk is usable or not. The FORMAT command also divides a disk into tracks and sectors and creates the *File Allocation Table* (FAT). The FAT indicates where data is saved on a disk.

When you format a disk, that disk is completely erased. Make sure the disk you are formatting is either a new disk or an old disk with files for which you have no need. Figure 2–5 shows the formatting procedure. At the C> prompt we typed *FORMAT A:*, pressed Enter, and followed the prompt.

You can format a disk in a different drive than A. For example, at the C> prompt type *FORMAT B:* and press the Enter key; the disk in drive B will be formatted.

Having a formatted disk at hand, you are ready to use it as a data disk or to copy other programs onto it.

2–9 DIFFERENT VERSIONS OF MS-DOS AND PC-DOS

PC-DOS is for IBM microcomputers and MS-DOS is for IBM compatibles. Both of these programs have gone through several revisions. The first version was 1.0 and the latest is version 6.0. Each version has added new commands and corrected some of the bugs in the earlier versions. Major enhancements occurred in version 3.0 and later versions. Versions 3.1 and later include commands for the local area network (LAN) environment. Minor revisions are indicated as .1, .2, and so on. Major revisions are indicated as 2, 3, and so forth.

Table 2–1
Special Keys on the Keyboard

Keys	Description
Backspace	Backs up and erases the character typed
Ctrl+Alt+Del	A key combination used to warm boot the system—equivalent to turning your computer off, then turning it back on (without memory check)
Ctrl+C or Ctrl+Break	Cancels a command while it is being executed (Note: Look for Break on the side of the Pause key.)
Ctrl+Print Scr or Ctrl+P	Sends a copy of each line on the screen to the printer as it is being displayed, assuming you are connected to a printer and the printer is on. This command toggles the printer on. (Toggle means the key combination remains in effect until you press Ctrl and PrtScr or P again.) When the printer is toggled on, everything displayed on the screen will be printed.
Ctrl+S or Ctrl+Num Lock	Pauses the directory listing for viewing
Esc	Erases the current command or statement
F1 (function key)	Displays one character of the previous command by each press. Useful for editing a DOS command.
F3 (function key)	Displays the entire previous command. You can perform editing or just press F3 and then the Enter key to execute the command again.
Print Scr (one key)	In enhanced keyboards, does the same job as Shift+Prtsc
Shift+Prtsc	Sends a copy of the screen to the printer. This command does not toggle the printer on.

Figure 2–5
Formatting procedure.

```
C>FORMAT A:
Insert new diskette for drive A:
and press ENTER when ready...

Checking existing disk format.
Formatting 1.2M
Format complete.

Volume label (11 characters, ENTER for none)?

   1213952 bytes total disk space
   1213952 bytes available on disk

       512 bytes in each allocation unit.
      2371 allocation units available on disk.

Volume Serial Number is 0362-1BEC

Format another (Y/N)?N


C>
```

Versions of MS-DOS and PC-DOS are upwardly compatible: all the commands in earlier versions are available in the newer versions, but not vice versa. To a typical microcomputer user, PC-DOS and MS-DOS are almost identical. To find out which version of DOS you are using, at the DOS prompt, type *VER* and press the Enter key. This command displays the current version of DOS in the default drive. Figure 2–6 illustrates this process. It shows this DOS is version 6.0. In this text, DOS version 6.0 is used. All the commands discussed in the text work with all versions of DOS unless otherwise specified.

2–10 BATCH AND AUTOEXEC FILES

Batch files are disk files designed for a specific use. A batch file can have any standard name, but the extension must always be BAT. In theory, batch files can be of any length. You can include any valid command or statement in a batch file. To enter a command, you must always press the Enter key after the specific command. To generate a batch file you can use EDLIN, the line editor available on DOS prior to version 5.0, or any word processing program. DOS 5.0 and 6.0 include an impressive full-screen editor called EDIT. For simple batch files, you can use a version of the COPY command, which allows you to copy one or a series of files. For example, if the default drive is C, to copy a file named TEST from drive C to drive A, type *COPY TEST A:* and press Enter. To generate a simple batch file using the COPY command, the process is as follows:

```
C>COPY CON MYFILE.BAT     (press Enter)
Command or statement      (press Enter)
Command or statement      (press Enter)
Command or statement      (press Enter)
```

To terminate a batch file, press Ctrl and Z together (or the F6 function key). To execute a batch file, all you need to do is to insert the disk that includes the batch file and type the name of the file at the C> prompt.

A simple batch file follows:

```
C>COPY CON HELLO.BAT      (press Enter)
DIR                       (press Enter)
CLS                       (press Enter)
BASICA                    (press Enter)
                          (press Ctrl and Z keys together or press F6)
```

If you type *HELLO* at the C> prompt, you will see a listing of a directory of drive C, the screen will clear, and BASICA will be loaded to RAM. (The assumption is that drive C includes BASICA, a programming language available in the majority of computers.)

Figure 2–6
Finding out your version of DOS.

```
C>VER

MS-DOS Version 6.00

C>
```

The only limitation with COPY CON is that you cannot edit a file that has been created. For editing, you have to redo the entire file or use EDLIN, EDIT, or use some other word processing or editor-type system.

To stop the execution of a batch file, press Ctrl and Break at the same time.

If you name your file AUTOEXEC.BAT, it will be executed automatically as soon as you start the system. As a matter of fact, DOS always looks for the **autoexec file** first. If you have such a file, all its commands and statements will be executed. This facility can be very helpful. In addition to designing a menu or customizing your system, you can help people who are unfamiliar with computers by providing a question-and-answer type environment. Batch files in general are very helpful if you have to do a series of repetitive operations.

2–11 DEFINING A DIRECTORY

When you format a disk, DOS automatically creates a directory for you. This directory usually is called the **root directory**.

As a result of advances in disk technology, more and more files can be stored on a disk. These files are stored based on the date that they were created. As the number of files increases, it becomes extremely difficult to manage them properly. It becomes a time-consuming process to locate one file among several hundred.

There is a limit to the number of files that can be stored on a floppy disk or a hard disk. The root directory on a single-sided disk can hold up to 64 files; on a double-sided disk there can be up to 112 files. The root directory of a high-density disk can hold up to 224 files, and on a hard disk, up to 512 files. To create a better mechanism for storing and maintaining files and to bypass these file limitations, you can create **subdirectories**. A subdirectory is similar to a folder that contains a listing of files that you have grouped together based on a given scheme. (Subdirectory names follow the same conventions as file names.)

Consider a file cabinet in your office. Suppose that you store all important sales documents in this file cabinet. One method of storage is to throw all the sales documents in the cabinet as they arrive. In this case, retrieving information is a very difficult task. Another method is to divide the file cabinet into three separate parts (three subdirectories) by using some type of folders. You can then divide these folders into more logical parts (lower-level subdirectories). After this segmentation, you can put each document into its proper folder. This method, which is illustrated in Figure 2–7, improves retrieval time.

The directory below the root directory is considered a subdirectory to the root directory. A directory immediately below a subdirectory is considered a subdirectory to that subdirectory. In Figure 2–7, the WEST, SOUTH, and EAST regions are subdirectories to the root directory. OREGON and CALIFORNIA are subdirectories to the WEST region. They can be broken down further into SOUTHERN and NORTHERN (California) and so on.

As another example, suppose that on your hard disk you create four subdirectories for WordPerfect, Lotus 1-2-3, dBASE, and Quattro Pro. All your word processing documents will be saved in the WordPerfect directory, all your spreadsheets will be saved in the Lotus 1-2-3 directory, and so forth. Under Lotus 1-2-3, you may want to create two subdirectories, one for graphics files and one for database files. You can continue this process for several levels based on your specific needs.

The root directory is always identified by a back slash (\). The current subdirectory is identified by a period (.) and the parent subdirectory (the directory immediately above the current directory) is identified by two periods(..).

Figure 2–7
Example of directory structure.

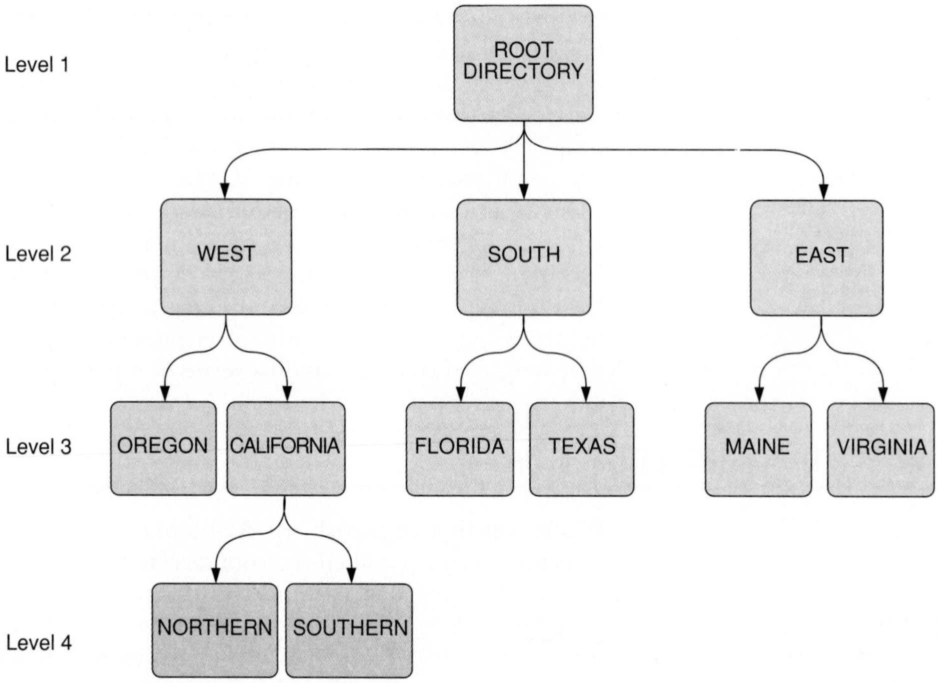

2–12 IMPORTANT COMMANDS FOR DIRECTORIES

To create a subdirectory, use the DOS command MKDIR (make directory) or MD. You must be in the directory immediately above the subdirectory you are creating. To change to a subdirectory or make a subdirectory the current directory, use the CHDIR (change directory) or CD command. The CD command uses several different parameters as shown in Table 2–2.

To remove a subdirectory, you first must erase all the files and subsequent subdirectories by using either the DEL or ERASE command. Then get in the root directory and use the RMDIR (remove directory) or RD command.

If you do not know in which directory you are working, use the PROMPT PG command. At the DOS prompt, type *PROMPT PG* and press Enter. The default prompt changes to a prompt that identifies the current directory. For example, if you are working in the OREGON directory, your new prompt will read C:\OREGON>.

To display the structure of your directory, use the TREE command. Type *TREE /F* to display each directory on your disk and the files stored within each directory.

Another powerful command that you can use with directories is the PATH command. This command establishes a search path. Suppose that the DOS disk is in drive A and you are working with a data disk in drive B. If you issue an external DOS command from drive B, you will receive an error message (because the DOS disk is in drive A). When you type *PATH A:* at the *A>* prompt, DOS searches the root directory on drive A for any commands that it cannot find in the current drive or directory (in this case drive B). You also can establish multiple search paths by using the PATH command and a semicolon (;). Suppose that you want to tell your computer to search for DOS commands in drive B and in a subdirectory on drive C called EXTERNAL. Type the following search path to do the job: *PATH B:\; C:\EXTERNAL.*

Table 2–2
Change Directory (CD) Command Parameters

Parameter	Function
CD.	Displays the current directory
CD..	Moves up one directory level
CD\	Moves up to the root directory from any directory level
CD..\..	Moves up two directory levels
CD\WEST\OREGON	OREGON becomes the current directory

When you establish a search path, it remains in effect until you turn off your PC. To cancel a search path, type *PATH* and press Enter. To make a search path permanent, enter the command into your AUTOEXEC.BAT file. Then, as soon as you start your computer, the search path will be activated.

2–13 DOS 5: AN OVERVIEW

In 1991, Microsoft Corporation released a new version of MS-DOS: **DOS 5.0**. In all ways, this release is a major improvement over the earlier releases of DOS. DOS 5 is uniquely identified by the following features:

- Memory management. DOS 5.0 allows the memory of your computer to be used more effectively. This is because DOS 5.0 loads itself to memory other than conventional memory. For example, DOS 5.0 loads drivers and TSR programs to the upper memory area, leaving you with more conventional memory.
- A shell program providing some of the features of Windows 3.0/3.1. Using the shell program, you enter a graphical-type environment. In this environment, you can access various options through the keyboard or simply through the mouse, which simplifies your DOS work.
- A DOS macro capability. Through a DOSKEY you can assign a series of options to a DOS command and then use this DOS command by only typing its name. This is almost like creating a mini batch file.
- Support for higher capacity disks. DOS 5.0 basically lets you utilize as much memory as your computer can support.
- Some command enhancement. Many new commands and new options in existing commands have been added in DOS 5.0. For example, two of the most important new commands are UNDELETE and UNFORMAT, which allow you to rescue your work erased mistakenly.
- Capability of task swapping. Using DOS 5.0, you can exit one application program such as a word processor and enter another application program such as Quattro Pro and easily get back to the word processor without closing the Quattro Pro program.
- A new and complete online help facility. DOS 5.0 enables you to receive online help for all DOS commands. At the DOS prompt, type *HELP* and press Enter for complete information on the help facility. Or type *HELP*, then the command name, and press Enter. This provides you with specific help on a given

command. For example, type *HELP DIR* and press Enter to receive online help for the DIR command.

- Full-screen editing feature. DOS 5.0 includes an impressive full-screen editing component that is similar to a word processor. (The EDLIN utility is still available for people who are familiar with it.)

All commands presented in this chapter work in DOS 5.0 and 6.0.. Consult Table 2–3 for summary of important DOS commands. The commands simplify DOS operations and your PC work.

Table 2–3
Important DOS Commands*

Command	Function
ATTRIB +R (Release 3 and higher)	Makes a file a read-only file, e.g., ATTRIB +R COMMAND.COM (press Enter). This makes COMMAND.COM a read-only file.
ATTRIB –R (Release 3 and higher)	Removes the read-only status, e.g., ATTRIB –R COMMAND.COM (press Enter)
CHDIR (CD)	Changes the current directory or displays the current directory path. For example, CD\ changes the current directory of a drive to its root directory
CHKDSK	Displays free space on diskette
CHKDSK B:	Displays free space on diskette in drive B
CLS	Clears the screen
COMP	Compares two files to determine if they are the same or if they are different, e.g., COMP A:TEXT.JOE B:TEXT.JAC
COPY Filename.ext B:	Copies Filename.ext to the B drive
COPY B:Filename.ext	Copies Filename.ext to the C drive
COPY *.ext B:	Copies all files with the same ext from the C drive to the B drive
COPY B:*.ext	Copies all files with the same ext from the B drive to the C drive
COPY *.* B:	Copies all files from the C drive to the B drive
COPY B:*.*	Copies all files from the B drive to the C drive
COPY Filename1.ext Filename2.ext	Copies a file from C to C with a different name
COPY B:Filename1.ext B:Filename2.ext	Copies a file from B to B with a different name
COPY Filename1.ext B:Filename2.ext	Copies a file from C to B with a different name

*To execute all of these commands, the C prompt is assumed. An A stands for A drive; B stands for B drive; ext stands for file extension (any three valid characters). Filename can be any valid file name.

Table 2–3 *(continued)*

<table>
<tr><th>Command</th><th>Function</th></tr>
<tr><td>COPY B:Filename1.ext Filename2.ext</td><td>Copies a file from B to C with a different name</td></tr>
<tr><td>COPY CON B:Filename.BAT</td><td>Creates a batch file in drive B. To terminate the file creation, press F6 then Enter.</td></tr>
<tr><td>CTRL-ALT-DEL</td><td>Resets the system (a warm boot)</td></tr>
<tr><td>DATE</td><td>Resets the system date</td></tr>
<tr><td>DEL Filename.ext</td><td>Erases Filename.ext from drive C</td></tr>
<tr><td>DEL B:Filename.ext</td><td>Erases Filename.ext from drive B</td></tr>
<tr><td>DEL B:Filename.*</td><td>Erases all Filenames with any extension from drive B</td></tr>
<tr><td>DEL B:*.ext</td><td>Erases all files with the same extension from drive B</td></tr>
<tr><td>DIR</td><td>Displays a directory of C</td></tr>
<tr><td>DIR B:</td><td>Displays a directory of B</td></tr>
<tr><td>DIR/P</td><td>Displays a complete directory of drive C with a pause before scrolling off the screen</td></tr>
<tr><td>DIR B:/P</td><td>Does the same as above for drive B</td></tr>
<tr><td>DIR/W</td><td>Displays a wide directory of drive C</td></tr>
<tr><td>DIR B:/W</td><td>Does the same as above for drive B</td></tr>
<tr><td>DIR|SORT (| This character is the broken line found on back-slash key)</td><td>Displays a sorted directory of drive C</td></tr>
<tr><td>DIR B:|SORT</td><td>Displays a sorted directory of drive B</td></tr>
<tr><td>DISKCOMP</td><td>Compares two diskettes track by track, sector for sector, to determine if their contents are identical, e.g., DISKCOMP A: B:</td></tr>
<tr><td>DISKCOPY A: B:</td><td>Copies a diskette in drive A to a diskette in drive B. The two drives must be identical.</td></tr>
<tr><td>ERASE Filename.ext</td><td>Erases Filename.ext on C</td></tr>
<tr><td>ERASE B:Filename.ext</td><td>Erases Filename.ext on B</td></tr>
<tr><td>ERASE *.ext</td><td>Erases all files with the same .ext on C</td></tr>
<tr><td>ERASE B:*.ext</td><td>Erases all files with the same .ext on B</td></tr>
<tr><td>FORMAT A:</td><td>Erases and formats a diskette in drive A</td></tr>
<tr><td>FORMAT B:</td><td>Erases and formats a diskette in drive B</td></tr>
<tr><td>FORMAT A:/V</td><td>Formats a diskette in drive A with a volume label (a name with up to 11 characters long)</td></tr>
<tr><td>FORMAT B:/V</td><td>Formats a new diskette with a volume label (a name with up to 11 characters long) in drive B</td></tr>
</table>

Table 2–3
(continued)

Command	Function
LABEL	Creates, changes, or deletes a volume label for a disk, e.g., type *LABEL* and press Enter; follow the prompt
MKDIR (MD)	Creates a subdirectory on C drive, e.g., MD CLIENTS
PATH	Instructs DOS to search a specified directory for a program that cannot be found in the current directory, e.g., PATH C:\
PROMPT	Customizes the DOS system prompt, e.g., PROMPT Hello
PROMPT PG	Displays the current subdirectory that you are in
RENAME Filename1.ext Filename2.ext	Renames a file on C
RENAME B:Filename1.ext B:Filename2.ext	Renames a file on B
RMDIR (RD)	Removes a subdirectory from a disk, e.g., RD C:CPA. Remember, the subdirectory must be empty
SHIFT-PrtSc or Print Scr	Prints a copy of the screen
SYS	Puts a copy of operating system files IBMDOS.COM and IBMBIO.COM on the specified diskette or hard disk, e.g., SYS B:
TIME	Resets system time
TREE	Displays the structure of the current directory
TYPE Filename.ext	Displays the content of Filename.ext
TYPE B:Filename.ext	Displays the content of Filename.ext on B
VER	Displays the DOS version number on the screen
VERIFY	Checks the data just written to a disk to be sure the data has been correctly recorded and then displays if the data has been checked, e.g., VERIFY ON sets verify status on, VERIFY OFF sets verify status off, and VERIFY shows verify status.
VOL	Displays the volume label of a disk, if the label exists

2–14 HIGHLIGHTS OF DOS 6.0

DOS 6.0, which was released in April 1993, offers features not available in the previous versions of DOS. Some of the important features of this release are listed next:

- Disk compression that can almost double the capacity of your hard disk
- Back-up facility for easy backing up of your hard disk
- Antivirus feature which eliminates known viruses. Computer viruses are a series of computer codes that can wipe out your computer hard disk.
- Memory management, more powerful than DOS 5.0, that can increase availability of your RAM by up to 100 K
- Advanced communications capabilities for accessing files and peripherals on other PCs with compatible software.
- Availability of electronic mail (E-mail) program. By means of this feature, you can send and receive mail through your computer
- File sharing utility for exchanging files with another microcomputer.
- Ease of use by improving online help
- New commands such as *MOVE* for moving files and DELTREE for deleting a directory and its contents and all its subdirectories

SUMMARY

This chapter introduced you to elementary DOS operations, beginning with differences between internal and external DOS commands. Types of DOS prompts and file name specifications in the DOS environment were described, and the DIR command with different switches was highlighted. Important keys used frequently in DOS environment were introduced. The chapter also examined the FORMAT command, which is necessary for preparing blank disks. After a brief discussion of different versions of MS-DOS and PC-DOS, DOS 5 and 6.0 were outlined briefly. The chapter featured with a table of the most commonly used DOS commands.

REVIEW QUESTIONS

*These questions are answered in Appendix A.

1. What is a cold boot?
2. What is a warm boot?
*3. Why is it important to enter the correct time and date at boot-up time (if the system does not have an internal battery)?
4. What are internal DOS commands?
5. What are external DOS commands?
6. How many different DOS prompts are there?
*7. How do you change from drive C to A and from A to C?
8. What is the default drive?
9. Describe a valid DOS file name.
10. Give three examples of file extensions.
11. How many different ways can you use the DIR command?
12. Name the two DOS wildcards.

13. Describe the functions of the F1, F3, and F6 keys.
14. Why must a new disk be formatted before it can be used?
*15. What is a batch file? What is an autoexec file?
*16. Give three examples of DOS internal and three examples of DOS external commands.
17. What is a directory?
18. Why should you use directories?
19. List some directory commands.
20. How do you get to the root directory from a three-layered subdirectory?
21. How do you remove a directory?
22. What are some of the features of DOS 5.0?
23. How can you receive online help in DOS 5.0?

HANDS-ON EXPERIENCE

1. Start your computer. At the C> prompt enter the date as *1-1-95*. Change it back to today's date.
2. Change the default drive from C to A or from A to C. Type *DIR* and press Enter. What are the contents of drive A and of drive C?
3. By using Ctrl+Alt+Del, warm boot your computer. Type *DIR* and press Enter. How many different types of file extensions do you see in the directory?
4. Type *DIR/W* and press Enter; then type *DIR/P* and press Enter. What is the difference between these two commands?
5. By using the asterisk wildcard (*), generate listings of all COM files, of all EXE files, and of all SYS files.
6. Format a new disk. Use the COPY command to copy all COM files from drive C to this formatted disk.
7. Use the VER command to determine the version of DOS that you are using.
8. Create two directories on a diskette in drive A; name them TEST1 and TEST2. Copy two COM files from drive C to TEST1. Now copy the contents of TEST1 to TEST2.
9. Remove TEST1 from your disk.

KEY TERMS

Autoexec files	DOS 5.0	Internal command
Batch files	DOS 6.0	Root directory
Cold boot	External command	Subdirectory
Directory	File allocation table (FAT)	Warm boot
Disk operating system (DOS)	File extension	
	File name	

KEY COMMANDS

See Tables 2–1 through 2–3

MISCONCEPTIONS AND SOLUTIONS

Misconception You turn on your PC and you see a message that is not familiar to you, for example:

```
NON-SYSTEM DISK
```

Solution You forgot to put the DOS disk in drive A, or you inserted your disk on the wrong side, or you inserted a data disk instead of the DOS disk. Insert the DOS disk into drive A properly and reboot the system.

Misconception You are trying to format a disk in the A drive and receive this error message:

```
ATTEMPTED WRITE-PROTECT VIOLATION
```

Solution The disk in drive A has the write-protection notch covered. Either remove the protection or insert another disk.

Misconception You are using the FORMAT command and receive this error message:

```
DRIVE NOT READY
```

Solution Either the target drive door is not closed or there is no disk in that drive. Insert a disk in this drive, close the drive door, and press Enter.

Misconception You are using a DOS command and receive one of these error messages:

```
SYNTAX ERROR   BAD COMMAND   FILENAME ERROR
```

Solution Check the spelling of the command. Most likely, you have misspelled a command.

ARE YOU READY TO MOVE ON?

Multiple Choice

1. The procedure known as warm boot means
   - **a.** inserting the DOS disk in drive A and turning on the computer
   - **b.** typing the name of the program to be run and pressing Enter
   - **c.** simultaneously pressing the Ctrl, Alt, and Del keys
   - **d.** formatting a disk
   - **e.** none of the above
2. Which of the following prompts are you most likely to see after performing a cold boot with the DOS disk in drive A?
   - **a.** A>
   - **b.** B>
   - **c.** C>
   - **d.** OK
   - **e.** C:/DOS>
3. If the correct date and time are not entered during the boot process or if you want to change them at any time, the commands are
   - **a.** HOUR and DAY
   - **b.** DAY and HOUR

   c. DATE and CLOCK
   d. DATE and TIME
   e. none of the above

4. To change the default drive from drive B to drive A, what should you type at the DOS prompt before pressing Enter?
   a. *A*
   b. *DRIVE=A*
   c. *B+A*
   d. *GO TO A:*
   e. *A:*

5. File names with these extensions can be executed by typing the name of the file. (Remember, both extensions in each pair must be correct.)
   a. COM and SYS
   b. COM and EXE
   c. EXE and SYS
   d. BAK and SYS
   e. BAK and BAT

6. The command DIR/P will yield
   a. the same as DIR
   b. a wide directory listing
   c. one screen at a time of the file listing
   d. a hard copy output to the printer
   e. nothing—it is not a valid command

7. The command to format a disk in drive B is
   a. ERASE B:
   b. DELETE *.*
   c. SYS B:
   d. FORMAT B:
   e. A or B

8. The file allocation table indicates
   a. where data are saved on a disk
   b. the maximum number of files that can be saved on disk
   c. how much disk space is available
   d. how much memory (RAM) is available
   e. none of the above

9. A typical computer response to the command VER is
   a. Disk Verified OK
   b. MS_DOS Version 5.0
   c. File Verified OK
   d. Insert new disk and strike Enter when ready
   e. A or B

10. When you format a disk,
   a. all data is erased
   b. the file allocation table is created
   c. the operating system checks for defective spots
   d. the disk is divided into sectors and tracks
   e. all of the above occur

True/False

1. If the computer is off and the system does not have a hard disk, the DOS disk must be placed in drive A to boot the computer.
2. A cold boot is faster than a warm boot because the computer does not check the memory.

3. To get back to the root directory from a subdirectory, type *CD* and press Enter.
4. External DOS commands are those loaded into the computer memory at boot-up time.
5. The DOS prompt indicates the current default drive.
6. The DIR command generates a listing of the files in the default directory.
7. DOS wildcards act as placeholders for other characters and include *, ?, @, $, %, and ¦.
8. DIR and DIR/W yield exactly the same information except that DIR/W places it in a wide format.
9. To move up two directory levels, type *CD..\..* and press Enter.
10. Versions of MS-DOS and PC-DOS are not upwardly compatible.

ANSWERS

Multiple Choice		True/False	
1.	c	1.	T
2.	a	2.	F
3.	d	3.	T
4.	e	4.	F
5.	b	5.	T
6.	c	6.	T
7.	d	7.	F
8.	a	8.	F
9.	b	9.	T
10.	e	10.	F

Lotus 1-2-3: A Quick Preview

3–1 INTRODUCTION

This chapter provides an overview of Lotus 1-2-3. We begin with the process of getting in and getting out of the program. Next, the help facility of 1-2-3 is described. After you develop a general familiarity with 1-2-3, we focus on how it functions as a decision support system tool. Mouse support for 1-2-3 is highlighted. Moving around the worksheet and correcting mistakes are discussed. The chapter concludes with an overview of a worksheet.

3–2 WHAT IS A SPREADSHEET?

A **spreadsheet,** or **worksheet,** is simply a table or a matrix of rows and columns. It is similar to an accounting journal. The intersection of each row and column is called a cell. A cell in any spreadsheet can hold any type of data or information—numbers, formulas, or text. The major differences between an electronic spreadsheet and an accounting journal are the enhanced flexibility, speed, and accuracy provided by the electronic spreadsheet.

Lotus 1-2-3 features a worksheet of 8,192 rows and 256 columns. Rows are numbered from 1 to 8,192 and columns are indicated by the letters A to IV. The intersection of a row and a column is called a cell. A cell or **cell address** is uniquely identified by a column letter and a row number. Figure 3–1 illustrates an empty 1-2-3 worksheet showing a table of 20 rows and 8 columns. Figure 3–2 illustrates an empty 1-2-3 worksheet in text mode. By default Lotus 1-2-3 Release 2.4 activates a WYSIWYG add-in program. You can return to the text mode by detaching the WYSIWYG add-in program. We will talk about WYSIWYG in detail

Figure 3–1
1-2-3 blank worksheet in WYSIWYG.

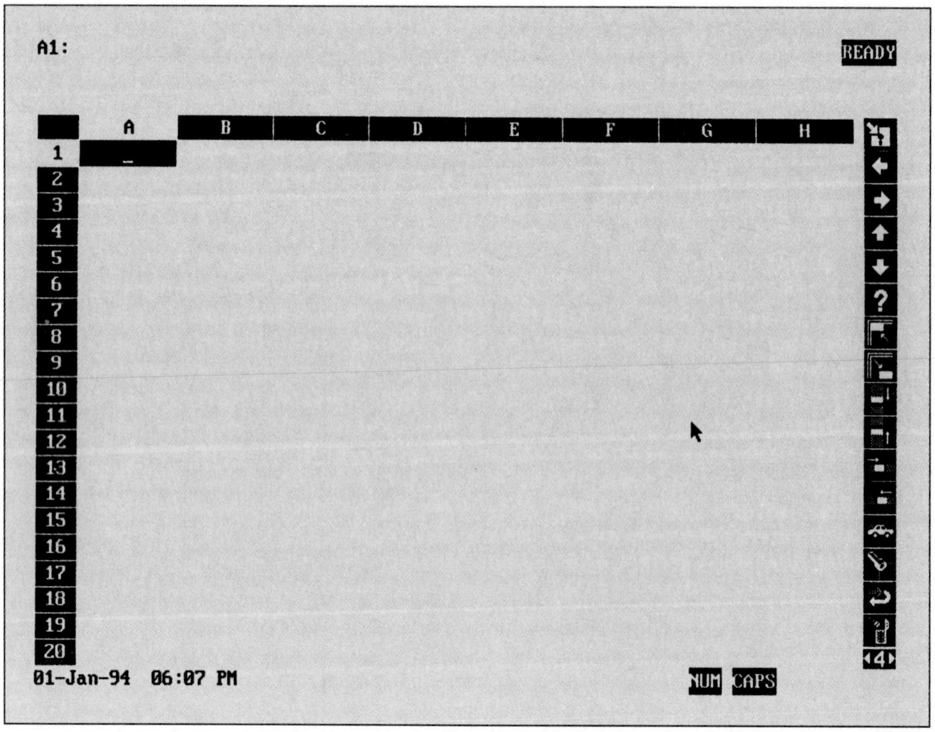

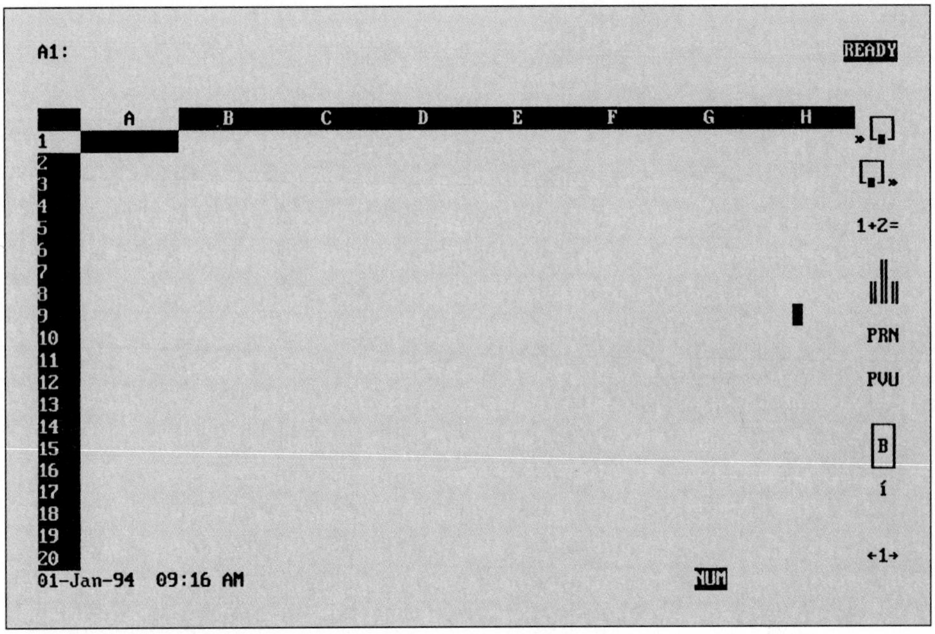

Figure 3–2
1-2-3 blank worksheet in text mode (WYSIWYG is not attached).

in Chapter 9. In this text all the screens are displayed in WYSIWYG mode. WYSIWYG mode allows you to see all formatting and text enhancements on the screen as well as on the printout.

Theoretically, the number of applications that can be handled by an electronic spreadsheet is unlimited. In general terms, any application that can fit into a row and column setting can be handled by a spreadsheet program. This includes balance sheets, income statements, budgeting analyses, mailing lists, databases, and sales analyses. The size and sophistication of a spreadsheet depends on the type of program. Some are just dedicated spreadsheets (e.g., VisiCalc), whereas others are integrated packages that perform many more applications. Lotus 1-2-3 is able to perform graphics and database operations in addition to spreadsheet analysis.

3–3 GETTING IN AND OUT OF 1-2-3

To begin, you must install 1-2-3 on your hard disk. Consult the 1-2-3 user's guide for the installation procedure. By using the DOS CD command, change the directory to the directory that includes 1-2-3 (for example, type *CD 123R24* and press Enter), then type *123* and press Enter. After a few seconds you will be presented with a screen similar to the one in Figure 3–1 or Figure 3–2. 1-2-3 commands can be accessed either through the keyboard or by use of the mouse. We will discuss these two methods later in this chapter.

To activate the 1-2-3 menu, either press the / (forward slash) key or move the mouse cursor to the top of the screen. In either case you will be presented with Figure 3–3. To use the mouse, put the mouse cursor on a given option then click its left button. To get out of 1-2-3, invoke the menu (by using the / key or the mouse), press Q (for Quit), then select Y (for Yes). Now you will be back to DOS or your starting menu.

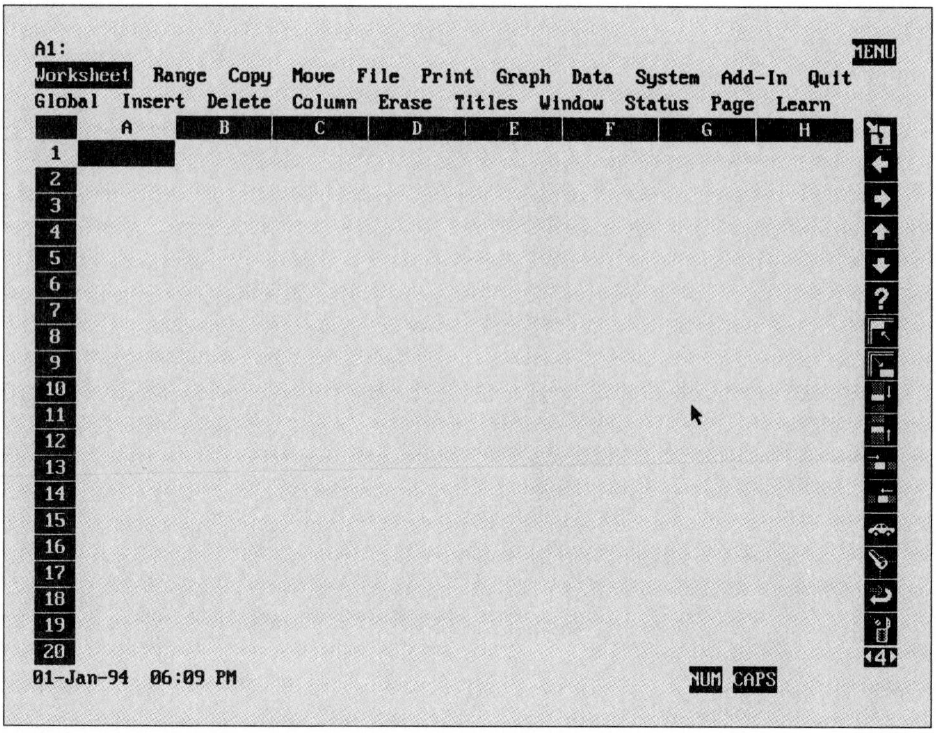

Figure 3–3
1-2-3 main menu.

3–4 HELP FACILITIES

When you are using 1-2-3, you can always receive help by accessing the online Help menu. Say you have a blank worksheet on the screen without a menu displayed. If you press the F1 function key, the 1-2-3 Main Help Index menu is brought up (see Figure 3–4). You can move the cursor to any of the topics, and when you press Enter, the help facilities on that topic will be displayed. This index is organized alphabetically and you can only see one screen at a time. Use the down-arrow key to move through the list alphabetically. As you can see at the bottom of Figure 3–4, you can press F1 for the listing of index, F3 for a listing of all the keys and their functions, F8 to go back, and Esc to get out of the help facility. Throughout your 1-2-3 work, press F1 to receive online help for any command or function. As an example, move the cursor to 1-2-3 Keys on the Main Help Index menu and press Enter. (You have to move down to see 1-2-3 Keys.) You are presented with Figure 3–5. From this menu select the first option (Function Keys), which gives you Figure 3–6. To see the rest of the function keys, move the cursor down.

3–5 WHAT 1-2-3 CAN DO FOR YOU

The number of applications handled by a spreadsheet such as 1-2-3 is practically unlimited. Although the major applications of 1-2-3 have been in the areas of finance and accounting, many other disciplines have effectively utilized this powerful software. In the next few pages we will concentrate on some of the most common applications.

Figure 3–4
1-2-3 Main Help Index.

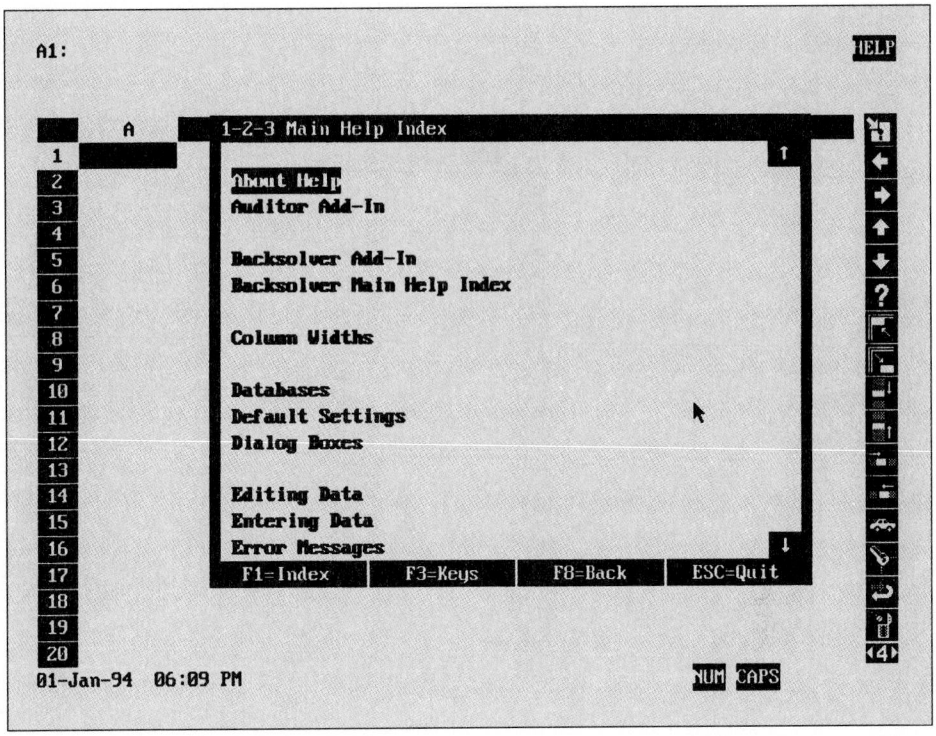

Figure 3–5
Help facility on 1-2-3 Keys.

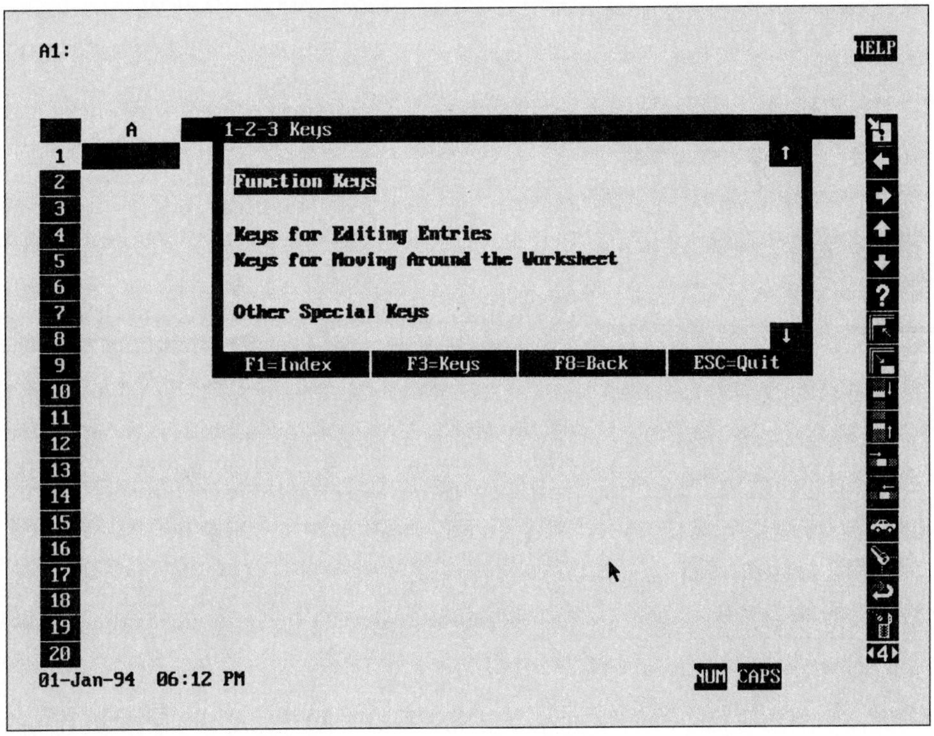

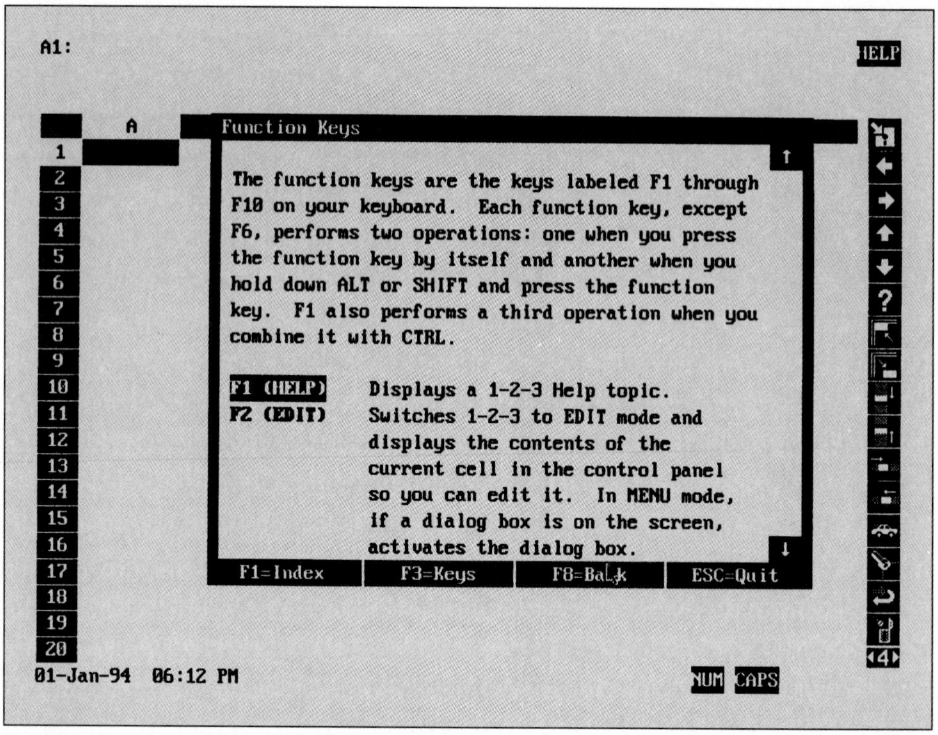

Figure 3–6
Help facility on function keys.

3–5–1 A Decision Support System Tool

1-2-3 has been used and evaluated as a **decision support system** (DSS) tool. A DSS tool or product is any software package that can help make a decision or a better decision. The minimum requirement of a DSS product or tool is the capability of performing what-if analyses, goal-seeking operations, sensitivity analyses, and modeling analyses. As you will see throughout this book, 1-2-3 can perform all of these functions. These capabilities are either readily available in the 1-2-3 command structure or can be developed within 1-2-3.

3–5–2 What-If Analysis

What-if analysis is useful for calculating the effects of a change in one variable on other variables or on the entire worksheet. A simple example is the case of break-even analysis. The break-even point is the number of units produced at which the total cost is equal to the total revenue. For example, if the fixed cost of a company's operation is $500, the variable cost of a unit is $10, and the selling price per unit is $15, the break-even point is 100 units. If the company produces and sells this quantity, it neither loses nor gains. If the company produces and sells more than 100 units, it gains. If it produces and sells fewer than 100, it loses. What-if analysis shows what happens to the break-even point if changes are made to the selling price per unit and/or to the fixed and variable costs. Lotus 1-2-3 can easily perform the calculations when changes to these variables are made.

The what-if feature can be used in a much more complex environment such as in budgeting. Let us say you have projected the budget of your company for the next five years. It includes projected incomes and projected costs. Suddenly you notice that the projected income for one year will be reduced by 5 percent. What is the impact of this income reduction on the entire budget? Thousands of calculations must be done to answer this question. The accuracy of the entire process is a critical concern. Don't worry. If your budget is on a 1-2-3 spreadsheet, the program will do all the recalculations in a blink of an eye and with no errors! Just change the old value to the new value and press the Enter key.

What-if analysis works with graphics and tables as well. Change any data item and press the F10 (Graph) key in the READY mode and bingo! Your graph will instantly be redrawn (refer to Chapter 8). As you will see in Chapter 10, 1-2-3 provides you with table-handling procedures; that in itself is a good application of what-if analysis. You can monitor the impact of one or two variables on the entire worksheet or on a specific block.

3–5–3 Goal-Seeking Analysis

Goal-seeking analysis is the reverse of what-if analysis. Here you may ask a question such as, to generate $5 million in total sales, how much advertising should I do? If you build an advertising model (1-2-3 provides you with facilities to do so), then performing such goal-seeking analysis is easy. One variable or many variables can be changed depending on the complexity of your model. Fairly complex mathematical models can be built, and once built, the user can leave recalculations to the speed and accuracy of 1-2-3.

3–5–4 Sensitivity Analysis

Sensitivity analysis is basically the monitoring of the range, elasticity, or variation within a model. Let us say that in a production setting you are paying $25 per hour to workers on the assembly line. If the workers ask for more money, how much more can you pay and still make a profit? Sensitivity analysis studies the range of variation for a variable and calculates its effect over the entire system. Again, 1-2-3 provides you with such a facility.

3–5–5 Building an Integrated DSS

1-2-3, by its combination of a powerful spreadsheet, database management, and graphics, can serve as an integrated DSS package. The database component can be used for storing data and for basic database operations (see Chapter 10). Data can be organized in different orders, sorted, or searched. Data can also be used for modeling analysis; 1-2-3 provides many different models (built-in formulas). Many of the built-in functions, especially the financial functions, can be used directly. In addition, the Matrix and Regression commands can help build sophisticated forecasting models. After analysis and model building is complete, in no time at all the graphics portion of 1-2-3 can provide various graphs. Even though all operations (database, spreadsheet, and graphics) are done within one package, the speed and effectiveness is extremely high.

3–6 MOVING AROUND YOUR WORKSHEET

Start with a blank worksheet; the cursor is at column A, row 1, or cell A1. Now you are able to move around the entire worksheet by using the following keys:

→ (right arrow)	Moves the cursor one cell to the right.
← (left arrow)	Moves the cursor one cell to the left.
↑ (up arrow)	Moves the cursor up one cell.
↓ (down arrow)	Moves the cursor down one cell.

PgUp	Moves the cursor up one screen.
PgDn	Moves the cursor down one screen.
Goto (F5)	Takes you to any location in the worksheet. To activate Goto, press the F5 function key and 1-2-3 will request a position. Type the address of the desired cell, press the Enter key, and there you go!
Home	Takes you to the "home cell" (the cell in the upper left corner of worksheet, e.g., cell A1).
End	Moves the cursor to a place indicated by another key. Used with arrow keys. Press End first, release your finger, and then press the other key; or press them simultaneously.
End + Home	Moves the cursor to the bottom right cell of your active worksheet. For example, if you have some information in cell A1 and in cell C2, the End + Home combination puts you in cell C2.
End + ↑	Moves the cursor up to the last cell above the current position (occupied or empty).
End + ↓	Moves the cursor down to the last empty cell or last occupied cell below the current position.
End + →	Moves the cursor to the last right cell of the worksheet to the right of the current position (occupied or empty).
End + ←	Moves the cursor to the last left cell of the worksheet to the left of the current position (occupied or empty).

Also see the SmartIcons for moving around presented in Table 3–1 at the end of the chapter. We will talk about SmartIcons in this chapter and Chapter 4.

3–7 MOUSE SUPPORT FOR 1-2-3

The commands of 1-2-3 can be accessed either through the keyboard by use of the forward slash key (/) or by use of a mouse. For example, to activate the help facility, move the mouse cursor to the question mark in the Number 4 Palette SmartIcon and click the left button of the mouse.

To make the mouse function, place your hand over the mouse, gently grasping the sides between your thumb and ring finger. The small rectangle that appears on the screen is called the mouse cursor (see Figure 3–2). In WYSIWYG mode it takes the shape of an arrow (see Figure 3–1). Its movements correspond to the movements of the mouse across your desk or table. The cursor allows you to make selections from menus or objects on the screen. You may select a menu option or screen item by first "pointing" to any object on the screen, then "shooting" (pressing the button)—the "point and shoot" technique. By moving the mouse so that the cursor is pointing (highlighting) the desired object and pressing Enter, you eliminate the need to keep your hands on the keyboard at all times. This method may make a program easier to learn and quicker to use, because the mouse can move across the screen very rapidly to perform the desired actions. Furthermore, you need not learn complicated keyboard sequences or combinations to use a program effectively.

Another use of the mouse is cursor movement. Rather than using the arrow keys to reposition the cursor within a spreadsheet, you can simply point the mouse cursor to the new position you wish to move to, then click the left button. The flashing cursor will automatically reposition itself to the new location. If you hold down the left button and move the cursor to the top, bottom, left side, or right side of your screen, the spreadsheet will automatically scroll up, down, left, or right, depending on your direction of movement. Release the mouse button when you have scrolled to the desired location in your document. You can also use the icons presented in Table 3–1 to move around using a mouse.

Blocking areas of the spreadsheet can also be done easily using the mouse. By holding down the left button and moving the mouse cursor, you can automatically block areas to prepare them for operations such as moving, copying, erasing, and so forth. To try this, type some numbers into cells A1 through A5. Position the mouse cursor at cell A1, hold down the left button, then move the mouse cursor down through cell A5. Notice that 1-2-3 blocks the cells for further action. With your hand still holding down the left button, move the mouse cursor back toward cell A1. As you can see, the blocking feature follows the movements of the mouse. By using this method, you can block as much or as little of the spreadsheet as you desire.

3–8 YOUR FIRST WORKSHEET

You can enter data items in your worksheet by two methods: (1) typing the data item, pressing the Enter key, and moving the cursor to the next cell, or (2) typing the data item and moving the cursor to the next cell. Option 2 is faster, but both will get the job done.

Let's create a worksheet.

1. Move the cursor to cell A1 and type *L.A.*
2. Move the cursor to cell B1 and type *1000.*
3. Move the cursor to cell A2 and type *DENVER.*
4. Move the cursor to cell B2 and type *2000.*
5. Move the cursor to cell A3 and type *PORTLAND.*
6. Move the cursor to cell B3 and type *3000.*

Your spreadsheet should be similar to Figure 3–7. As the worksheet illustrates, L.A. is in row 1 and column A (cell A1), 1000 is in row 1 and column B (cell B1), Denver is in row 2 and column A (cell A2), and so on.

A new entry will replace an old entry. For example, if you move the cursor to cell A3, type *Orlando,* and press the Enter key, the content of cell A3 will become Orlando. Try this on your worksheet. Remember, in any worksheet, regardless of its size, you can only see 20 rows and 8 columns (columns in default setting). To see the rest of your worksheet, you must move the cursor down or use the PgDn key to see one screen of your worksheet at a time.

To erase the current worksheet, choose /, then W (for Worksheet), then E (for Erase), and Y (for Yes).

3–9 CORRECTING MISTAKES

If you make an error, do not panic; there are two ways of **correcting mistakes.** The first method is to replace the contents of the cell by reentering the data item. This method may not be efficient, however, especially if the content of a cell is a long series of characters. The second method—the preferred one—is to edit the content of the cell that contains the mistake(s). This is how **editing** is done:

Figure 3–7
Sample worksheet with some data items.

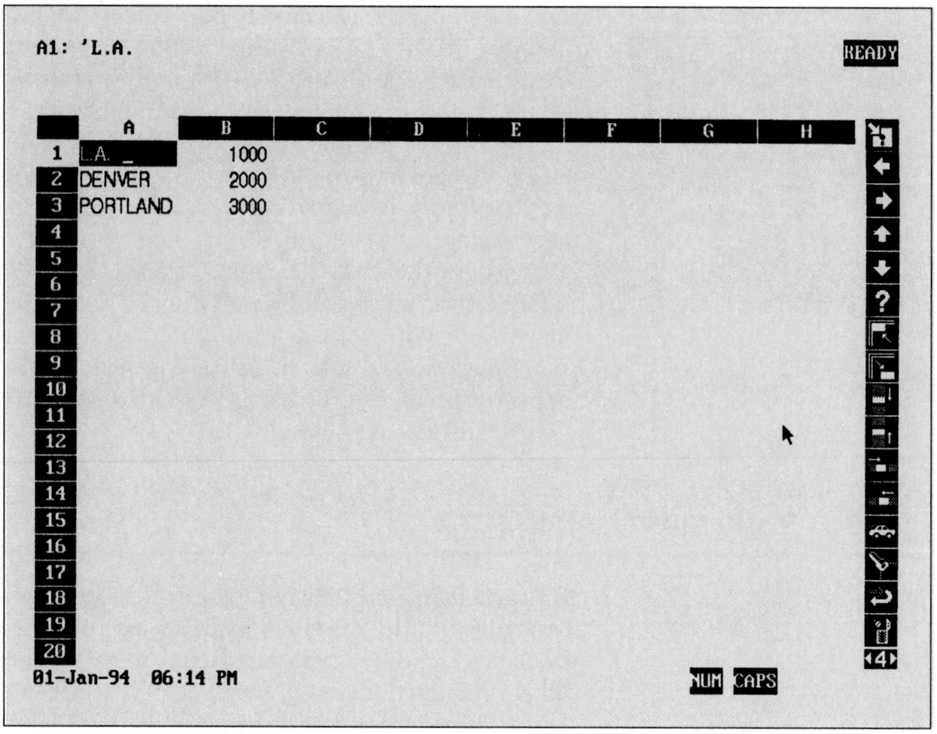

1. Move the cursor to the cell that contains the error.
2. Press the F2 function key (Edit key); now the cursor is at the end of the last character in that cell in the control panel.
3. The control panel is the area on the top of the worksheet; you can display data or 1-2-3 menus in this area. Use the left- or the right-arrow key to move to the position where the mistake occurs and retype that particular character(s). The new character will be inserted to the left of the cursor position.
4. Delete the unwanted character(s) by moving to those characters and pressing the Del key.
5. Press Enter to signal the end of editing.

Let us assume that in Figure 3–7 you mistakenly typed Denver as *Dennver* and you wish to correct the spelling.

1. Move the cursor to cell A2.
2. Press the F2 key.
3. Use the ← (left arrow) to move the cursor to one of the Ns.
4. Press Del and then press the Enter key.

Other keys are helpful for editing data:

Backspace	Erases the character to the left of the cursor
Insert (Ins)	Toggles the INSERT mode on and off. If the key is not pressed down, text will be inserted by moving existing characters to the right. If the key is pressed down, old characters will be replaced by the new ones typed in.
Escape (Esc)	Cancels the entire line where the cursor resides if pressed while editing or replacing a cell entry. The length of the line does not

matter. Pressing Esc before pressing Enter results in keeping the old entry. Pressing Esc when entering data into a blank cell cancels the data entry for that cell. Think of pressing Esc as a way of changing your mind about your current data entry.

3–10 IMPORTANT AREAS ON THE WORKSHEET

Consider the blank worksheet presented in Figure 3–8. At the top of the screen on the second line is the Main menu of 1-2-3. This menu includes 11 options:

`Worksheet Range Copy Move File Print Graph Data System Add-In Quit`

The cursor is in cell A1: column A and row 1. It can be moved to any location by using the mouse or the arrow movement keys. On the right border of the worksheet, notice the **SmartIcons palette.** The 1-2-3 SmartIcons add-in provides a total of 77 icons organized in palettes. A **palette** is a column of icons that appears to the right of the worksheet. The total number of palettes that you can have depends on your screen display type (CGA, EGA, or VGA) and on whether or not WYSIWYG is attached. We will talk about these icons in detail in the next chapter. For now, remember that commonly used 1-2-3 tasks can be simplified by using these icons.

At the top right of the worksheet, you can see the mode indicator, which says MENU. As soon as you press Esc, the mode indicator changes to READY. A listing of all mode indicators appears in Appendix A. The NUM at the bottom of the screen indicates that the Num Lock key is pressed down. This is called the status indicator; there are several, and they are discussed in Appendix A. If you press the Num Lock key again, NUM will disappear from the screen. To the bottom left, you can see the date and time. This indicates the system date and time, which can be changed through DOS. You can remove them by typing */WGDOCNQ.* Toward the center of the screen, note the mouse cursor.

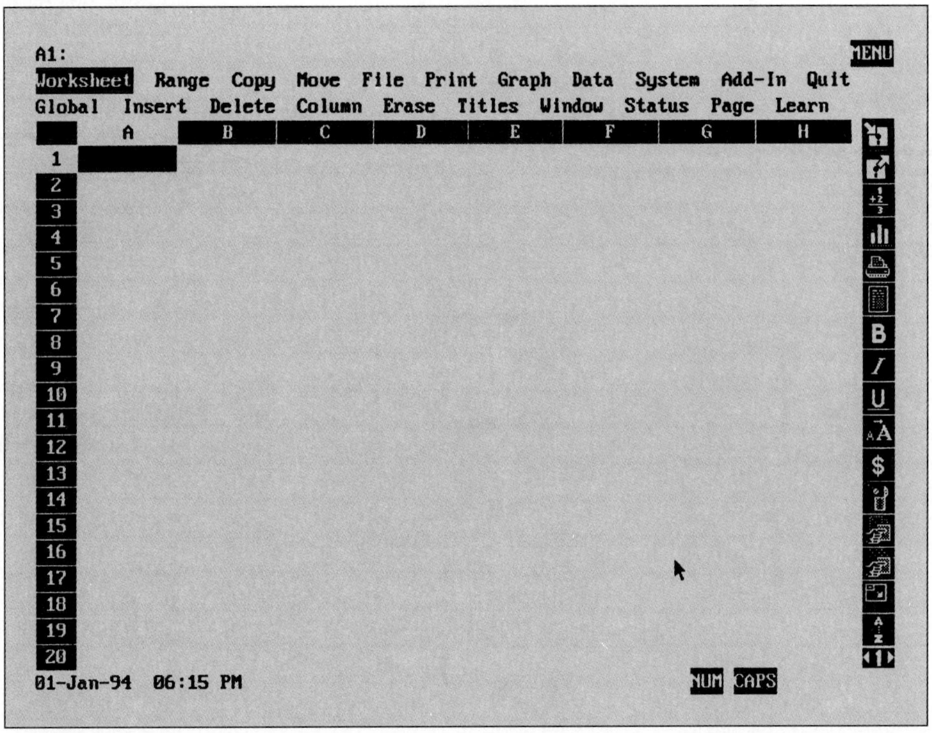

Figure 3–8
Sample blank worksheet with 1-2-3 main menu activated.

SUMMARY

In this chapter you had a quick review of the functions of a spreadsheet. You also learned about several features of 1-2-3: the help facility, the process of getting in and getting out of the program, and 1-2-3 as a DSS tool. In addition, the chapter described mouse support for 1-2-3, moving around in a worksheet and correcting mistakes, and the important areas of a worksheet. As you will see in the following chapters, the 1-2-3 package is capable of doing many things—it is limited only by your imagination!

See Table 3–1 for arrow movement SmartIcons.

Table 3–1
Arrow Movement Icons

WYSIWYG Mode	Text Mode	Description
	◀	Moves the cell pointer left one cell.
	▶	Moves the cell pointer right one cell.
	▲	Moves the cell pointer up one cell.
	▼	Moves the cell pointer down one cell.
	?	Starts the 1-2-3 Help system in READY mode.
		Moves the cell pointer to cell A1. Equivalent to pressing HOME.
		Moves the cell pointer to the lower right corner of the active area (the rectangular area between cell A1 and the lowest and rightmost nonblank cell in the worksheet).
	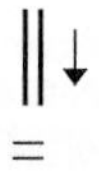	Moves the cell pointer down to the intersection of a blank and a nonblank cell. Equivalent to pressing END and then ↓.
		Moves the cell pointer up to the intersection of a blank and a nonblank cell. Equivalent to pressing END and then ↑.
	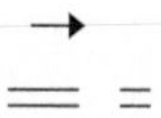	Moves the cell pointer right to the intersection of a blank and a nonblank cell. Equivalent to pressing END and then →.
	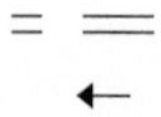	Moves the cell pointer left to the intersection of a blank and nonblank cell. Equivalent to pressing END and then ←.
	GOTO	Lets you move the cell pointer to a specified cell range. Equivalent to pressing F5.

Column 1 shows icons if WYSIWYG is attached. Column 2 shows icons as they appear when WYSIWYG is either not attached or is set to: Display Mode Text.
The icons identified by **W** work only when WYSIWYG is attached.

REVIEW QUESTIONS

*These questions are answered in Appendix A.

*1. How would you compare 1-2-3 to a manual accounting spreadsheet?
2. How do you define a spreadsheet?
3. How do you get 1-2-3 started?
*4. How do you get out of 1-2-3?
5. Mention 10 specific applications of 1-2-3.
6. Why is 1-2-3 considered a DSS product?
7. Give an example of what-if analysis using 1-2-3.
8. What is goal-seeking analysis and how can 1-2-3 perform such a task?
9. Describe two examples of using 1-2-3 as an integrated DSS package.
10. What is the advantage of the mouse over the keyboard while working with 1-2-3?
*11. How do you correct your mistakes in 1-2-3?
12. What is the role of the Home key?
13. How do you move the cursor to the last row of the worksheet?
14. Which function key performs the editing task?
*15. What is the role of the Esc key?
16. Which function key moves you to any location of the worksheet?
17. What is the mode indicator? What is the status indicator?
18. What is a SmartIcon? How many SmartIcons does 1-2-3 have?
19. What is a palette?

HANDS-ON EXPERIENCE

1. Get 1-2-3 started and access the online help facility.
2. What is available in the Main Help Index of 1-2-3?
3. From the 1-2-3 Main Help Index retrieve the information related to the function keys. (Hint: select the 1-2-3 Keys option first.) What is the application of F2? Of F5? Of Alt-F4?
4. Consult computer magazines to determine some other spreadsheet packages on the market. Which package is a close competitor to 1-2-3? Why is 1-2-3 so popular?
5. Compare and contrast 1-2-3 with an accounting journal. What are some of the unique advantages of 1-2-3?
6. Try all the arrow movement keys. What are the applications of arrow keys when combined with the End key?
7. In a blank worksheet in cell A1, type *Portland.* By using the F2 function key, change the P to *S.* Press Enter. Now in this cell you should see Sortland. Change S back to *P.*
8. By using /WEY, erase this worksheet.

KEY TERMS

Cell address	Goal-seeking analysis	Spreadsheet
Correcting mistakes	Palette	What-if analysis
Decision support system	Sensitivity analysis	Worksheet
Editing	SmartIcons	WYSIWYG

KEY COMMANDS

F1 function key (to invoke the online help facility)

F2 function key (to edit the content of a cell)

F5 function key (to move the cursor to any location)

/ forward slash (to invoke 1-2-3 command menu)

End + ↓ (to move the cursor down to the last empty cell or last occupied cell below the current position)

End + Home (to move the cursor to the bottom right cell of the active worksheet)

End + ← (to move the cursor to the last left cell of the worksheet to the left of the current position—occupied or empty)

End + → (to move the cursor to the last right cell of the worksheet to the right of the current position—occupied or empty)

End + ↑ (to move the cursor up to the last cell above the current position—occupied or empty)

Home (to move the cursor to cell A1)

PgDn (to move the cursor one screen down)

PgUp (to move the cursor one screen up)

MISCONCEPTIONS AND SOLUTIONS

Misconception 1-2-3 provides a very large spreadsheet: 8,192 rows and 256 columns. At the present time there is no way to use all this capacity with a typical PC because of the memory requirements.

Solution To utilize most of this capacity, some computers can be upgraded to a bigger memory, up to 64 or more megabytes.

Misconception The processing power of 1-2-3 is higher than that of other spreadsheets. Even so, this speed is not adequate when dealing with very large spreadsheets.

Solution Install a coprocessor chip, which will immensely increase the speed of calculation. This is very helpful when a worksheet includes a lot of mathematical calculations, sorts, or table handling.

Misconception When you perform editing, you move around as usual, back and forth, by using left or right arrows. This may be time consuming for long labels.

Solution Use the Home key to move to the beginning of the label and use the End key to move to the end of the label.

Misconception Sometimes the arrow keys do not move.

Solution Press the Esc key till you get back to the READY mode. If the arrow keys still do not work, check if the Num Lock key is pressed down. If this is the case, press the Num Lock key again.

ARE YOU READY TO MOVE ON?

Multiple Choice

1. 1-2-3 includes
   a. graphics and spreadsheet capabilities
   b. database capabilities
   c. communications capabilities
   d. a and b
   e. none of the above
2. The 1-2-3 Main Help Index screen presents
   a. 5 options
   b. 10 options

c. 3 options
d. 2 options
e. none of the above

3. The intersection of a row and a column is called a

a. cell
b. pointer
c. function
d. formula
e. none of the above

4. Using 1-2-3 for what-if analysis, you can

a. change one value and see the result on the rest of the worksheet
b. change one value and create a new graph
c. do both a and b
d. change one graph and create a new value
e. do none of the above

5. After changing to the directory that includes 1-2-3, you can start 1-2-3 by

a. typing *Help* followed by Enter
b. typing *123* followed by Enter
c. typing *Start* followed by Enter
d. typing *Spreadsheet* followed by Enter
e. all of the above followed by Enter

6. The 1-2-3 help facility is accessed through

a. F1
b. F2
c. F5
d. F9
e. F10

7. Some consider 1-2-3 a DSS tool because it can be used to perform

a. what-if analyses
b. goal-seeking analyses
c. sensitivity analyses
d. a and c only
e. all of the above

8. To begin 1-2-3 directly from a hard disk, change the directory to the proper subdirectory (or use a modified path) and type

a. *1-2-3* and press Enter
b. *WK1* and press Enter
c. *123* and press Enter
d. *WKE* and press Enter
e. none of the above

9. The edit function is accessed through

a. F1
b. F2
c. F3
d. F4
e. F5

10. To move to any location of the 1-2-3 worksheet, press

a. F1
b. F2
c. F3
d. F4
e. F5

True/False

1. 1-2-3 has 10 SmartIcons.
2. 1-2-3 has 256 columns.
3. The Home key puts you in cell A1 no matter where the cursor is currently located.
4. A spreadsheet is simply a table or a matrix of rows and columns.
5. 1-2-3 can only handle accounting applications.
6. 1-2-3 cannot be used as a database manager.
7. To use 1-2-3's graphics capabilities, you must have a graphics adapter in your computer.
8. A cell is the intersection of a row and a column.
9. When you are not in the EDIT mode, you always use the End key with one of the arrow keys.
10. The PgUp key always moves the cursor up by 20 rows if there are at least 20 rows available.

ANSWERS

Multiple Choice		True/False	
1.	d	1.	F
2.	e	2.	T
3.	a	3.	T
4.	c	4.	T
5.	b	5.	F
6.	a	6.	F
7.	e	7.	T
8.	c	8.	T
9.	b	9.	T
10.	e	10.	T

Getting Started with 1-2-3

4

4–1 INTRODUCTION

This chapter covers the fundamentals of 1-2-3. We begin by discussing types of data and label prefixes. After studying the chapter, you should be able to build some simple worksheets, save and print them, and correct your errors. The chapter introduces the UNDO feature of 1-2-3 for recovering your mistakes. The chapter concludes with 1-2-3 SmartIcons.

4–2 TYPES OF DATA

Throughout your 1-2-3 work, you will encounter three **types of data:** numbers, formulas, and labels.

Numbers, or values, are any data items starting with digits 0 through 9 and +, –, and . (period). Numbers can be up to 254 digits per cell. They cannot include spaces, dollar signs, or commas. (Later, however, you will learn to use the Format command to include commas and/or dollar signs in your numbers.) Numbers can have up to 15 decimal places. Very small and very large numbers are presented in scientific notation. For those of you who have forgotten scientific notation, Table 4–1 presents some examples.

Formulas must begin with digits 0 through 9 and these symbols: ., +, –, (, @, #, or $. They can be up to 254 characters. For example, +A7+A8 is a valid formula. Formulas cannot contain spaces. If the first part of a formula is a cell address, the formula must start with a plus or minus sign.

Data items that are neither formulas nor numbers are considered **labels.** Labels, or nonnumeric data, can be up to 254 characters per cell. Labels either begin with a prefix (see the next section) or start with characters that are not included in the starting position of numbers or formulas. Labels can, however, be made up of numeric digits (e.g., phone numbers, street addresses, etc.) as long as the data will not be used in any arithmetic operations. To enter numeric data as a label, precede the data by a label prefix. Long labels occupy the next right cell(s). If the next right cell is already occupied, 1-2-3 truncates the label on the screen but not in memory.

4–3 TYPES OF LABEL PREFIXES

Labels can be **left justified, right justified,** or centered in a cell. By default, 1-2-3 left justifies a label. Labels begin with one of four different **label prefixes:**

' (apostrophe)	Left justify
" (quotation)	Right justify
^ (caret)	Center (this character is the uppercase of key 6, i.e., press the Shift key and then the 6 key)

Table 4–1
Examples of Scientific Notation

Regular Numbers		Scientific Notation		Equivalent
5,000	=	5E + 03	=	$5 * 10^3$
2,500,000	=	2.5E + 06	=	$2.5 * 10^6$
.0000006	=	6E – 07	=	$6 * 10^{-7}$
.00007	=	7E – 05	=	$7 * 10^{-5}$

Figure 4–1
Examples of different types of prefixes.

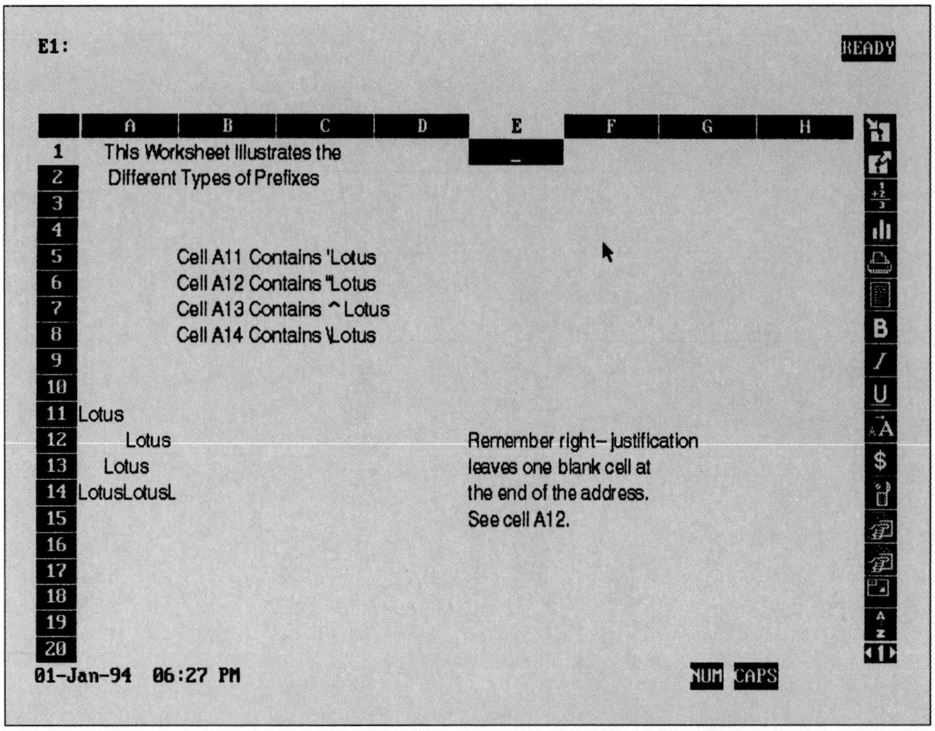

\ (back slash)	Repeat the same character or number until the length of the cell is filled out

Two words in these descriptions may not be familiar to you. The word "default" means the computer performs a task automatically without input from the user. For example, by default, the width of a cell in 1-2-3 is nine characters. You can override this rule any time you wish. The word "justified" refers to the way in which the computer fills a cell. Right justified means the characters occupy the cell from right to left. If you type *COBOL* in cell A1 as a right-justified data item, 1-2-3 will display three empty spaces first, then COBOL. (Right justification leaves the last space in the cell empty.) Remember, prefixes are only for labels. Numbers are always right justified and don't need a prefix. Figure 4–1 illustrates different prefixes.

Table 4–3 at the end of the chapter shows the SmartIcons to use for aligning labels in cells.

4–4 A BUSINESS EXAMPLE

Now that you have learned how to walk through your worksheet and perform simple tasks, let us construct a simple worksheet. Figure 4–2 lists three salespersons who have sold four products for Always Smile Merchant. You have been asked to calculate the total sales for each product, for each salesperson, and finally, the total sales for the business.

In cells B10, C10, D10, and E10 the following identifications were entered: PROD 1, PROD 2, PROD 3, and PROD 4. Cells A11, A12, and A13 contain the three salespersons' names. Cells B11, C11, . . .E13 contain the total sales for each salesperson for the different products.

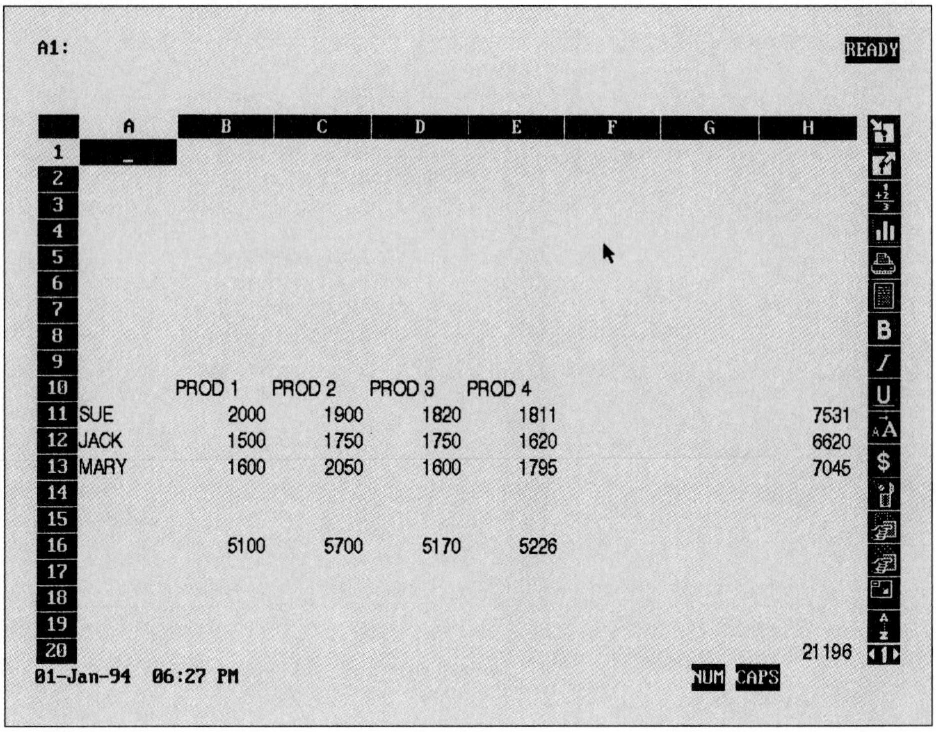

Figure 4–2
Sales analysis using 1-2-3.

In this particular example, we added up cells by using the plus sign. To produce the answer for the total sales generated by Sue, we entered +B11+C11+D11+ E11 in cell H11. Jack's total sales is in cell H12; we entered +B12+C12+D12+E12. Cell H13 contains Mary's total sales; we entered +B13+C13+D13+E13. In cell B16 we entered +B11+B12+B13; in cell C16 we entered +C11+C12+C13; in cell D16 we entered +D11+D12+D13; in cell E16 we entered +E11+E12+E13. Cells B16, C16, D16, and E16 contain the total sales for four products. What did we enter in cell H20? As you will see in future chapters, there is a much easier way to do this task. For now, just remember that you can use the @SUM function or the Sum SmartIcon, which will be discussed in Chapter 7. Type *@SUM (H11..H13)* and press Enter. Cells H11 through H13 will be added.

4–5 ENTERING FORMULAS

In the previous example, we entered the formula for addition in different cells by typing the actual formula. This process is straightforward; however, remember to start a formula with a plus sign.

There is another way of entering formulas. It is called **pointing.** Let us say that in the next worksheet (Figure 4–3) we would like to add cells A1, B1, C1, and D1 and store the result in cell G1 by pointing. Do the following:

1. Enter *1, 2, 3,* and *4* in cells A1 through D1, respectively.
2. Move the cursor to cell G1 and type a plus sign.
3. Move the cursor to cell A1 (you will see A1 in the cell now) and type another + sign.
4. Move the cursor to cell B1 and type another + sign.

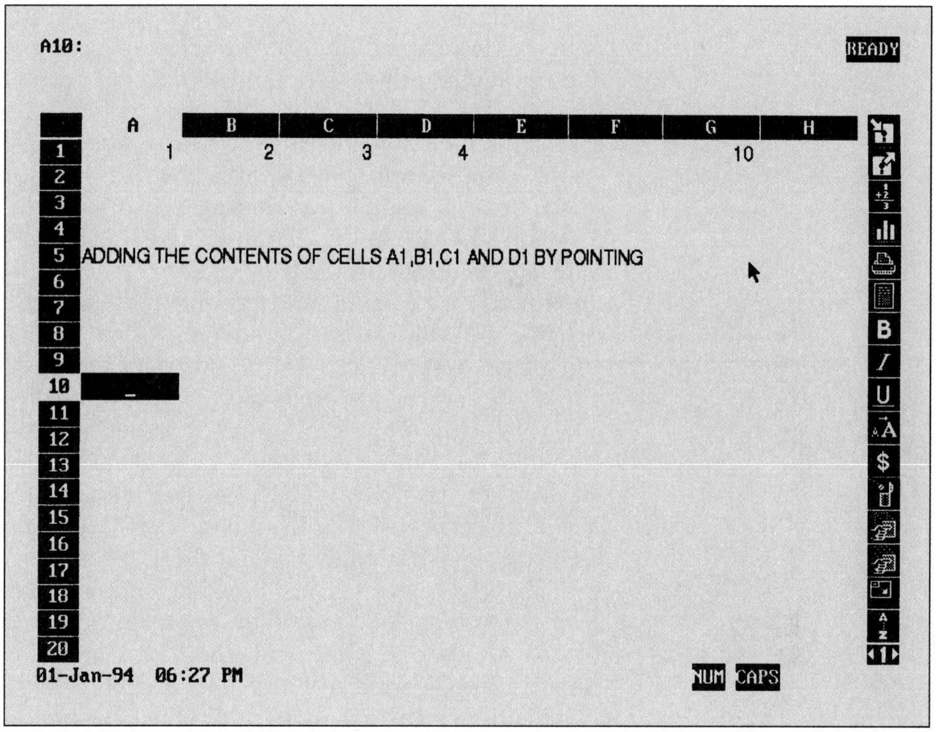

Figure 4–3
Adding the contents of four different cells by pointing.

5. Move the cursor to cell C1 and type another + sign.
6. Move the cursor to cell D1.

You are done adding; just press the Enter key. You will see the result, 10, stored in cell G1.

When you design a formula, always use the cell address instead of the cell value (D1 versus 4 or C1 versus 3 in this example). Why? Because you can change the content of the cells and the result will be recalculated automatically. If you use values instead of cell addresses, you have to change the formula whenever you change the values. Pointing can be very helpful if you are dealing with long and complicated formulas. You can copy the content of one cell to another by just starting with a plus sign in the destination cell, then moving the cursor to the source cell and pressing the Enter key. Pointing is more accurate than typing the formulas because we are all prone to transpositions and typographical errors.

4–6 1-2-3 AS A BLACK BOX

Throughout this book 1-2-3 is viewed as a **black box.** In other words, don't be concerned about what is happening inside 1-2-3. Think of driving a car: you do not need to know how the engine functions to drive your car. You send some information to 1-2-3, it performs some calculations, and the result is given to you either in printed form or on a screen. To use this black box, you should be able to answer the following three questions:

1. How is information sent to 1-2-3?
2. How does 1-2-3 perform calculations?
3. How is output received from 1-2-3?

Sending data to 1-2-3, as you have already seen, is easy. You have two options: (1) you can enter data directly by typing data, moving to the next cell, and continuing this process until all data has been entered, or (2) if your data is a formula, you can enter it directly or by pointing. If you make a mistake, you can correct it either by reentering the data or editing the content of a cell.

The second question asks how 1-2-3 performs calculations. It performs calculations in many ways, and we will discuss these methods throughout this text. For now, remember that most basic calculations by 1-2-3, or any other software, are done by arithmetic operations. 1-2-3 can perform addition, subtraction, multiplication, division, and exponentiation (raising to power). Chapter 7 will describe 1-2-3 functions (predefined formulas) that can perform mathematical and logical (comparison) operations. You can translate any mathematical formula into 1-2-3, and very quickly 1-2-3 will give you the result.

The third question concerns output from 1-2-3. You have seen the output of 1-2-3 on a monitor, but how do you generate a paper report (hard copy) from the data on the screen? There are two methods for generating reports or hard copies. For now, learn the simplest way. If you have an IBM PC or compatible keyboard, press the Shift key and the PrtSc (Print Screen) key at the same time. On enhanced keyboards, just press the dedicated Print Screen key. What you have on the monitor will be sent to the printer.

Another convenient method for generating a report involves the Print command. All operations accomplished by 1-2-3 are done through a series of commands (we will talk about this in the next section).

Before we go any further, let us look at an example of the entire input-process-output cycle of the black box approach. Here are some of the students in our 1-2-3 class. You have been asked to generate a worksheet with their names, their grades on the exam, and the average on the exam for this group:

Craig Johnson 95

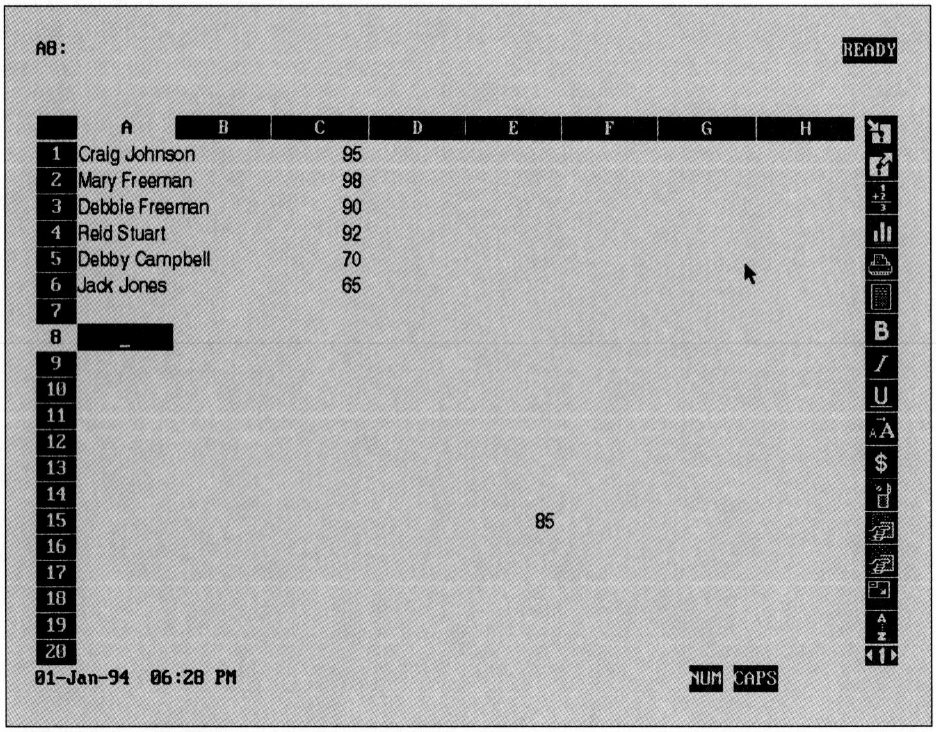

Figure 4–4
Students' average on exam in 1-2-3 class.

Mary Freeman	98
Debbie Freeman	90
Reid Stuart	92
Debby Campbell	70
Jack Jones	65

Figure 4–4 is the worksheet generated for this task. Data was entered as usual; then the formula (C1+C2+C3+C4+C5+C6)/6 was entered in cell E15. Please notice the parentheses.

4–7 THE COMMAND MENU

To activate the 1-2-3 Command menu (which is the same as the Main menu), press the forward slash (/) key (which is also the question mark key). You are given the screen shown in Figure 4–5. Any of the menu items can be selected by either typing the first letter of each command or pointing to them using the arrow keys and pressing the Enter key. You can also move the mouse pointer to the option and then click the left mouse button.

The first line at the top of the screen displays the present position of the cursor. The second line displays the Main menu of 1-2-3, which has 11 options:

```
Worksheet  Range  Copy  Move  File  Print  Graph  Data  System  Add-In  Quit
```

The third line displays all the options under a given menu item. In our example in Figure 4–5, all the options under the Worksheet menu are displayed as follows:

```
Global  Insert  Delete  Column  Erase  Titles  Window  Status  Page  Learn
```

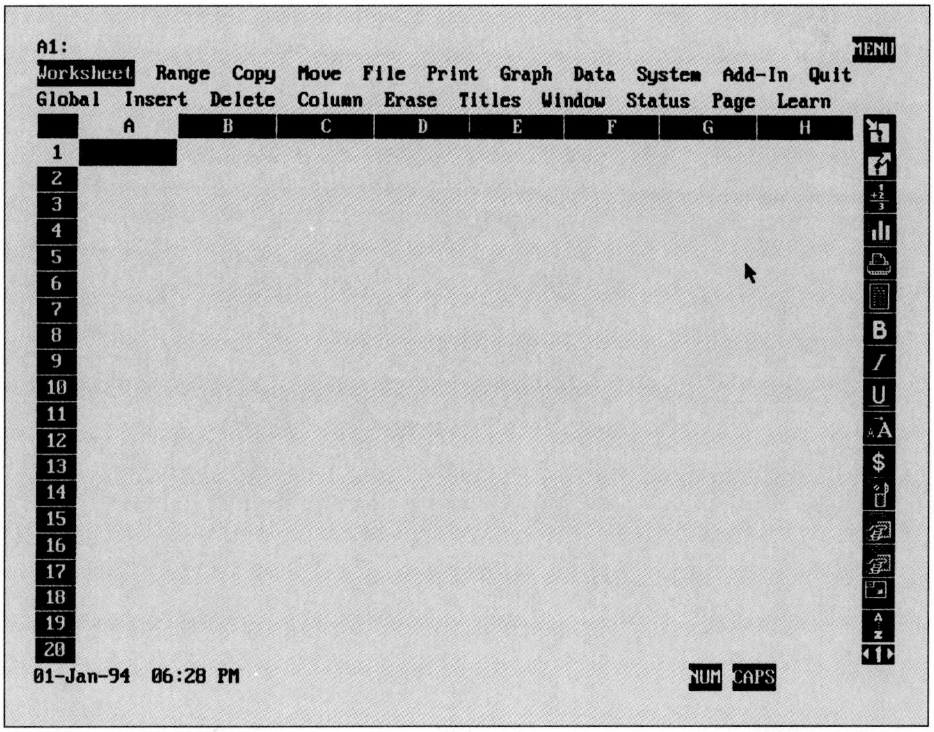

Figure 4–5
1-2-3 Command menu.

Figure 4–6
1-2-3 as a black box.

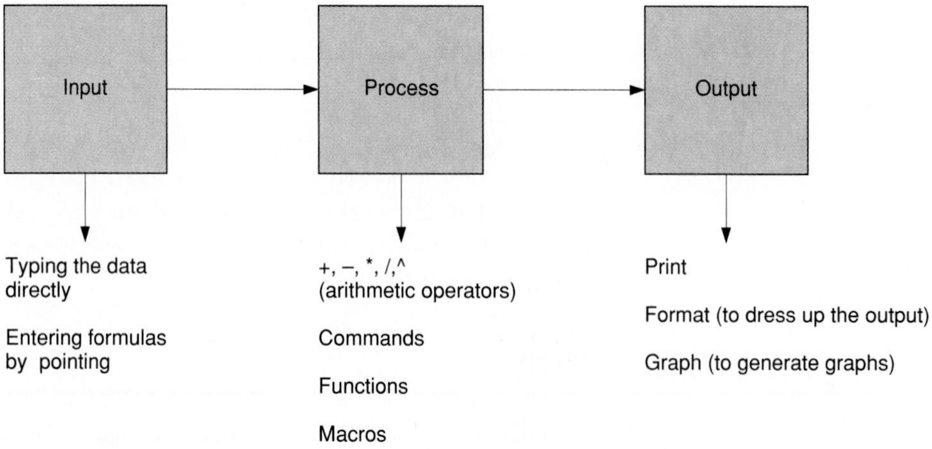

4–8 A SECOND LOOK AT THE BLACK BOX

All you need to do to use 1-2-3 as a spreadsheet program is enter data and ask 1-2-3 to perform calculations. No matter how simple or how complicated your application is, it always includes three distinct components: input, process, and output (see Figure 4–6). After you have accomplished this process, your next question should be how to save your work for future reference. And, how do you recall your previous work? We will answer these questions in the next section.

4–9 CREATING A WORKSHEET

The following students have taken three tests in our 1-2-3 class:

	Test 1	**Test 2**	**Test 3**
Craig	90	78	75
Mary	92	95	80
Debbie	80	85	96
Reid	95	75	94
Debby	70	85	76
Jack	65	75	85

You have been asked to do the following:

1. Create a new worksheet for the class.
2. Add an additional column for the average score of each student.
3. Add an additional row for the average of each test.
4. Generate a hard copy of the worksheet.
5. Save your worksheet for future reference.

Figure 4–7 shows how your worksheet should look. Entering data and calculating averages should not pose any problems. For example, Craig's average is calculated by the formula (B3+C3+D3)/3. Mary's average is calculated by (B4+C4+D4)/3. The average score for the class on the first test is calculated by (B3+B4+B5+B6+B7+B8)/6, and so on.

Figure 4–7
More comprehensive problem of students' averages.

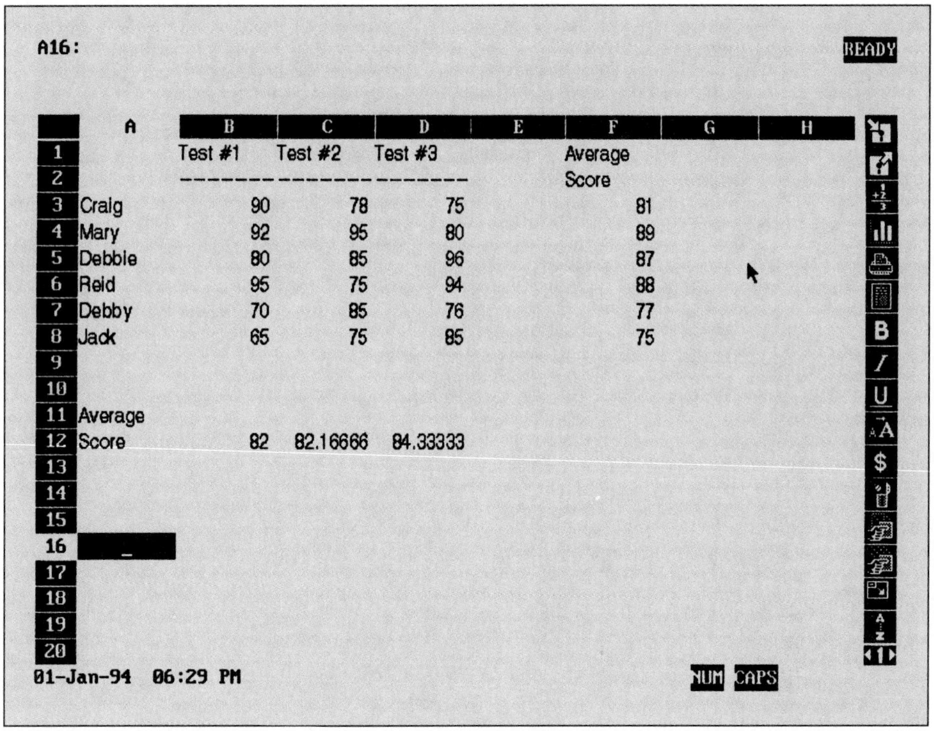

As mentioned earlier, you have two options available to generate a hard copy. The first option if you have a standard keyboard is to press the Shift and the PrtSc keys at the same time. If you have an enhanced keyboard, just press the dedicated Print Screen key. The second option is to use the Print command. As you can see in Figure 4–5, one of the selections available in the Main menu of 1-2-3 is the Print command. If you choose Print, Figure 4–8 will be displayed. It indicates several options. You can print through the printer or print to a file for future printing. If you print to a file, this file will be saved with a PRN extension. You can also send the output to an encoded file. An encoded file can include 1-2-3 data and printer codes that tell your printer how to format output. The Background option sends the print output to an encoded file and prints it in the "background," that is, while you are doing something else on the computer. Use the background option when you want to continue working in 1-2-3 as your work is printing. Now from this menu, select Printer and 1-2-3 presents Figure 4–9.

The first option, Range, refers to the part of the worksheet you want to print. Select Range, then specify the desired area by typing the upper left and lower right cell addresses of the selected area. For example, A1..B5 means everything from cell A1 to cell B5, inclusive—the entire rectangle. (Chapter 6 describes how to define a range.) Then choose Go. Your worksheet will be printed. In the next chapter we discuss the Print command in detail. The Quit option gets you out of the Print menu.

The next step is to save your worksheet for future reference. First you must have a formatted disk. Put the formatted disk in the default drive and choose the File command from the Main menu. You are presented with Figure 4–10. Choose Save from this submenu. You are given the default directory. If you do not want to save your file to your default directory, use the Esc key to erase this drive and then type your desired directory. For example, A:JACK will save your file in drive A and under the name JACK. Save your worksheet using a

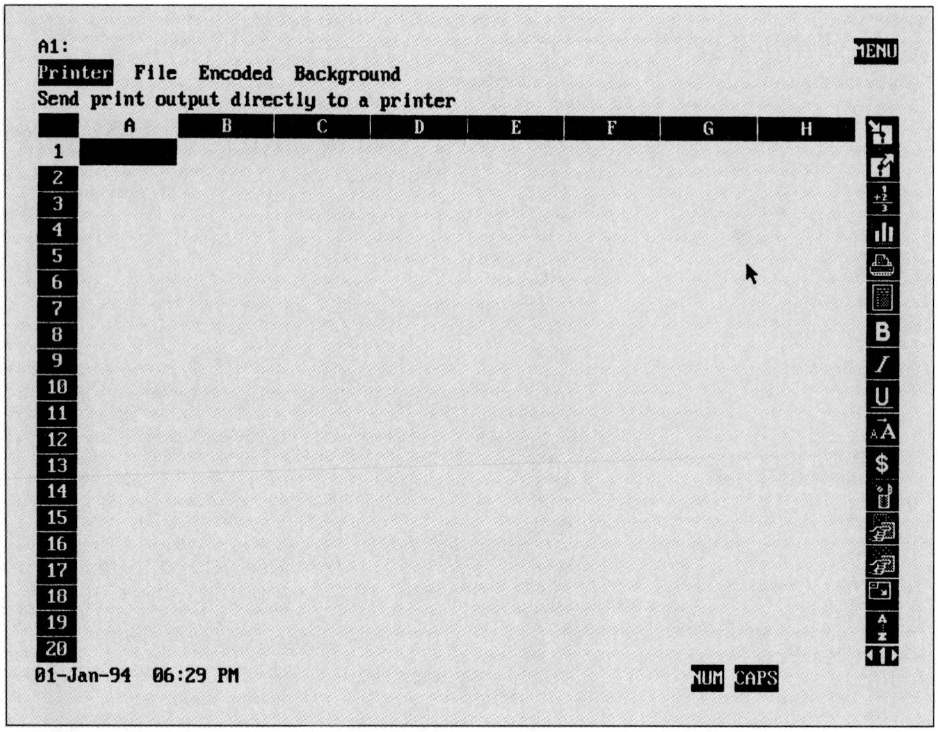

Figure 4–8
Options available under the Print command.

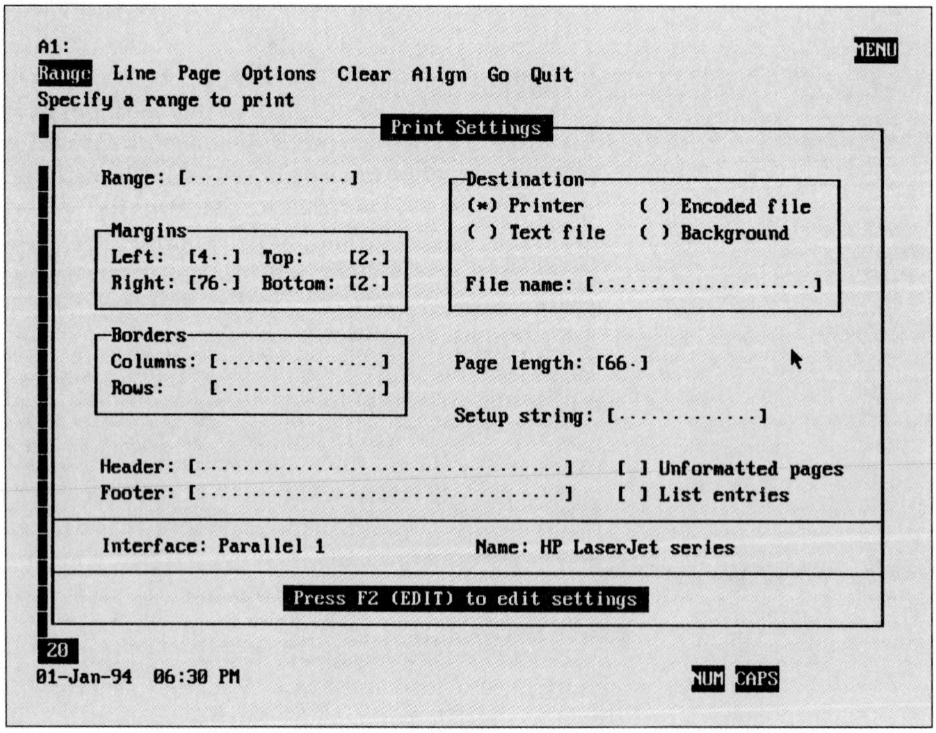

Figure 4–9
Print settings.

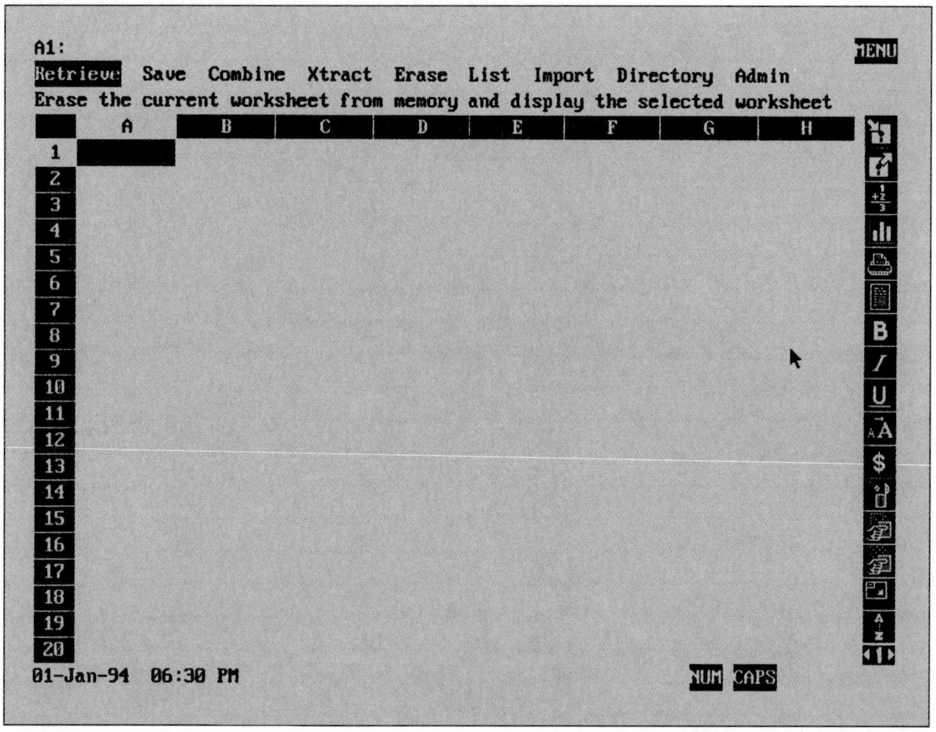

Figure 4–10
Options available under the File command.

unique file name of up to eight characters. (The extension .WK1 will automatically be added to your file name.) If you have access to a hard disk, you can save your worksheet on it. When you save your worksheet on a floppy or a hard disk, you have made a permanent copy of your worksheet, which will remain saved until you erase it.

Now, how do you recall a previously saved worksheet? Look at the choices given to you under the File command (Figure 4–10); Retrieve is among them. When you choose the Retrieve option, you are given the names of all the files in the default directory where the extension is WK1 (the extension for worksheet files). By typing the name of a file (and pressing Enter), or by pointing to it (and pressing Enter), you bring a file (a worksheet) back from disk to memory. Remember, when you bring a file to memory (to screen), this file replaces the current worksheet in memory. In other words, the file on the screen is lost. If you don't want to lose this worksheet, you must save it first and then retrieve the other file. A more detailed overview of the File command is presented in the next chapter.

4–10 THE UNDO FEATURE

The UNDO feature enables you to reverse the most recent change made to the worksheet. When you get 1-2-3 started, the UNDO feature is either enabled or disabled, depending on your setup. If the UNDO feature is enabled, the status indicator at the bottom of the screen displays UNDO (see Figure 4–11). If you need to invoke the UNDO feature, press Alt+F4.

You can disable the UNDO feature by using the /Worksheet Global Default Other UNDO Disable command. To make this change permanent, you must use the /Worksheet Global Default Update command.

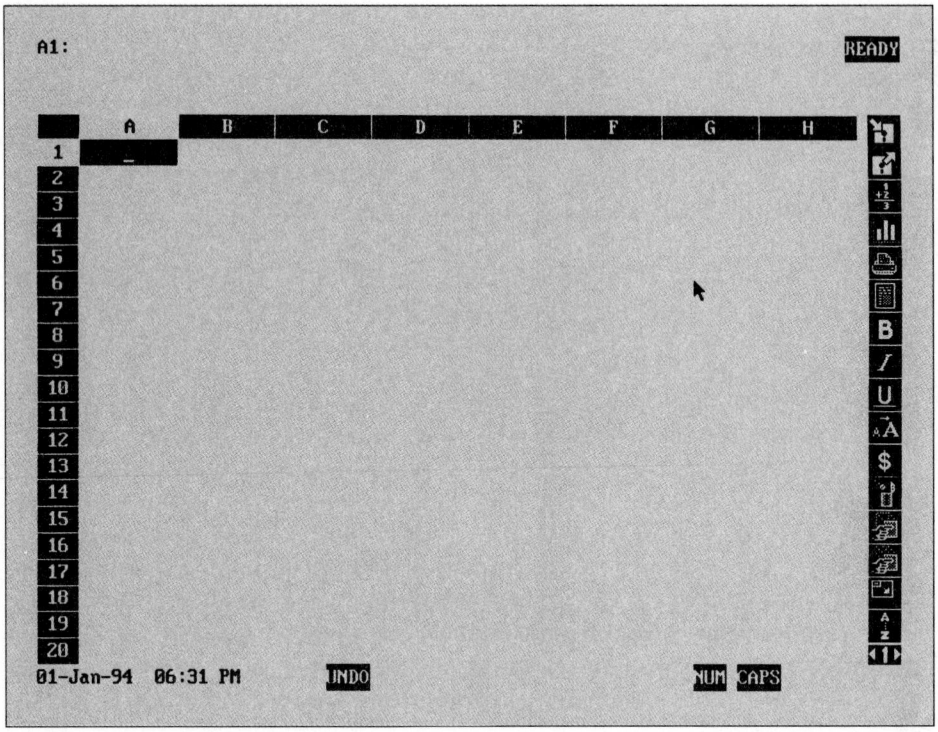

Figure 4–11
Blank worksheet with the UNDO feature displayed.

Remember, the UNDO feature reverses only the last change made to the worksheet. Understanding the last change can be a tricky matter. The last change includes a cycle from one READY mode to the next READY mode. Let us look at a couple of examples to make this feature more understandable.

In a blank screen (the mode is READY), type *CHECK.* While you are typing, the mode indicator displays LABEL. As soon as you press the Enter key, the mode indicator is changed back to READY. This is one cycle. Now, if you press Alt-F4, the worksheet returns to a blank worksheet. (CHECK is erased.)

In some cases the cycle may include several commands. For example, you may enter /Graph, Type, Pie, A, Cl..C3, Enter, View, Esc, Quit. At this point you are back in READY mode. This is one cycle. By pressing the UNDO keys (Alt-F4), you reverse all these commands.

Depending on the complexity of the operations, the UNDO feature consumes various amounts of memory. Whenever there is not enough memory to save the current status in the UNDO buffer before the change, 1-2-3 pauses and presents you with the following message:

```
YOU WILL NOT BE ABLE TO UNDO THIS ACTION..DO YOU WISH TO PROCEED?
```

Answer yes to disable the UNDO feature temporarily and complete the command. Now you will not be able to undo this command; however, the UNDO feature is reenabled as soon as the command is completed. If you answer no, you cancel the command in progress, and you are returned to the READY mode.

If you press the UNDO keys, you can change your mind and press the UNDO keys again to undo the UNDO! In this manner, 1-2-3 allows you to use the UNDO key like a toggle switch.

4–11 1-2-3 SMARTICONS

The 1-2-3 SmartIcons add-in provides you with a series of icons that can simplify commonly used tasks. For example, instead of using /Range Format Percent to format a range with percent option, you can highlight a range and click the icon for Percent format. Icons can be used with a mouse or the keyboard. However, using them with the mouse is easier.

If for any reason you do not want to see these SmartIcons, you can detach them from your worksheet. To do this, select /Add-In, Detach, Icons, Quit. If you change your mind, you can attach them again by selecting /Add-In, Attach, Icons.ADN, Quit. Lotus 1-2-3 Release 2.4 automatically attaches these icons for you.

As mentioned in the last chapter, there are a total of 77 icons organized in palettes. A palette is a column of icons that is displayed to the right of the worksheet. The number of palettes that you can see depends on the type of monitor in use (CGA, EGA, or VGA) and on whether or not WYSIWYG is attached. As you saw in the last chapter, at the end of each chapter we have provided a table of all the popular icons related to that chapter.

The Palette Number 1 is the custom palette. This means you can modify it to display the icons you want to use most frequently. The custom palette is identified by ←1→. As soon as you select another palette, this number is changed to ←2→, ←3→, and so on. The other palettes and their icons are fixed. You can copy them to the custom palette, but you cannot move or delete them.

The last palette contains the icons U1 through U12. These are customized icons (user icons) to which you can assign macros. We will discuss these icons in Chapter 11.

To select an icon using a mouse, move the mouse pointer to the desired icon and then press the left mouse button. For the majority of icons, you first must highlight a range, then select the icon. To select an icon using the keyboard, press Alt+F7 or the key you assigned to SmartIcons when you attached them. 1-2-3 highlights the first icon on the current palette. Use one of the keys listed in Table 4–2 to move to the desired icon, then press the Enter key.

To change the palette using a mouse, click the arrow to the left or right of the palette number displayed at the bottom of each palette.

If you do not know what function a particular icon performs, you can always receive online help. Using the keyboard, when an icon is highlighted you see a brief description about the icon on the top of the screen on the Control Panel. To receive help when using a mouse, move the mouse pointer to the desired icon and press the right mouse button.

Table 4–2
Keys for Using SmartIcons

Key	Function
←	Moves the highlight to the previous icon palette.
→	Moves the highlight to the next icon palette.
↑	Moves the highlight up to the previous icon.
↓	Moves the highlight down to the next icon.
END	Moves the highlight to the last icon on the current palette
HOME	Moves the highlight to the first icon on the current palette
ENTER	Executes the highlighted icon.

4–12 CUSTOMIZING SMARTICONS

You can customize the 1-2-3 SmartIcons in two ways:

1. Modify the custom palette (Palette Number 1) to display the icons that you frequently use.
2. Assign your own 1-2-3 macros to use icons U1 through U12. We will talk about this in Chapter 11. The first method will be discussed below.

To add an icon to the custom palette, follow these steps:

1. Select the Add icon. This icon is usually in Palette Number 6, right before the last palette (see Figure 4–12). This is selected by moving the mouse pointer to the icon and clicking it or highlighting the icon and pressing the Enter key. At this time you will be presented with a screen similar to the one presented in Figure 4–13.
2. Select the icon that you want to add to your custom palette by moving the mouse pointer to the icon and pressing the left mouse button or highlighting the icon and then pressing the Enter key.

1-2-3 inserts a copy of the icon that you selected at the bottom of the custom palette and displays the custom palette on the screen. If the custom palette was full before you added the new icon to it, 1-2-3 removes the bottom icon to make room for the new icon.

To remove an icon from the custom palette, follow these steps:

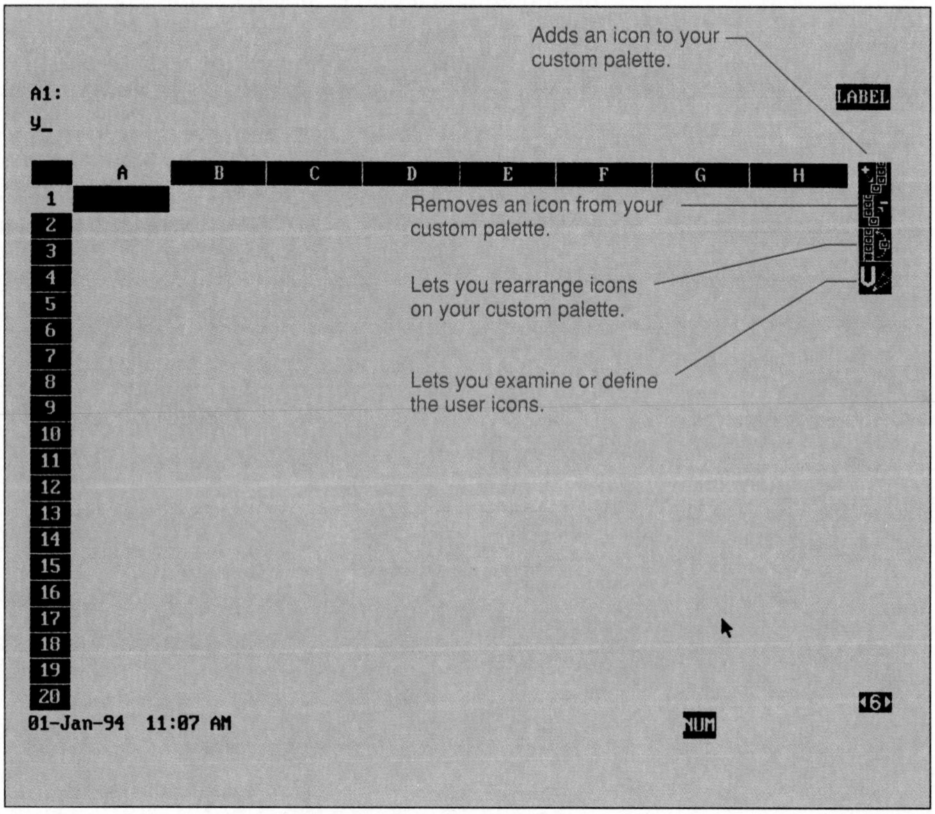

Figure 4–12
Icons for customizing.

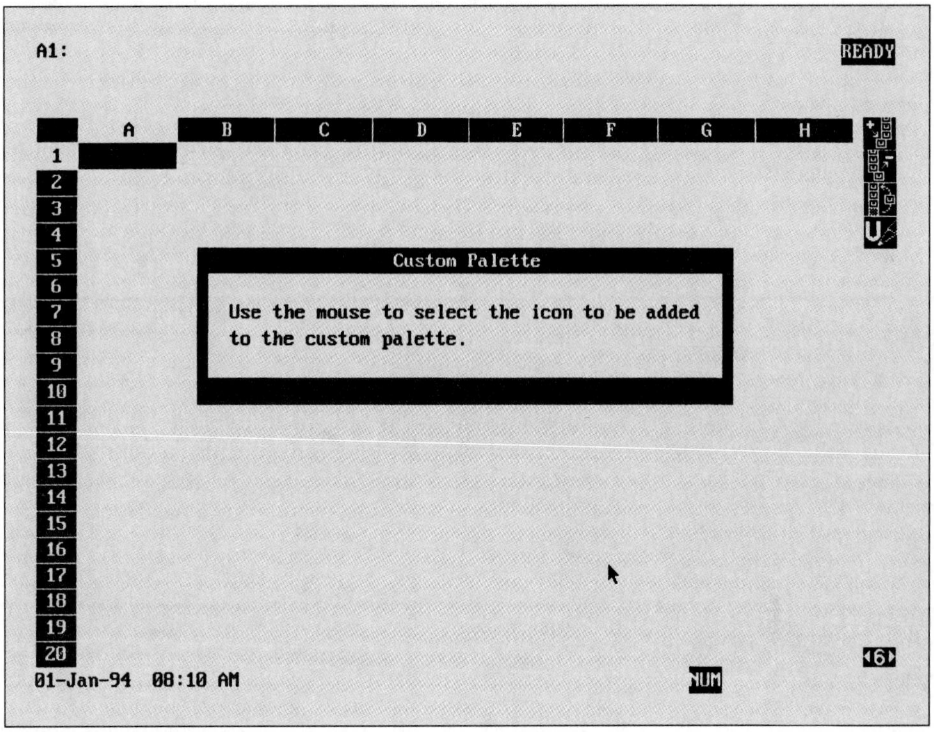

Figure 4–13
Adding an icon to the custom palette dialog box.

1. Select the Delete icon. This is the icon right after the Add icon (see Figure 4–12).
2. Select the icon that you want to remove from the custom palette.

To rearrange the icons on the custom palette, follow these steps:

1. Select the Move icon (see Figure 4–12). 1-2-3 displays your custom palette.
2. Select the icon you want to move. 1-2-3 replaces the icon with a blank icon.
3. Select the icon at the location where you want the icon that you are moving to appear. At this time the icon that you selected in step 2 appears in the new location, and 1-2-3 repositions the other icons to make room for the icon you moved.

If you moved an icon to a position below its original position, the icons above the new location move up one slot to make room for the repositioned icon. If you moved an icon to a position above its original position, the icons below the new location move down one slot to make room for the repositioned icon.

4–13 EXITING 1-2-3

After you save your worksheet and you are through with 1-2-3, exit 1-2-3 by choosing Quit from the Main menu. If you have not saved your worksheet, 1-2-3 responds by asking

```
Worksheet changes not saved! End 1-2-3 anyway?
```

You will be presented with two options to choose from in response to this prompt:

```
No  Yes
```

Choosing No enters you to your spreadsheet without exiting. Then you can save the worksheet by using the /File Save command (discussed in Section 4–9 and Chapter 5). Choosing Yes ends your 1-2-3 session without saving your spreadsheet. The Quit option helps maintain control over worksheet content and provides some security for the system. Quit puts you back to DOS or to your starting menu, depending on how you got into 1-2-3 in the first place.

SUMMARY

In this chapter you learned the basics of 1-2-3. You learned how to build, print, and save simple worksheets. In addition, the chapter introduced types of data and label prefixes for 1-2-3. The chapter introduced a discussion on the UNDO feature. It concluded with a discussion on 1-2-3 SmartIcons and the process of creating a customized icon palette. See Table 4–3 for editing and customizing SmartIcons.

Table 4–3
Editing and Customizing SmartIcons

WYSIWYG Mode	Text Mode	Description
	<L	Left justifies labels in a range.
	<C>	Centers labels in a range.
	R>	Right justifies labels in a range.
	ALIGN TEXT	**W** Centers text in a text range, aligns text evenly at both the left and right of a text range, right aligns text, left aligns text, or clears the alignment settings for a range, depending on the current alignment setting.
	UNDO	Cancels your previous action or command if the undo feature is enabled.
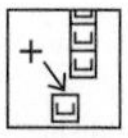	■ + ■ ■→	Adds an icon to your custom palette.
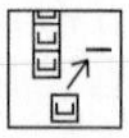	■ ■ – ■→	Removes an icon from your custom palette.
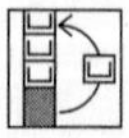	■← ■ ■ ■→	Moves an icon to another location on your custom palette.
	U ■ ■ ■	Displays descriptions of user icons U1 through U12, lets you assign one or more macros and descriptions to one or more user icons, and lets you copy the text of one or more macros to the worksheet so you can debug the macros.

Column 1 shows icons if WYSIWYG is attached. Column 2 shows icons as they appear when WYSIWYG is either not attached or is set to: Display Mode Text.
The icons identified by **W** work only when WYSIWYG is attached.

REVIEW QUESTIONS

*These questions are answered in Appendix A.

1. How many types of data does 1-2-3 have?
2. How do you make a data item right justified?
3. How do you center a data item?
*4. How do you get 1-2-3 started?
5. How do you enter labels into a worksheet?
6. How do you enter numbers into a worksheet?
*7. Is entering numbers different from entering labels?
*8. How do you invoke an option in the 1-2-3 Command menu?
9. How many options are available in the 1-2-3 Main menu?
10. What is a mode indicator?
11. What is usually displayed on the top of the screen?
*12. How do you generate a hard copy of a worksheet?
13. How do you save a worksheet on the default drive?
*14. How do you save a worksheet on your hard disk (assuming it is not your default drive)?
15. How do you recall an old worksheet?
16. How do you exit 1-2-3?
17. When you recall a file from a disk to memory, do you still have the file on the disk or is the file destroyed?
18. What are the options under the File command?
19. What are the options under the Print command?
*20. Let us say you want to enter 15 minus signs (–) in cells A1 through A2. Why must you start with one of the label prefixes?
21. How do you enable the UNDO feature?
22. How do you disable the UNDO feature?
23. What key combination is used to invoke the UNDO, for example, to unerase an erased worksheet?
24. What are SmartIcons? How many palettes of icons are there?
25. How do you customize an icon palette? How do you remove an icon from a palette?

HANDS-ON EXPERIENCE

1. Get 1-2-3 started and do the following arithmetic operations in cells A1, A2, A3, and A4, respectively:

   2+2/2
   (2+2)/2
   2*2/2
   2^2/2

   Check your answers manually and see if 1-2-3 is correct!
2. Using a 1-2-3 worksheet, calculate the average of the following test scores:100, 95, 85, and 80.

3. Design a worksheet with 10 salespersons in cells A1 through A10. For each salesperson, enter four-digit sales data in column C. In cell H1, calculate the average sales for these 10 individuals.
4. Jack's Social Security number is 524-13-1439. Is this numeric or nonnumeric data? How do you enter this data into the worksheet? Do you enter it as a number or label?
5. Enter *555* in cell A10 as nonnumeric (label) data (e.g., use one of the label prefixes). How does it look? Is it right or left justified? Can you do calculations with this cell now? Discuss.
6. The area of a triangle is calculated by B1*H1/2 where B1 is the base and H1 is the height. Enter a value for the base in cell B1 and a value for the height in cell H1; now enter the formula for the area in cell A1. Try to enter different values for the base and the height and see how quickly 1-2-3 calculates the area.
7. Mary receives a base salary of $560 a week and three different commissions of 5, 7, and 10 percent on Persian rugs, color TVs, and general appliances, respectively. Last week she sold $12,000, $5,000, and $10,000 on these three items, respectively. Using 1-2-3, calculate her total pay.
8. Save this worksheet under the name First. By using the Print command, print the worksheet. By using the /Worksheet Erase Yes command, erase this worksheet. Now by using the /File Retrieve command, bring the file back to the screen.
9. Add five icons of your choice to Palette Number 1.
10. Insert an icon of your choice to Palette Number 1. Now remove this icon.
11. Create a worksheet similar to Figure 4–14. Enter data of your choice and generate comparable results. Generate a hard copy of the worksheet.

KEY TERMS

Black box	Label prefix	Pointing
Formula	Left justified	Right justified
Label	Number	Types of data

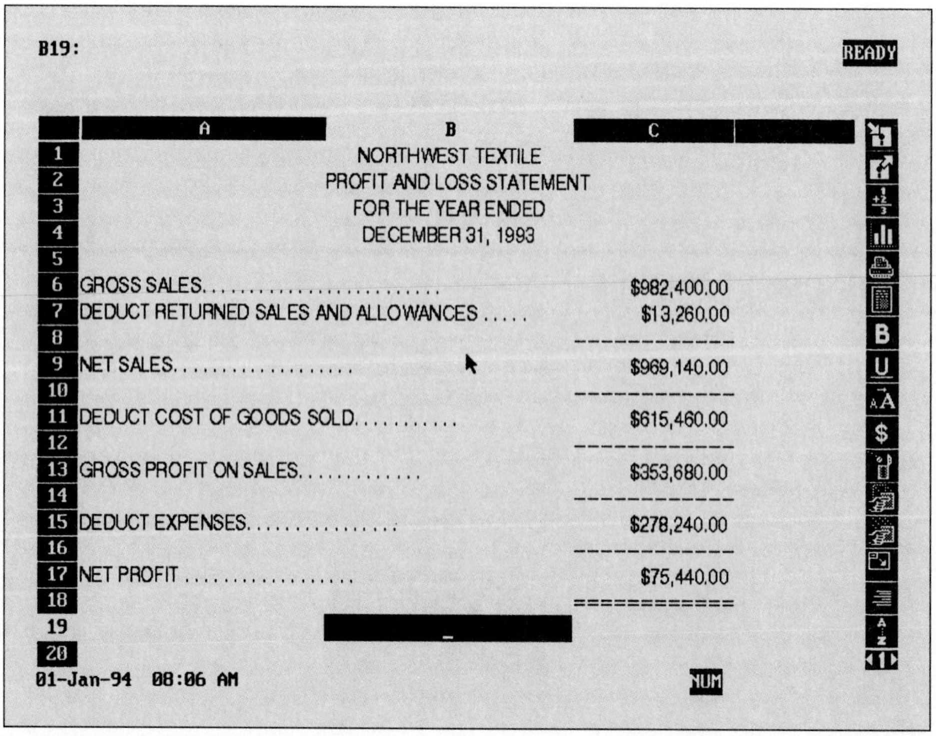

Figure 4–14
A sample worksheet.

KEY COMMANDS

Print (to print a worksheet)

Print Screen (to print one screen at a time)

Save (to save a worksheet)

Retrieve (to retrieve a worksheet)

Shift+PrtSc (to print one screen at a time)

Quit (to exit from 1-2-3)

MISCONCEPTIONS AND SOLUTIONS

Misconception Entering long formulas is time consuming and accuracy may be jeopardized.

Solution Use the pointing technique to enter long formulas.

Misconception Nonnumeric data that starts with numbers (e.g., 29 Broadway Avenue) is considered numeric data. Watch the mode indicator at the top right of the screen; it tells you what type of data you are entering. The mode indicator for numbers is VALUE; for labels it is LABEL. (All mode indicators are discussed in Appendix A at the end of the book.)

Solution Enter such data with one of the label prefixes, for example, ′ (apostrophe), ″ (quotation), ^ (caret).

Misconception Cell addresses (e.g., A5, A69) are considered nonnumeric data by 1-2-3.

Solution These values must be preceded by a + sign (e.g., +A9) or any numeric character: 0 through 9, +, –, ., (, $, or #.

Misconception You are entering a formula and at the end you press the Enter key. Then 1-2-3 gives you a beep and you cannot get out of the EDIT mode.

Solution Check your parentheses; make sure every left parenthesis is matched with a right one.

Misconception Label justifications are only for labels. If a number is entered with one of the label prefixes, the entry is not considered a number by 1-2-3. It will assign the value of zero to this entry and continue calculation.

Solution Check your cells with numeric entries. They all must be right justified without using the right justification symbol (i.e., ″).

ARE YOU READY TO MOVE ON?

Multiple Choice

1. To create a permanent electronic copy of your worksheet you must use the
   - **a.** Print command
   - **b.** Save command
   - **c.** Retrieve command
   - **d.** Shift+PrtSc command
   - **e.** none of the above
2. By default, nonnumeric (label) data is always
   - **a.** left justified
   - **b.** centered
   - **c.** right justified
   - **d.** repeated over and over
   - **e.** none of the above
3. Quotes are used for
   - **a.** left justification
   - **b.** centering

c. right justification
d. repeating over and over
e. none of the above

4. 1-2-3 data types include

a. numbers
b. labels
c. formulas
d. all of the above
e. a and b only

5. The maximum number of characters allowed in a cell is

a. 1,000
b. 9
c. 100
d. 10
e. 254

6. To repeat the same character or characters until the length of the cell is filled, begin with the prefix

a. '
b. "
c. ^
d. \
e. none of the above

7. Which of the following is *not* a valid 1-2-3 formula?

a. +A1+B1+C3+H5
b. (C20/D3)
c. B25 – A3
d. +C1/(B10/F3)
e. (H15 – (D3+D4)/C4)*2

8. When designing a formula, always use the

a. cell address
b. cell value
c. arrow keys
d. a and b
e. all of the above

9. Numeric data cannot include

a. the digits 0 through 9
b. spaces, commas, and dollar signs
c. parentheses
d. all of the above
e. none of the above

10. Depending on whether or not you have pressed the Enter key, data can be edited by using the

a. Edit key (F2)
b. Backspace key
c. Escape key (Esc)
d. a and b
e. all of the above

True/False

T 1. The Print command is one of the options in the Main menu of 1-2-3.
F 2. You can only save your file in the default drive.
F 3. Numeric data is always left justified.

4. By default, very large and very small numbers are presented in scientific notation.
5. 1-2-3 provides only two types of label prefixes.
6. Entering formulas by using the pointing technique is generally less accurate than typing the formula directly.
7. The only way to correct a mistake in a worksheet is to use the Edit key.
8. To enter a cell address in a formula, you must always start with either a + or –.
9. A number such as the number 55 *cannot* be entered as a label and still be considered numeric data.
10. All the palettes can be customized.

ANSWERS

Multiple Choice		True/False	
1.	b	**1.**	T
2.	a	**2.**	F
3.	c	3.	F
4.	d	4.	T
5.	e	**5.**	F
6.	d	**6.**	F
7.	c	**7.**	F
8.	a	**8.**	T
9.	b	**9.**	T
10.	e	**10.**	F

More on File Operations and Printing

5

5–1 INTRODUCTION

In this chapter we focus on the File and Print commands. Creating files with password and autoexecute (executed automatically) files is described. By means of examples, various file operations under the File command are explained. The chapter then covers various options under the Print command.

5–2 POPULAR FILES

1-2-3 manipulates several types of files. The popular types and their extensions are worksheet files (WK1), graph files (PIC), and print files (PRN). The PRN files are ASCII files that can be exported to other software that accepts this type of file.

When you save a worksheet (by selecting File from the Main menu and then Save), 1-2-3 automatically attaches an extension WK1 to it. If you wish, you can type your own extension when you save a file. Be aware, however, that such a file will not be automatically retrieved by 1-2-3 nor will it show up in your File Retrieve window. (The File Retrieve window appears when you press /File Retrieve. At this time all your WK1 files are displayed on the control panel.) To retrieve a file that has your own extension, you must first issue the Retrieve command, then type the file name with its extension. You can also make your 1-2-3 files **self-booting.** This is practical for files that you use frequently. You make a file self-booting by saving it under the name AUTO123.WK1. 1-2-3 will automatically load this file as soon as you start the 1-2-3 worksheet.

The PIC files are generated by /Graph Save command (discussed in Chapter 8). The PRN files are generated by /Print File command.

5–3 ERASING A FILE FROM DISK

To erase a file from disk, choose File from the Main menu and then Erase. Next select the file type (option), which is either Worksheet, Print, Graph, or Other, and highlight the file that you wish to erase (either move the cursor to the file or just type the file name), then press Enter. If you erase a file, that file is gone for good.

You can have one current file (on screen) and many permanent files (on disk) at any time. A current file is your current worksheet, and the permanent files are the files saved on your disk. When you retrieve another file, the current worksheet is erased. If you do not want to lose this worksheet, you must first save it before retrieving another file. To erase the current file from the screen, select Worksheet from the Main menu then Erase and Yes.

5–4 SAVING A FILE WITH A PASSWORD

1-2-3 allows you to save a file with a **password.** To do this, execute the following steps:

1. Create or load a file.
2. Choose File from the Main menu then Save.
3. Type the desired file name.
4. Press the space bar.
5. Type *P* (for password).
6. Press the Enter key.

7. Type the desired password. (Your password can be any of the valid characters, up to 15 characters. Do not use spaces.)
8. Press the Enter key.
9. Type the password again to verify it and press the Enter key.

Remember that when you type your password for the first time or when you verify it, 1-2-3 does not display the characters that you typed on the screen. For security reasons, it displays nonreadable characters. If you change your mind, you can always change or delete the password. To delete a password, but save the file itself, first retrieve the file with the present password. When you are ready to save it again, select File from the Main menu and then Save. You will be given the following message:

```
A:Myfile.WK1 [Password Protected]
```

(Myfile is your file name.) Press the backspace key to erase [Password Protected], then press the Enter key. In our example, A is the default drive. You will be presented with three options: Cancel, Replace, and Backup. Choose Replace and your file will be saved under the desired name, in this case, Myfile. To change a password, first delete the password (as we just did), press the space bar, type *P*, and press the Enter key. Follow the rest of the steps as described.

If you use a password, you must always remember it or you won't be able to retrieve the file. Every time you retrieve the file, you must type the password exactly as you created it. Uppercase characters are considered to be different than lowercase characters.

5–5 BACKING UP A FILE

Sometimes you save a file and later you would like to modify it. When you save a file for the first time, the file is saved with the WK1 extension. When you perform modifications and get ready to save your file again by selecting File from the Main menu and then Save, 1-2-3 gives you three options: Cancel, Replace, and Backup.

If you select Cancel, your new changes are not saved and your original file remains intact on the disk. If you select Replace, this new file with all the changes replaces the original file regardless of differences in size. If you select Backup, your original file is saved with the BAK extension (file with no changes) and your modified file (with all the changes) is saved with the WK1 extension. Therefore, the file with BAK extension is one version older than your most recent file.

5–6 FILE COMBINE

The Combine option from the File menu gives you three choices: Copy, Add, and Subtract.

The Copy option enables you to copy an entire file or a portion of a file to the current worksheet. Be aware that the position of the cursor is important; the Copy option can overwrite the current worksheet. If you select Copy, you will receive the following two choices: Entire-File and Named/Specified-Range. An entire file or a specific range can be copied. If you choose either of these options, 1-2-3 asks you either the name of the file, the range name, or the range coordinates. The Copy command does not change the current worksheet if the cursor is in an empty location of the current worksheet.

The Add option enables you to add a file or a portion of a file to the current worksheet. Again, the position of the cursor is important. When you choose Add, you receive two choices: Entire-File and Named/Specified-Range.

You can choose either of these. The difference between Add and Copy is that the Add option adds the contents of the incoming file/range to the current worksheet. For example, if the cursor is at cell A1 and contains 5, and if cell A1 from the incoming file contains 15, the final value of cell A1 in the current worksheet will be 20.

The Subtract option gives you the opportunity to subtract an entire file or a portion of a file from the current worksheet. Remember the importance of the present position of the cursor. In each of the three options we are discussing, the incoming data is entered in the worksheet from the present position of the cursor to the right and down.

When you use the Add option, if an incoming file overlays a cell that contains a label or a formula, 1-2-3 discards the incoming value and retains the label or formula in the current worksheet. For example, if cell A1 in the current worksheet contains the label, COBOL, the incoming data does not have any effect on it.

To make this discussion clearer, consider the sample worksheet presented in Figure 5–1 (saved under CH5-1 in the default directory). The cursor is in cell A10. We issued the following commands:

1. /File
2. Combine
3. Copy
4. Entire-File
5. CH5-1
6. Enter

Figure 5–1
Sample worksheet.

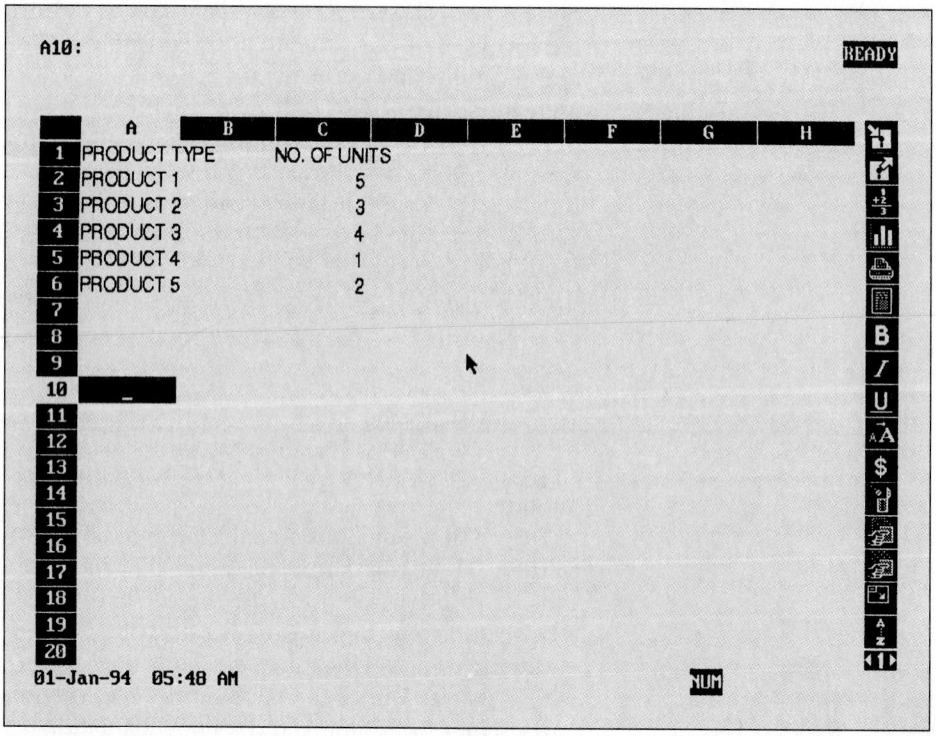

The result is presented in Figure 5–2. As you can see, the entire file (CH5-1) was copied from cell A10 downward.

As an example of the Combine Add command, again consider Figure 5–1. The cursor is in cell A1. We issued the following commands:

1. /File
2. Combine
3. Add
4. Entire-File
5. CH5-1
6. Enter

The final result is presented in Figure 5–3. As you can see, the incoming data was added to the existing data. If the cursor had been in cell A10, or in any other cells outside of your active worksheet, the Add option would not have changed your original numbers. If the cursor had been in cell A10, Add would have generated a result identical to Figure 5–2.

As an example of Combine Subtract, consider Figure 5–1 again. The cursor is in cell A1. We issued the following commands:

1. /File
2. Combine
3. Subtract
4. Entire-File
5. CH5-1
6. Enter

Figure 5–2
Combine Copy operations.

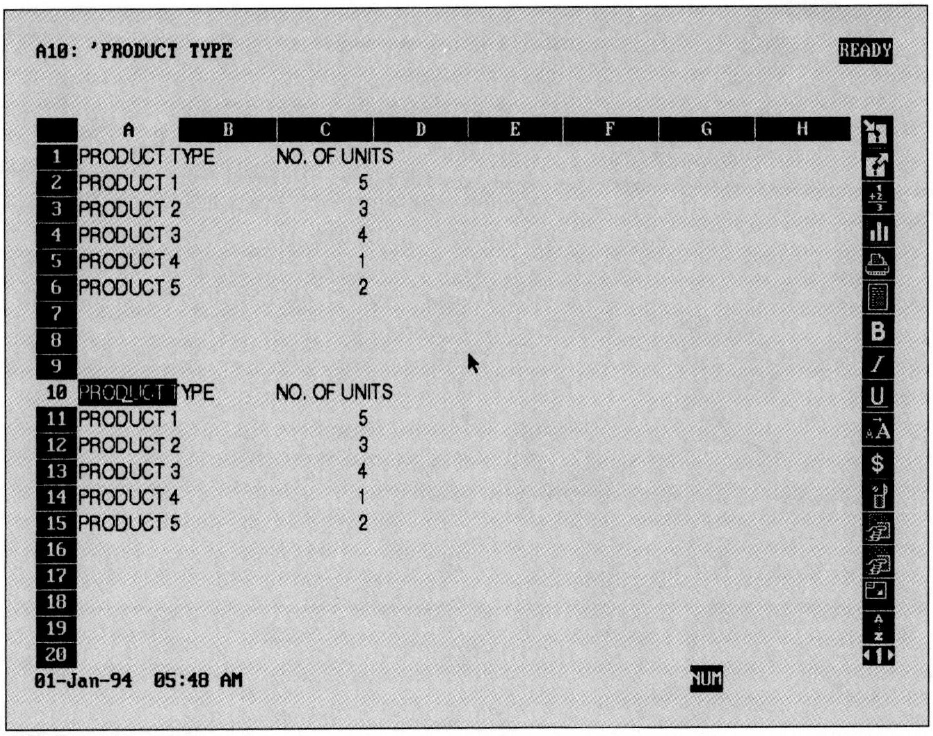

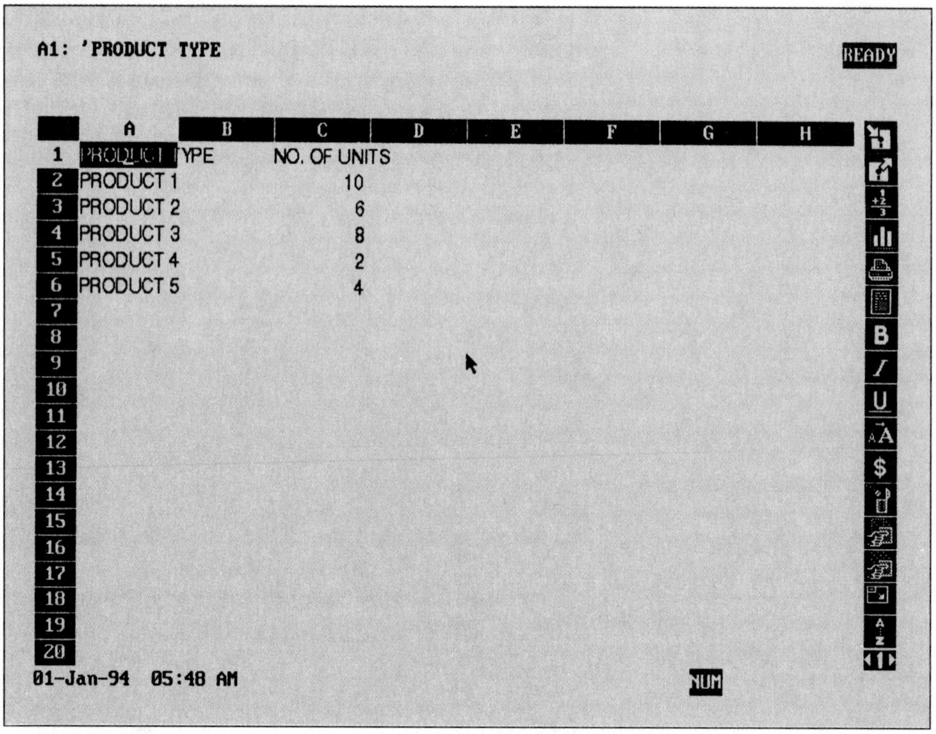

Figure 5–3
Combine Add operations.

The final result is presented in Figure 5–4. As you can see, the incoming data was subtracted from the original data.

5–7 FILE XTRACT

The Xtract option from the File menu extracts and saves a portion of or the entire current worksheet in a file on a disk. Unlike the Combine command, the Xtract command does not change information in the current worksheet. Two choices are given under Xtract: Formulas and Values. If you select Formulas, 1-2-3 saves the worksheet with any formulas from the current worksheet to the extracted file. For example, if cell A1 and A2 contain 5 and 10 and cell A3 contains their sum (e.g., +A1+A2), the Formulas option allows you to save this worksheet and the formula. If you select Values, 1-2-3 saves the worksheet with only the calculated values of the formula. In our example, 15 will be extracted and saved with the worksheet, not +A1+A2. This means you will not know how the value was generated.

Let us say you want to extract range C1..C6 in Figure 5–1. To do so issue these commands: /File, Xtract, Values, Sample, C1..C6, Enter. There is no change in the current worksheet. Only a copy of range C1..C6 has been transferred to a file called Sample in your default drive. Later you can bring the sample file to any other worksheet by using /File Combine Copy or /File Combine Add.

5–8 FILE IMPORT

The Import option from the File menu enables you to bring in files from other programs. These files are imported as text or numbers. The imported files must be in ASCII format, which are considered standard file format for most of the

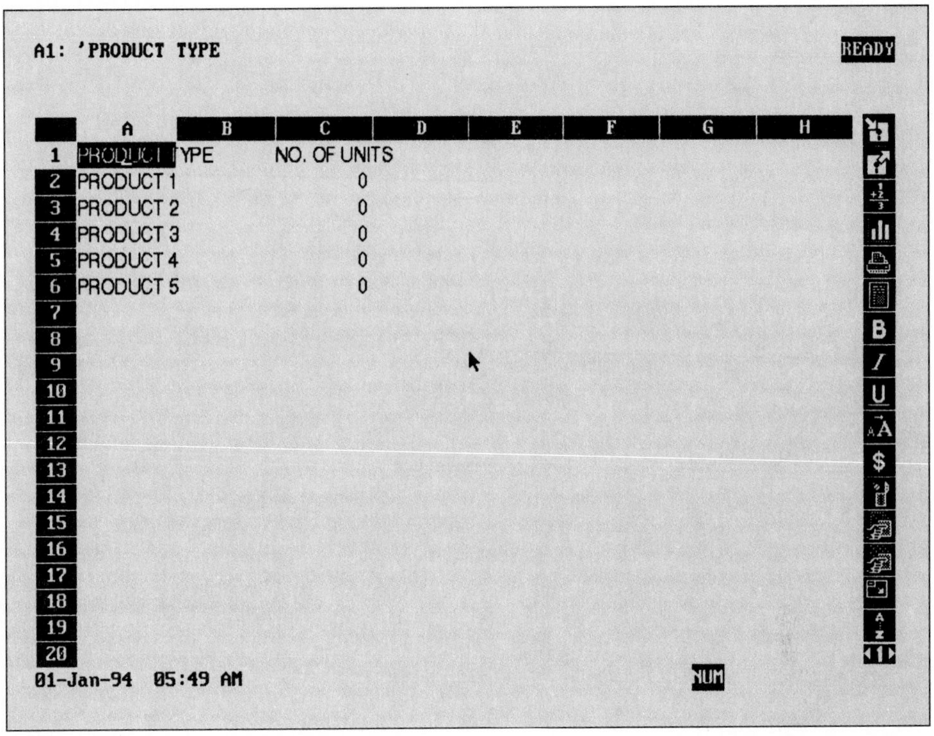

Figure 5–4
Combine Subtract operations.

software on the market. The Text option brings everything as text. The Numbers option keeps numbers in their numeric format, which means you can later perform calculations with these numbers. Import is a powerful feature because it enables you to share data between 1-2-3 and different application programs.

5–9 FILE DIRECTORY

The file directory tells you the current directory of your system. In a hard drive system, usually your directory is drive C. This directory can be changed to A or B. If your computer has a hard disk, you must issue /File Directory A: if you wish to access files on a floppy disk in drive A.

To permanently change your default directory from C to A, invoke these commands: /Worksheet, Global, Default, Directory (erase the current directory by using the Esc key), A:, Enter, Update, Quit. From now on your default directory will be A.

5–10 PRINT COMMAND

When you select Print from the Main menu and then Printer, you will be presented with Figure 5–5—the Print Settings menu. Remember that in 1-2-3 Release 2.4, you can press the F2 key and edit the settings shown in Figure 5–5. Now let's look at the options given at the top of the screen.

Range allows you to print either a specific portion of the worksheet or the entire worksheet.

Line allows you to skip a line.

Page allows you to skip a page.

Figure 5–5
Print Settings menu.

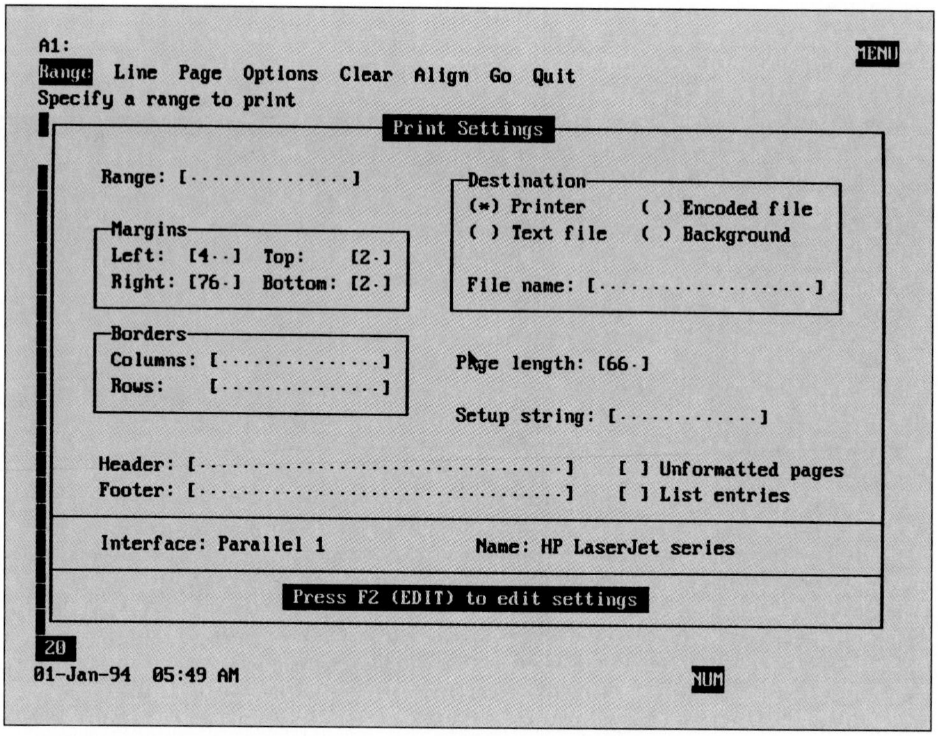

Options gives you several choices. Header prints a line of text up to 240 characters below the top margin. This line is printed at the top of each page. Footer prints a line of text up to 240 characters above the bottom margin. This line is printed at the bottom of each page. By default, headers and footers are left justified. However, by using special characters (discussed later), you can center or right justify them. Margins allows you to define left, right, top, and bottom margins. Borders prints designated column or row headings on every page. They can be either above or to the left of the specified range you are printing. With this option you can choose rows or columns. The areas you have identified as borders are not supposed to be included in your print range. If they are, you get duplicate information. Setup specifies the style and font size for a printer. The **setup string** represents control codes or commands to the printer. It lets you use printer attributes or features that are not on 1-2-3 menus. For example, a setup string enables you to use compressed print or double strikes if these features are available on your printer. Consult your printer manual for specifics. This setup code is preceded by a back slash (\). Pg-Length specifies the number of lines per page. The default is 66 lines.

Other under Options gives you the following four choices: As-Displayed, Cell-Formulas, Formatted, and Unformatted. As-Displayed prints the report as it appears on the monitor. Cell-Formulas prints the content of each occupied cell in the specified print range, one cell per line. Formatted restores the format settings for headers, footers, and page breaks. Unformatted prints a specified range without headers, footers, and page breaks. This option can be very helpful when printing to a file, because it generates a so-called plain ASCII file.

Clear in the Print Settings menu gives four options: All, Range, Borders, and Format. All returns all print settings to defaults, Range clears the current print range, Borders clears border column and row ranges, and Format returns margins, page length, and setup string to default.

Align in the Print Settings menu resets to the top of the page after adjusting paper.

Go sends the specified range to the printer.

Finally, Quit takes you back to the Print menu.

As an example of some of these options, consider the sample worksheet in Figure 5–6. In column E we added data for Division1 and Division2. We would like to print this sample worksheet using the following two options: As-Displayed and Cell-Formulas.

Figure 5–7 illustrates the result from using As-Displayed. To create this figure, we issued the following commands:

> /Print, Printer, Range, A1..E6, Enter, Options, Other, As-Displayed, Quit, Align, Go

Figure 5–8 illustrates the result from using Cell-Formulas. To create this figure, we issued the following commands:

> /Print, Printer, Range, A1..E6, Enter, Options, Other, Cell-Formulas, Quit, Align, Go

Also see Table 5–1 presented at the end of the chapter for print icons.

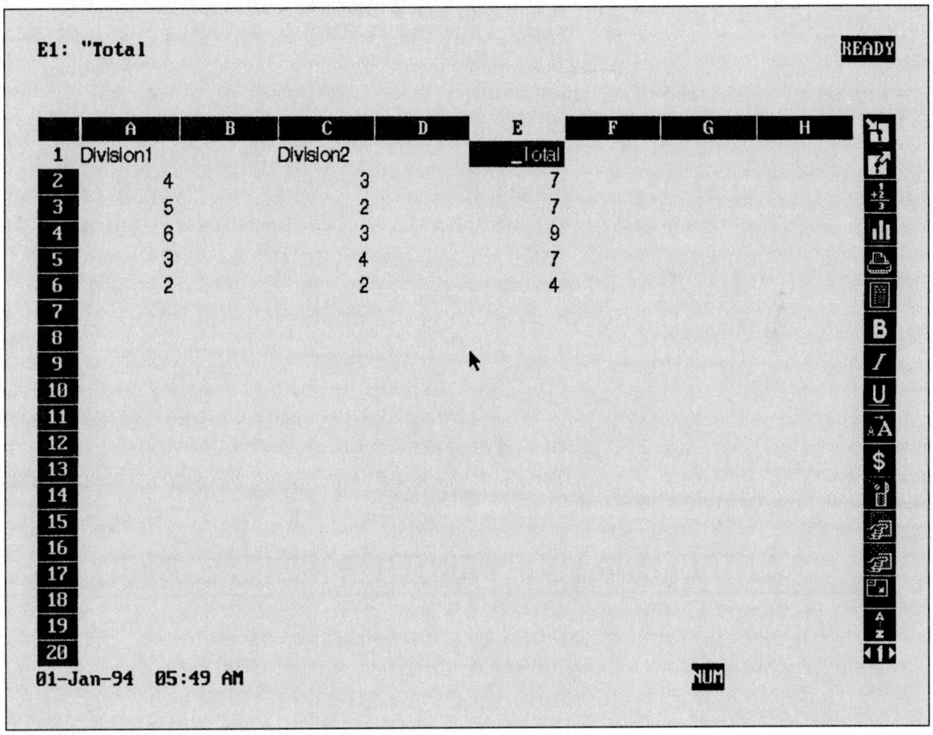

Figure 5–6
Sample worksheet.

Division1	Division2	Total
4	3	7
5	2	7
6	3	9
3	4	7
2	2	4

Figure 5–7
Sample worksheet in Figure 5–6 printed with As-Displayed option.

Figure 5–8
Sample worksheet in Figure 5–6 printed with Cell-Formulas option.

```
A1: 'Division1
C1: 'Division2
E1: "Total
A2: 4
C2: 3
E2: +A2+C2
A3: 5
C3: 2
E3: +A3+C3
A4: 6
C4: 3
E4: +A4+C4
A5: 3
C5: 4
E5: +A5+C5
A6: 2
C6: 2
E6: +A6+C6
```

5–11 DEFAULT SETTINGS

In most cases, the **default print settings** of the Print command should satisfy your needs. The default settings, as Figure 5–5 indicates, include the following:

Page length	66 lines
Left margin	4 characters from the left side of the paper
Right margin	76 characters from the left side of the paper
Top margin	2 lines from the top of the page
Bottom margin	2 lines from the bottom of the page

As you have seen in the Print Command menu, any of these settings can be changed, either temporarily or permanently. For temporary changes, issue these commands: /Print, Printer, Options. Then select any of the options displayed in Figure 5–5. You can also press F2 (the Edit key), then use the arrow keys to move to any of these options and change them. When done, move to OK and press Enter. For permanent changes you must first change whatever you would like to change, then issue /Worksheet, Global, Default, Printer, Update.

5–12 CONTROLLING YOUR PRINTER MORE EFFECTIVELY

Several commands that we have already discussed can be used individually or collectively to enhance the effectiveness of your printer. They reduce manual intervention and generate more readable output.

The enhanced features will become clearer when you design a macro (Chapter 11) for printing and/or when you print to a file rather than to the printer.

The /Print, Printer, Line command skips a line. If you would like to skip a page you should issue /Print, Printer, Page. After printing a report, it is advisable to issue /Print, Printer, Align. This command tells 1-2-3 that the paper in your printer is at the top of the form and that the printer is ready to accept data.

The /Worksheet Page command puts a **page break** in a desired location; that is, the command starts a new page no matter how much of the present page is empty. When you use this command, you must check to see how many lines you have specified in the /Print, Printer, Options, Pg-Length command. The Worksheet Page command may not override this command if the number of lines specified by /Print, Printer, Options, Pg-Length is less than the number of lines covered by Worksheet Page. To issue Worksheet Page command, the cursor must be in column A.

5–13 SPECIAL CHARACTERS

Three special characters can be utilized for entering page numbers and the current date and to specify the position of the header or footer:

# (number sign)	Enters a page number starting at 1
@ (at sign)	Enters current date in international format (e.g., 01/01/94)
¦ (split vertical bar)	(This character is found on the back slash key.) Separates portions of the header or footer, either left justified, centered, or right justified. Text by itself will be left justified; if preceded by a ¦ (one split vertical bar) text will be centered; if preceded by two ¦¦ (two split vertical bars), the text will be right justified.

5–14 PLANNING YOUR PRINTED REPORT MORE ACCURATELY

A standard page is 66 lines; standard means 11 inches and 6 lines per inch. By default, 1-2-3 leaves two lines blank between the text and the header or footer. If your printed line is longer than the right margin, 1-2-3 wraps around to the next line. If you need to print wider worksheets, one solution is to request **compressed output** in your setup string (the Setup option under Options). The other option for printing wide worksheets is to use Landscape printing in WYSIWYG mode. See Chapter 9 for a detailed discussion of WYSIWYG printing.

Different printers have different setup options. With the Epson FX80 printer, for example, \015 is used to generate compressed output.

Of the total 66 lines on a standard page, only 56 lines are available for the text:

Lines 1–2	Top margin
Line 3	Header, if any
Lines 4–5	Blank—by default
Lines 6–61 (56 lines)	Your text
Lines 62–63	Blank—by default
Line 64	Footer, if any
Lines 65–66	Bottom margin

To stop a printing session, press the Ctrl and Break keys simultaneously. The printer may not stop immediately, but it will stop as soon as the printer buffer is empty.

5–15 EXAMPLE OF THE PRINT COMMAND

Now let us consider an example of how the Print command works. Figure 5–9 is a balance sheet for four quarters of the Ocean City Tourist Attraction. In Figure 5–10 we printed these three worksheets in one report. By using some of the fancy

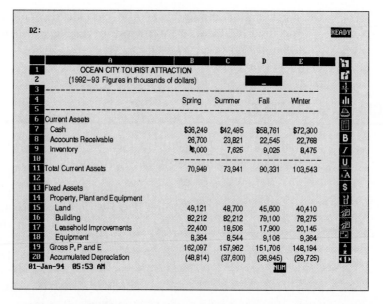

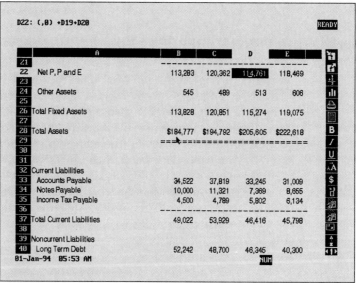

Figure 5–9
Ocean City Tourist Attraction balance sheet in three worksheet forms.

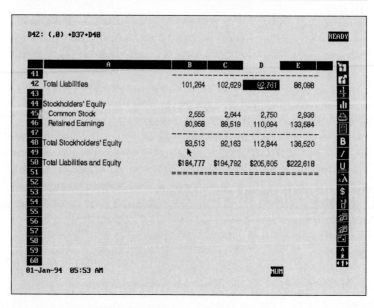

D2: READY

	A	B	C	D	E
1	OCEAN CITY TOURIST ATTRACTION				
2	(1992–93 Figures in thousands of dollars)				
3	----------	----------	----------	----------	----------
4		Spring	Summer	Fall	Winter
5	----------	----------	----------	----------	----------
6	Current Assets				
7	Cash	$36,249	$42,495	$58,761	$72,300
8	Accounts Receivable	26,700	23,821	22,545	22,768
9	Inventory	8,000	7,625	9,025	8,475
10		----------	----------	----------	----------
11	Total Current Assets	70,949	73,941	90,331	103,543
12					
13	Fixed Assets				
14	Property, Plant and Equipment				
15	Land	49,121	48,700	45,600	40,410
16	Building	82,212	82,212	79,100	78,275
17	Leasehold Improvements	22,400	18,506	17,900	20,145
18	Equipment	8,364	8,544	9,106	9,364
19	Gross P, P and E	162,097	157,962	151,706	148,194
20	Accumulated Depreciation	(48,814)	(37,600)	(36,945)	(29,725)

01-Jan-94 05:53 AM NUM

D22: (,0) +D19+D20 READY

	A	B	C	D	E
21		----------	----------	----------	----------
22	Net P, P and E	113,283	120,362	114,761	118,469
23					
24	Other Assets	545	489	513	606
25					
26	Total Fixed Assets	113,828	120,851	115,274	119,075
27					
28	Total Assets	$184,777	$194,792	$205,605	$222,618
29		==========	==========	==========	==========
30					
31					
32	Current Liabilities				
33	Accounts Payable	34,522	37,819	33,245	31,009
34	Notes Payable	10,000	11,321	7,369	8,655
35	Income Tax Payable	4,500	4,789	5,802	6,134
36		----------	----------	----------	----------
37	Total Current Liabilities	49,022	53,929	46,416	45,798
38					
39	Noncurrent Liabilities				
40	Long Term Debt	52,242	48,700	46,345	40,300

01-Jan-94 05:53 AM NUM

D42: (,0) +D37+D40 READY

	A	B	C	D	E
41		----------	----------	----------	----------
42	Total Liabilities	101,264	102,629	92,761	86,098
43					
44	Stockholders' Equity				
45	Common Stock	2,555	2,644	2,750	2,936
46	Retained Earnings	80,958	89,519	110,094	133,584
47		----------	----------	----------	----------
48	Total Stockholders' Equity	83,513	92,163	112,844	136,520
49					
50	Total Liabilities and Equity	$184,777	$194,792	$205,605	$222,618
51		==========	==========	==========	==========
52					
53					
54					
55					
56					
57					
58					
59					
60					

01-Jan-94 05:53 AM NUM

Figure 5–10
Figure 5–9 printed as a report.

01-Jan-94

OCEAN CITY TOURIST ATTRACTION
(1992-1993 Figures in thousands of dollars)

	Spring	Summer	Fall	Winter
Current Assets				
Cash	$36,249	$42,495	$58,761	$72,300
Accounts Receivable	26,700	23,821	22,545	22,768
Inventory	8,000	7,625	9,025	8,475
Total Current Assets	70,949	73,941	90,331	103,543
Fixed Assets				
Property, Plant, and Equipment				
Land	49,121	48,700	45,600	40,410
Building	82,212	82,212	79,100	78,275
Leasehold Improvements	22,400	18,506	17,900	20,145
Equipment	8,364	8,544	9,106	9,364
Gross P, P, and E	162,097	157,962	151,706	148,194
Accumulated Depreciation	(48,814)	(37,600)	(36,945)	(29,725)
Net P, P, and E	113,283	120,362	114,761	118,469
Other Assets	545	489	513	606
Total Fixed Assets	113,828	120,851	115,274	119,075
Total Assets	$184,777	$194,792	$205,605	$222,618
Current Liabilities				
Accounts Payable	34,522	37,819	33,245	31,009
Notes Payable	10,000	11,321	7,369	8,655
Income Tax Payable	4,500	4,789	5,802	6,134
Total Current Liabilities	49,022	53,929	46,416	45,798
Noncurrent Liabilities				
Long Term Debt	52,242	48,700	46,345	40,300
Total Liabilities	101,264	102,629	92,761	86,098
Stockholders' Equity				
Common Stock	2,555	2,644	2,750	2,936
Retained Earnings	80,958	89,519	110,094	133,584
Total Stockholders' Equity	83,513	92,163	112,844	136,520
Total Liabilities and Equity	$184,777	$194,792	$205,605	$222,618

Page 1

features of the Print command, this figure was generated by issuing the following commands:

/Print, Printer, Range, A1..E52, Enter, Options, Header, ¦¦ @, Enter, Footer, ¦ Page #, Enter, Pg-Length, 64, Enter, Margins, Right, 78, Enter, Margins, Top, 2, Enter, Margins, Bottom, 4, Enter, Quit, Align, Go

SUMMARY

In this chapter we discussed File and Print commands in detail. Various file operations were described. Different options available under the Print command were highlighted. See Table 5–1 for File and Print SmartIcons.

REVIEW QUESTIONS

*These questions are answered in Appendix A.

1. How many file extensions can be manipulated by 1-2-3?
2. How do you create a password for a file?

Table 5–1
File and Print Icons

WYSIWYG Mode	Text Mode	Description
	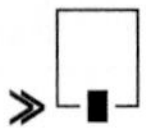	Saves the current worksheet file to a disk.
	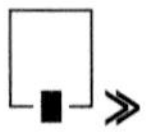	Lets you retrieve an existing worksheet file from a disk.
	PRN	Prints the range you specified with :Print Range or /Print Printer Range; or , if a range is highlighted, prints the highlighted range.
	PVU	W Displays a preview of the range you specified with :Print Range or /Print Printer Range; or, if a range is highlighted, displays a preview of the highlighted range.

Column 1 shows icons if WYSIWYG is attached. Column 2 shows icons as they appear when WYSIWYG is either not attached or is set to: Display Mode Text.
The icons identified by **W** work only when WYSIWYG is attached.

***3.** Can you remove a password after it has been defined?
4. What is the convention for a file name? For a password?
5. How do you erase the current worksheet?
6. How do you erase a file from a disk?
7. How do you change the default drive from C to A?
8. When you erase a file from disk, is this file gone forever?
***9.** What options are available under the File Combine command?
10. What is the difference between /File Combine Copy and /File Combine Add?
***11.** What does File Xtract do?
12. What are the differences between Values and Formulas in Xtract operations?
13. What is the difference between printing to a printer and printing to a file?
14. What are all the options under either Print Printer or Print File?
15. What does Align do?
16. What are the applications of special characters in the Print command?
17. How do you enter a date to your report?
18. How do you enter a page number into your report?
19. What is the role of the Worksheet Page command?
20. How do you create a backup file?
21. What is the file extension of a backup file?
22. What is the difference between /File Xtract and /File Combine Copy?
***23.** How do you bring an ASCII file to your worksheet?
24. How do you center a date in a printed report?

HANDS-ON EXPERIENCE

1. Generate a worksheet with 10, 20, and 30 in cells A1, A2, and A3. Create a formula in cell H10, by using the pointing method, that will show the sum of the cells given. Erase the worksheet.

2. Design a worksheet with your first name in cell A1, your last name in cell A2, and your Social Security number in cell A3. Generate a hard copy of this worksheet both by using the Shift and PrtSc keys (or Print Screen) and by using the Print command.
3. Save the worksheet in question 2 under the name First. Exit 1-2-3. Turn the computer off.
4. Get 1-2-3 started again and retrieve the worksheet named First. In cell A4 enter your age and in cell A5 enter your street address. Save this worksheet under the name Second.
5. When you enter a long label such as street address, what will happen? Will your data occupy more than one cell or will your data be truncated? Try entering a street address.
6. Generate compressed output from the worksheet in question 4. Put the correct date and page number on this worksheet.
7. In cell A1 and B1 type the numbers *5* and *10*. Save this worksheet under the name Try. Perform /File Combine operations with Try and the current worksheet. What is the difference between the Copy and Add commands? Will the Xtract command change the appearance of your current worksheet? Try these commands.
8. Design the following worksheet for the students in your 1-2-3 class:

	A	B	C	D	E	F	G	H
1	Name	Major	Sex	Standing	Age	Test 1	Test 2	Test 3
2	Brown	MIS	M	JR	20	90	85	75
3	Jones	CS	M	JR	25	95	70	60
4	Smith	CS	M	SO	19	85	90	90
5	Rudd	MKT	F	SO	20	99	85	100
6	Gerlads	MIS	F	SR	23	100	85	80
7	Moseley	CS	F	SR	28	80	90	100
8	Erb	CS	M	FR	18	80	90	100
9	Thomson	MIS	F	GD	35	95	80	80
10	Sapp	MGT	M	GD	45	100	90	65
11	Lopez	FIN	M	JR	22	95	92	95

   a. Using the correct label prefix, line up all the headings.
   b. Calculate the average of each test.
   c. Calculate the average of each student.
   d. Save this worksheet under the name CHAPT5.

KEY TERMS

Default print setting
Compressed output
Page break
Password
Self-booting
Setup string

KEY COMMANDS

Combine (to combine files or portions of files, e.g., /File Combine)

Erase (to erase a file from disk, e.g., /File Erase)

File (to invoke the File command)

Import (to import an ASCII file into your worksheet, e.g., /File Import)

Print (to invoke the Print command)

Quit (to exit 1-2-3)

Retrieve (to retrieve a file, e.g., /File Retrieve)

Save (to save a file, e.g., /File Save)

Xtract (to extract a worksheet or a part of it into a file, e.g., /File Xtract)

MISCONCEPTIONS AND SOLUTIONS

Misconception If you save a file with a password and then forget the password, you will never be able to retrieve that file.

> **Solution** Use a password that has a special meaning to you.

Misconception One of the options in the 1-2-3 Main menu is Quit. When you choose Quit, you leave 1-2-3 and your work is not saved.

> **Solution** True, 1-2-3 does not save your worksheet automatically. However, you are given the opportunity to save your work after you select Quit.

Misconception A common error message is FILE NOT FOUND.

> **Solution** Either the particular file is not on the disk, or you spelled the name wrong, or you have the wrong disk in the drive, or. . . . Type the correct file name and drive identifier. If you still don't get the file, there probably is no such file.

Misconception You try to save or retrieve a file and an error message appears: DRIVE NOT READY.

> **Solution** Check if there is a disk in your default drive and if the door is closed.

Misconception You try to use the /Print Printer command and receive the message: ERROR.

> **Solution** Check your printer. It may be loosely connected, not connected at all, out of paper, or turned off!

Misconception Some commands display a setting screen. This may block your worksheet.

> **Solution** To see the worksheet, press the F6 (window) key to temporarily remove the setting screen. Press F6 again to bring the setting screen back.

ARE YOU READY TO MOVE ON?

Multiple Choice

1. The Main menu of 1-2-3 includes:
   - a. 10 options
   - b. 11 options
   - c. 9 options
   - d. 13 options
   - e. 14 options
2. The line at the top of the screen tells you about
   - a. the present cursor position
   - b. the Main menu
   - c. the selected option from the Main menu
   - d. the memory status
   - e. none of the above
3. In a hard disk system, when you exit 1-2-3, you
   - a. get back to DOS
   - b. get back to your starting menu
   - c. get back to the OK prompt
   - d. a or b
   - e. any of the above
4. How many options are there in the File Combine menu?
   - a. 1
   - b. 2

c. 3
d. 4
e. none of the above

5. When you first get 1-2-3 started and before you strike any key, the mode indicator shows
   a. READY
   b. MENU
   c. POINT
   d. LABEL
   e. EDIT
6. If you want to save your worksheet and use another program to print it, use
   a. /Print Printer
   b. Shift+Print Screen
   c. /File Save
   d. /Range Format
   e. /Print File
7. The Goto command is found on
   a. F5
   b. F1
   c. F6
   d. F4
   e. F10
8. 1-2-3 supports all of the following except
   a. a file with one password
   b. a report with headers and footers
   c. a file with two passwords
   d. sideways printing
   e. all of the above
9. 1-2-3 generates and manipulates files with the extension(s)
   a. WK1
   b. PIC
   c. PRN
   d. all of the above
   e. none of the above
10. File Erase allows you to erase
    a. BAK files
    b. WK1 files
    c. PIC files
    d. PRN files
    e. all of the above

True/False

T 1. After pressing the forward slash key (/), the screen displays the 1-2-3 Main menu.

F 2. If you type *25* in cell A1, as the number is being entered the mode indicator is LABEL.

T 3. The mode indicator is found at the upper right of the worksheet.

T 4. The status indicator is on the lower right of the worksheet.

T 5. When you retrieve a worksheet from the disk, that file still remains on the disk in its original format.

F 6. The 1-2-3 Command menu is invoked by pressing any key.

F 7. There is only one method to print a 1-2-3 worksheet.

F 8. 1-2-3 automatically saves your worksheet to disk.
T 9. A file password can be up to 15 characters.
F 10. The line at the top of the screen tells you the options available under a given menu.

ANSWERS

Multiple Choice		True/False	
1.	b	1.	T
2.	a	2.	F
3.	d	3.	T
4.	c	4.	T
5.	a	5.	T
6.	e	6.	F
7.	a	7.	F
8.	c	8.	F
9.	d	9.	T
10.	e	10.	F

Important 1-2-3 Commands

6

6–1 INTRODUCTION

This chapter reviews important 1-2-3 commands including Copy, Move, Worksheet, and Range. Detailed descriptions highlight the specific use of each command. We also discuss relative, absolute, and mixed addressing. You will see that the majority of 1-2-3 operations are done by these commands.

6–2 DEFINING A RANGE

A **range** is a rectangular block within a worksheet. A range can be a cell, a row, a part of a row, a column, a part of a column, or an entire worksheet.

A range in 1-2-3 is indicated by the upper left and lower right corners. To identify a range, type the cell address of the first corner, enter two periods, and then type the cell address of the second corner. For example, the range A1..B5 means the rectangle that extends from cell A1 to B5. The following are some more examples of a range:

A1..A1	Cell
A1..A8192	Column
A1..A50	Part of a column
A1..IV1	Row
A1..H1	Part of a row
A1..H30	Block (8 columns by 30 rows)
A1..IV8192	Entire worksheet

6–3 COPY COMMAND

The /Copy command enables you to copy a portion of a worksheet to another section of the same worksheet. The origin and the destination cell(s) do not need to be symmetrical. This means that you can copy one cell to many cells, one cell to another cell, or many cells to many cells.

To use this command, choose Copy from the Main menu of 1-2-3. 1-2-3 will ask you to enter the range to copy FROM (Copy what). It shows the present cell address. Type the address of the cells you want to copy (the origin cells), then press Enter. If you want to make a copy of the cell in which the cellpointer is residing, just press Enter—you do not need to type the address. (The cellpointer is the cursor position on the screen that tells the user about his or her position in the worksheet.) 1-2-3 will ask you to enter the range to copy TO (To where, the destination cells). Type the destination range, then press Enter. You can also point to the original and destination cells.

Figure 6–1 illustrates an example of the Copy command. In this example, we entered *Lotus* in cell A4 and chose Copy from the Main menu. We entered *A4* as the original cell and selected A8..H20 as the range to copy to.

Because the Copy command is very important, let's summarize the steps involved in using it:

1. First, enter your data.
2. From the Main menu choose Copy.
3. Enter the range that you want to copy.
4. Press Enter.

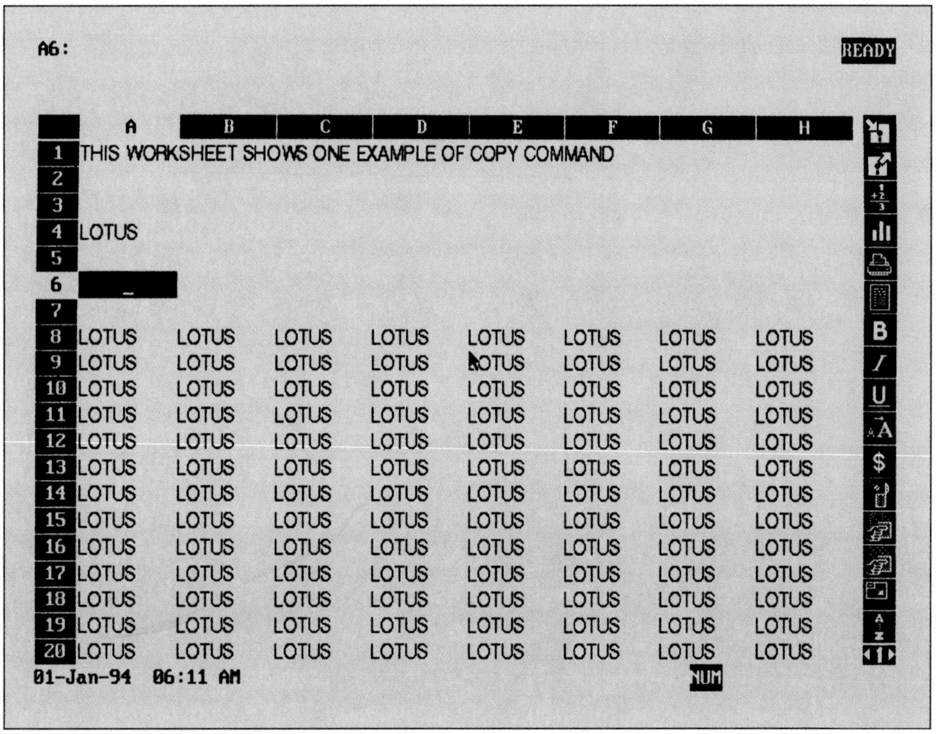

Figure 6–1
Example of the Copy command.

5. Enter the range that you want to copy to.
6. Press Enter.

Also see the SmartIcon for the Copy command presented in Table 6–1 at the end of the chapter.

6–4 MOVE COMMAND

With the /Move command, you can move a portion of a worksheet to another section of the same worksheet. Choose the Move command from the Main menu, and 1-2-3 prompts you to enter an address for the FROM (Move what) range. Enter the cell or range of cells that you want to move and press Enter. Next, 1-2-3 asks for the destination range (To where). Enter the destination range, or point to it, and press Enter. Figure 6–2 illustrates a sample worksheet. We generated Figure 6–3 by moving row 1 to row 15. We typed */MA1..G1* and pressed Enter, then typed *A15* and pressed Enter.

Also see the SmartIcon for the Move command in Table 6–1 presented at the end of the chapter.

6–5 POINTING

To define a range in a worksheet, you have two options. The first option is to enter the address of a range, for example, A1..A5. The second option is to use the pointing technique. To use the pointing technique, you must be in POINT mode. The easiest way to get into POINT mode is to press F5 (the GoTo key). Next, press the period key. This anchors the first corner of the range. Now you

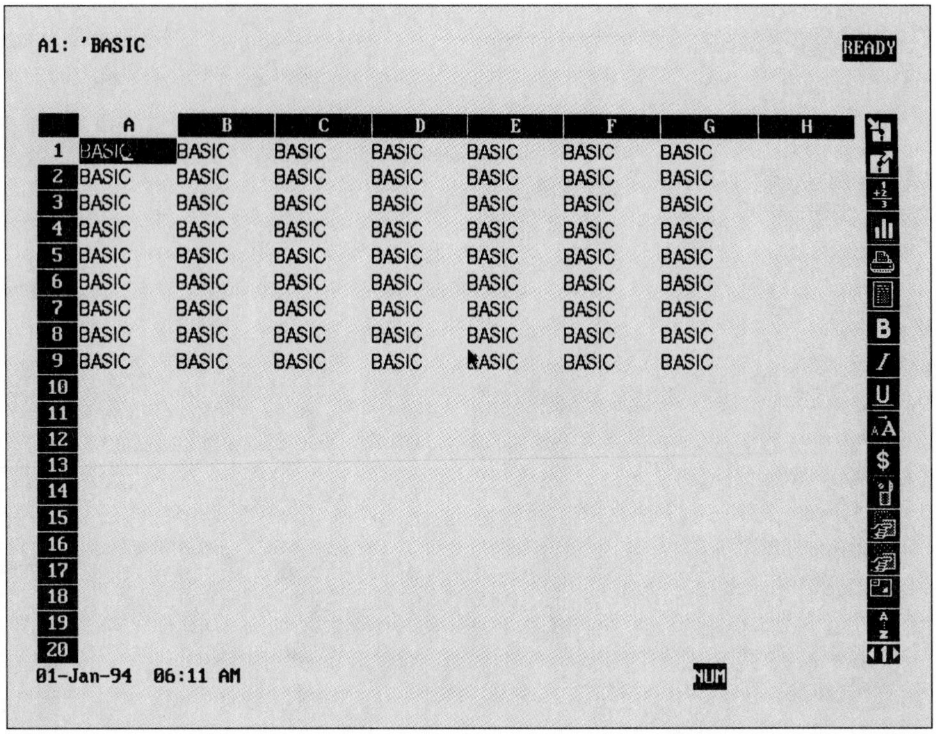

Figure 6–2
Sample worksheet before using the Move command.

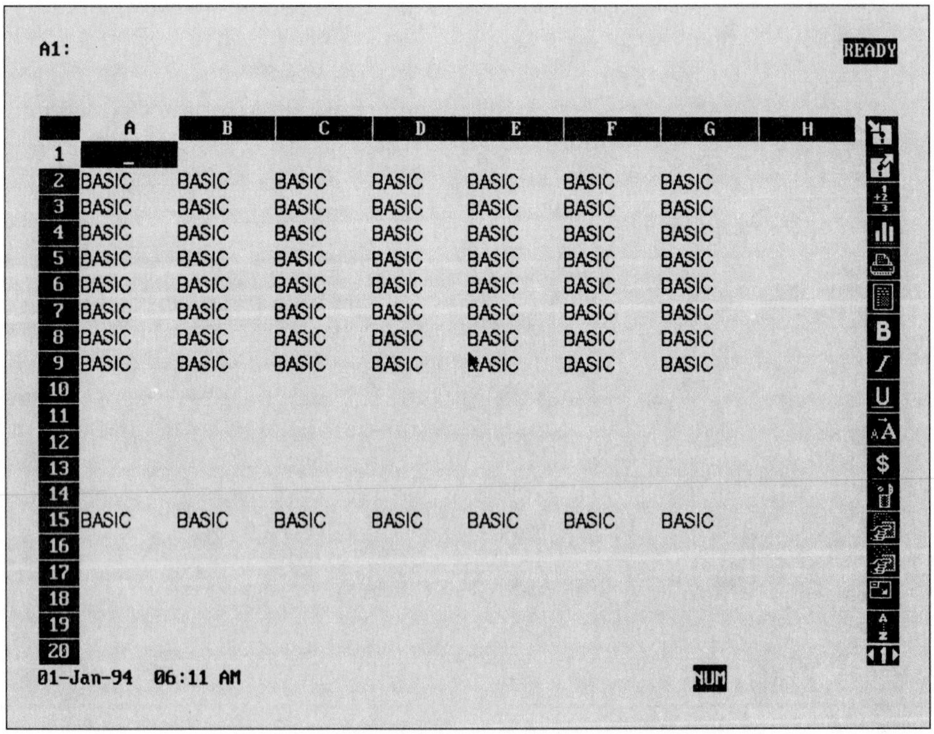

Figure 6–3
Sample worksheet after using the Move command.

can move the cellpointer in any direction until you have specified the range. When the desired range is established, press Enter.

Use the Esc key to unanchor a range or break off the pointing process. The Backspace, Home, and End keys can also be used with pointing. For example, use Home to anchor the cellpointer to cell A1. To make the pointing technique clearer, consider the following example.

In cell A1, enter *system.* You want to copy cell A1 into range A11..H20. With the cellpointer in cell A1, perform the following steps:

1. From the Main menu choose Copy.
2. Press Enter.
3. Move the cellpointer to cell A11.
4. Press the period key to anchor the cell.
5. Move the cellpointer from cell A11 to cell H20.
6. Press Enter.

6–6 WORKSHEET INSERT

Use the /Worksheet Insert command to insert either a row or a column into your worksheet. Choose /Worksheet, then Insert. 1-2-3 displays the options Column and Row. Choose either and then press Enter. Or you could type *C* for column or *R* for row. 1-2-3 asks for the cell address of the row or the column. For column or row insertion, all you need is the address of one cell.

If you have chosen to insert a column, selecting D1..D1, for example, inserts a blank column in front of the current column D and names it column D. If you want to insert a row, choose A1..A1, for example, to insert a blank row above row 1 (the current row 1 will be moved down).

Figure 6–4 shows a sample worksheet. Figure 6–5 shows this same worksheet after inserting a blank row in row 5 and a blank column in column C. For row insertion we typed */WIR A5..A5* (press Enter). For column insertion we typed */WIC C1..C1* and pressed Enter.

Figure 6–4
Sample worksheet.

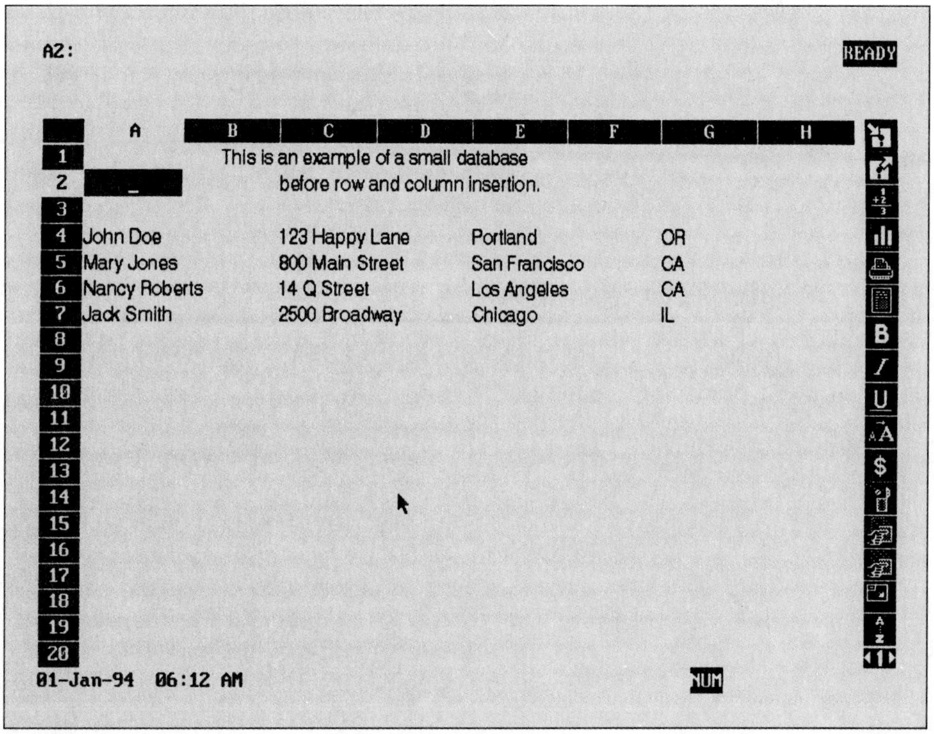

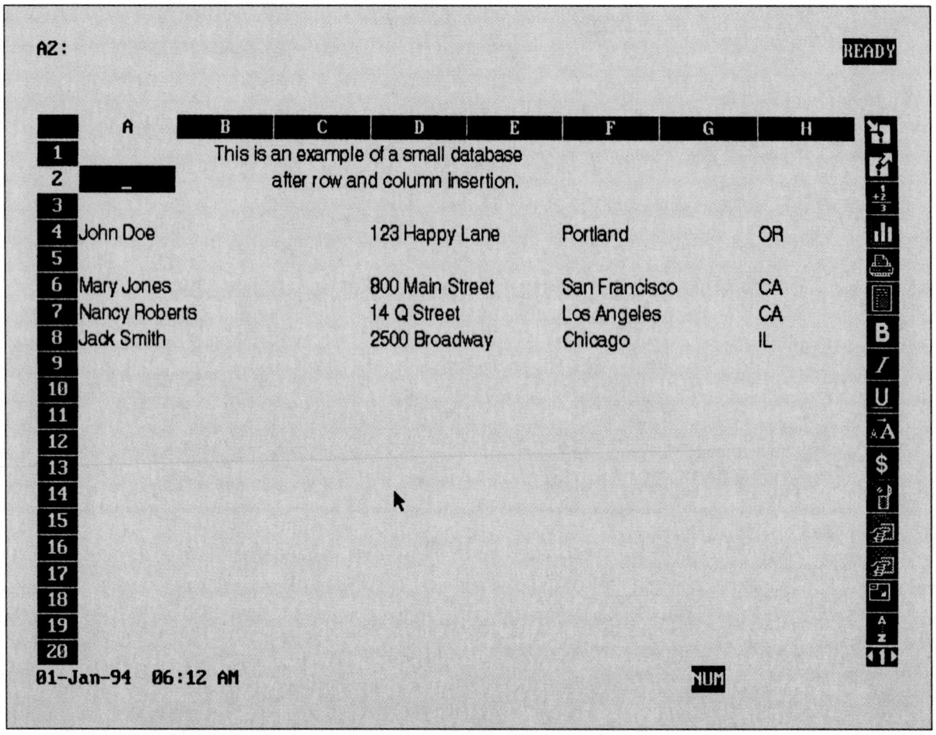

Figure 6–5
Worksheet with a row and column inserted.

Also see the SmartIcon for the Insert command presented in Table 6–1 at the end of the chapter.

6–7 WORKSHEET DELETE

The /Worksheet Delete command enables you to delete rows or columns. When you invoke this command, you are given two options: Column and Row.

To return the worksheet shown in Figure 6–5 to its original condition, you can delete the row and column that were added. For row deletion we typed */WDR A5..A5* Enter. For column deletion we typed */WDC C1..C1* Enter.

Also see the SmartIcon for the Delete command presented in Table 6–1 at the end of the chapter.

6–8 WORKSHEET COLUMN

If you choose /Worksheet Column from the Main menu, you will see the following options:

```
Set-Width  Reset-Width  Hide  Display  Column-Range
```

Use the Set-Width option to change the width of a column. The default width setting is 9 characters. You can set the width of a column from 1 to 240 characters. You can also use the mouse to change the width of a column. To do this, move the mouse pointer to the column letter right at the column divider, then press the left mouse button and click and drag in any direction. Use the Reset-Width option to return the column width to its default setting.

The Hide option allows you to hide a portion of the worksheet without erasing. This command is useful when you are printing a worksheet containing information you do not want displayed on the printout. The hidden columns will be marked with asterisks.

Use the Display option to redisplay the hidden columns.

The Column-Range option allows you to adjust several columns at a time.

6–9 WORKSHEET ERASE

The /Worksheet Erase command allows you to erase the entire worksheet. When you select /Worksheet Erase, you are given two options: No and Yes. Choose Yes to erase the worksheet. Be careful, however. The erased worksheet is gone permanently if it has not been saved.

6–10 RANGE ERASE

The /Range Erase command can be used for erasing a specified portion of a worksheet. To erase a single cell, move the cellpointer to that particular cell, select the /Range Erase command, then press Enter. To erase a portion of a worksheet, select the /Range Erase command, enter a range address to erase, and press Enter.

Also see the SmartIcon for the Range Erase command presented in Table 6–1 at the end of the chapter.

6–11 RELATIVE ADDRESSING

When you use cell addresses in formulas, you need to be aware of the fact that 1-2-3 remembers a cell by its position in the spreadsheet. For example, in relation to cell E10, cell G4 is the cell two columns to the right and six rows above cell E10. To make this clear, look at Figure 6–6. In cell B11 is the formula

+B9+B8+B7+B6

If you copy this formula to cell C11, 1-2-3 changes the formula to read

+C9+C8+C7+C6

The new cell addresses in the formula maintain the same relationship to cell C11 as the old addresses did to cell B11.

This powerful feature is called **relative addressing.** You can use relative addressing with the Copy command to facilitate calculations. Suppose that you have sales data related to 100 different businesses in the first 100 columns of a worksheet. To calculate the sum of each column, all you need to do is type a formula for one column and then copy the same formula to the other 99 columns. 1-2-3 automatically changes the cell addresses for you.

6–12 ABSOLUTE ADDRESSING

Relative addressing is a powerful feature. There are many times, however, when you want to refer to an exact location or an exact value. Sometimes you may even want to use predefined numbers or ratios. In these cases, you must use **absolute addressing**.

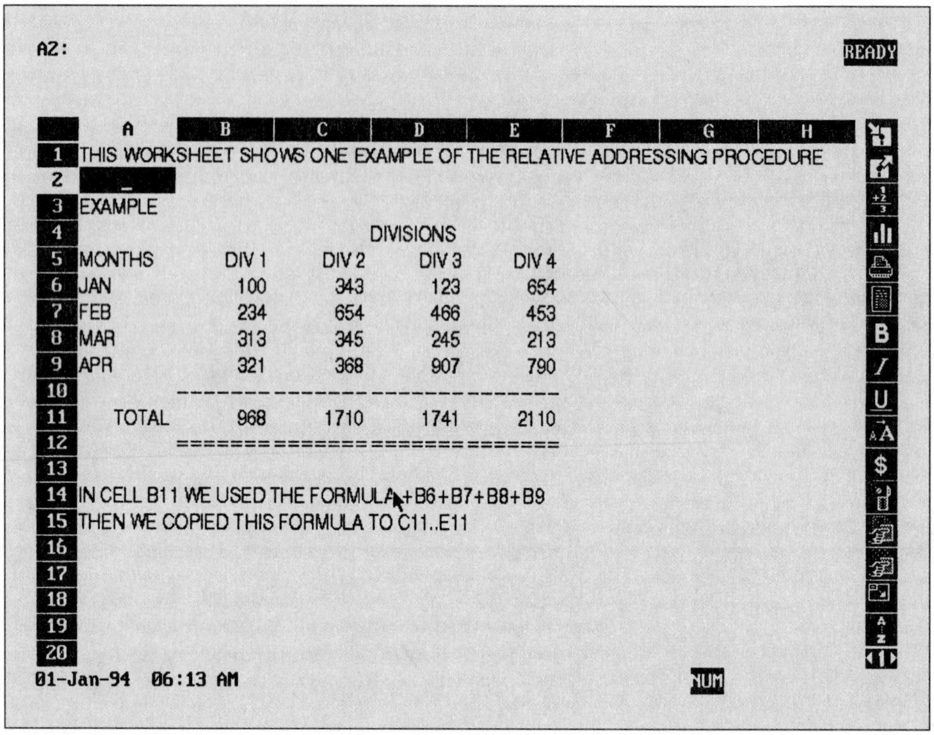

Figure 6–6
Example of relative addressing.

To make this distinction clear, look at Figure 6–7. Five divisions of XYZ company sold different numbers of a particular product. Your task is to calculate each division's percentage of total sales, and you have used the formula +B5/B11 in cell C5. However, if you copy this formula to range C6..C9, you will receive an error because, in each case, the division's units must be divided by the total units in cell B11. When you copy the formula, the B11 cell address changes to reflect the formula's new location, which produces the error. You must make the reference to cell B11 absolute (fixed). You do this by placing a dollar sign in front of the row number and one in front of the column letter ($B$11). You can either enter the $ sign or use the F4 function key. To use this key, you must be in POINT mode.

In Figure 6–7, first we entered +B5/$B$11 in cell C5; then we copied this formula to range C6..C9.

6–13 MIXED ADDRESSING

Sometimes you are interested in using both relative and absolute addressing. You can make the row reference absolute and leave the column reference free to change as you copy the formula, or vice versa. For example, $A10 means the column remains the same but the row changes. B$10 means the row is fixed but the column changes.

Figure 6–8 illustrates two examples of mixed addressing. The first example shows the discounted prices under different discount rates for two products with original prices of $12 and $30. The second example in this figure shows the same information with a different format. Can you tell what is different?

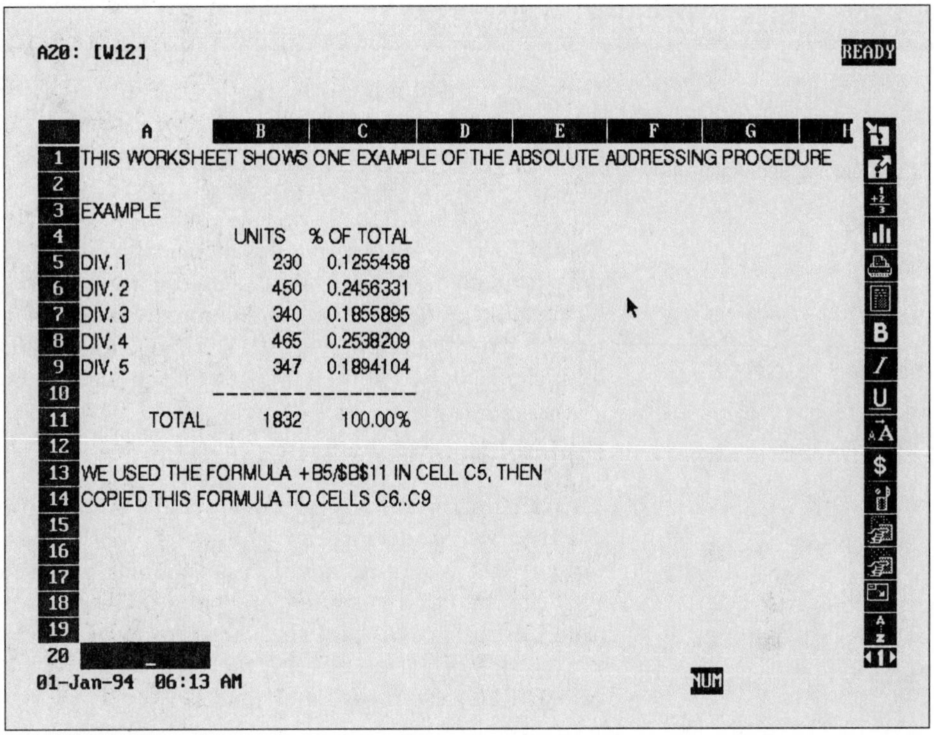

Figure 6–7
Example of absolute addressing.

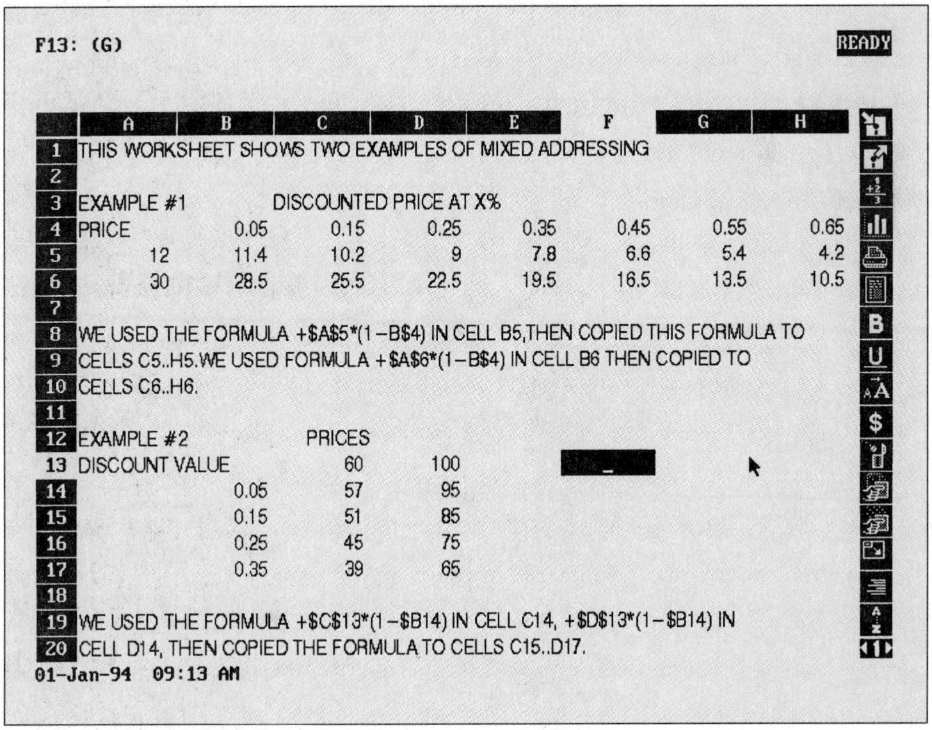

Figure 6–8
Two examples of mixed addressing.

6–14 UNDERSTANDING FORMATS

To generate usable reports, the look of the report plays as important a role as does accuracy, especially in the business world. The format of the report is extremely important. 1-2-3 provides a number of formatting options so that a variety of reports can easily be generated.

You can use the Format command in two ways: /Worksheet Global Format or /Range Format. /Worksheet Global Format is used when the entire worksheet needs to be formatted. /Range Format is used if a specific portion of the worksheet is to be formatted. Figure 6–9 shows the options available under the Format command.

The Reset option is used to change the existing setting to the global default setting. The Reset option is available only under the /Range Format command.

6–14–1 General Option

The General option is the Format default. In this format, the insignificant zeros to the right of the decimal are eliminated, very large and very small numbers are presented in scientific notation, and labels (nonnumeric data) are left justified. You can change this setting manually by inserting one of the label prefixes, by using /Worksheet Global Label-Prefix, or by using /Range Label (see Figure 6–10).

To format a cell with the General option, move the cursor to the cell, invoke /RFG, and press Enter.

6–14–2 Fixed Option

The Fixed option format does not display commas or dollar signs in the formatted worksheet. Numbers can include up to 15 decimal places. If you specify fewer decimal places, the number will be rounded up. For example, if you specify three decimal positions, the number 6.778642 will be displayed as 6.779. This option is

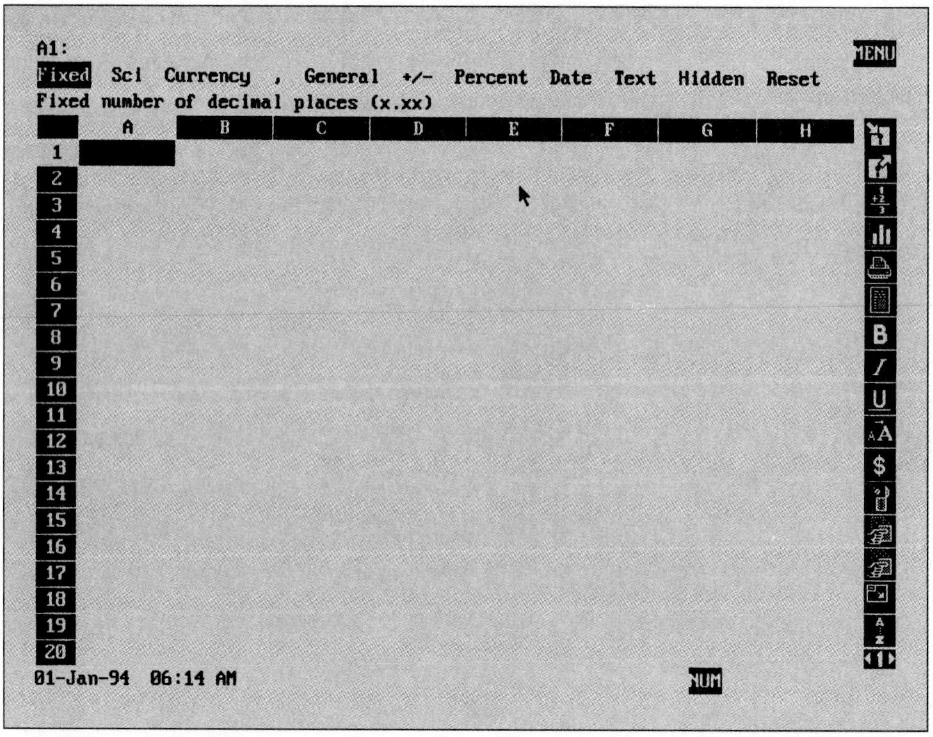

Figure 6–9
Different format options available in 1-2-3.

Figure 6–10
Example of format options.

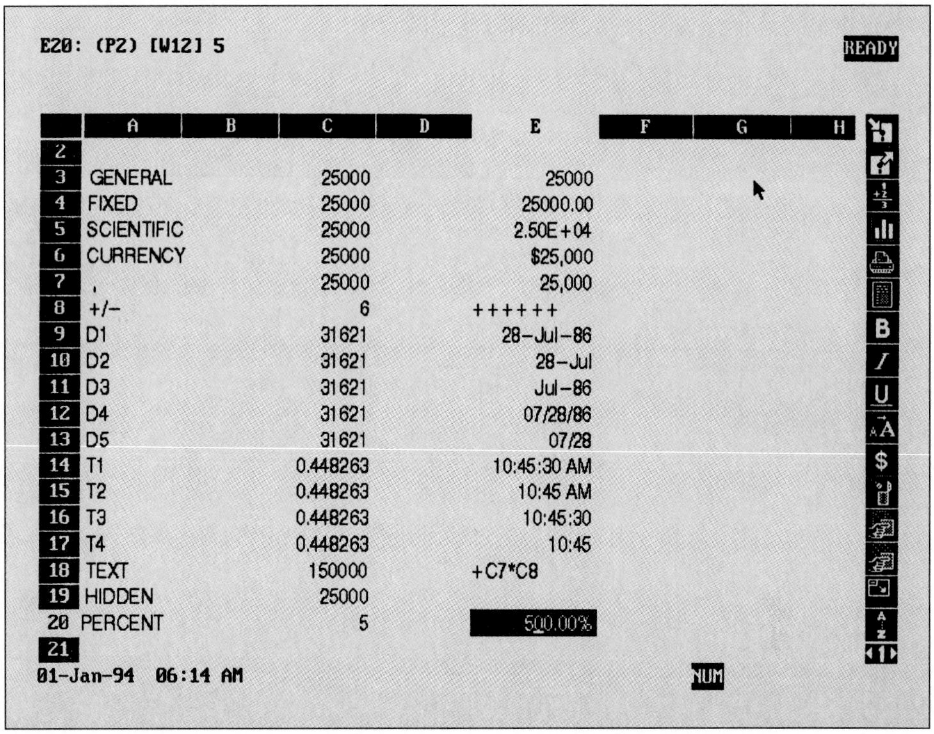

E20: (P2) [W12] 5 READY

	A	C	E
2			
3	GENERAL	25000	25000
4	FIXED	25000	25000.00
5	SCIENTIFIC	25000	2.50E+04
6	CURRENCY	25000	$25,000
7	,	25000	25,000
8	+/-	6	++++++
9	D1	31621	28-Jul-86
10	D2	31621	28-Jul
11	D3	31621	Jul-86
12	D4	31621	07/28/86
13	D5	31621	07/28
14	T1	0.448263	10:45:30 AM
15	T2	0.448263	10:45 AM
16	T3	0.448263	10:45:30
17	T4	0.448263	10:45
18	TEXT	150000	+C7*C8
19	HIDDEN	25000	
20	PERCENT	5	500.00%
21			

01-Jan-94 06:14 AM NUM

suitable for printing checks or financial statements, such as an income statement or balance sheet (see Figure 6–10).

To format a cell with the Fixed option, move the cursor to the cell, invoke /RFF, specify the number of places to the right of the decimal point, and press Enter twice.

6–14–3 Scientific Option

The Scientific option is used for very large or very small numbers. You can specify up to 15 decimal places (see Figure 6–10).

To format a cell with the Scientific option, move the cursor to the cell, invoke /RFS, specify the number of places to the right of the decimal point, and press Enter twice.

6–14–4 Currency Option

In the Currency option, a dollar sign appears immediately to the left of the number. A comma (,) separates groups of three digits, and negative numbers appear in parentheses. You determine the placement of the decimal. If the specified column is not wide enough to display the entire number, 1-2-3 displays a series of asterisks. (This is true of all the options.) In such a case you must increase the column width by using either the /Worksheet Column Set-Width or the /Worksheet Global Column-Width command (see Figure 6–10).

To format a cell with the Currency option, move the cursor to the cell, invoke /RFC, specify the number of places to the right of the decimal point, and press Enter twice.

Also see the Currency SmartIcon presented in Table 6–1 at the end of the chapter.

6–14–5 Comma (,) Option

The Comma option is similar to the Currency option. The only difference is that the dollar sign is suppressed. This option is suitable for nonfinancial reports (see Figure 6–10).

To format a cell with the comma (,) option, move the cursor to the cell, invoke /RF,, specify the number of places to the right of the decimal point, and press Enter twice.

Also see the Comma SmartIcon presented in Table 6–1 at the end of the chapter.

6–14–6 +/– Option

In the +/– format, a positive number is presented by + signs, negative numbers by – signs, and zero by a period. This option is considered a limited graphics option and makes the job of comparing different numbers an easy task. For example, the number 5 is displayed as five + signs, the number –2 as two – signs, and so forth (see Figure 6–10).

To format a cell with the +/– option, move the cursor to the cell, invoke /RF +/–, and press Enter.

6–14–7 Percent Option

The Percent option presents numbers as percentages of 100. For example, .05 is displayed as 5%. This option can be very useful when comparing a data item to a total, for example, when comparing the raw material cost to the total cost of production (see Figure 6–10).

To format a cell with the Percent option, move the cursor to the cell, invoke /RFP, specify the number of places to the right of the decimal point, and press Enter twice.

Also see the Percent SmartIcon presented in Table 6–1 at the end of the chapter.

6–14–8 Date Option

1-2-3 has five different formats for date. The beginning date in the 1-2-3 calendar is December 31, 1899 and the last date is December 31, 2099. December 31, 1899 is defined by 1-2-3 as the number zero, January 1, 1900 as the number 1, and December 31, 2099 equals 73050. Using these various date options, you can create the majority of standard formats for different reports (see Figure 6–10).

To format a cell with the Date option, move the cursor to the cell, invoke /RFD, select 1, or 2, or 3, or 4, or 5, and press Enter.

6–14–9 Time Option

1-2-3 has four time options. In time formats, fractional parts of serial numbers represent time (.000 indicates midnight, .500 indicates noon, .833 indicates 8:00 p.m. and so on). You can use the @TIME and @NOW functions to generate these numbers (see Figure 6–10). @TIME and @NOW are discussed in Chapter 7.

To format a cell with the Time option, move the cursor to the cell, invoke /RFDT (Time), select 1, or 2, or 3, or 4, and press Enter.

6–14–10 Text Option

The contents of each cell is displayed as text when you use the Text option. For example, if cell A30 contains +H1*P1 (hours multiplied by pay rate), instead of displaying the result of this formula, 1-2-3 will show it as text. This option can be helpful in debugging long formulas (see Figure 6–10).

To format a cell with the Text option, move the cursor to the cell, invoke /RFT, and press Enter.

6–14–11 Hidden Option

The Hidden option is useful for hiding a portion of the worksheet or the entire worksheet. The hidden portion is still a part of the worksheet and is included in any calculations. This format provides security by hiding some portions of a worksheet from unauthorized users. To reveal the hidden portion, reformat the worksheet using any other format option (see Figure 6–10).

6–14–12 Override Option

As we mentioned earlier, the Format command can be accessed by either the /Worksheet Global Format or the /Range Format command. /Range Format always has priority over /Worksheet Global Format. This means the portion of the worksheet that has been formatted by /Range Format is not affected by /Worksheet Global Format. Also, /WCS has priority over /WGC.

6–15 WORKSHEET GLOBAL LABEL-PREFIX

If you choose the /Worksheet Global Label-Prefix command from the Main menu, you will be presented with the following three choices:

```
Left  Right  Center
```

As discussed in Chapter 4, either manually enter a label prefix or use these commands for inserting left, right, or center justification. Remember, by default, numbers are right justified and labels are left justified. You should always first issue the command and then enter data into the worksheet. The command has no effect on data already entered in the worksheet.

6–16 WORKSHEET GLOBAL PROTECTION

The /Worksheet Global Protection command works in conjunction with /Range Protect and /Range Unprotect to protect a worksheet or a portion of a worksheet from unwanted changes. When you issue this command, you are given two choices: Enable and Disable. With Enable, only unprotected areas can be accessed and modified. The /Worksheet Erase command can always erase your worksheet, whether it's protected or unprotected.

To make this discussion clearer, consider the following example. From the Main menu choose /Worksheet Global Protection Enable. The control panel will display

```
PR
```

which means that your worksheet is now protected. To verify this, try to enter a data item in the worksheet. For example, type *check* and press Enter. 1-2-3 beeps and the words

```
Protected cell
```

appear at the middle of the screen. To cancel this facility, again choose /Worksheet Global Protection from the Main menu. This time choose the Disable option.

You may want to protect just a portion of the worksheet, leaving a range, such as A1..H10, unprotected. To do this follow these steps:

1. Select /Worksheet Global Protection from the Main menu.
2. Choose Enable.
3. Choose /Range Unprotect from the Main menu.
4. Select range A1..H10 to be unprotected.
5. Press Enter.

Now data may only be entered in range A1..H10. The rest of the worksheet is protected.

6–17 WORKSHEET TITLES

The /Worksheet Titles option freezes rows or columns along the top or left side of the screen. This enables you to see either the top portion, the side portion, or both, of your worksheet as you move around the worksheet.

Select /Worksheet Titles and you will be given the following options:

```
Both  Horizontal  Vertical  Clear
```

Both freezes the rows above and the columns to the left of the cellpointer.

Horizontal freezes the rows above the cellpointer. This means you can move around the cellpointer vertically in the worksheet, but the rows above the cellpointer stay fixed.

Vertical freezes the columns to the left of the cellpointer. This means you can move around the cellpointer horizontally in the worksheet but the columns to the left of the cellpointer stay fixed.

Clear unfreezes the worksheet.

Remember, the data to be frozen must be to the left and above the cellpointer.

6–18 WORKSHEET WINDOW

Using the /Worksheet Window command allows you to split the screen so that you can view two versions of a worksheet at the same time. When you invoke /Worksheet Window, you are given the following choices:

```
Horizontal  Vertical  Sync  Unsync  Clear
```

The Horizontal option creates a split screen with two horizontal windows. To create such a worksheet, move the cellpointer to a particular row (row 2 or any row below this), and then select /Worksheet Window Horizontal. If you invoke this command in row 1, you will hear a beep telling you that you cannot split the screen in row 1.

The Vertical option creates a split screen with two vertical windows. To create such a worksheet, move the cellpointer to column B or any column to the right of column B, then select /Worksheet Window Vertical.

The Sync option allows two windows to move together. This means that the data items in the two windows scroll across the screen together. The default for scrolling is Sync.

The Unsync option allows independent movement in either window.

The Clear option removes the second window from your worksheet.

To move the cellpointer between the two windows, press F6.

6–19 WORKSHEET PAGE

You use the /Worksheet Page command to insert a page break into the worksheet. When you print a worksheet, a new page will start at the page break. To use this command, move the cellpointer to the row below where you want to have a page break, then select /Worksheet Page. The location of the break will be shown by :: (these symbols must be in column A). This feature can be useful for report generation. You can remove a page break by using /Range Erase, /Worksheet Delete Column, and so forth.

6–20 RANGE LABEL

As we discussed in Chapter 4, 1-2-3 by default enters numbers as right justified and labels as left justified. The format of a label can be changed either by including a label prefix (', ", or ^) or by using the /Range Label command. This command has no effect on numbers. When you invoke the /Range Label command, you can choose from these options: Left, Right, Center.

6–21 RANGE NAME

To perform any 1-2-3 operations in a certain range, there are two options available. Suppose that you are trying to add the contents of cells A1, A2, A3, and A4. You can either refer to these four cells as A1..A4, or you can give this range a name.

To name a range, you use the /Range Name Create command. A range name can be up to 15 characters long. Try to use meaningful names and avoid names that might also be cell names, such as A14 or G23.

You can use /Range Name Labels to name an adjacent cell. With this command, you can use the options Right, Down, Left, and Up. For example, if cell G1 contains

```
Commission Rate
```

cell H1 contains

```
22%
```

and if the cellpointer is in cell G1, you can use the /Range Name Labels Right command to assign the label "Commission Rate" as the name for cell H1.

To delete a range name, use /Range Name Delete. To erase all the range names in your worksheet, use /Range Name Reset.

What happens if you duplicate a range name? 1-2-3 assigns the most recent range to the specific range name.

To see a listing of all the range names with their addresses, use /Range Name Table. This command lists the names of all the ranges in your current worksheet in alphabetical order. When you invoke this command, you must position the cellpointer in a blank area of the worksheet so that the table of range names does not overwrite your data. You need not define an address for the entire table. All you need is the upper left corner cell.

If you want to use a new range name and you are not sure which names you have already used, you can press F3 in the POINT mode to display all the range names already used in your worksheet. Whenever you save a worksheet, the range names also are saved.

Using range names can be much easier than using range addresses, and they make your spreadsheet work more meaningful.

6–22 RANGE JUSTIFY

You can use the /Range Justify command to break a long title or heading into several lines instead of one long line. Type your title and select /Range Justify. Then specify the range for justification and press Enter. If there is data underneath the line that you are justifying, that data will also be justified and moved down. Therefore, your data will not be destroyed. Figure 6–11 shows an example of this command.

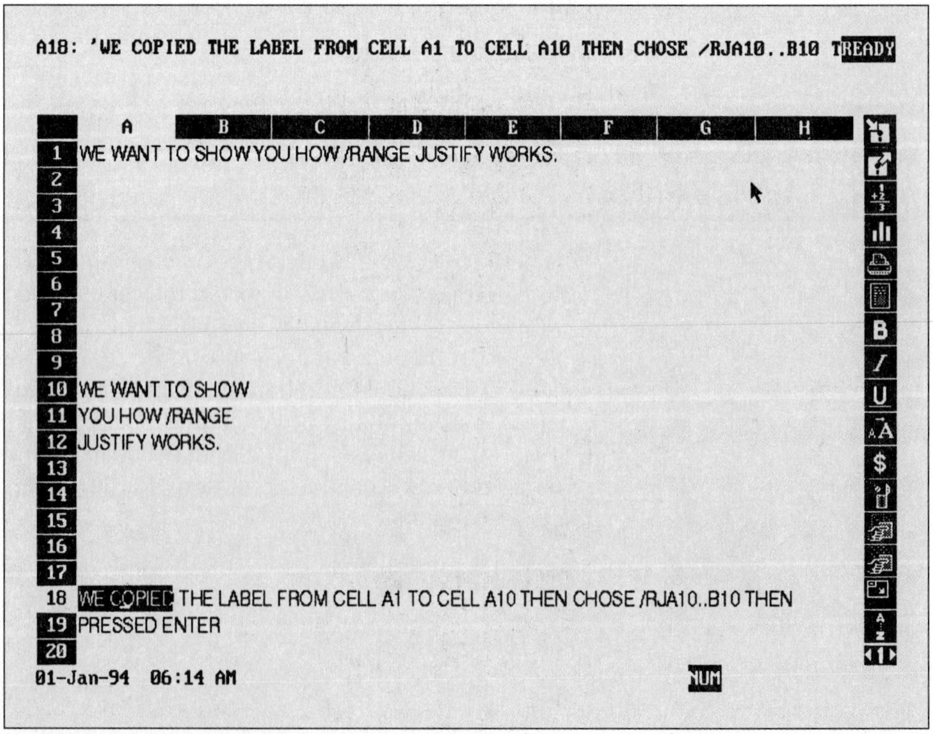

Figure 6–11
Examples of /Range Justify command.

SUMMARY

This chapter reviewed important 1-2-3 commands, including Copy, Move, Worksheet, and Range. A discussion of relative, absolute, and mixed addressing also was presented. Practice to become more familiar with these commands.

See Table 6–1 for Worksheet and Range SmartIcons.

REVIEW QUESTIONS

*These questions are answered in Appendix A.

1. What is the difference between Worksheet commands and Worksheet Global commands?
2. What does global mean?
*3. What is the default value for column width in your worksheet?
*4. When you use /Worksheet Global Label-Prefix, should the data be entered first (before issuing the command) or does it matter?
5. How do you activate global protection for your worksheet?
6. If a worksheet is protected, can you erase it?
7. What is the difference between the /Worksheet Delete and /Range Erase commands?
8. How many options are available under the /Worksheet Column command?
9. What are some applications of the /Worksheet Titles command?
10. How many ways can /Worksheet Window be utilized?
11. How do you move the cellpointer between two split screens?
12. What are some applications of /Worksheet Window?
*13. What does /Worksheet Page do? Is there any specific column for a page break or can it be placed anywhere?
14. What is a range?
*15. Can a range and a worksheet be the same?
16. What is the function of the /Range Label Center command?
17. How do you erase a range?
18. How do you name a range?
*19. How do you know a range name has not been used already (to avoid duplication or erasing a range name)?
20. How do you erase all range names?
21. How many characters can be used in a range name?
22. What are some applications of the /Range Justify command?
23. What does the /Range Protect command do?
*24. When can you actually see the effect of the /Range Protect command?
25. What is relative addressing?
26. Why can't relative addressing be used all the time?
27. What is mixed addressing?
*28. How do you make a range name absolute?
29. Can a cell have both absolute and relative addresses at the same time?
30. Why is formatting necessary?
31. How many format options are available?
32. What is the difference between the Currency option and the Comma (,) option?
*33. How many Date options are available? What is the application of each?

34. How many Time options are available? What is the application of each?
35. What are some applications of the Text format?
36. What are some applications of the Hidden format?
37. What is the difference between /Worksheet Global Format and /Range Format?
38. What are the beginning and ending dates in the 1-2-3 calendar?
*39. Can you do arithmetic operations with dates and times (can you subtract two dates or two times from each other)?

Table 6–1
Worksheet and Range Icons

WYSIWYG Mode	Text Mode	Description
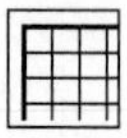	+ROW	Inserts one or more rows above the highlighted range.
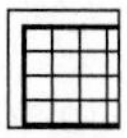	+COL	Inserts one or more columns to the left of the highlighted range.
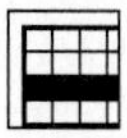	–ROW	Deletes all rows in the highlighted range.
	–COL	Deletes all columns in the highlighted range.
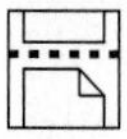	— - - - —	Inserts a page break in the row that contains the cell pointer.
	| ¦ |	**W** Inserts a page break in the column that contains the cell pointer.
	DEL	Erases the highlighted range.
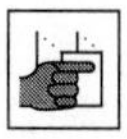	COPY	Lets you specify a range where you want the highlighted range to be copied.
	MOVE	Lets you specify a range where you want the highlighted range to be moved.
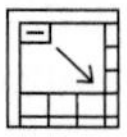	REP DATA	Copies the contents of the current cell of the highlighted range in all other cells in the range.
0,0	0,0	Formats values in a range with 2 decimal places, the default currency symbol, and the default thousands separator or restores the global format in the range.
$	$	Formats values in a range with the default thousands separator and no decimal places or restores the global format in the range.
%	%	Formats values in a range as % (percent) with 2 decimal places or restores the global format in the range.

Column 1 shows icons if WYSIWYG is attached. Column 2 shows icons as they appear when WYSIWYG is either not attached or is set to: Display Mode Text.
The icons identified by **W** work only when WYSIWYG is attached.

HANDS-ON EXPERIENCE

1. Create a worksheet with your first name in cell A1; then copy your name into cells A1..H20.
2. In the worksheet you created in question 1, move rows 1 and 2 to rows 50 and 51.
3. Repeat the process in question 2, only this time use the pointing technique.
4. Extend all the column widths in the worksheet to 30.
5. Split your worksheet both vertically and horizontally.
6. Using the /Worksheet Erase command, erase your worksheet.
7. Generate a worksheet in which both row 1 and column A are frozen.
8. Generate a protected worksheet. Then, by using the /Range Unprotect command, unprotect cell H10. Enter your last name in cell H10.
9. Select the /Worksheet Global Default Status command. What is the status of your system?
10. Enter the number 10 in cells A1 and A2. In cell A3 enter the formula +A1 – A2. Because there is no data in these cells, you will see 0 in A3. Suppress the 0 using the /Worksheet Global Zero command.
11. In the worksheet you created in question 10, first hide column A and then reveal it. Erase the worksheet.
12. Create the following worksheet:

A	B	C . . .
1	Financial Data	
2 Branch A		
3 Branch B		
4 Branch C		
.		
.		
.		

    Using the /Worksheet Titles command, freeze both horizontal and vertical titles. Now to verify your work, move the cellpointer to the right and then downward.
13. Erase the screen then enter *COBOL* into cell A1; then center it using /Range Label Center.
14. Erase the screen then enter *10, 20, 30,* and *40* into cells A1 to A4. Using the appropriate command, give this range a valid name.
15. Enter *5, 66, 777, 8888,* and *99999* into cells A1 to A5. Now do the following:
    a. Format the worksheet using the Comma (,) option with three decimals.
    b. Format the worksheet using the Fixed option with two decimals.
    c. Format the worksheet using the Scientific option with two decimals.
    d. Format the worksheet using the Currency option with two decimals.

    In some of these cases, you may see a series of asterisks. Why is this? Extend the cell width using /WCS or /WGC.
16. In cell A1, using the /Range Format Date 3 command, enter *33970* to indicate Jan-93. Now generate the next 11 months by using the Copy command. (Hint: in cell A2, enter +A1+30.)
17. In cells H1 and H2, enter *500* and *1000.* In cell H3 enter *+H1+H2.* 1-2-3 displays

Which format option will display the actual formula

+H1+H2

and not its numeric value?

18. Enter the numbers *2, 22, 222, 2222,* and *22222* into cells A1 to A5. Copy these numbers to cells F1..F5. Now split the screen vertically in column D. Format the first screen using the Currency option. Format the second screen using the Comma (,) option. Do you see the difference?
19. Retrieve CHAPT5 and perform the following:
    - **a.** Move all graduate students to the top of the worksheet.
    - **b.** Adjust the length of each column to display the data more clearly. For example, the length of the SEX column should be 3; the length of MAJOR should be 5, and so on.
    - **c.** Using /Worksheet Titles, freeze both horizontal and vertical titles.
    - **d.** Make it so that a user can enter information in only the test scores area. (Hint: use /Range Input.)
    - **e.** Return the worksheet to normal.
    - **f.** Move the entire worksheet down four rows.
    - **g.** Enter the following title for the entire worksheet:

      This worksheet illustrates the performance of a group of students in the 1-2-3 class.

    - **h.** Using /Range Justify, justify this title into four lines.
    - **i.** Using the appropriate Format command, add one decimal place to each test score.
    - **j.** Using /File Xtract, extract the name and major of all the students into a file called NAME.
    - **k.** Save the final worksheet as CHAPT6.
    - **l.** Save this file once again with a password. This time use SECRET as the password and IMPORTANT as the file name.
    - **m.** Retrieve IMPORTANT and change the password to SECRET1.
20. Complete the worksheet in Figure 6–12.
21. Complete the worksheet in Figure 6–13.
22. Either type or load the worksheet presented in Figure 6–14. Do the following:
    - **a.** Using the Copy command, calculate and complete the TOTAL column.
    - **b.** Freeze the worksheet horizontally and vertically by moving to the right and then downward. Verify your work.

KEY TERMS

Absolute addressing
Format
Mixed addressing
Range
Relative addressing

KEY COMMANDS

Copy
Move
Range Erase
Range Format
Range Justify
Range Label
Range Name
Worksheet Column
Worksheet Delete
Worksheet Erase
Worksheet Global Format
Worksheet Global Label-Prefix
Worksheet Global Protection
Worksheet Insert
Worksheet Page
Worksheet Titles
Worksheet Window

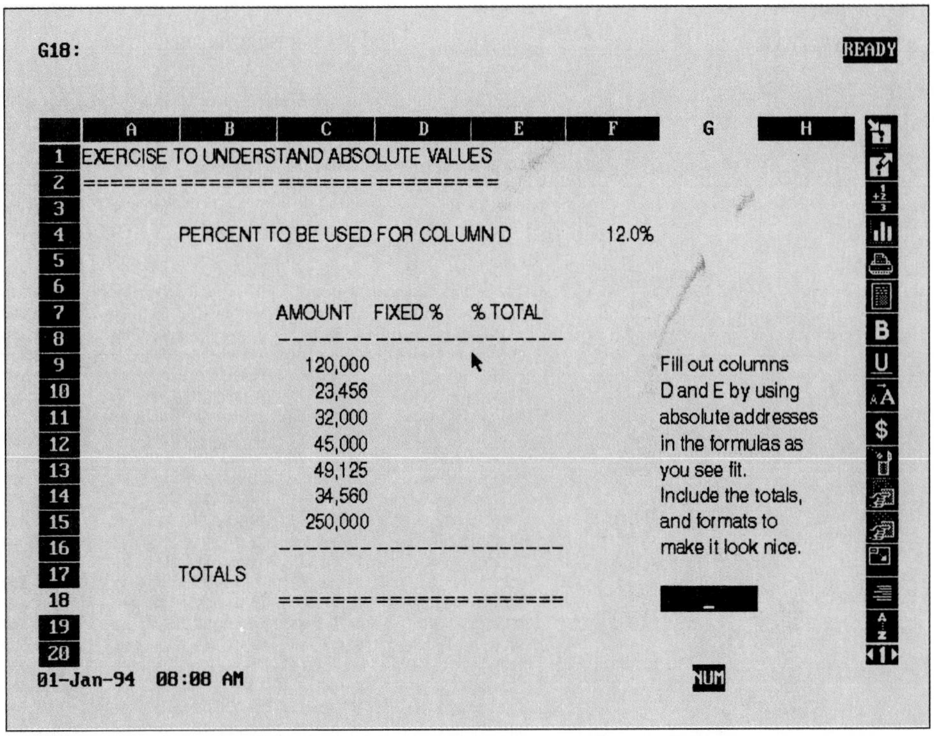

Figure 6–12
A sample worksheet.

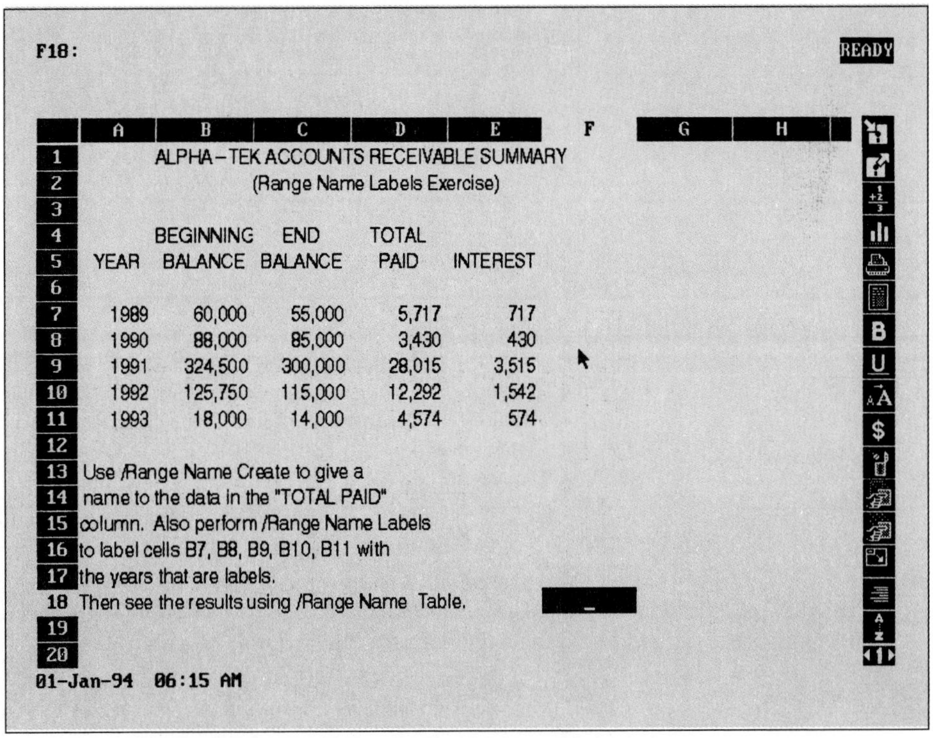

Figure 6–13
A sample worksheet.

Figure 6–14
A sample worksheet.

ON-LINE MARKETING
SALES RESULTS - 1994

EMP.NO.	NAME	DATE/HIRED	BRTHDATE	RANK	REGION	1ST QTR	2ND QTR	3RD QTR	4TH QTR	TOTAL
1001	Lyman,Emerson	20-Nov-61	24-June-24	JR	NE	$34,500	$24,450	$40,500	$41,350	
1002	Nesbit,LeRoy	26-Jun-79	16-Jun-55	MGR	SE	$32,100	$26,850	$21,850	$16,400	
1003	Healy,Harold	24-Sep-78	13-Sep-56	JR	MW	$16,300	$31,000	$32,450	$29,500	
1004	Lloyd,June	13-Aug-82	30-Sep-61	JR	SW	$47,500	$19,950	$24,700	$16,700	
1005	Stubbs,Sharron	18-Nov-80	06-Apr-54	JR	SW	$18,900	$23,500	$23,700	$34,800	
1006	Maag,Lisa	11-Jul-66	31-May-61	JR	MOU	$23,570	$34,650	$39,670	$25,050	
1007	Harris,Phil	18-Nov-67	25-Dec-47	NE	SW	$32,150	$21,350	$31,500	$18,600	
1008	Lynn,Grant	19-Ju;-76	29-Aug-52	MGR	NE	$39,210	$48,100	$34,780	$21,200	
1009	Reynolds,Donald	14-Aug-74	11-Aug-51	JR	SW	$24,400	$15,650	$23,950	$45,850	
1010	Leavitt,Leo	28-Feb-68	07-Mar-42	JR	PAC	$24,300	$41,000	$21,000	$23,000	
1011	Farley,Cheryl	27-May-83	21-Oct-59	SR	MW	$21,000	$17,500	$28,600	$39,050	
1012	Wade,Elaine	02-Apr-71	26-Feb-47	SUP	SW	$26,550	$39,600	$24,700	$21,500	
1013	Thomas,Kenny	11-Mar-64	03-Sep-31	SR	SE	$39,950	$19,100	$21,350	$23,800	
1014	Hurst,Connie	14-Aug-75	25-Apr-49	MGR	PAC	$15,000	$16,350	$22,780	$32,200	
1015	Park,Clara	15-May-69	22-Nov-44	SR	MOU	$45,100	$32,200	$35,800	$27,150	
1016	Ritchie,Marc	30-Nov-72	04-Sept-44	SR	MOU	$27,000	$23,700	$24,600	$49,600	
1017	Tanner,Amy	21-Jul-77	29-Oct-51	SR	NE	$21,000	$23,550	$19,250	$45,600	
1018	Larse,Max	21-Dec-79	02-Nov-58	JR	SW	$19,500	$15,400	$41,300	$16,600	
1019	Turner,Wayne	07-Dec-65	17-Jun-34	JR	NE	$38,950	$21,200	$41,800	$23,750	
1020	Rodney,Luella	29-Mar-62	19-May-33	SR	SW	$43,000	$24,550	$27,350	$15,900	
1021	Dixon,Linda	15-Dec-69	29-Aug-41	SR	MOU	$27,000	$43,750	$18,350	$30,100	
1022	Payne,Shirley	10-Oct-71	15-May-45	SR	SE	$23,450	$49,200	$15,700	$35,000	
1023	Price,Kevin	21-Sep-82	01-Feb-53	MGR	MOU	$15,400	$45,300	$49,450	$32,400	
1024	Harson,Craig	03-Feb-60	20-Jan-29	JR	ME	$29,500	$27,850	$21,500	$44,600	
1025	Clark,Gus	04-Oct-63	20-Jan-30	SUP	SE	$43,400	$26,300	$38,600	$17,000	
1026	Adams,Robert	01-Jan-80	02-Nov-60	JR	SW	$15,500	$21,750	$30,440	$25,150	
1027	Whitehead,Aaron	26-Jul-76	01-Sep-49	JR	MW	$21,560	$24,500	$26,900	$42,900	
1028	Pace,Alfred	12-Oct-71	11-Apr-37	SR	SW	$35,600	$21,600	$32,300	$27,100	
1029	Bowen,Glen	10-Mar-73	12-Oct-38	SR	SE	$21,500	$30,250	$16,200	$27,300	
1030	Cox,Nathan	19-Mar-73	24-Jul-47	JR	MOU	$17,000	$38,000	$43,900	$23,900	
1031	Madsen,Linda	24-Oct-66	04-Oct-39	SUP	SE	$24,500	$39,400	$23,900	$52,500	
1032	Seamons,Jackie	22-May-72	24-Jan-47	MGR	SW	$34,500	$43,200	$35,950	$24,650	
1033	Shelley,Scott	08-Feb-61	13-Jun-32	JR	PAC	$44,400	$35,800	$34,770	$27,500	
1034	Carlile,Kay	17-Apr-82	18-May-52	JR	MOU	$37,800	$22,100	$29,250	$30,650	
1035	Marks,Merlin	04-Jan-71	27-Sep-50	SR	SE	$41,000	$23,770	$25,400	$34,800	
1036	Nelson,Henry	05-Dec-77	03-Dec-48	JR	SW	$19,550	$26,850	$26,950	$16,600	
1037	Slater,Derek	02-Sep-76	04-Apr-49	JR	MW	$23,450	$34,650	$44,850	$43,650	
1038	McCurdy,Steven	18-Oct-81	29-Aug-53	MGR	MW	$16,300	$43,500	$31,600	$24,100	
1039	Savage,Brian	13-Jan-78	22-Dec-44	JR	PAC	$35,670	$27,100	$43,410	$24,100	
1040	Wilde,Stuart	15-Oct-70	23-Dec-44	JR	SW	$30,100	$26,800	$21,950	$42,300	
1041	Vincent,Bret	25-Jun-75	27-Jun-52	JR	NE	$23,450	$41,200	$41,600	$19,350	
1042	Marshall,Clyde	23-Mar-73	21-May-42	JR	SW	$30,000	$24,750	$44,000	$39,910	
1043	Sperry,Bruce	23-Mar-76	16-Jul-43	SR	NE	$23,450	$44,650	$23,650	$40,100	
1044	Miller,Paula	04-Jan-65	18-Jul-36	SR	SE	$26,700	$16,350	$16,300	$46,000	

MISCONCEPTIONS AND SOLUTIONS

Misconception In very large worksheets, if you enter a new data item, 1-2-3 immediately recalculates the entire worksheet. If you keep entering different values, the entire process may slow down.

> **Solution** If you use the /Worksheet Global Recalculation Manual command, you can turn the automatic recalculation off. Calculations can be done by entering all your numbers, then pressing F9 (Calc).

Misconception When you use either the Move or the Copy command to copy or move a data item or formula to a cell, the content of the cell is replaced by the new data item. Any formula that refers to this cell now uses this new value.

> **Solution** Move or copy the data item to an empty cell or an area of the worksheet that does not have any relationship to your earlier formulas.

Misconception If you have a series of range names in a worksheet and you delete a portion of that worksheet by using the /Worksheet Delete or /Range Erase command, your range becomes undefined but the range names are still intact.

> **Solution** First check the address and listing of all your range names by using F3 in POINT mode, then issue the command for erasing.

Misconception The Move command does not transfer cell addresses in the same way that the Copy command does. The Copy command transfers relative addresses of cells. Absolute cell addresses are transferred as absolute with Copy but not with Move. For example, in cells A1 and B1, enter the numbers *1* and *2,* respectively, then use the formula $A$1+$B$1 in cell C1. Copy this entire row to row 10 by using the Copy command. The formula in cell C10 is the same as that in cell C1. If you move the original row to row 10, you will see

```
$A$10+$B$10
```

in cell C10.

> **Solution** Do not try to transfer absolute addresses with the Move command.

Misconception If you try to erase a portion of a row or a column of a worksheet, do not use /Worksheet Delete Row or /Worksheet Delete Column. This command erases the entire row or the entire column.

> **Solution** Use /Range Erase to erase a portion of a worksheet.

Misconception /Range Name Table gives you a listing of all the range names. This command may overwrite a part of your worksheet.

> **Solution** Before invoking this command, find an empty location in your worksheet, then invoke the command.

Misconception You cannot use /Range Justify if any cells in the range are protected.

> **Solution** First use /Worksheet Global Protection Disable to turn off the protection facility, then use /Range Justify.

Misconception If you use the /Range Transpose command and the range contains formulas with relative addresses, 1-2-3 does not adjust the relative addresses to refer to the same cells. (The /Range Transpose command changes rows to columns and columns to rows.)

> **Solution** Use the /Move command instead.

Misconception In the middle of your spreadsheet session you see the error message

```
ILLEGAL CELL OR RANGE ADDRESS
```

> **Solution** Check your range specification to see if this is what you wanted to do. You may have typed an undefined range.

Misconception You invoke a particular Format command and press Enter. The particular cell may give you a solid line of asterisks.

> **Solution** The cell is not wide enough. Use the appropriate command to widen the cell width.

Misconception Sometimes 1-2-3 beginners make the mistake of clearing a cell in the worksheet by positioning the cursor to the cell, pressing the space bar, then pressing Enter. This does not clear the cell; rather, it places a space in the cell. If you look in the upper left corner of the screen, you can still see an apostrophe in the cell. This indicates that the cell is indeed occupied.

> **Solution** To clear a cell, first position the cell pointer to the cell to be cleared, then use /RE (Range Erase) and press Enter.

Misconception Sometimes when you are using the Copy command you lose some of your data.

> **Solution** Make sure that your FROM (Copy what) cell range does not overlap your TO (To where) cell range. If this happens, 1-2-3 will overwrite the previous contents of the cell(s), and the previous contents are lost for good.

Misconception Sometimes when you use the /WGF (Worksheet Global Format) command some of your numbers are displayed with an * (asterisk), while others are formatted properly.

> **Solution** Select the largest number in the spreadsheet and use this cell width for the entire worksheet.

Misconception When you issue /WDR or /WDC you damage your worksheet permanently.

Solution In these cases if you do not want to get rid of a complete row or a column, use /RE (Range Erase) instead of the above commands.

Misconception You use the Move command and damage your worksheet permanently.

Solution Make sure that the receiving range does not overlap any valuable cells in your worksheet.

Misconception If the CALC indicator is displayed, it means that recalculation mode is set to manual. If you generate a printout or if you transpose some data by using /RT (Range Transpose), you may end up with erroneous results.

Solution Press the F9 key first then proceed with your spreadsheet work.

ARE YOU READY TO MOVE ON?

Multiple Choice

1. Column widths can be extended from 1 character wide to
   a. 100 characters wide
   b. 180 characters wide
   c. 200 characters wide
   d. 240 characters wide
   e. none of the above
2. To insert a page break using the /Worksheet Page command, the cellpointer must be in column
   a. A
   b. B
   c. AA
   d. AB
   e. any column
3. The /Worksheet Titles command can freeze titles
   a. horizontally
   b. vertically
   c. only in a protected worksheet
   d. both a and b
   e. all of the above
4. The Fixed format option
   a. displays commas
   b. displays a dollar sign
   c. does not display commas or dollar sign
   d. always displays two decimal places
   e. none of the above
5. The Currency format option
   a. displays dollar sign only
   b. displays dollar sign and commas
   c. displays only two decimal places
   d. both b and c
   e. none of the above
6. One way to see the actual formula in a cell is to use the
   a. Currency format option
   b. Text format option
   c. Comma format option
   d. Fixed format option
   e. none of the above

7. Compared to /Range Format, /Worksheet Global Format has
   a. lower priority
   b. higher priority
   c. equal priority
   d. priority determined by the type of calculation
   e. none of the above
8. 1-2-3 allows up to
   a. 6 decimal places
   b. 10 decimal places
   c. 12 decimal places
   d. 14 decimal places
   e. 15 decimal places
9. To enter a range of cells, you always use
   a. A1 and IV8192
   b. the top and bottom of the column
   c. the upper left and bottom right cells of the range
   d. @RANGE
   e. none of the above
10. To make the cell address D4 absolute, you type
    a. D4
    b. +D4
    c. $D4
    d. D$4
    e. $D$4

True/False

1. The Copy command can only copy one cell to one other cell.
2. The Move command can transfer a portion of a worksheet to another location.
3. To protect a worksheet from accidental erasure of data, you must first enable the protection facility.
4. By default, each column in 1-2-3 is 11 characters long.
5. Depending on the format desired, there are two options to access the Format command: /Worksheet Global Format and /Range Format.
6. The General option is the default format.
7. When using the General option format, the insignificant zeroes to the right of the decimal are retained.
8. Very large or very small numbers are displayed in scientific notation.
9. The Comma option and the Currency option generate the same output.
10. When the +/– option is used, no provision is made for zero values.

ANSWERS

Multiple Choice		True/False	
1.	d	1.	F
2.	a	2.	T
3.	d	3.	T
4.	c	4.	F
5.	b	5.	T
6.	b	6.	T
7.	a	7.	F
8.	e	8.	T
9.	c	9.	F
10.	e	10.	F

1-2-3 Functions

7

7–1 INTRODUCTION

In this chapter we discuss the general format of 1-2-3 functions. Mathematical, financial, statistical, logical, special, string, date, and time functions are summarized. Appendix A lists all 1-2-3 functions.

7–2 DEFINING A 1-2-3 FUNCTION

A 1-2-3 **function** is a built-in formula for the calculation of a specific task. 1-2-3 offers eight function groups. Each group has been designed to perform a unique task. For example, so far you have learned how to add the contents of cells A1, A2, A3, and A4 by using the formula +A1+A2+A3+A4. Instead, you could use the function @SUM(A1..A4).

All functions follow this format:

@Function(argument1,argument2, . . .)

Functions must begin with the at sign (@), and they contain the name of the function and one or a series of arguments. An **argument** is the information that 1-2-3 needs to perform the calculation. Some functions need no arguments. For example, the function @PI is equal to 3.141592.

7–3 ARGUMENT TYPES

1-2-3 accepts three types of arguments: numeric, range, and string. Numeric values can have one of the following forms:

Actual value	@ABS(–5)
Cell address	@ABS(A11)
Cell range name	@SUM(ASSET)
Formula	@ABS((–20/4)/5)
Function	@INT(ABS(A11)+@SQRT(64))
Combination	@INT(@SUM(A1..A10)+ASSET+2500)

Range values can have one of the following forms:

Range name	@SUM(DIVISION1)
Range address	@SUM(A1..A10)
Combination	@SUM(DIVISION1,A1..A9,DIVISION9)

And finally, string values can have one of the following forms:

Cell address	@LOWER(A1)
Cell name	@LOWER(STREET) (STREET is a cell name)
Actual value	@LOWER("I AM A STUDENT")
Formula	@LENGTH("TITLE"&"SUB-TITLE")

When you are working with functions, you must keep in mind the type of argument accepted by each function. For example, if you try to use the function @SUM("TITLE"), you will receive an error message because the @SUM function requires a numeric value or a range value.

7–4 MATHEMATICAL FUNCTIONS

1-2-3 offers seventeen **mathematical functions.** All of them, except @PI and @RAND, require arguments. The arguments can be values, cell addresses, range names, formulas, or other functions. Arguments for sine, cosine, and tangent must be expressed in radians. (To convert degrees to radians, multiply the number of degrees by @PI/180.) The trigonometric functions arc sine, arc cosine, and arc tangent return all angles in radians. (To convert radians to degrees, the number must be multiplied by 180/@PI.)

7–4–1 @INT(A)

The @INT function returns the integer portion of the argument:

Function	Returns
@INT(5.5645)	5
@INT(–6.45698)	–6
@INT(9.9)	9
@INT(9.9+.50)	10

This function does not round the number—if you want to round a number, either use the @ROUND function or add .50 to the argument of the @INT function.

7–4–2 @MOD(A,B)

The @MOD function calculates the remainder of A/B. Argument A can be any number, and argument B can be any number except 0. The sign returned by this function will be always the same as the sign of A. For example,

Function	Returns
@MOD(13,7)	6
@MOD(11,3)	2
@MOD(–14,2)	0
@MOD(–15,4)	–3
@MOD(15,–4)	3
@MOD(7,0)	ERR (invalid argument)

7–4–3 @RAND

@RAND generates a random number between zero and one. You can use this function to generate a random number in any range as follows:

@INT(@RAND*(U–L+1)+L)

where U is the upper bound and L is the lower bound. For example, if you are interested in a random number between 1,000 and 100, your formula would be

@INT(@RAND*(901)+100)

You can use this function to generate six random numbers for a lotto game.

7–4–4 @ROUND(A,n)

The @ROUND function rounds number A to n places. This function can round on either side of the decimal point. Argument n must be a value between –15 and 15. For example:

Function	Returns
@ROUND(2.435678,3)	2.436
@ROUND(5.567564,3)	5.568
@ROUND(145.267,–1)	150
@ROUND(145.267,–2)	100
@ROUND(145.267,–3)	0

7–4–5 @SQRT(A)

@SQRT returns the positive square root of A. The argument of this function must be a positive number. For example,

Function	Returns
@SQRT(16)	4
@SQRT(25)	5
@SQRT(56)	7.483314
@SQRT(–4)	ERR (invalid argument)

7–5 FINANCIAL FUNCTIONS

1-2-3 offers eleven **financial functions.** These functions can be used for cash flow analysis, investment analysis, loan payment analysis, and three kinds of depreciation analyses. To use these functions, you must express the term and interest rate using the same time frame (to calculate monthly payment, for example, the yearly interest rate must be divided by 12 and the term must be multiplied by 12).

The interest rate can be entered as either a percent (10%) or a decimal (.10). 1-2-3 assumes ordinary annuity. This means payment is made at the end of each period and annuity due is made at the beginning of each period.

7–5–1 @FV(Payment,Interest Rate,Term)

The @FV function calculates the future value of a series of equal payments using the given interest rate over a period of time. The @FV function uses the following formula:

$$FV = Payment^{*}\ \frac{(1 + interest)^{n} - 1}{interest}$$

where n = number of periods.

Figure 7–1 shows the future value of an IRA plan over 20 years with a $2,000 yearly payment, and an interest rate of 9 percent. This function can be very helpful for calculating the future value of an investment.

Figure 7–1
Future value of an IRA investment.

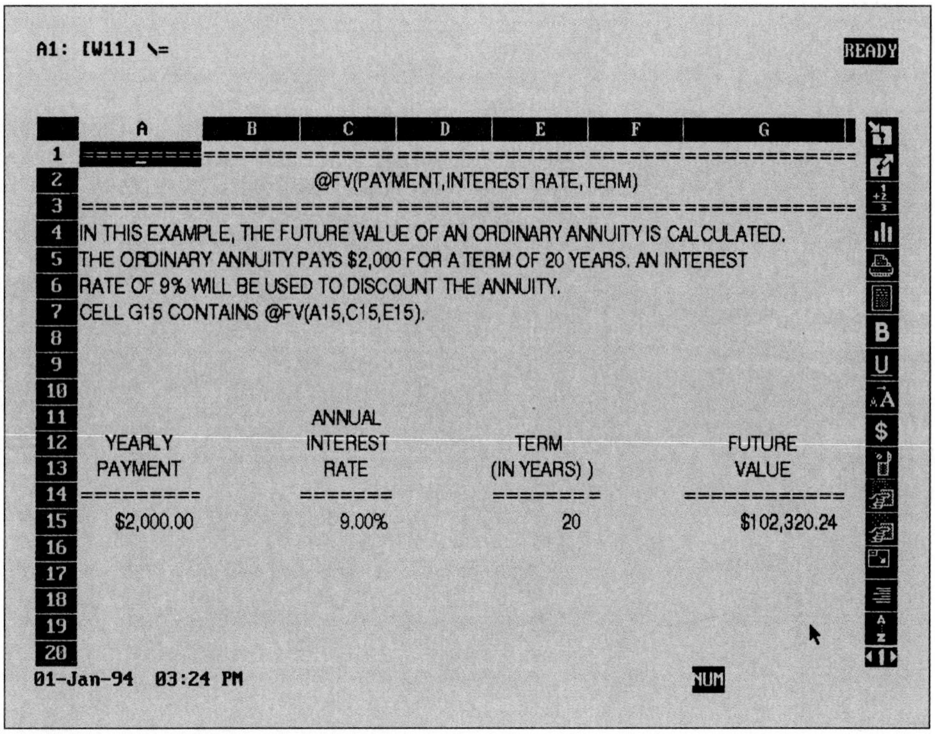
A1: [W11] \=
READY
A B C D E F G
@FV(PAYMENT,INTEREST RATE,TERM)
IN THIS EXAMPLE, THE FUTURE VALUE OF AN ORDINARY ANNUITY IS CALCULATED.
THE ORDINARY ANNUITY PAYS $2,000 FOR A TERM OF 20 YEARS. AN INTEREST
RATE OF 9% WILL BE USED TO DISCOUNT THE ANNUITY.
CELL G15 CONTAINS @FV(A15,C15,E15).
YEARLY PAYMENT
ANNUAL INTEREST RATE
TERM (IN YEARS))
FUTURE VALUE
$2,000.00
9.00%
20
$102,320.24
01-Jan-94 03:24 PM
NUM

7–5–2 @NPV(Interest Rate,Range)

@NPV calculates the present value of a series of future cash flows discounted at a fixed interest rate. The assumption is that each cash flow occurs at the end of each period. This function uses the following formula:

$$\Sigma \frac{Vi}{(1 + \text{interest})^{i}}$$

where

Vi . . .Vm = series of cash flows
m = number of cash flows
i = number of iterations (1 to m)

The cash inflows and outflows need not be equal. This function is very helpful for calculating today's worth of an investment that may generate different future cash inflows and outflows. Figure 7–2 illustrates an example of this function.

7–5–3 @PMT(Principal,Interest Rate,Term)

@PMT calculates the amount of the periodic payment for a loan. This function uses the following formula:

$$\text{PMT} = \text{Principal}^{*} \frac{\text{interest rate}}{1 - (\text{interest rate} + 1)^{-n}}$$

where n = term.

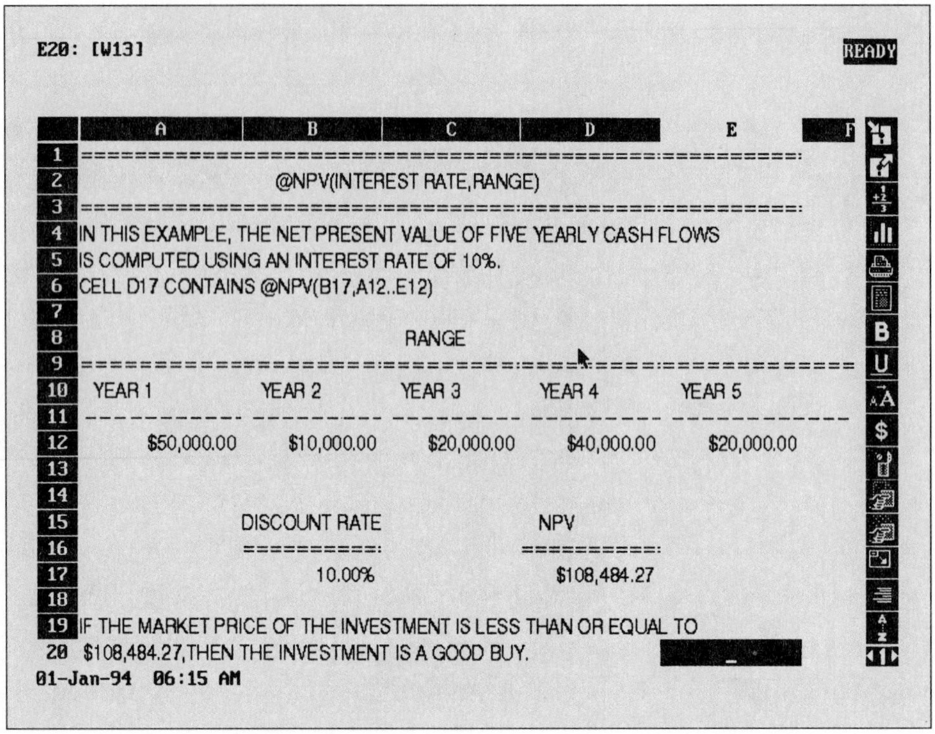

Figure 7–2
Net present value analysis.

This function is very helpful for determining the payment for a new car, house, or boat, for example. Figure 7–3 illustrates one example of this function.

7–5–4 @SLN(Cost,Salvage Value,Life)

This function calculates the straight-line depreciation of a piece of equipment for one period. This method assumes the same amount of depreciation for every period. This function uses the following formula:

$$\frac{\text{(cost – salvage value)}}{\text{useful life of the asset}}$$

Figure 7–4 illustrates an example of this function.

7–5–5 @SYD(Cost,Salvage Value,Life,Period)

@SYD calculates the sum-of-the-years' digits depreciation for a selected period. This function uses the following formula:

$$\frac{\text{(cost – salvage value)} * \text{(useful life} - P + 1)}{(n * (n + 1)/2)}$$

where

n = useful life of the equipment
P = period for which depreciation is being computed

This method accelerates the rate of depreciation; therefore, more depreciation expenses occur in earlier periods than in the later periods. Because maintenance costs are minimal in the first few years, this method balances out the total

Figure 7–3
Payment analysis of a loan.

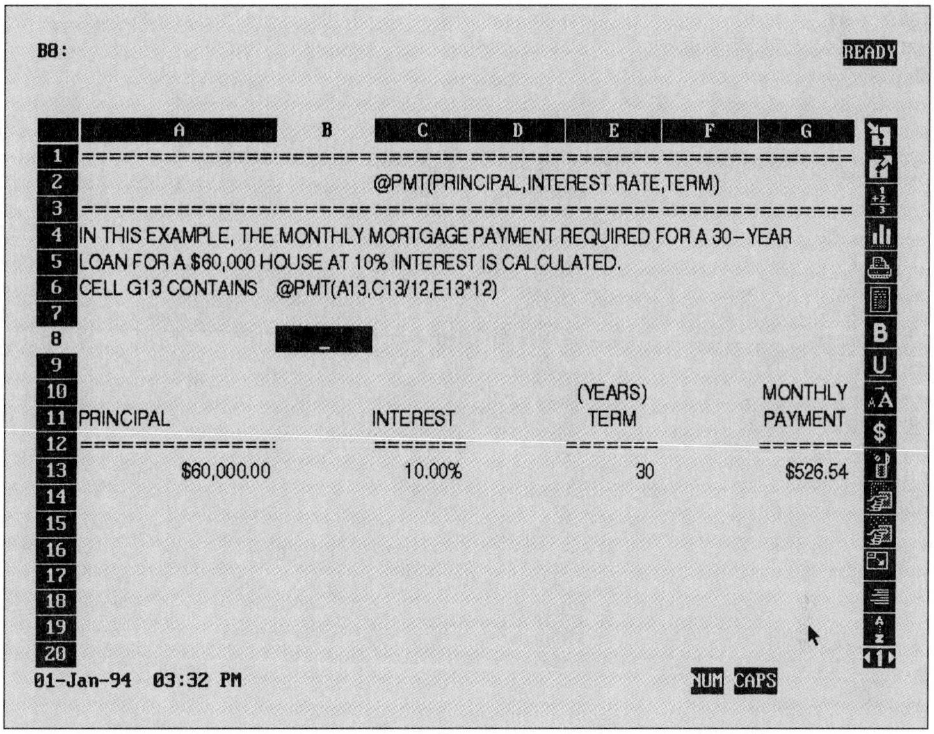

Figure 7–4
Straight-line depreciation.

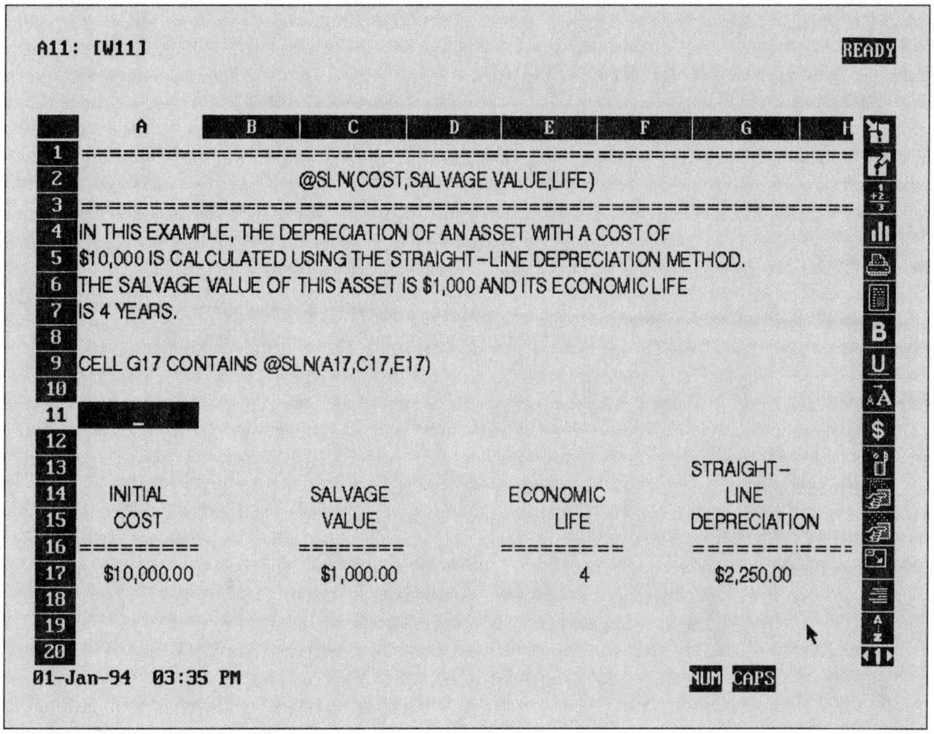

Figure 7–5
Sum-of-the-years' digits depreciation.

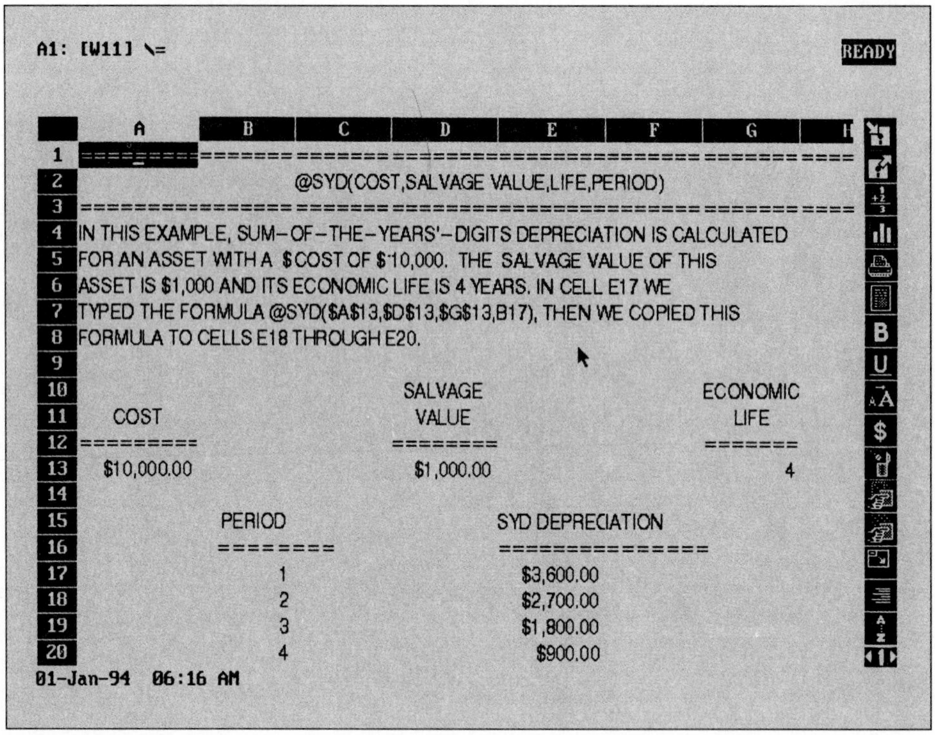
A1: [W11] \=
READY
A B C D E F G H
@SYD(COST,SALVAGE VALUE,LIFE,PERIOD)
IN THIS EXAMPLE, SUM-OF-THE-YEARS'-DIGITS DEPRECIATION IS CALCULATED
FOR AN ASSET WITH A $COST OF $10,000. THE SALVAGE VALUE OF THIS
ASSET IS $1,000 AND ITS ECONOMIC LIFE IS 4 YEARS. IN CELL E17 WE
TYPED THE FORMULA @SYD($A$13,$D$13,$G$13,B17), THEN WE COPIED THIS
FORMULA TO CELLS E18 THROUGH E20.
COST
SALVAGE VALUE
ECONOMIC LIFE
$10,000.00
$1,000.00
4
PERIOD
SYD DEPRECIATION
1 $3,600.00
2 $2,700.00
3 $1,800.00
4 $900.00
01-Jan-94 06:16 AM

cost of a piece of equipment. In later years there are fewer depreciation costs and more maintenance costs. Figure 7–5 illustrates an example of this function.

7–6 STATISTICAL FUNCTIONS

1-2-3 offers seven **statistical functions,** including @AVG, @COUNT, @MAX, @MIN, @STD, @SUM, and @VAR. All of these functions except @COUNT accept numeric values and range values for arguments. The @COUNT function accepts numeric as well as string values as arguments. In all these functions, an argument can be a single address or a group of addresses. For example, the function @SUM(A1..A9,B5,ASSET) is valid. 1-2-3 considers that a blank cell has the value of zero when used as an argument.

7–6–1 @AVG(Range)

@AVG calculates the average of all values included in a list or range. For example,

@AVG(A1..A15)
@AVG(ASSET)

If you do not want to use the @AVG function, you can always use its equivalent, which is @SUM(range)/@COUNT(range).

7–6–2 @COUNT(Range)

@COUNT counts the number of occupied (nonblank) cells in the range. For example, if cells A1, A2, and A5 are occupied, the function @COUNT(A1..A5)

returns 3. If the range includes only blank cells, the result is zero. However, if you use the function @COUNT(A10), even if A10 is empty, you will still receive a response of 1.

7–6–3 @MAX(Range)

@MAX returns the maximum value in the range.

7–6–4 @MIN(Range)

@MIN returns the minimum value in the range.

7–6–5 @STD(Range)

@STD calculates the standard deviation of all values in the range.

7–6–6 @VAR(Range)

@VAR calculates the variable of all values in the range.

7–6–7 @SUM(Range)

@SUM calculates the sum of all the values in the range. You can also highlight a range, then use the sum SmartIcon. Make sure to leave one blank cell at the end of the range for the result of the sum icon. See Table 7–1 at the end of the chapter. Figure 7–6 illustrates an example of these statistical functions.

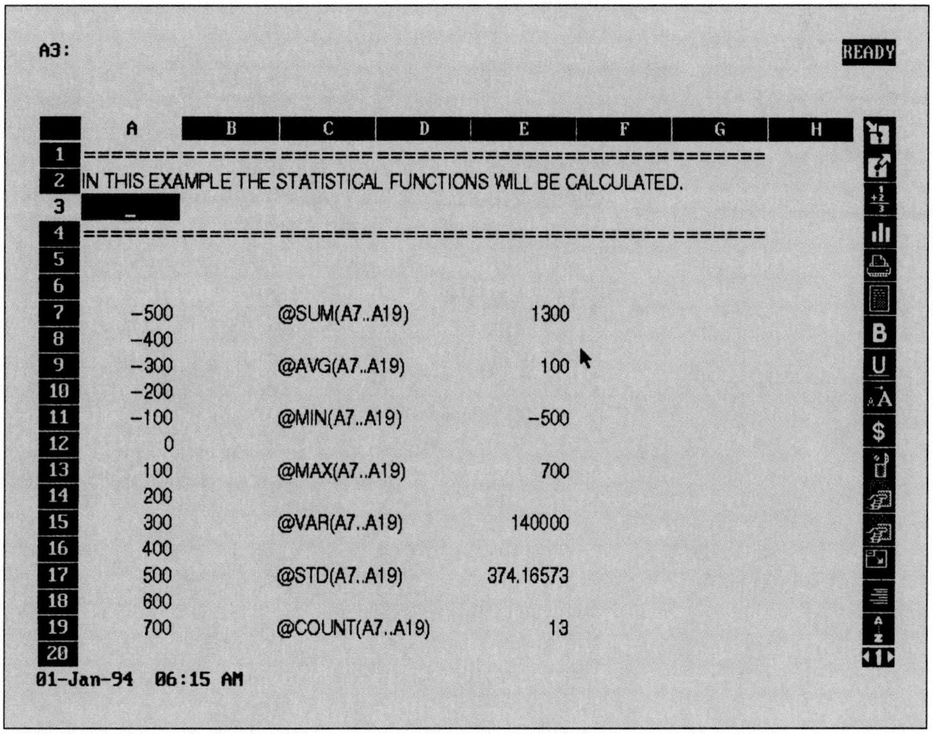

Figure 7–6
Statistical functions.

7–7 LOGICAL FUNCTIONS

1-2-3 Release 2.4 offers nine **logical functions**. These functions generate values based on the results of conditional statements. When you use logical functions, remember that a blank cell has the value of zero. If you use a range name that represents a range of cells, 1-2-3 examines the upper left cell.

7–7–1 @IF(Condition,A,B)

This function returns the value A if the condition is true or the value B if the condition is false. The condition must be either a numeric value or calculations that result in a numeric value. For example,

Function	**Returns**
@IF(3<5, 10, – 50)	10
@IF((10+5)/2<10,"T","F")	T

Another example is a function to calculate the total pay of an employee:

@IF(H1>40,R1*40+(H1–40)*1.5*R1,H1*R1)

The total pay is rate (R1) multiplied by hours (H1). However, if the employee works more than 40 hours, overtime pay is calculated at the rate of 1.5 times regular pay. Overtime pay is only for the hours over 40.

There are many applications of the @IF function. You could use this function to check your customer's credit limit, for example. If the customer's credit is good, you would send one message; if it is bad, you would send a different message. You also could use the @IF function for inventory management—if the inventory on-hand is below 500 units, you know to reorder. If it isn't, then you don't need to reorder.

Using @IF with the logical operators #NOT#, #AND#, and #OR# adds a strong decision-making facility to 1-2-3. When you use AND, all the conditions must be true. When you use OR, only one of the conditions must be met. You use NOT to screen out everything not meeting the condition.

Consider the information shown in Figure 7–7. In row 4, the student is accepted because he has met both conditions—his GMAT is greater than 600 and his GPA is greater than 3.3. In row 6, the student is accepted because her GMAT score is greater than 600 and the GPA condition does not matter. In row 9, the student is rejected because both conditions must be true and, in this case, they aren't. (In this figure, we used the Text format in column A to display the actual formulas instead of their results.)

Figure 7–8 shows another example of the @IF function. Northwest Lumber Company pays commission to its employees as follows:

Under $15,000 total sales	No commission
$15,000 to $20,000 total sales	$800
Over $20,000 total sales	$800 + 15% of sales over $20,000

This example illustrates a nested @IF function. In column C, we used the Text format to show the actual cell entry.

Figure 7–7
An @IF example.

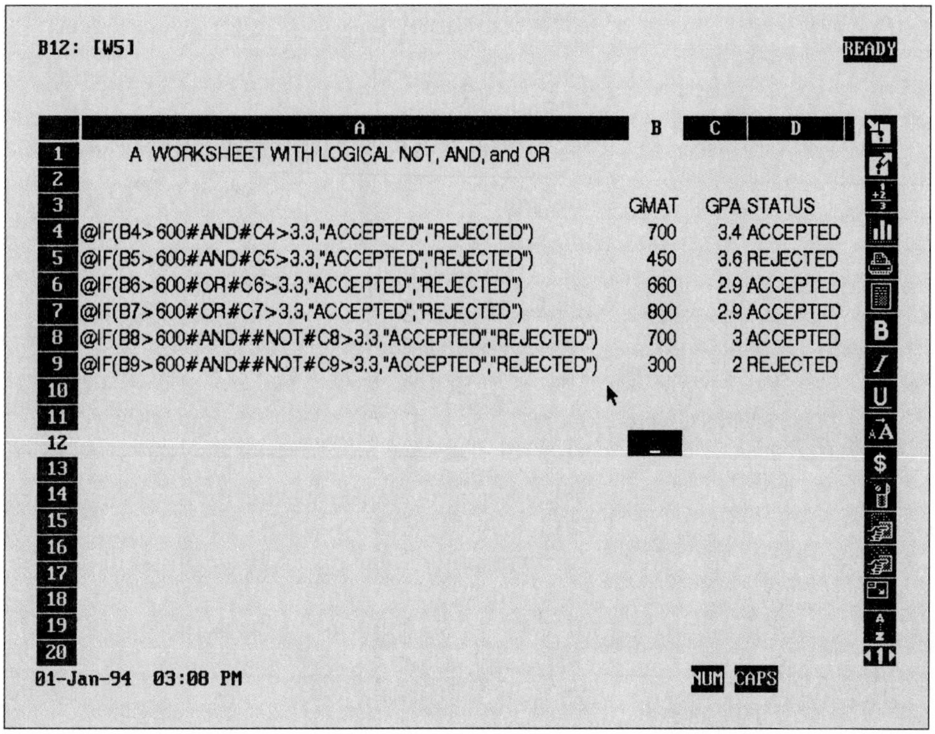

B12: [W5] READY

	A	B	C	D
1	A WORKSHEET WITH LOGICAL NOT, AND, and OR			
2				
3		GMAT	GPA	STATUS
4	@IF(B4>600#AND#C4>3.3,"ACCEPTED","REJECTED")	700	3.4	ACCEPTED
5	@IF(B5>600#AND#C5>3.3,"ACCEPTED","REJECTED")	450	3.6	REJECTED
6	@IF(B6>600#OR#C6>3.3,"ACCEPTED","REJECTED")	660	2.9	ACCEPTED
7	@IF(B7>600#OR#C7>3.3,"ACCEPTED","REJECTED")	800	2.9	ACCEPTED
8	@IF(B8>600#AND##NOT#C8>3.3,"ACCEPTED","REJECTED")	700	3	ACCEPTED
9	@IF(B9>600#AND##NOT#C9>3.3,"ACCEPTED","REJECTED")	300	2	REJECTED

01-Jan-94 03:08 PM NUM CAPS

Figure 7–8
Using @IF to calculate commissions.

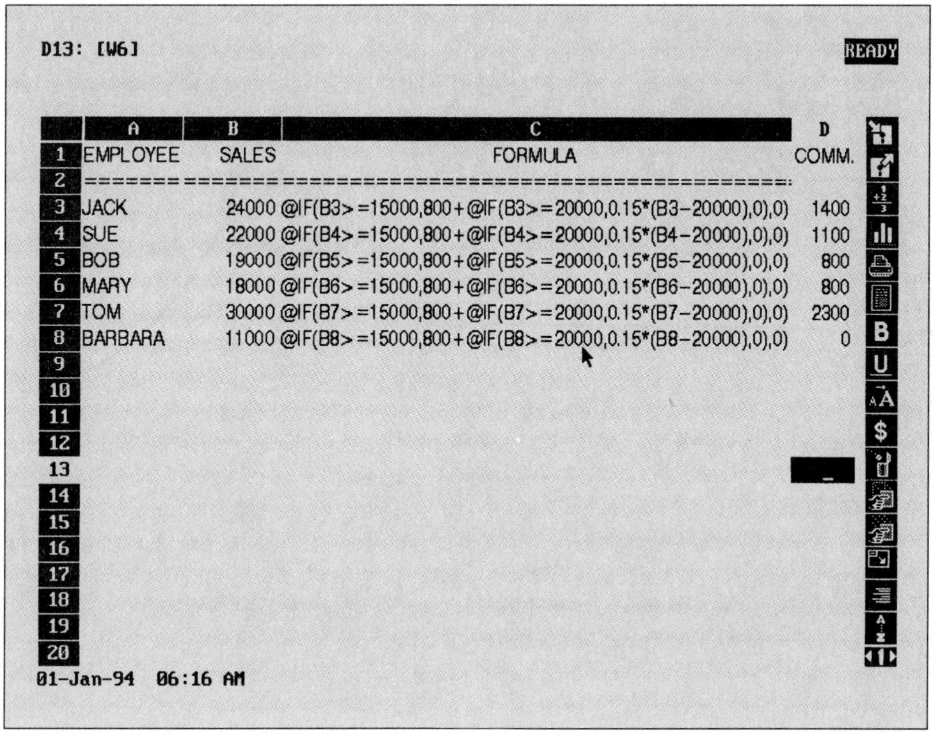

D13: [W6] READY

	A	B	C	D
1	EMPLOYEE	SALES	FORMULA	COMM.
2	=======	=======	=======================================	=====
3	JACK	24000	@IF(B3>=15000,800+@IF(B3>=20000,0.15*(B3-20000),0),0)	1400
4	SUE	22000	@IF(B4>=15000,800+@IF(B4>=20000,0.15*(B4-20000),0),0)	1100
5	BOB	19000	@IF(B5>=15000,800+@IF(B5>=20000,0.15*(B5-20000),0),0)	800
6	MARY	18000	@IF(B6>=15000,800+@IF(B6>=20000,0.15*(B6-20000),0),0)	800
7	TOM	30000	@IF(B7>=15000,800+@IF(B7>=20000,0.15*(B7-20000),0),0)	2300
8	BARBARA	11000	@IF(B8>=15000,800+@IF(B8>=20000,0.15*(B8-20000),0),0)	0

01-Jan-94 06:16 AM

7-7-2 @ISNUMBER(A)

You use this function to test cell A to see whether it contains a numeric value. The function returns a 1 if cell A contains a number or a calculation (formula) resulting in a numeric value; otherwise it returns a 0. For example:

Function	Returns
@ISNUMBER(5)	1
@ISNUMBER("7")	0
@ISNUMBER(68/8+@SQRT(16))	1
@ISNUMBER("PORTLAND")	0

7-8 STRING FUNCTIONS

1-2-3 offers nineteen **string functions.** These functions are helpful for nonnumeric manipulations. If a string is used as an argument, that string must be enclosed in a pair of quotation marks. Strings enclosed in quotation marks are numbered beginning with zero. For example, the string "DISK" is numbered from 0 to 3. The "D" is number 0, "I" is number 1, "S" is number 2, and "K" is number 3.

7-8-1 @LENGTH(String)

@LENGTH returns the number of characters included in the string. For example,

Function	Returns
@LENGTH("JACK")	4
@LENGTH("YESTERDAY WAS COLD")	18
@LENGTH(" ")	0
@LENGTH(555)	ERR (the argument must be in double quotation marks)

7-8-2 @LOWER(String)

This string function converts all the letters in the string to lowercase. For example,

Function	Returns
@LOWER("LOTUS")	lotus
@LOWER("JACK")	jack

7-8-3 @UPPER(String)

This function converts all the letters in a string to uppercase. For example,

Function	Returns
@UPPER("jack jones")	JACK JONES
@UPPER("happy")	HAPPY

7-9 DATE AND TIME FUNCTIONS

1-2-3 offers eleven **date and time functions.** These functions generate or use numbers to represent dates and times so that you can use dates and times in calculations. For example, you can calculate how many days there are between December 10 and January 23. To use these functions, remember these rules:

- Any date between January 1, 1900 and December 31, 2099, inclusive, is valid and has an integer serial number equivalent.
- January 1, 1900 is equivalent to 1, and December 31, 2099 is equivalent to 73050.
- Each hour has a serial number equivalent as well (for example, midnight = 0, noon = .5, and so on).
- The following functions generate serial numbers: @DATE, @DATEVALUE, @NOW, @TIME, and @TIMEVALUE.
- The following functions use serial numbers: @DAY, @MONTH, @YEAR, @HOUR, @MINUTE, and @SECOND.

7–9–1 @DATE(Year,Month,Day)

The @DATE function returns the serial number corresponding to a certain year, month, and day. Although there was no February 29, 1900, 1-2-3 assigns a date number to this particular day. This error will not invalidate any of your calculations unless you use any dates between January 1 and March 1, 1900. You can use these serial numbers in conjunction with the Date formats, D1, D2, D3, D4, and D5, to produce calculated dates in your worksheet. For example,

Function	Returns	Which equals
@DATE(94,7,1)	34516	01-Jul-94 in D1 format
@DATE(93,12,1)	34304	1-DEC in D2 format
@DATE(93,6,1)	34121	Jun-93 in D3 format
@DATE(92,10,1)	33878	10/01/92 in D4 format
@DATE(91,1,1)	33239	01/01 in D5 format

7–9–2 @DATEVALUE(Date String)

The @DATEVALUE function returns the serial number of a date written as a string. This function is very similar to the @DATE function, but @DATEVALUE uses a single string value as its argument. The date string must be in one of the five Date formats (discussed in Chapter 6). For example,

Function	Returns
@DATEVALUE("01-JUL-93")	34151
@DATEVALUE("01-DEC-80")	29556
@DATEVALUE("JUN-87")	31929
@DATEVALUE("10/01/87")	32051
@DATEVALUE("02-JUN-94")	34487

7–9–3 @YEAR(Date Number)

This function returns the year of the argument. It will return any year between 0 and 199. For example:

Function	Returns
@YEAR(@DATEVALUE("1-SEP-87"))	87
@YEAR(36000)	98

7–9–4 @NOW

The @NOW function returns the current date and time. For example, if you enter *@NOW* in your 1-2-3 worksheet, the function will return some number such as 29221.02. This particular number indicates that the date is January 1, 1980 and the time is 12:28 a.m. The integer part of the number is the date, and the decimal portion is the time.

You can also use the date SmartIcon to enter the system time and date into your worksheet (see Table 7–1 at the end of the chapter).

7–9–5 @TIME(Hour,Minute,Second)

@TIME returns a serial number between 0 and 1 for the hour, minute, and second. The serial number is a fraction of the day. In this function, the hours must be between 0 and 23, minutes must be between 0 and 59, and seconds must be between 0 and 59. For example:

Function	Returns	Which equals
@TIME(10,52,40)	0.453240	10:52:40 a.m. in T1 format
@TIME(2,10,59)	0.090960	02:10 a.m. in T2 format
@TIME(22,50,50)	0.951967	22:50:50 in T3 format
@TIME(23,1,1)	0.959039	23:01 in T4 format

7–9–6 @TIMEVALUE(Time String)

The @TIMEVALUE function returns a serial time number for the string. This function is similar to the @TIME function, except that the argument is only one string. The time string must be in one of the four 1-2-3 time formats (discussed in Chapter 6) and must be enclosed in double quotation marks. For example:

Function	Returns
@TIMEVALUE("12:30:45")	0.5213541667
@TIMEVALUE("12:30")	0.5208333333

7–10 SPECIAL FUNCTIONS

1-2-3 offers 11 **special functions,** most of which are used for searching for a value in a table (a **lookup table**).

7–10–1 @HLOOKUP(Test Variable,Range,Row Number)

The @HLOOKUP function performs a horizontal table search (see Figure 7–9). The function compares the value of the test variable to each cell in the top row of a specified range. The top row of the table used by @HLOOKUP function must be sorted in ascending order.

When 1-2-3 finds a number larger than test variable, it stops and backs up one cell. Then 1-2-3 moves down the specified number of rows and returns the contents of that cell. If there is an exact match to the test variable, the search stops at this cell and no back-tracking takes place.

If the test variable is smaller than the first value, this function returns ERR. If the test variable is larger than all the values, the search stops at the last

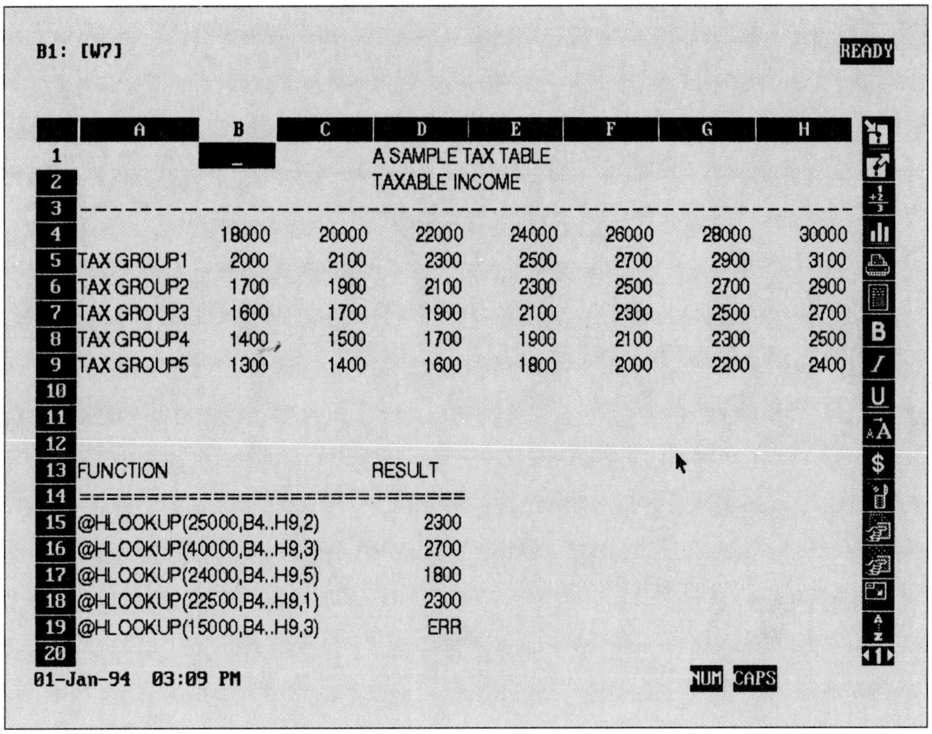

Figure 7–9
Using the @HLOOKUP function.

cell in the top row of the range, and then 1-2-3 moves down the specified number of rows and returns the contents of that cell.

Using the information shown in Figure 7–9, the following @HLOOKUP functions return the values shown:

Function	Returns
@HLOOKUP(25000,B4..H9,2)	2300
@HLOOKUP(40000,B4..H9,3)	2700
@HLOOKUP(24000,B4..H9,5)	1800
@HLOOKUP(22500,B4..H9,1)	2300
@HLOOKUP(15000,B4..H9,3)	ERR

7–10–2 @VLOOKUP(Test Variable, Range, Column Number)

The @VLOOKUP function performs a vertical search much like the @HLOOKUP function. @VLOOKUP compares the value of the test variable to each cell in the first column of a specified range (see Figure 7–10). Again, to work correctly, these cells must be in ascending order.

When 1-2-3 finds the first number that is either not greater than the test variable or an exact match, it moves across the search table the specified number of columns and returns the contents of that cell.

If the test variable is smaller than the first value in the search column, this function returns ERR. Using the information shown in Figure 7–10, the following @VLOOKUP functions return the values shown:

Function	Returns
@VLOOKUP(26500,A4..G10,2)	3000
@VLOOKUP(45000,A4..G10,3)	7100

Figure 7–10
Using the @VLOOKUP function.

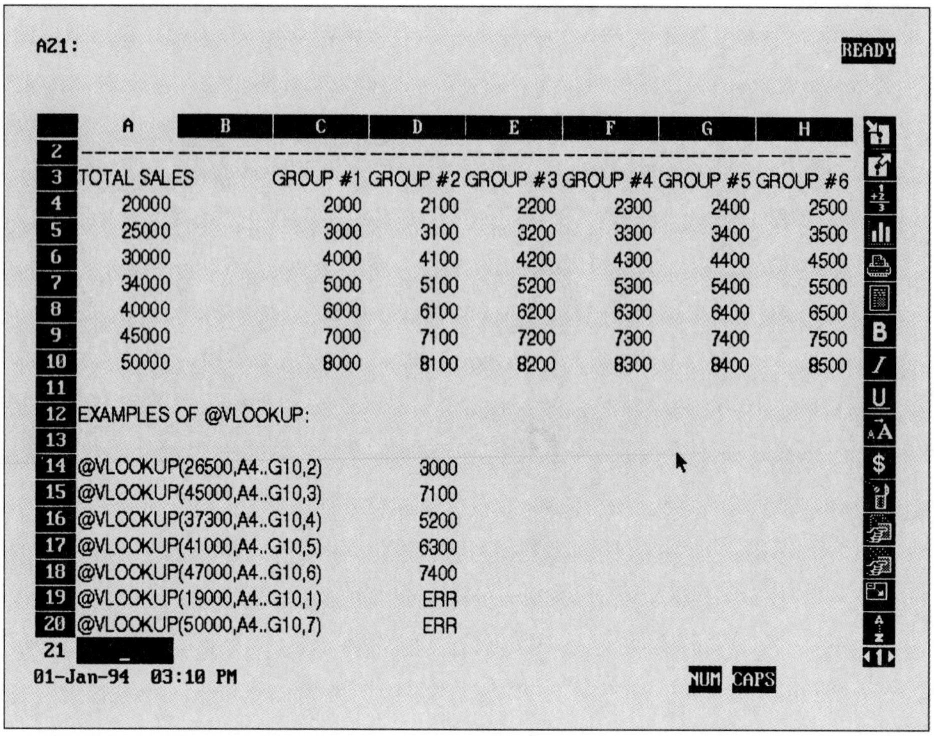

A21: READY

	A	B	C	D	E	F	G	H
2	--------	--------	--------	--------	--------	--------	--------	--------
3	TOTAL SALES		GROUP #1	GROUP #2	GROUP #3	GROUP #4	GROUP #5	GROUP #6
4	20000		2000	2100	2200	2300	2400	2500
5	25000		3000	3100	3200	3300	3400	3500
6	30000		4000	4100	4200	4300	4400	4500
7	34000		5000	5100	5200	5300	5400	5500
8	40000		6000	6100	6200	6300	6400	6500
9	45000		7000	7100	7200	7300	7400	7500
10	50000		8000	8100	8200	8300	8400	8500
11								
12	EXAMPLES OF @VLOOKUP:							
13								
14	@VLOOKUP(26500,A4..G10,2)			3000				
15	@VLOOKUP(45000,A4..G10,3)			7100				
16	@VLOOKUP(37300,A4..G10,4)			5200				
17	@VLOOKUP(41000,A4..G10,5)			6300				
18	@VLOOKUP(47000,A4..G10,6)			7400				
19	@VLOOKUP(19000,A4..G10,1)			ERR				
20	@VLOOKUP(50000,A4..G10,7)			ERR				
21								

01-Jan-94 03:10 PM NUM CAPS

@VLOOKUP(37300,A4..G10,4)	5200
@VLOOKUP(41000,A4..G10,5)	6300
@VLOOKUP(47000,A4..G10,6)	7400
@VLOOKUP(19000,A4..G10,1)	ERR
@VLOOKUP(50000,A4..G10,7)	ERR

SUMMARY

This chapter reviewed important 1-2-3 functions: mathematical, financial, statistical, logical, special, string, date, and time. Several examples highlighted the versatility of these functions. See Table 7–1 for functions SmartIcons.

REVIEW QUESTIONS

*These questions are answered in Appendix A.

1. What is a 1-2-3 function?
*2. What is the major task performed by a 1-2-3 function?
3. How many groups of functions are offered by 1-2-3?
4. What is a function argument?
5. How many types of arguments are accepted by 1-2-3?
*6. What is an invalid argument?
7. Do all 1-2-3 functions require arguments?
*8. What are some of the uses of the @ABS function?
9. What are some of the uses of the @INT function?

Table 7–1
Functions Icons

WYSIWYG Mode	Text Mode	Description
	DATE	Enters a number that corresponds to the current date and time in the current cell. If the cell is formatted with a date format, the date appears in the cell in that format. If the cell is not formatted with a date format, the date appears in a cell in the default date format. If the cell is formatted with a time format, the time appears in the cell in that format.
1 +2 3	1 + 2 =	Sums values in the highlighted range, if you include empty cells below or to the right of the range; or, if the highlighted range is blank, sums values in the nearest area of data and places the results in the highlighted range.

Column 1 shows icons if WYSIWYG is attached. Column 2 shows icons as they appear when WYSIWYG is either not attached or is set to: Display Mode Text.
The icons identified by **W** work only when WYSIWYG is attached.

***10.** Can you do rounding by the @INT function?

11. What does the @MOD function do?

12. The @RAND function has many business applications. Discuss three of these applications.

***13.** If you don't want to use the @SQRT function [@SQRT(B10), for example], what is its equivalent?

***14.** What are some of the applications of @FV and @NPV?

15. If you are trying to buy a house, which function in this chapter can help you the most? Why?

16. What depreciation method assumes an accelerated rate in the first few years?

17. How many statistical functions are offered by 1-2-3?

18. Among all the statistical functions, which one allows for string arguments?

19. What is the main purpose of logical functions?

20. What are some of the uses of @LENGTH?

21. What is the main purpose of @DATE functions?

***22.** What is the difference between @DATE and @DATEVALUE?

***23.** What is the difference between @HLOOKUP and @VLOOKUP?

***24.** What are some of the practical applications of @HLOOKUP and @VLOOKUP functions?

HANDS-ON EXPERIENCE

1. Using the @RAND function, generate five random numbers between 100 and 200.
2. Perform the seven statistical functions discussed in the chapter on the following data:

   10, 15, 20, 90, 60, 70, 85, 5, 85

3. What is the future value of a pension plan over 30 years with a $1,500 yearly payment, if the interest rate is 8.25 percent?

4. Assuming an interest rate of 10 percent, what is the NPV of a portfolio with the following cash flows:

   –25,000, –22,000, 1000, 20,000, 36,000, 40,000

5. If you buy a car for $30,000 with no down payment and a fixed interest rate of 9.25 percent, how much is your monthly payment in a five-year agreement?

6. Using the straight-line method, how much is the yearly depreciation of a piece of equipment with an original price of $10,000, a salvage value of $2,000, and six years' economic life?

7. Using the information in question 6, how much is the sum-of-the-years' digits depreciation for the next six periods?

8. What does the function @UPPER("Database") return?

9. What does the function @LENGTH("Database") return?

10. Using Figure 7–9, what do the following functions return:

    @HLOOKUP(25000,B4..H9,3)
    @HLOOKUP(20000,B4..H9,3)
    @HLOOKUP(27000,B4..H9,5)

11. Using Figure 7–10, what do the following functions return:

    @VLOOKUP(2000,A4..G10,3)
    @VLOOKUP(60000,A4..G10,2)
    @VLOOKUP(47000,A4..G10,5)

12. Retrieve the CHAPT6 file and do the following:

    a. Print the file using the Shift and PrtSc keys or Print Screen (in enhanced keyboard.)
    b. Print the existing file into an ASCII file called CHAPT7 (remember that the extension of this file will be PRN). (You must use the /Print File command.)
    c. Using the /Print Printer command, print this file with default settings.
    d. Print the existing file with 10 as the left margin and 60 as the right margin.
    e. Using the appropriate commands, generate a page number and today's date on the printed file.
    f. Using the appropriate commands, generate a printout in compressed print.
    g. Print the file using cell formulas.
    h. Save the file as CHAPT7.
    i. Using /File Import, retrieve CHAPT7.PRN. Erase the screen.
    j. Retrieve CHAPT7, add an additional column to the worksheet (column I); add the title "Total" to the column.
    k. Using the @SUM function, calculate the total score of each student and store the result in this column.
    l. Generate another column (column J); add the title "Statistics" to this column.
    m. Generate the seven statistical functions for the total scores of all the students.
    n. Using the @NOW and @INT functions, generate the system time and date in cells E19 and E20, respectively.
    o. Save this worksheet as CHAPT7 (by using the Replace option).

13. Load Figure 7–11 from the disk supplied by your instructor. Complete and print it.

Figure 7–11
A sample worksheet.

ACME SALES PERSONNEL

DPT	SALESPERSON	1993	1994	TOTAL SALES	1994 %TOTAL
111	Jim Thomas	$435,200	$490,250	$925,450	
113	Don Smith	$234,525	$375,255	$609,780	
106	Bill Green	$175,675	$225,500	$401,175	
112	Sharon Moon	$345,525	$385,750	$731,275	
109	Jack Traves	$672,900	$825,345	$1,498,245	
118	John Bowin	$575,000	$585,255	$1,160,255	
114	Bob Wood	$670,100	$627,450	$1,297,550	
117	Rich Asborne	$450,000	$465,275	$915,275	
124	Shelli Hansen	$375,255	$325,225	$700,480	
121	Lisa Myers	$401,250	$398,700	$799,950	
126	Gary June	$275,750	$325,725	$601,475	
104	Linda Smith	$297,655	$310,755	$608,410	
116	Pam Greene	$372,500	$375,210	$747,710	
129	Ann Thompson	$497,500	$150,000	$647,500	
	TOTAL				
	NO OF SALES STAFF				
	STD.DEVIATION				
	VARIANCE				
	MAXIMUM VALUE				
	MINIMUM VALUE				

NOTE: Use pointer and cell formula to do departmental totals as you are not familiar with any Database tools yet.

10X	DPT-10 TOTAL				
20X	DPT-11 TOTAL				
12X	DPT-12 TOTAL				
	VERIFY TOTAL	$0	$0	$0	

KEY TERMS

- Argument
- Date and time function
- Financial function
- Function
- Logical function
- Lookup table
- Mathematical function
- Special function
- Statistical function
- String function

KEY COMMANDS

- @AVG(range)
- @COUNT(range)
- @DATE(year,month,day)
- @DATEVALUE(date string)
- @FV(payment,interest rate,term)
- @HLOOKUP(test variable,range,row number)
- @IF(condition,A,B)

@INT(A)
@LOWER(string)
@MAX(range)
@MIN(range)
@MOD(A,B)
@NOW
@NPV(interest rate,range)
@PMT(principal,interest rate,term)
@RAND
@ROUND(A,n)
@SQRT(A)
@SLN(cost,salvage value,life)
@SYD(cost,salvage value,life,period)
@SUM(range)
@TIME(hour,minute,seco nd)
@TIMEVALUE(time string)
@UPPER(string)
@VLOOKUP(test variable,range,column number)
@YEAR(date number)

MISCONCEPTIONS AND SOLUTIONS

Misconception In a mortgage problem, the interest rate usually is stated as yearly and the payment is stated as a monthly figure. However, using a yearly interest rate and a monthly payment causes mistakes in payment calculation.

Solution Divide the yearly interest rate by 12 and multiply the number of payments by 12. These adjustments result in the correct payment.

Misconception You want to enter a function, but when you press Enter, 1-2-3 beeps.

Solution Check the syntax of any @ functions that you have used to make sure that you have typed the name and the syntax of the function correctly.

Misconception When you use lines of dashes (-), the equal sign (=), or any other symbol to dress up your worksheet, these cells have the value of zero.

Solution Make sure not to include these cells in your data range when you are using @COUNT, @AVG, @MIN, @MAX, @VAR, and @STR functions.

ARE YOU READY TO MOVE ON?

Multiple Choice

1. Argument types for 1-2-3 functions include
   - **a.** numeric values
   - **b.** range values
   - **c.** string values
   - **d.** both a and b
   - **e.** all of the above
2. The function @MOD(12,7) returns
   - **a.** 1
   - **b.** 5
   - **c.** 12
   - **d.** undefined (ERR)
   - **e.** none of the above
3. Arguments for sine, cosine, and tangent functions must be expressed in
   - **a.** whole numbers
   - **b.** degrees
   - **c.** radians
   - **d.** either b or c
   - **e.** none of the above
4. @NPV is an example of a
   - **a.** mathematical function
   - **b.** special function
   - **c.** logical function

d. statistical function
e. financial function

5. @PMT(A,B,C) computes the amount of a periodic payment on a loan where argument B is the
   a. interest rate
   b. principal
   c. term
   d. salvage value
   e. none of the above
6. @SUM(A1..D4)/@COUNT(A1..D4) returns the same result as
   a. @NPV(A1,D4)
   b. @AVG(A1..D4)
   c. @MAX(A1..D4)
   d. @STD(A1..D4)
   e. none of the above
7. If you have entered 5 in cell A1 and 10 in cell A2, the result of @IF(+A1+A2>20,"CORRECT","WRONG") is
   a. 15
   b. ERR
   c. CORRECT
   d. WRONG
   e. none of the above
8. Functions that generate values based on the results of conditional statements are best classified as
   a. mathematical functions
   b. statistical functions
   c. logical functions
   d. special functions
   e. date/time functions

Questions 9 and 10 refer to the worksheet example given in Figures 7–12 and 7–13.

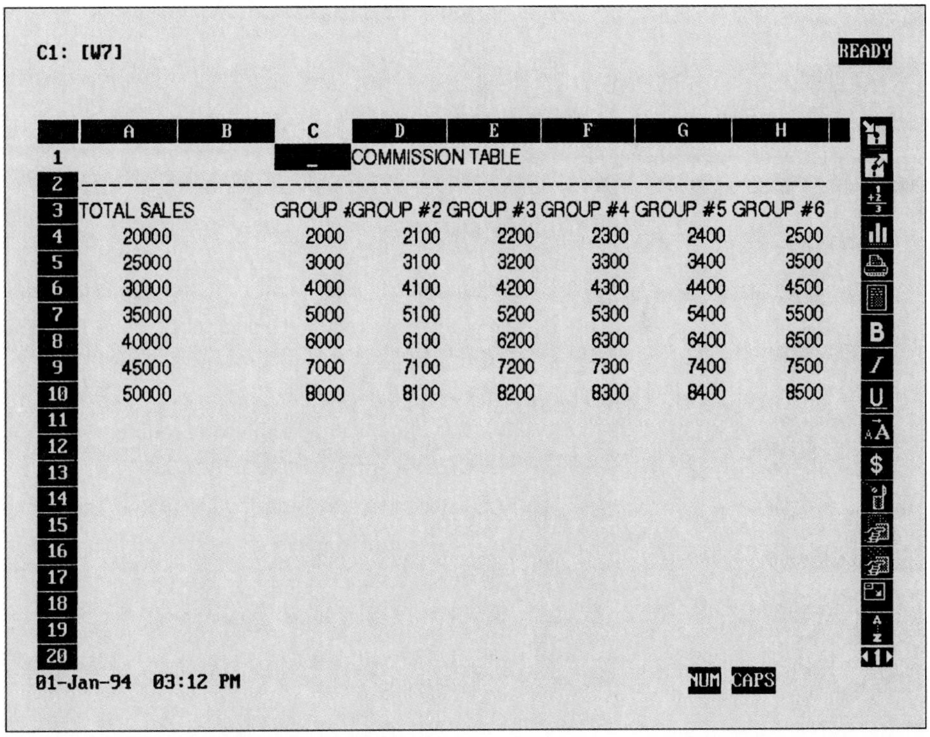
C1: [W7] READY

	A	B	C	D	E	F	G	H
1			_	COMMISSION TABLE				
2	--------	--------	--------	--------	--------	--------	--------	--------
3	TOTAL SALES		GROUP #	GROUP #2	GROUP #3	GROUP #4	GROUP #5	GROUP #6
4	20000		2000	2100	2200	2300	2400	2500
5	25000		3000	3100	3200	3300	3400	3500
6	30000		4000	4100	4200	4300	4400	4500
7	35000		5000	5100	5200	5300	5400	5500
8	40000		6000	6100	6200	6300	6400	6500
9	45000		7000	7100	7200	7300	7400	7500
10	50000		8000	8100	8200	8300	8400	8500
11								
12								
13								
14								
15								
16								
17								
18								
19								
20								

01-Jan-94 03:12 PM NUM CAPS

Figure 7–12
Sample worksheet.

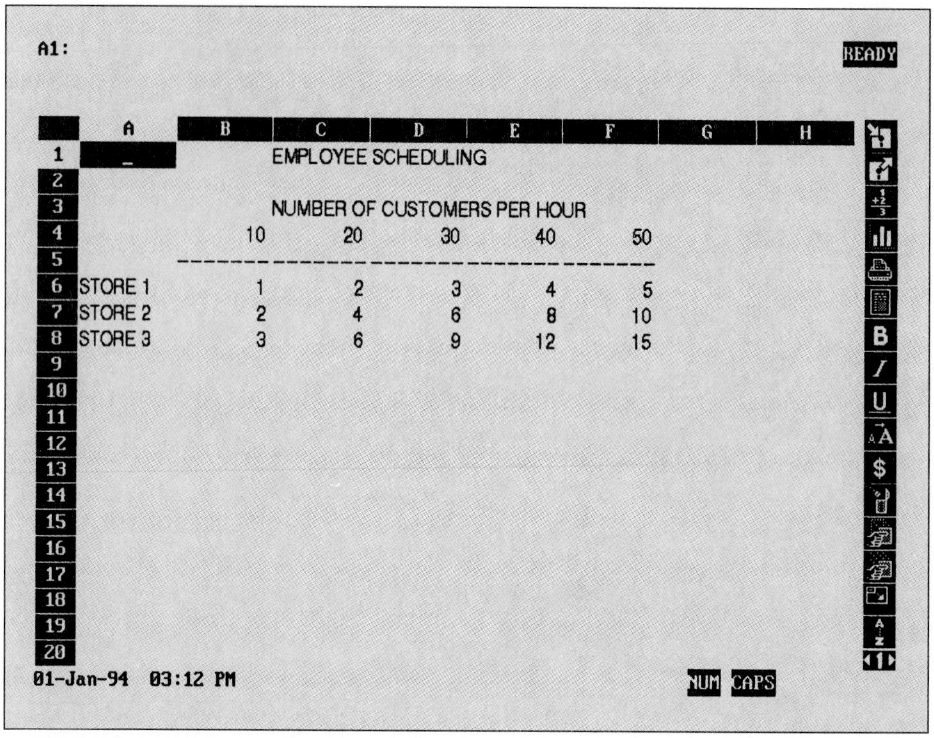

Figure 7–13
Sample worksheet.

9. The result of @VLOOKUP(30000,A4..H10,3) is
   a. 4100
   b. 4200
   c. 4300
   d. ERR
   e. none of the above
10. The result of @HLOOKUP(40,B4..F8,4) is
    a. ERR
    b. 4
    c. 8
    d. 12
    e. none of the above

True/False

1. The arguments of a function can be numeric values, strings, or range values.
2. The argument of a function cannot be another function.
3. If the argument of a function is a string, it must be enclosed in double quotation marks.
4. All 1-2-3 functions must have an argument.
5. @INT(9.9) is equal to @ROUND(9.9,0).
6. 1-2-3 @functions can simplify calculations significantly.
7. The @SUM function can be used to add a range of cells.
8. Unfortunately, 1-2-3 has no function to generate random numbers.
9. @SQRT(–25) is a valid expression.
10. 1-2-3 financial functions include several methods for calculating depreciation.

ANSWERS

Multiple Choice		True/False	
1.	e	1.	T
2.	b	2.	F
3.	c	3.	T
4.	e	4.	F
5.	a	5.	F
6.	b	6.	T
7.	d	7.	T
8.	c	8.	F
9.	a	9.	F
10.	d	10.	T

1-2-3 Graphics

8

8–1 INTRODUCTION

In this chapter we focus on 1-2-3 graphics and the types of graphs generated by 1-2-3. We discuss line, bar, XY, stacked-bar, pie, high-low-closed-open, and mixed graphs and the specific applications of each graph. We also discuss the PrintGraph program for printing graphs using a graphics printer or plotter.

8–2 USING 1-2-3 GRAPHS

To compete in today's world, business executives and decision makers need to get information in the most effective and efficient way. Graphs achieve these goals by condensing massive amounts of data into a simple form.

With 1-2-3 Release 2.4, you can generate seven different types of graphs:

- Line graphs show changes in data over time. These graphs are suitable for time series analysis. In this type of analysis, one variable is time and the other variable could be total sales, total cost, total advertising budget, and so on. Using line graphs, you can easily depict advertising budget trends, total sales trends, or administrative cost trends.
- Bar graphs emphasize differences among data items. For example, you can use these graphs effectively when comparing the total sales figures for five products from a particular company, oil production levels for five oil wells, the student populations of six state universities, and so on.
- XY graphs show relationships between two sets of data—sales and advertising budgets, or years of education and yearly income, for example.
- Pie charts compare all the parts to the whole—advertising expenses compared to total expenses, for example.
- Stacked-bar graphs show differences among data items by stacking the bars on top of each other. This method may help you better visualize data, for example, when a comparison is made between the incomes generated by different products in four regions.
- HLCO (high-low-close-open) graphs track changes in data over time. They are useful for stock market analysis to display fluctuations in the high, low, closing, and opening prices of a stock over time.
- A mixed graph combines a bar graph with a line graph. It is used to show different types of data, such as sales volume and advertising expenses, in the same graph.

The many graphics programs on the market may offer more variety and more sophistication than 1-2-3 graphics. Nevertheless, because 1-2-3 graphs are based on the data available in the spreadsheet, you can use the graphs to perform what-if analyses.

8–3 CREATING A GRAPH

If you select Graph from the 1-2-3 Main menu, the following options are presented:

```
Type X A B C D E F Reset View Save Options Name Group Quit
```

Choose Type to pick the type of graph you want to create. The X range is used for labeling the x-axis or the pieces of a pie chart; it is also used in XY graphs. Ranges A through F are used to set up six different data ranges. Use Reset to erase all previous graph parameters. Choose View to display the graph on screen. Use Save to save a graph for printing. Use Options to dress up your graph. Use Name for naming graph settings. Use Group to specify several data ranges at once, and use Quit to return to the worksheet.

To create and display a graph, enter your data first, then follow this procedure:

1. Select /Graph and choose Type.
2. Choose one of the graph types.
3. Select one or more data ranges (X and A through F).
4. Specify the data for each range either by pointing or by typing the address.
5. Select View to display the graph.
6. Press any key to return to the worksheet and the Graph menu.

8–4 CREATING A SIMPLE PIE CHART

Sunset Travel Agency has the following three expenses as part of its operating costs for 1992–1993. Enter them into a worksheet.

Utilities	1850
Rent	1250
Supplies	700

Plot these expenses using a pie chart. Figure 8–1 shows this graph. The graph was generated by /Graph, Type, Pie, X, A4..A6, Enter, A, C4..C6, Enter, View.

Also see Table 8–1 at the end of the chapter for graph SmartIcons.

8–5 SAVING GRAPH PARAMETERS

Once the graph is created, you can give it a name for later reference and retrieval. To save a graph's parameters, select /Graph Name Create. You can save a graph parameter under any name up to 15 characters long. Once you have saved a graph, you can change the parameters and save it under another name. You must always name the graph first with the /Graph Name Create command, and then save the worksheet with the /File Save command. If you do not name your graph or if you forget to save your worksheet, your graph will be lost.

To make a graph active (to bring it into memory), use the /Graph Name Use command. The Graph Name Table allows you to generate a listing of all your named graphs. You can have only one graph active at a time. You can generate as many graphs as you want from one worksheet.

8–6 SAVING A GRAPH FOR PRINTING

1-2-3 spreadsheet program is not capable of printing your graph. To print your graph, you first must save it using the /Graph Save command. 1-2-3 creates a

Figure 8–1
Simple pie chart

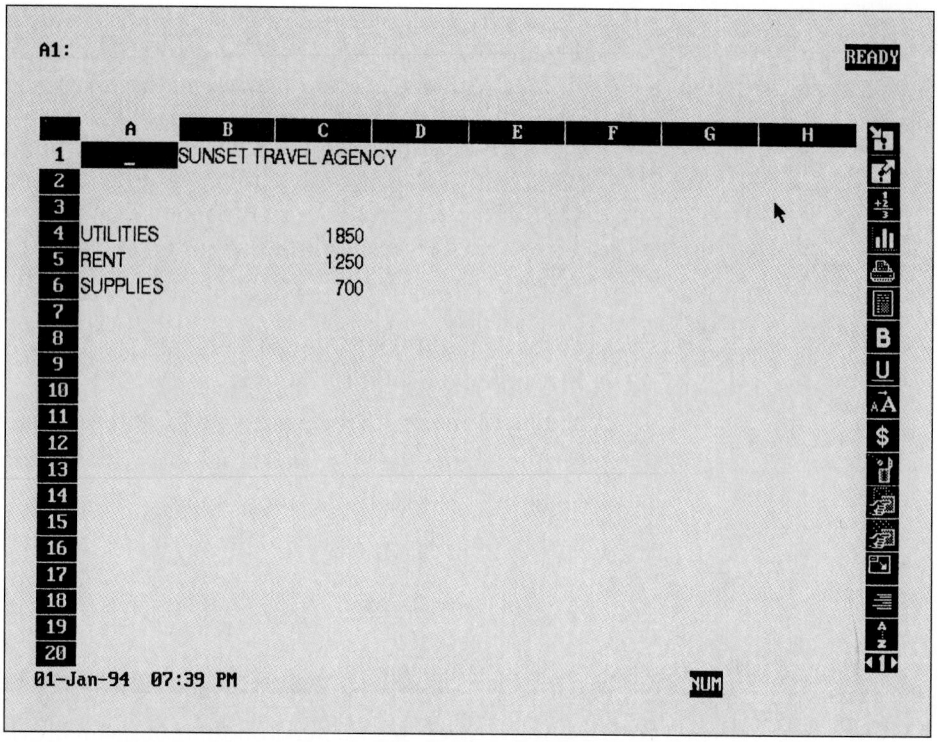

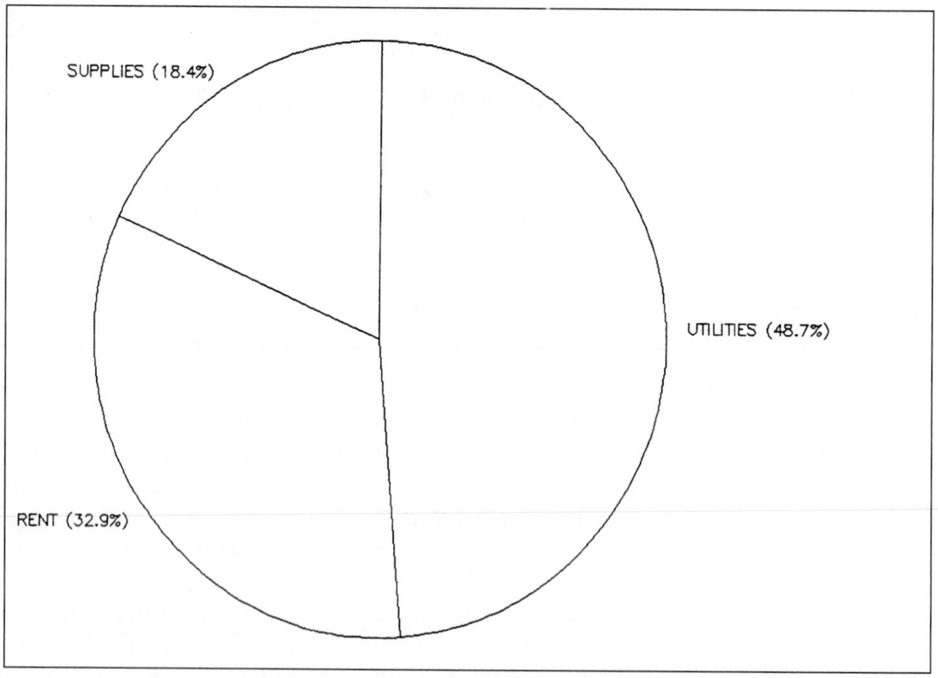

graphics file with a PIC extension. When the graph is saved in a graphics file, you can access it only from the PrintGraph program. With Release 2.4, you can use the WYSIWYG add-in program to print your graphs in addition to using the PrintGraph. WYSIWYG will be discussed in the next chapter.

8–7 DELETING A GRAPH

To delete a graph, choose /Graph Name Delete. 1-2-3 will display all the graph names for the current worksheet. You can either type the name or move the cursor to the specific graph name and press Enter. If you want to delete all the graphs under the current worksheet, use the /Graph Name Reset command. Be careful, however. When you issue this command, all the graphs under the current worksheet will be erased and there is no way to retrieve them.

8–8 PIE CHARTS: A SECOND LOOK

Pie charts are useful when you want to compare parts of data to the data as a whole. To create a pie chart, select /Graph Type Pie. Specify the X range (the labels), specify the A range (the data), and choose View.

Figure 8–2 is a pie chart of a simple regional analysis. The sales of each region is compared to the total sales. This graph was generated by using

/Graph, Type, Pie, X, A11..A13, Enter, A, E11..E13, Enter, View

8–8–1 Creating a Pie Chart Using Crosshatches

1-2-3 can generate eight different **crosshatches,** or fillers, to make data comparison an easy task. Each type of crosshatching is different. If you are using color, each type has a unique color. To generate a graph with crosshatching, use the codes 0 to 7. Place these codes in a separate data range outside the original data range. The location of this data range is not important. If you are creating a pie chart, you must specify this data range as the B range.

Figure 8–3 illustrates these crosshatches. To generate this figure, select /Graph Type Pie. Choose X, indicate range B2..I2, and press Enter. Next, choose range A, indicate B3..I3, and press Enter. Finally, choose range B, indicate range B6..I6, and press Enter.

8–8–2 Exploding a Pie Chart

Sometimes you may want to highlight a portion of your pie chart. 1-2-3 gives you a way to **explode** one, or all, of the pieces of your pie chart. To do so, add 100 to the codes for the crosshatching. As you can see in Figure 8–4, we added 100 to cell B18—it now contains 101. This code will explode that particular section of the pie chart and fill in the appropriate crosshatching.

8–9 BAR GRAPHS

Bar graphs are useful for comparing data items, for example, comparing the oil production levels for OPEC for the past 10 years. 1-2-3 allows you to choose up

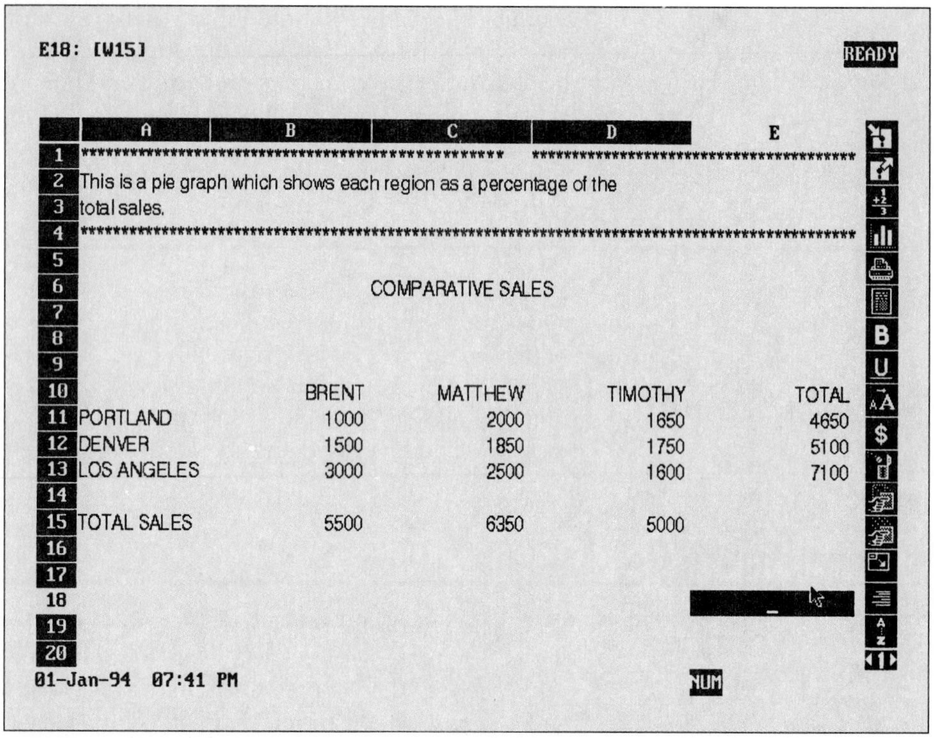

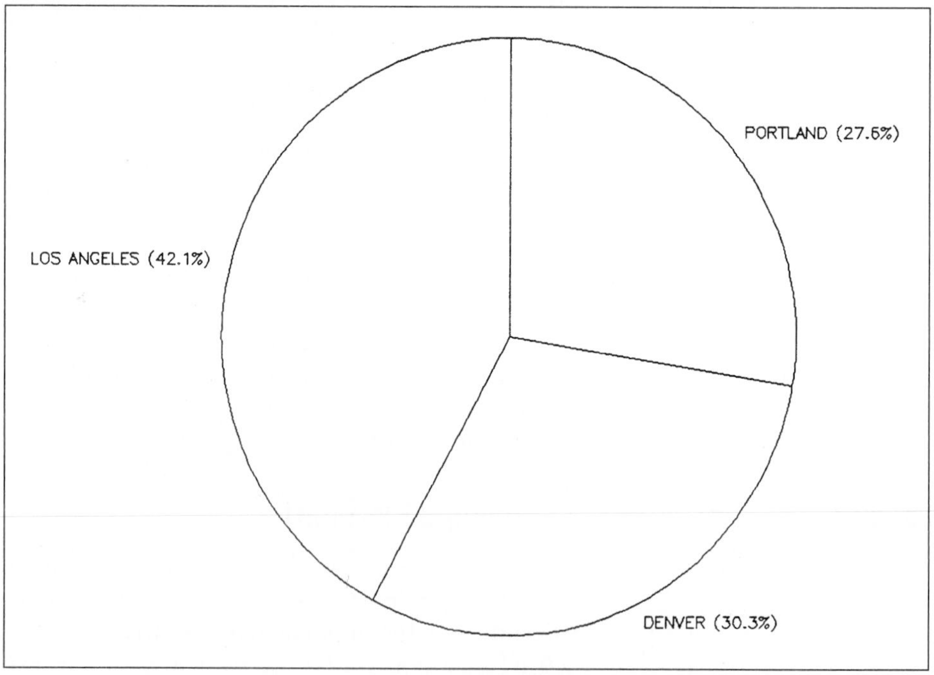

Figure 8–2
Regional analysis using a pie chart.

to six data ranges for bar graph presentation. Figure 8–5 shows a bar graph that charts the performances of three salespersons in three regions.

As you can see, the X data range shows the names of the three salespeople. The A range shows the performance of the first salesperson, Brent, in three regions. The B and C ranges are the performances of the second and third salespeople, respectively. We entered the heading *COMPARATIVE SALES* and the

Figure 8–3
Crosshatching options.

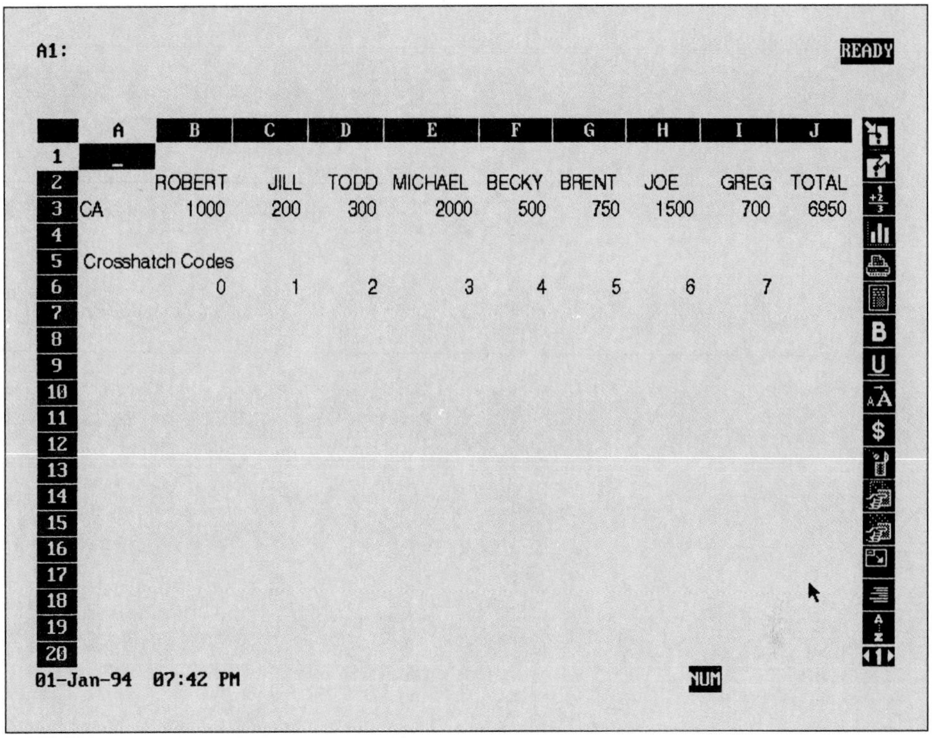

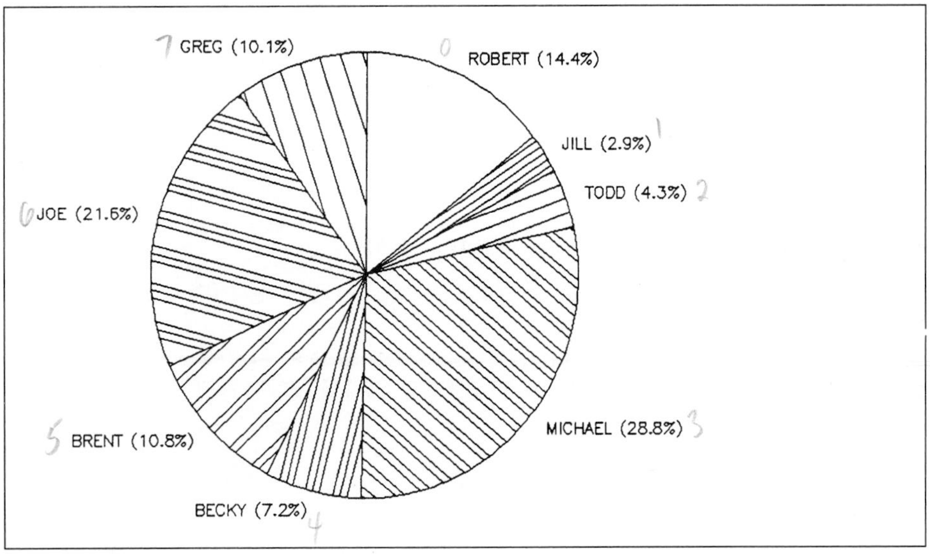

subtitle *FOR THE HAPPY TRAVELER*. We put the title *SALESMEN* on the x-axis and *SALES* on the y-axis.

To make the presentation clearer, you can choose up to six **legends** for your graph. We entered *PORTLAND* for legend A, *DENVER* for legend B, and *LOS ANGELES* for legend C.

You can generate this graph by selecting /Graph Type Bar. Choose X, indicate B10..D10, and press Enter. Next, choose range A, indicate B11..D11, and press Enter. Select range B, indicate B12..D12, and press Enter. Choose range C, indicate range B13..D13, and press Enter.

Figure 8–4
Exploding one section of a pie chart.

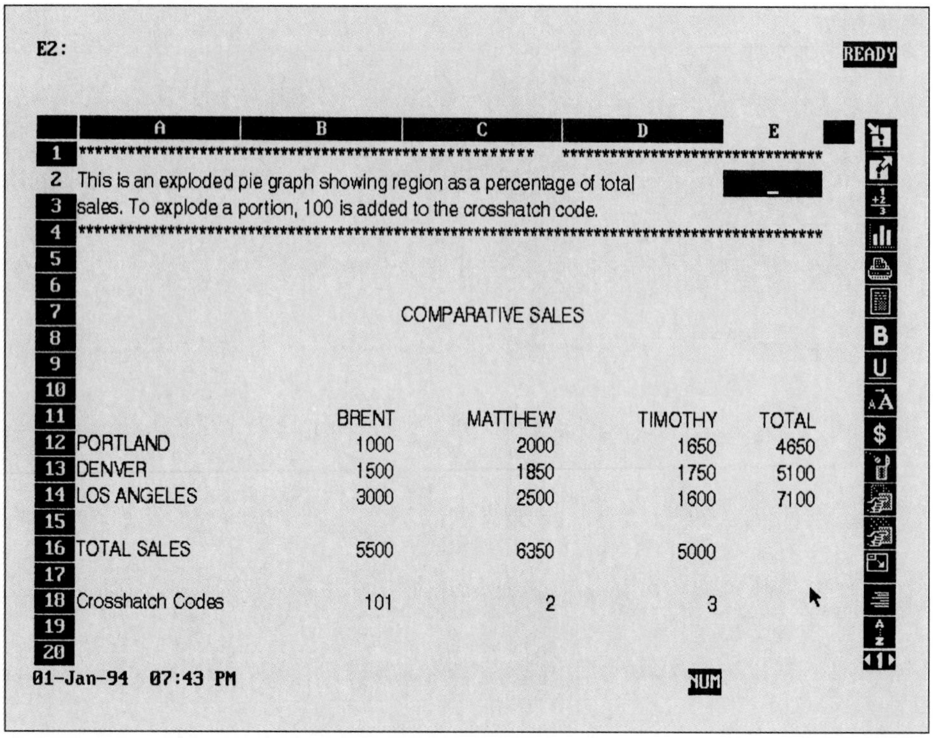

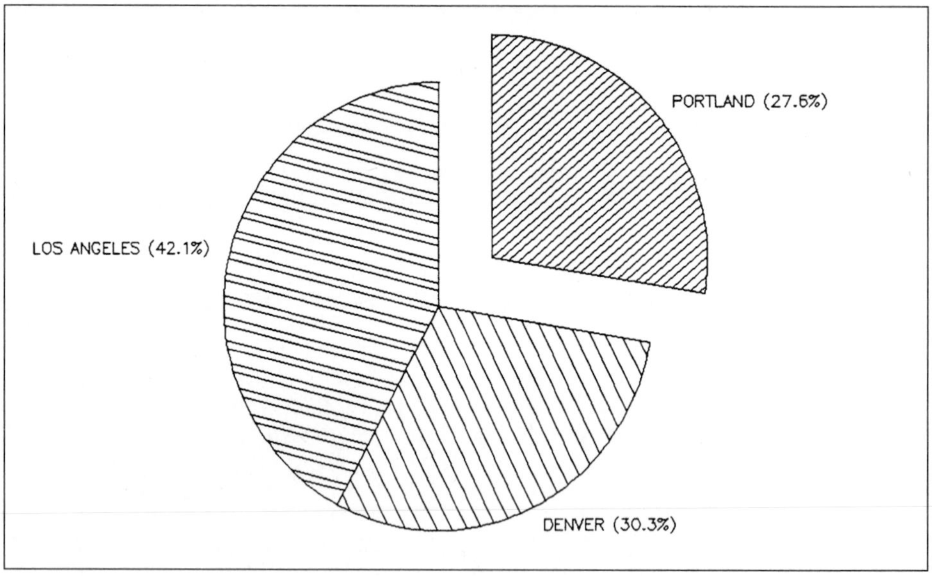

Next, to add the titles, choose Options Titles First, type *COMPARATIVE SALES,* and press Enter. Select Titles Second, type *FOR THE HAPPY TRAVELER,* and press Enter. Choose Titles X-Axis, type *SALESMEN,* and press Enter. Pick Titles Y-Axis, type *SALES,* and press Enter.

Choose Legend, press A, type *PORTLAND,* and press Enter. Next, select Legend, press B, type *DENVER,* and press Enter. Finally, choose Legend, press C, type *LOS ANGELES,* press Enter, and choose Quit and then View.

In Release 2.4, by selecting /Graph, Type, Features, 3D-Effect, you can add or remove three-dimensional effects (drop shadow) in your bar, stacked-bar, and mixed graphs.

Figure 8–5
Bar graph for sales performance analysis.

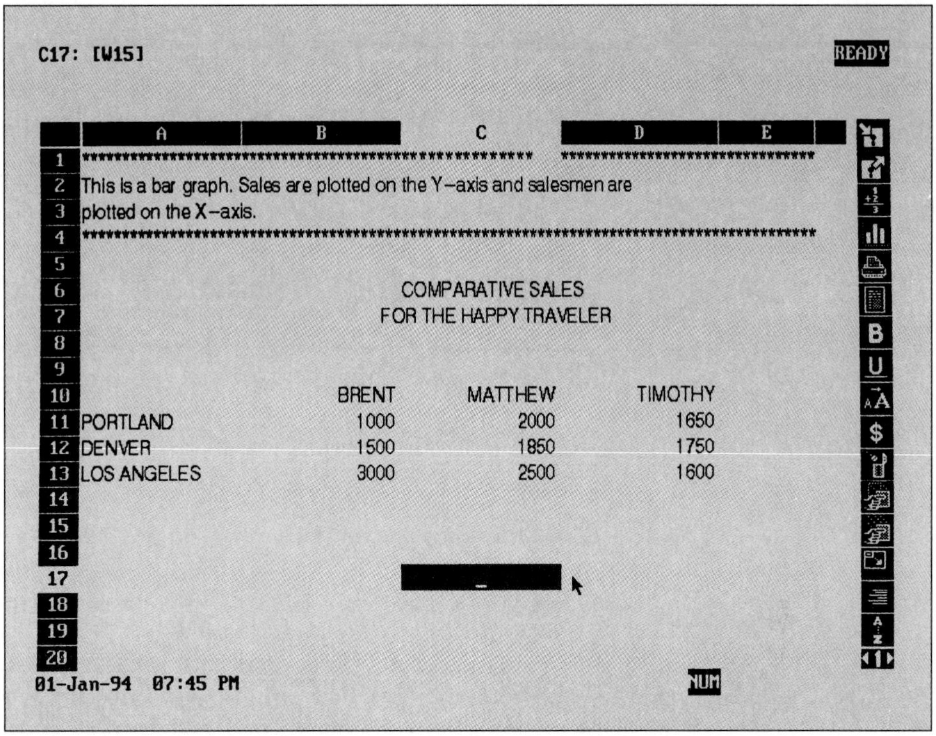

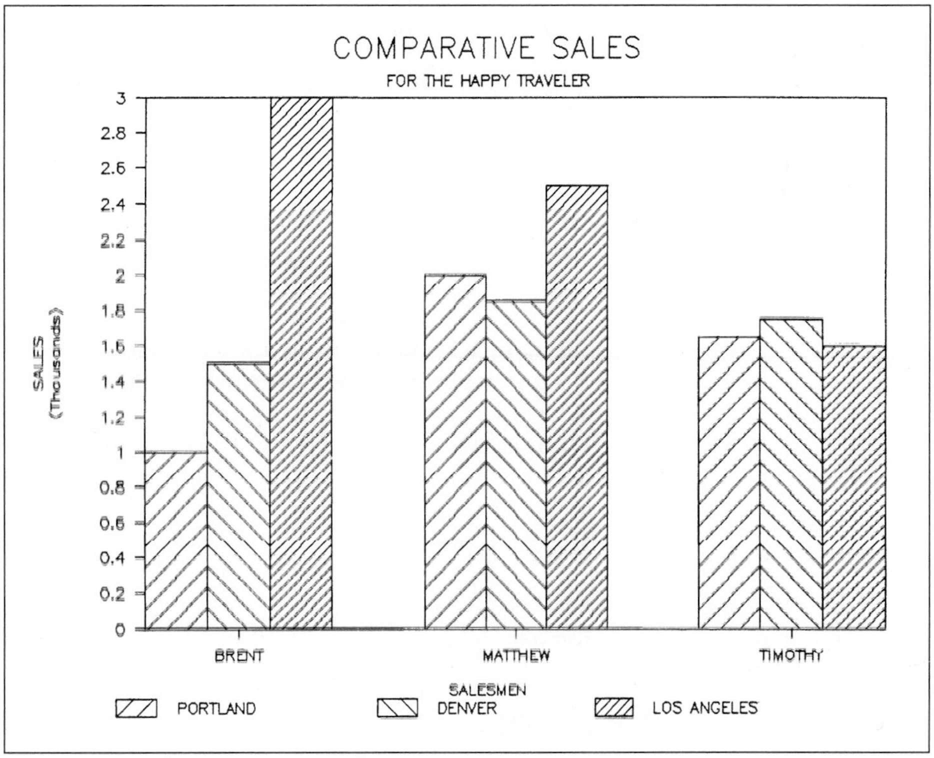

8–10 LINE GRAPHS

Line graphs are useful when one variable is observed over a period of time, such as when the total advertising budget of a company is observed from 1988 to 1992. Use the Format option to draw lines or symbols in line or XY graphs. When you choose the Format option from the Options menu, the following menu is presented:

```
Graph A B C D E F Quit
```

Use the Graph option to set the format for all ranges. Options A through F set the format for each particular range. If you choose Graph, you are given the following choices:

```
Lines Symbols Both Neither Area
```

Use Lines to draw lines between data points; use Symbols to draw symbols at data points. The Both option will draw both lines and symbols, and the Neither option will display data labels only. The Area option fills the area under lines in line graphs.

You can use horizontal and vertical grid lines to make graphs easier to read. You draw grid lines with the Grid option from the Options menu. You have a choice of horizontal or vertical grid lines, or both.

You use the Data-Labels option from the Options menu to specify a label corresponding to the data range. Up to six data ranges can be labeled. If you choose this option, you will be presented with:

```
A B C D E F Group Quit
```

When you select one of these options, then you can align your labels in five convenient ways:

```
Center Left Above Right Below
```

Figure 8–6 is an example of a line graph. It shows the total sales trend for Alpha-Talk Company from 1988 to 1992. We generated this graph by choosing /Graph Type Line. Next, we chose X, indicated range C11..C15, pressed Enter, selected range A, indicated F11..F15, and pressed Enter. Then we selected Options Titles First, typed *ALPHA-TALK COMPANY,* pressed Enter, picked Titles X-Axis, typed *YEAR,* and pressed Enter. Finally, we chose Titles Y-Axis, typed *TOTAL SALES,* pressed Enter, and picked Format Graph Lines, Quit, and Quit and then View.

Figure 8–7 plots data using Data-Labels. We used the /Graph Options Scale Skip 2 command to print every other item of data on the x-axis. You can use Skip 3 to print every third number on the x-axis, and so on.

8–11 STACKED-BAR GRAPHS

In a **stacked-bar graph,** 1-2-3 displays the values for each data range stacked on top of each other. 1-2-3 allows you to build a stacked-bar graph with six data items, one on top of the other. It also uses shadings or colors to represent the data items. When you define your data ranges, remember that the A range corre-

Figure 8–6
Line graph with line only.

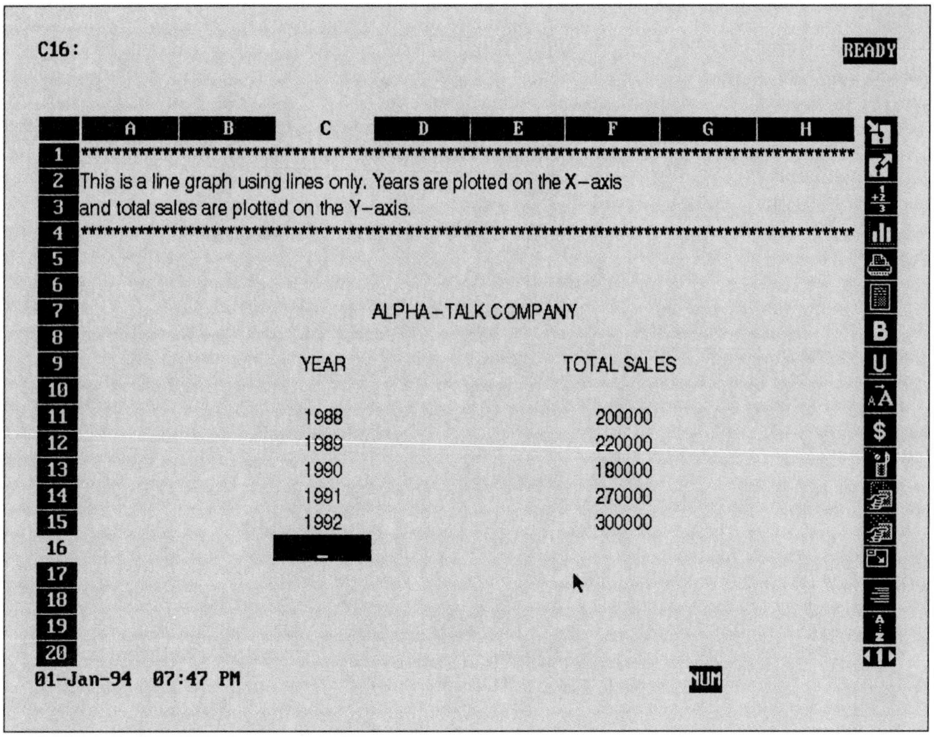

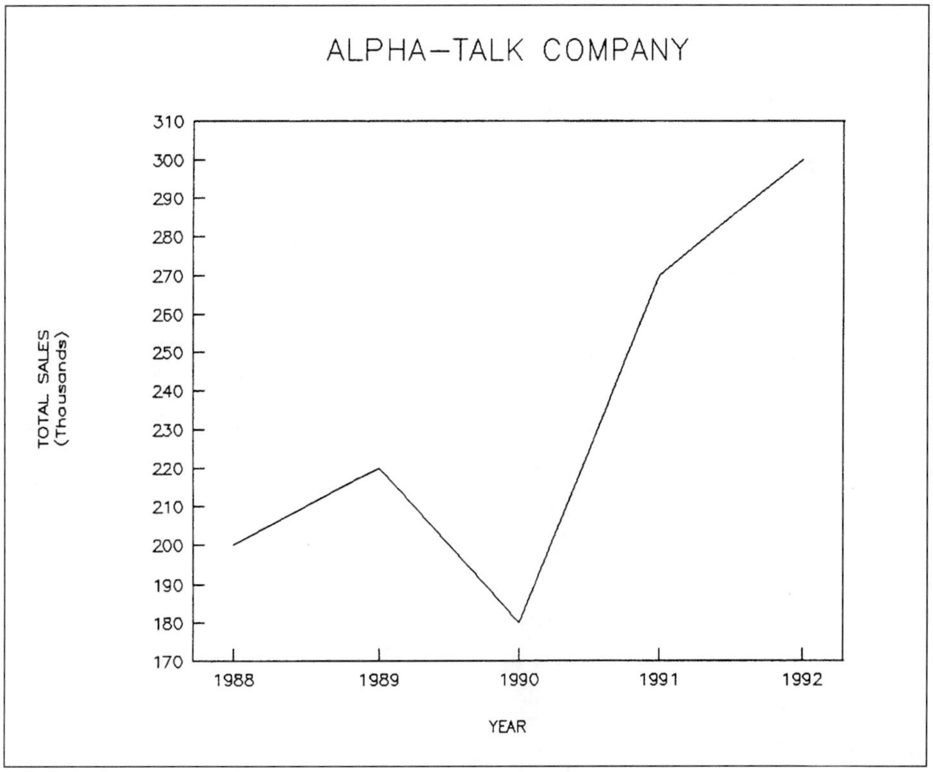

Figure 8–7
Plotting an advertising budget using data-labels.

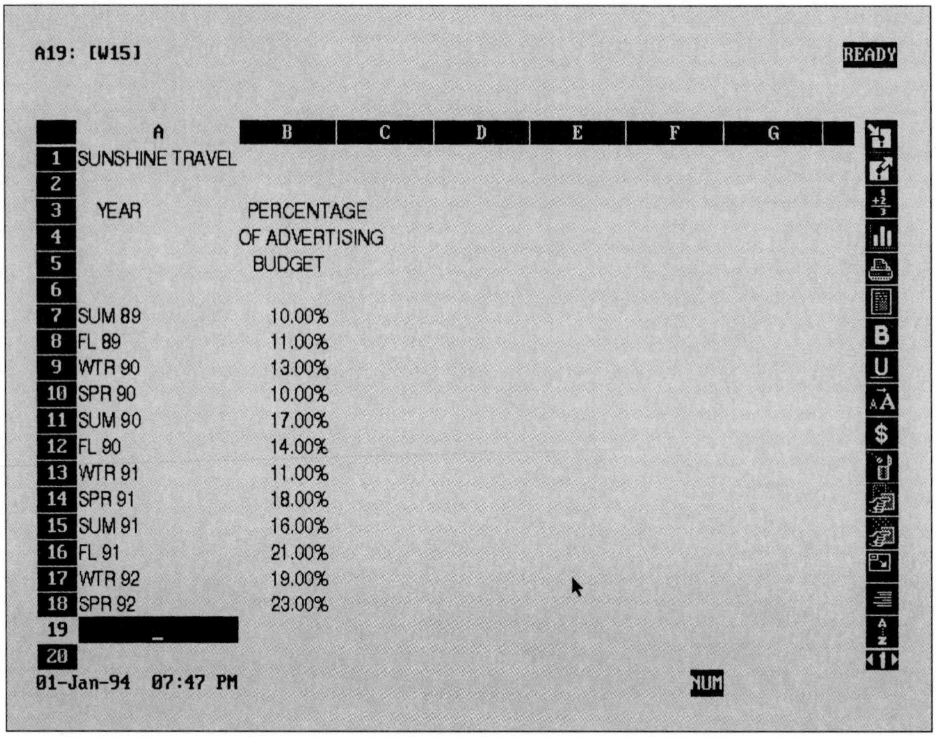

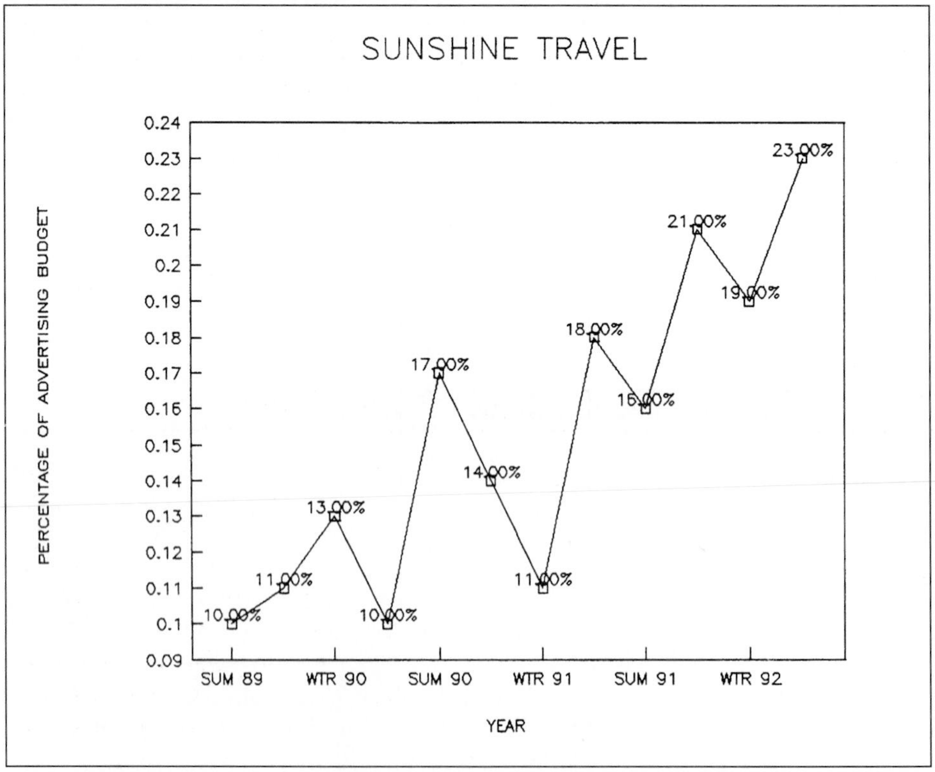

sponds to the lowest value of data and the F range corresponds to the highest. As usual, the X range is used for the data label on the x-axis.

Figure 8–8 is an example of the stacked-bar graph. The performances of each salesperson in all the regions are displayed on top of one another. The first bar from the left is Brent's performance in Portland (the bottom portion), Denver, and Los Angeles. This figure was generated using the following commands:

> /Graph, Type, Stacked-Bar, X, B11..D11, Enter, A, B12..D12, Enter, B, B13..D13, Enter, C, B14..D14, Enter, Options, Legend, A, \A12, Enter, Legend, B, \A13, Enter, Legend, C, \A14, Enter, Titles, First, COMPARATIVE SALES, Enter, Titles, X-Axis, SALESMEN, Enter, Titles, Y-Axis, SALES, Enter, Quit, View.

In this example, using \ is a shortcut. You can also type in the data directory. For example, instead of \A12, you could type *PORTLAND.*

8–12 XY GRAPHS

In an **XY graph,** 1-2-3 pairs each value from the X data range with the corresponding data item from each of the ranges A through F to plot the graph. You can generate up to six data ranges in an XY graph. 1-2-3 uses a different symbol to show each distinct range.

Figure 8–9 shows one example of an XY graph. Total sales are shown on the y-axis, and advertising is shown on the x-axis. In an XY graph, one of your data ranges must be the X range. This is the major difference between a line graph and an XY graph. In a line graph, one set of data generates a graph, but in an XY graph, you must have two sets of data, one for the X range and one for ranges A, B, C, D, E, and F. We have used both lines and symbols. The following commands were used to generate this figure:

> /Graph, Type, XY, X, C11..C16, Enter, A, A11..A16, Enter, Options, Titles, First, SALES AND ADVERTISING, Enter, Titles, X-Axis, ADVERTISING, Enter, Titles, Y-Axis, TOTAL SALES, Enter, Format, Graph, Both, Quit, Quit, View.

8–13 HIGH-LOW-CLOSE-OPEN (HLCO) GRAPHS

HLCO graphs track changes in data over time. They are most commonly used to display fluctuations in the high, low, closing, and opening prices of a stock over time.

In an HLCO graph, 1-2-3 uses the A data range as the high values, the B data range as the low values, the C data range as the closing values, and the D data range as the opening values. Each set of high, low, closing, and opening values is one vertical line on the graph. The line extends from the high value to the low value and includes tick marks for the closing and opening values. The number of vertical lines in the graph depends on the number of time periods for which you recorded the high-low-close-open data.

This type of graph can also be used for recording the atmospheric temperature for several years for given dates. The graph shows the highest and lowest temperature recorded for a given day. In this graph type you must specify at

Figure 8–8
Comparing sales in three regions using a stacked-bar graph.

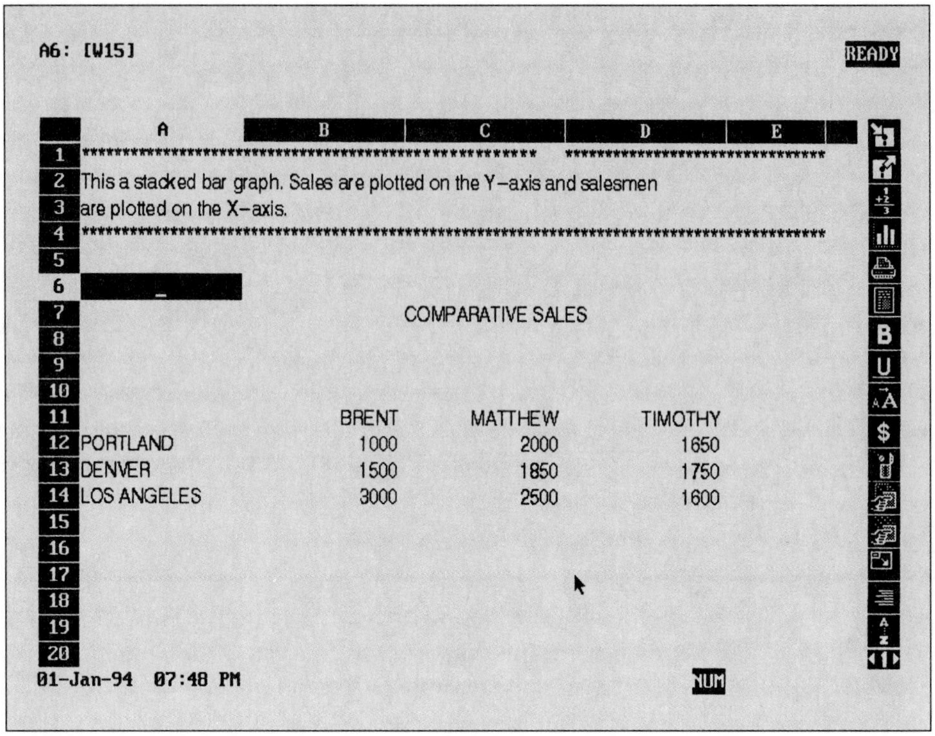

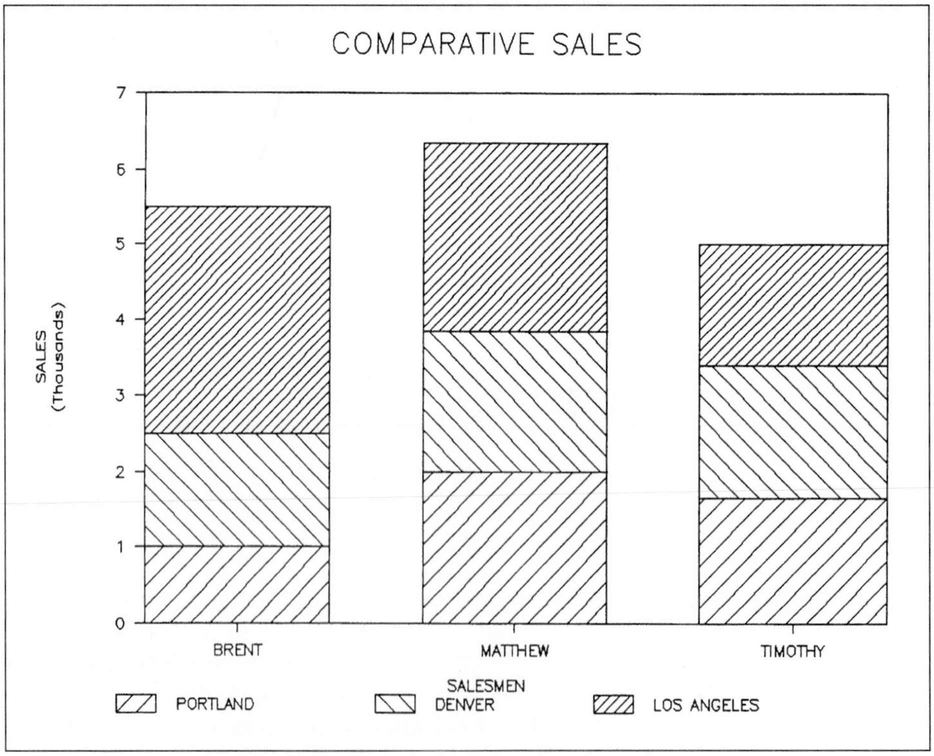

Figure 8–9
XY graph for total sales and advertising.

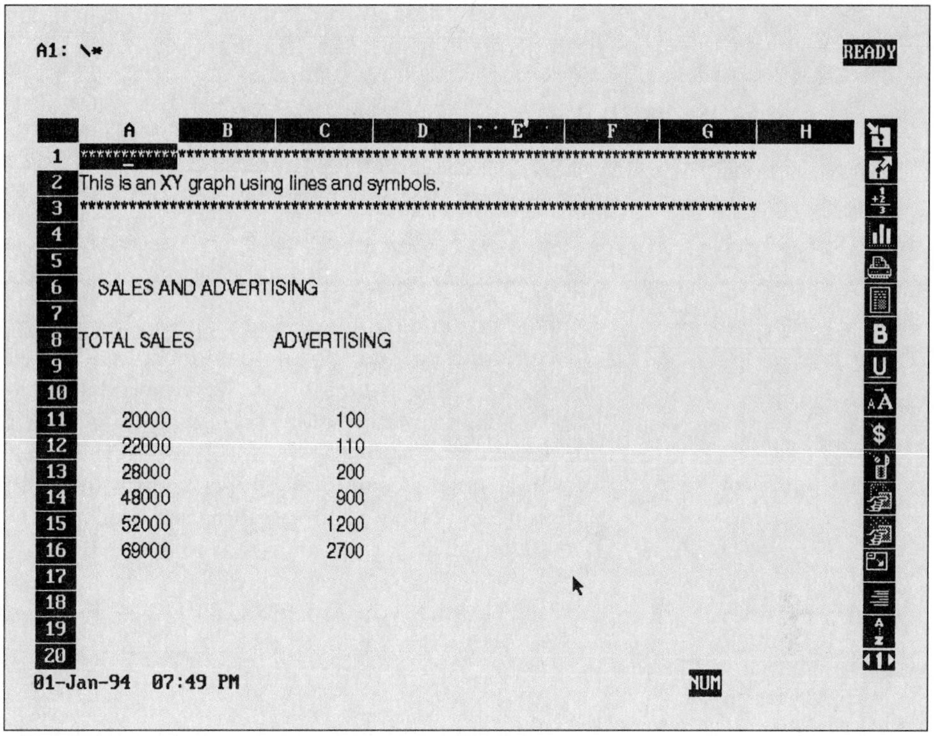

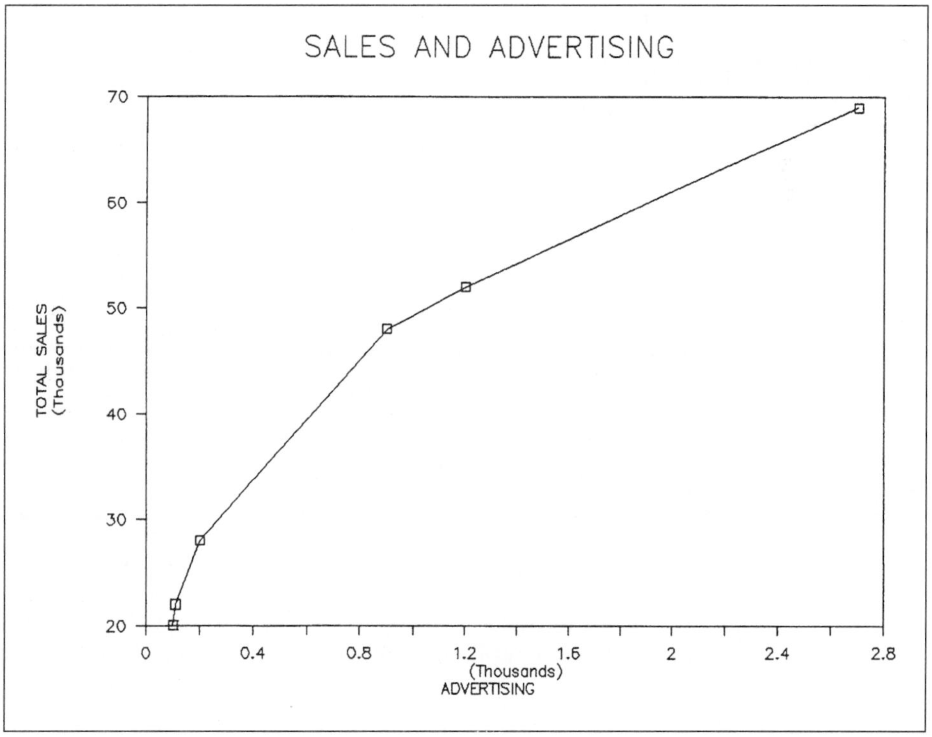

least two sets of data; the other two are optional. Figure 8–10 shows one example of this type of graph. This graph was generated by the following commands:

> /Graph, Type, HLCO, A, C4..C9, Enter, B, D4..D9, Enter, X, A4..A9, Enter, Options, Titles, First, \B1, Enter, Titles, Second, \B2, Enter, Titles, X-Axis, MONTH, Enter, Titles, Y-Axis, PRICE, Enter, Quit, View.

8–14 MIXED GRAPHS

A **mixed graph** combines a bar graph with a line graph. It is used to show different types of data, such as sales volume and advertising expenses, or sales volume and sales in different regions or different quarters, in the same graph. In a mixed graph, 1-2-3 uses the A, B, and C data ranges for the sets of bars and the D, E, and F data ranges for the lines. Figure 8–11 is an example. In this figure the bars show different sales amounts generated in three different regions in three different quarters. The line graph indicates that quarter 2 has generated the largest sales. This graph was generated as follows:

> /Graph, Type, Mixed, X, B10..D10, Enter, A, B11..D11, Enter, B, B12..D12, Enter, C, B13..D13, Enter, D, B15..D15, Enter, Options, Titles, First, COMPARATIVE SALES, Enter, Titles, Second, FOR THE HAPPY TRAVELER, Enter, Titles, X-Axis, QUARTER, Enter, Titles, Y-Axis, SALES, Enter, Legend, A, PORTLAND, Enter, Legend, B, DENVER, Enter, Legend, C, LOS ANGELES, Enter, Quit, View.

8–15 USING COLOR

We have not talked about the color option yet because the majority of 1-2-3 users probably do not have access to color graphics. However, if you do, the /Graph Options Color command provides this facility. This command displays data range bars, graph lines, and symbols in different colors only if your monitor is capable of displaying color graphics.

The /Graph Options B&W command displays data ranges in contrasting monochrome crosshatching. You should use /Graph Options B&W only if you have previously selected /Graph Options Color and are interested in returning to a monochrome display.

8–16 USING PRINTGRAPH

As you have seen, operations performed by 1-2-3 are stored on the 1-2-3 disk (the system disk). The only function not stored on this disk is the PrintGraph program, which is stored on a separate disk to keep 1-2-3 a manageable size. **PrintGraph** enables you to generate hard copies of the graphs you have created.

You can use PrintGraph only if your printer is capable of printing graphics, such as the IBM Graphics printer, or if you have access to a plotter, such as an HP 7475.

To use the PrintGraph program, you first must save your graph with the /Graph Save command. You then exit 1-2-3 and enter the PrintGraph program. You can start PrintGraph from either DOS or the 1-2-3 Access System.

To load PrintGraph from DOS, put the PrintGraph disk in drive A, type *PGRAPH* at the A> prompt, and press Enter.

Figure 8–10
Example of high-low-close-open graph.

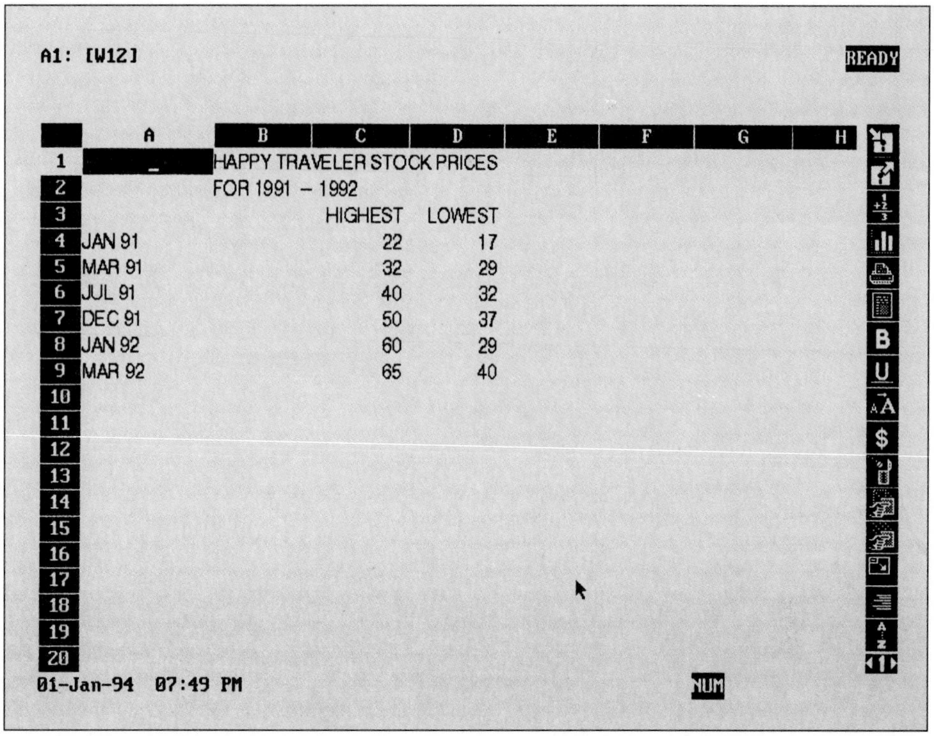

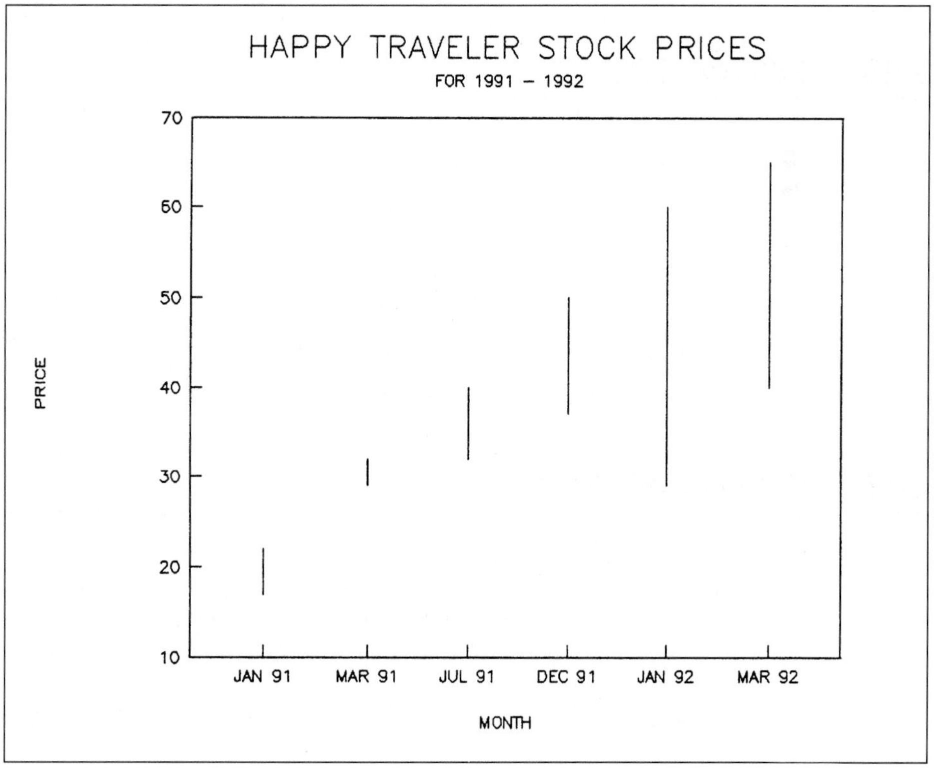

Figure 8–11
Example of mixed graph.

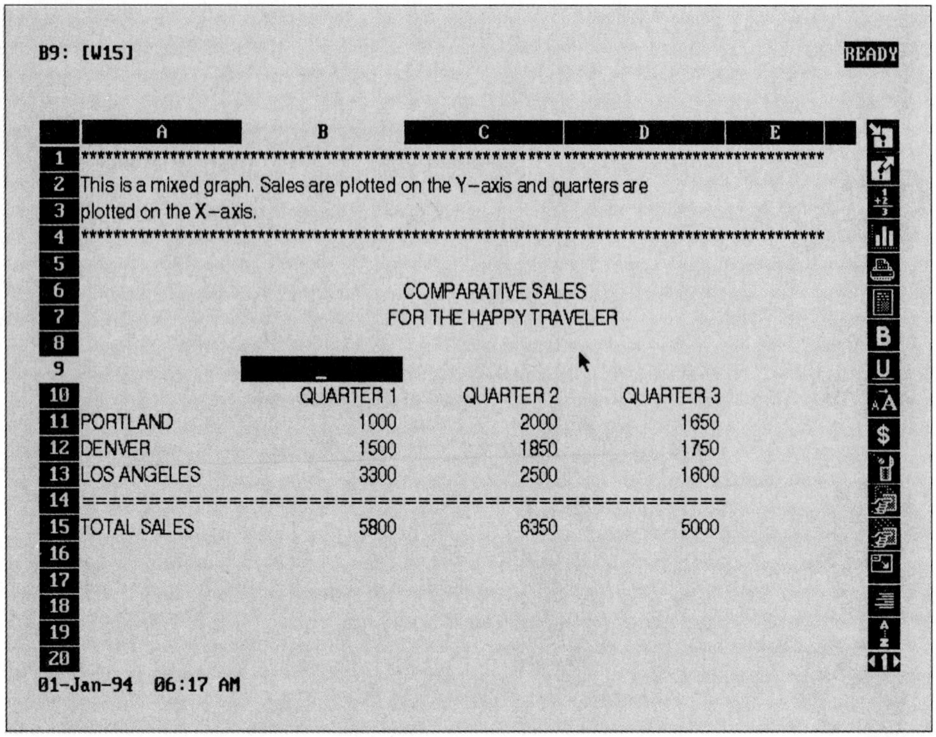

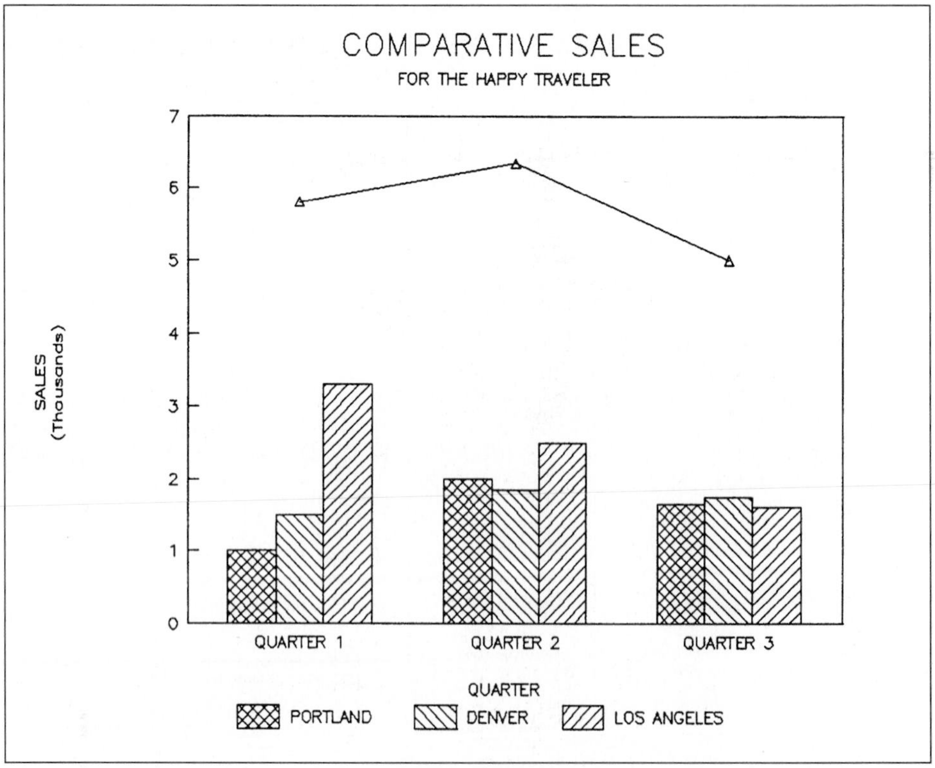

To load PrintGraph from the 1-2-3 Access System, select PrintGraph in the Access menu, press Enter, and follow the prompts.

8–16–1 PrintGraph Options

Once you have loaded the PrintGraph program, you will see the main menu, shown in Figure 8–12. As you can see, the menu gives you six options. Use the left- and right-arrow keys to highlight the option you want. Press Enter to select the option.

Image-Select allows you to choose the graphs to be printed. From the listing of your graph directory, move the cursor to the graph you want to print and press the space bar. Your graph will be marked with a # sign, which indicates that the graph has been selected for printing. To remove the # sign, press the space bar again. If you want to print a different graph, first remove the # sign from the selected graph, and then choose another graph.

Figure 8–13 shows the graph menu and the graph selected for printing. This menu also tells you when the graphs were generated, the time, and the size of the graphs in bytes. You can display your graph on the monitor (if you have graphics capability) by pressing F10.

Use the Settings option to choose the settings for the PrintGraph program, including size, fonts, and color. Use the Go option to begin printing. Use Align to tell PrintGraph that the paper is positioned on the top of the page. Use the Page option to advance the paper to the top of the next page.

When you choose a graph from the directory for printing, you cannot change any of the graph parameters. If you want to make changes, you must exit from PrintGraph, go back into 1-2-3, retrieve your worksheet file, make the changes on the file, and save it with /Graph Save. You cannot retrieve a PIC file in 1-2-3. You can only retrieve the worksheet file that generated the corresponding PIC file.

Under the Settings menu, there are six other options:

```
Image Hardware Action Save Reset Quit
```

Figure 8–12
PrintGraph main menu.

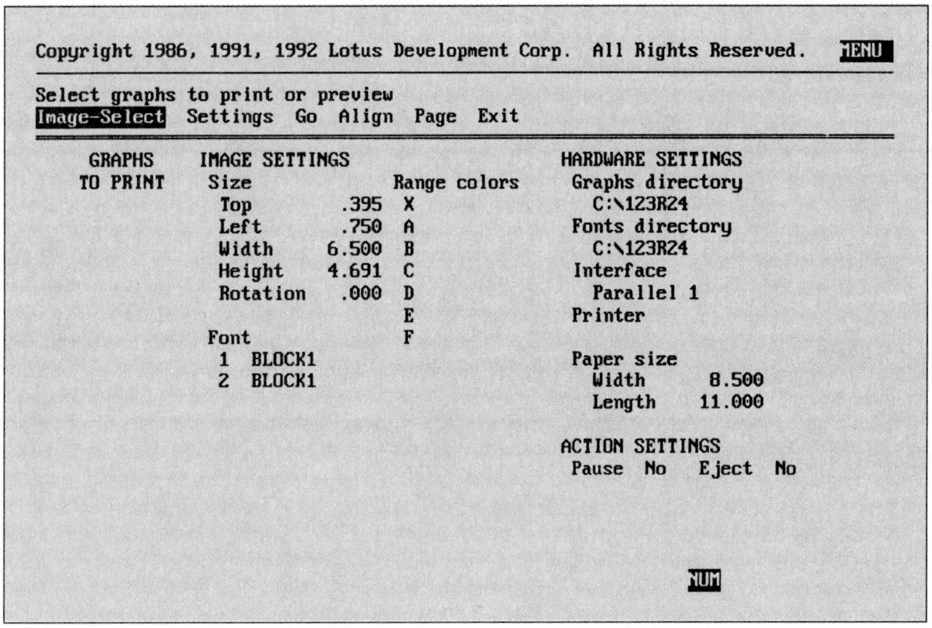

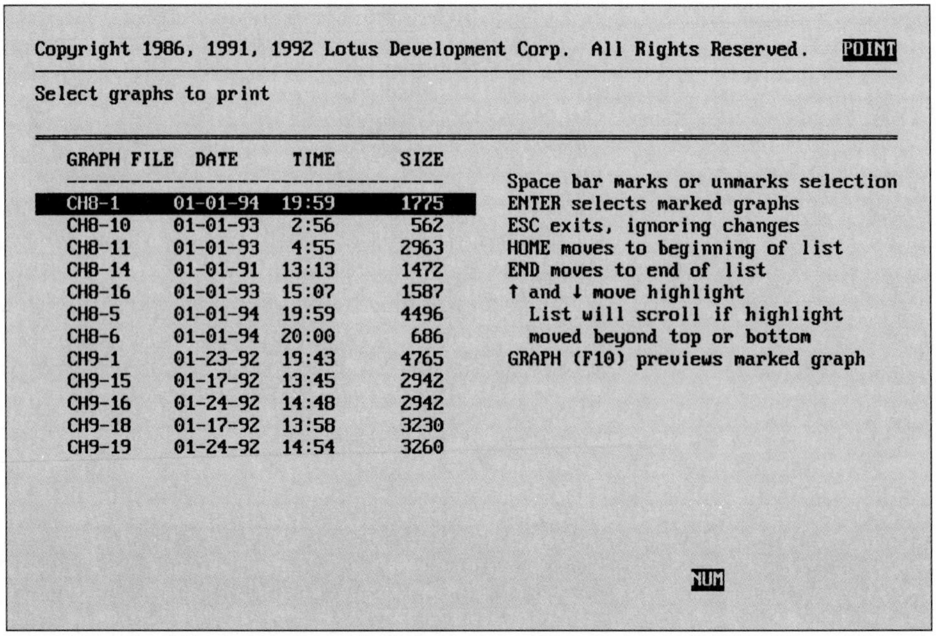
Copyright 1986, 1991, 1992 Lotus Development Corp. All Rights Reserved.
POINT
Select graphs to print
GRAPH FILE DATE TIME SIZE
CH8-1 01-01-94 19:59 1775
CH8-10 01-01-93 2:56 562
CH8-11 01-01-93 4:55 2963
CH8-14 01-01-91 13:13 1472
CH8-16 01-01-93 15:07 1587
CH8-5 01-01-94 19:59 4496
CH8-6 01-01-94 20:00 686
CH9-1 01-23-92 19:43 4765
CH9-15 01-17-92 13:45 2942
CH9-16 01-24-92 14:48 2942
CH9-18 01-17-92 13:58 3230
CH9-19 01-24-92 14:54 3260
Space bar marks or unmarks selection
ENTER selects marked graphs
ESC exits, ignoring changes
HOME moves to beginning of list
END moves to end of list
↑ and ↓ move highlight
List will scroll if highlight
moved beyond top or bottom
GRAPH (F10) previews marked graph
NUM

Figure 8–13
A graphs directory.

Use the Image option to define graph settings such as font, color, and size. Use the Hardware option to define printer and directories for fonts and graph files. The Action option controls printer options such as ejecting paper and pausing between graphs. Use the Save option if you want to save the present settings to use for another graph. If you don't choose this option, PrintGraph will not remember the most recent settings—it will use the default graph settings. Use the Reset option to return the current settings to their defaults. Use the Quit option to leave this menu.

Figure 8–14 shows a graph generated with 1-2-3's default settings.

8–16–2 Exiting from PrintGraph

To exit from the PrintGraph program, choose Exit from the PrintGraph main menu. You will be returned to the 1-2-3 Access System or to the DOS prompt, depending on how you entered PrintGraph.

SUMMARY

In this chapter we discussed 1-2-3 graphics. We examined the seven different graphs generated by 1-2-3—line, bar, XY, pie, stacked-bar, HLCO, and mixed. 1-2-3 presents a very impressive graphics operation. The last section of this chapter presented a quick view of the PrintGraph program, which you can use to generate hard copies of your graphs. See Table 8–1 for graphs SmartIcons.

REVIEW QUESTIONS

*These questions are answered in Appendix A.

1. How many types of graphs can be generated by 1-2-3?
2. What is the unique application of each type?

Figure 8–14
A graph generated with default settings.

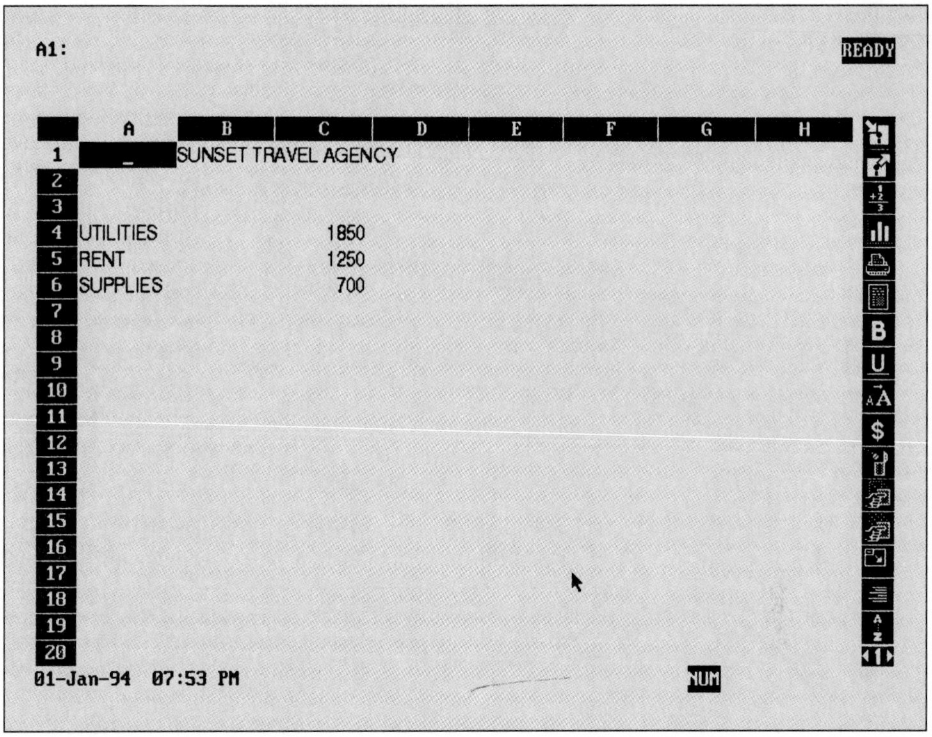

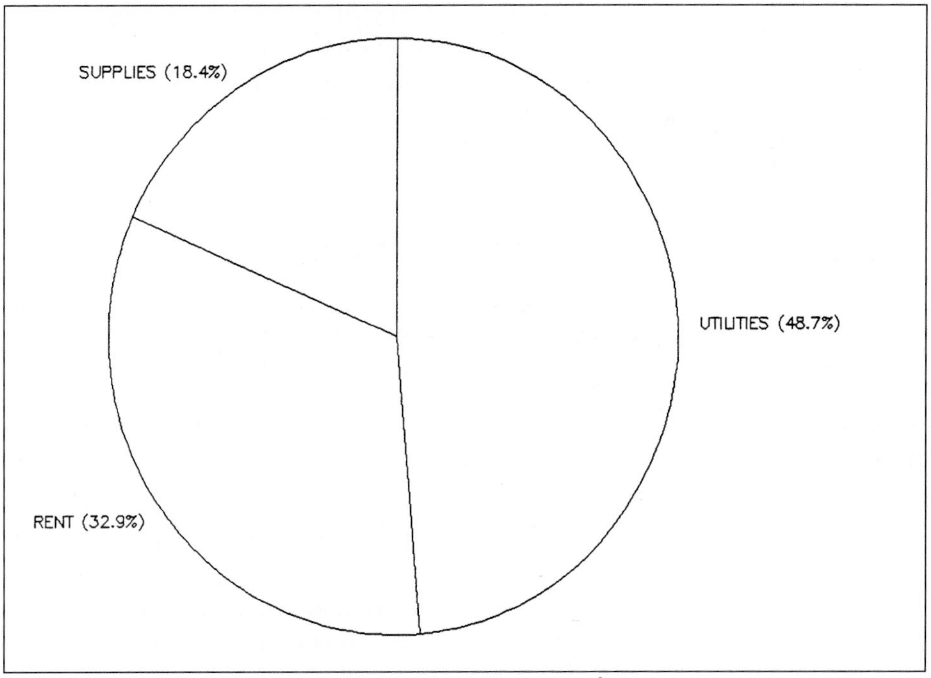

Table 8–1
Graph Icons

WYSIWYG Mode	Text Mode	Description
		Graphs the contents of the highlighted range or the data immediately adjacent to or surrounding the cell pointer. This icon displays the QuickGraph dialog box, which lets you change the settings for graph type, orientation, colors, and 3-D effect and lets you graph data in columns or rows. If the cell pointer is not currently in an area that contains data, this icon lets you make changes to the current graph settings and displays the current graph.
		**W** Adds the current graph to the highlighted range in the worksheet.
	VIEW GRPH	Displays the current graph. Equivalent to pressing F10 (GRAPH).

Column 1 shows icons if WYSIWYG is attached. Column 2 shows icons as they appear when WYSIWYG is either not attached or is set to: Display Mode Text.
The icons identified by **W** work only when WYSIWYG is attached.

***3.** What are some of the limitations of 1-2-3 graphics?
4. What is the difference between XY graphs and line graphs?
5. How many data ranges can be used in 1-2-3 graphics?
***6.** What is the specific use of the X range?
7. How do you save a graph for printing?
***8.** Can your graph and your worksheet be saved under the same name?
9. Can you retrieve a graphics file (a PIC file) from the 1-2-3 worksheet?
10. How do you delete a graph?
***11.** How many different graphs can be generated by a given worksheet?
12. What are the choices available under Options in the Graph menu?
13. How many types of crosshatching can you have?
14. How many symbols are available for line graphs?
15. What are data labels? What are their applications?
16. What is the function of the Reset command in the Graph menu?
17. How do you get PrintGraph started?
18. How do you exit the PrintGraph program?
19. When you exit PrintGraph, do you return to DOS or to the 1-2-3 Access System?
20. What is the purpose of Image-Select in the main menu of PrintGraph?
***21.** Can you see your graph on the monitor using the PrintGraph program? If yes, how?
22. What are the options under the Settings menu?
***23.** How do you modify a graph's parameters in the PrintGraph program?
24. What is the purpose of the Align command in the main menu?
25. What is the purpose of Save and Reset in the Settings menu?

HANDS-ON EXPERIENCE

1. The following are oil production figures for Exatec Oil Company:

1989	200,000 barrels
1990	250,000 barrels
1991	350,000 barrels
1992	400,000 barrels
1993	450,000 barrels
1994	400,000 barrels
1995	475,000 barrels

   Design and print a line graph, a bar graph, and a pie chart for this data.

2. Using the sample data in Figure 8–15, generate and print a bar, stacked-bar, and a line graph.
3. Retrieve CHAPT7 and perform the following tasks:
   a. Generate a line graph of the total scores of all the students. Name the graph G1, save it as G1, and save the worksheet as CHAPT8.
   b. Generate a bar graph for three tests. This graph should compare the total scores of three tests. Name this graph G2 and save it as G2. Save the worksheet as CHAPT8.
   c. Generate a stacked-bar graph for three test scores for six selected students. Name this graph G3, save it as G3, and save the worksheet as CHAPT8.
   d. Generate a pie chart comparing the total scores of each test. Name the graph G4, save it as G4, and save the worksheet as CHAPT8.
   e. Generate a pie chart with crosshatching to differentiate the pieces.
   f. Explode the pie chart.

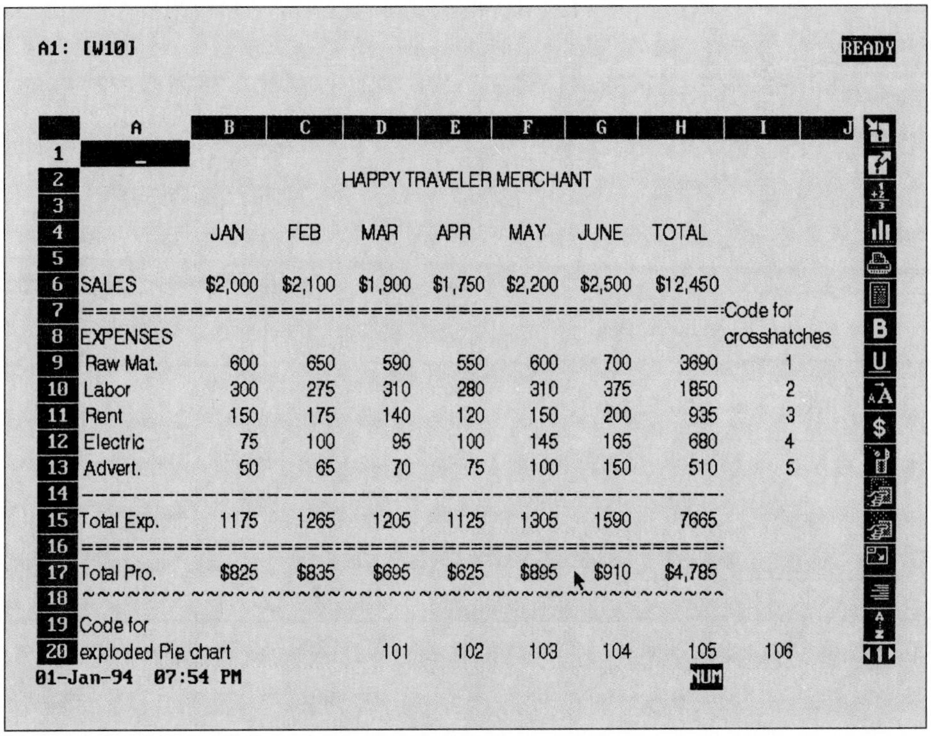
A1: [W10] READY

	A	B	C	D	E	F	G	H	I
1									
2				HAPPY TRAVELER MERCHANT					
3									
4		JAN	FEB	MAR	APR	MAY	JUNE	TOTAL	
5									
6	SALES	$2,000	$2,100	$1,900	$1,750	$2,200	$2,500	$12,450	
7	========	========	========	========	========	========	========	========:	Code for
8	EXPENSES								crosshatches
9	Raw Mat.	600	650	590	550	600	700	3690	1
10	Labor	300	275	310	280	310	375	1850	2
11	Rent	150	175	140	120	150	200	935	3
12	Electric	75	100	95	100	145	165	680	4
13	Advert.	50	65	70	75	100	150	510	5
14	--------	--------	--------	--------	--------	--------	--------	--------.	
15	Total Exp.	1175	1265	1205	1125	1305	1590	7665	
16	========	========	========	========	========	========	========	========:	
17	Total Pro.	$825	$835	$695	$625	$895	$910	$4,785	
18	~~~~~~~~	~~~~~~~~	~~~~~~~~	~~~~~~~~	~~~~~~~~	~~~~~~~~	~~~~~~~~	~~~~~~~~	
19	Code for								
20	exploded Pie chart			101	102	103	104	105	106

01-Jan-94 07:54 PM NUM

Figure 8–15
Income statement for Happy Traveler Merchant.

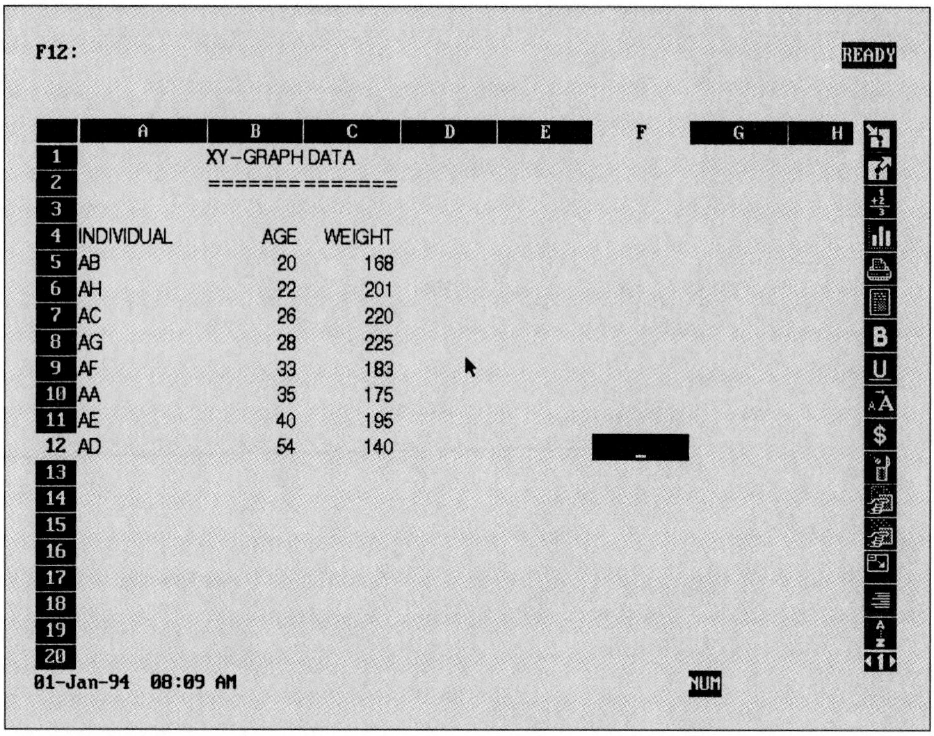

Figure 8–16
A sample worksheet.

g. Generate a line graph from the total scores of each student with a heading and subheading (any title); label both the x- and y-axes.

h. Name this graph G5, save it as G5, and save the final worksheet as CHAPT8.

4. Using the worksheet presented in Figure 8–16, plot an XY graph.

KEY TERMS

Bar graph
Crosshatch
Explode
HLCO graph
Legend
Line graph
Mixed graph
Pie chart
PrintGraph
Stacked-bar graph
XY graph

KEY COMMANDS

Graph
Name
Options
Reset
Save
Type (Line, Bar, XY, Stacked-Bar, Pie, HLCO, and Mixed)
View

MISCONCEPTIONS AND SOLUTIONS

Misconception When you select /Graph Name Delete, 1-2-3 immediately erases the present graph settings and automatically returns you to the Graph menu. There is no confirmation step.

Solution Before you use this command, make sure this is what you want to do.

Misconception Sometimes your graph does not show on the screen.

Solution Use /Graph Options Format Graph Neither. You may have accidentally formatted your graph to display neither lines nor symbols.

Misconception In a PrintGraph session, you have changed some of the default settings and you want to use these settings later, but PrintGraph will not save these settings automatically.

Solution Use the Settings Save command to save the current settings to the PGRAPH.CNF file before you exit the PrintGraph session.

ARE YOU READY TO MOVE ON?

Multiple Choice

1. The most suitable graph for time series analysis is a(n)
   a. pie chart
   b. exploded pie chart
   c. any graph that uses symbols
   d. line graph
   e. none of the above
2. 1-2-3 Release 2.4 can generate
   a. 4 types of graphs
   b. 5 types of graphs
   c. 7 types of graphs
   d. 10 types of graphs
   e. none of the above
3. Not counting the X range, some 1-2-3 graphs can use up to
   a. 10 data ranges
   b. 6 data ranges
   c. 5 data ranges
   d. 4 data ranges
   e. none of the above
4. A graph name can be up to
   a. 10 characters long
   b. 12 characters long
   c. 14 characters long
   d. 15 characters long
   e. 16 characters long
5. The X range is used in
   a. pie charts
   b. exploded pie charts
   c. graphs that use symbols
   d. line graphs
   e. all graphs
6. To explode a segment from a pie chart, you must
   a. add 100 to the crosshatching code
   b. choose Explode from the Options menu
   c. choose Exploded-Pie from the Type menu
   d. both b and c
   e. none of the above
7. To generate crosshatching in a pie chart, the codes must be in the
   a. X range
   b. D range

c. B range
d. any of the above
e. crosshatch codes are not necessary

8. To generate crosshatching in a bar chart, the codes must be in the
   a. X range
   b. D range
   c. B range
   d. any of the above
   e. crosshatch codes are not necessary

9. To generate a hard copy of your graph on a plotter or a graphics printer, you must
   a. in your worksheet, press F10 in the READY mode
   b. save your graph with the /Graph Save command
   c. exit 1-2-3 and select the PrintGraph utility or WYSIWYG
   d. both b and c
   e. use the /Print Printer command

10. Examine the graph of break-even analysis for the RLG Company in Figure 8–17. The straight line at $20 denotes fixed costs. This line was most likely created by
    a. choosing Lines from the Options Format menu in Graph mode
    b. choosing Grid from the Options menu in Graph mode
    c. setting the crosshatch code to 20
    d. drawing the line by hand
    e. none of the above

True/False

1. One of the major uses of a line graph is to show changes in data over time.
2. Bar graphs emphasize differences in data items.
3. A pie chart uses all six data ranges in one graph.

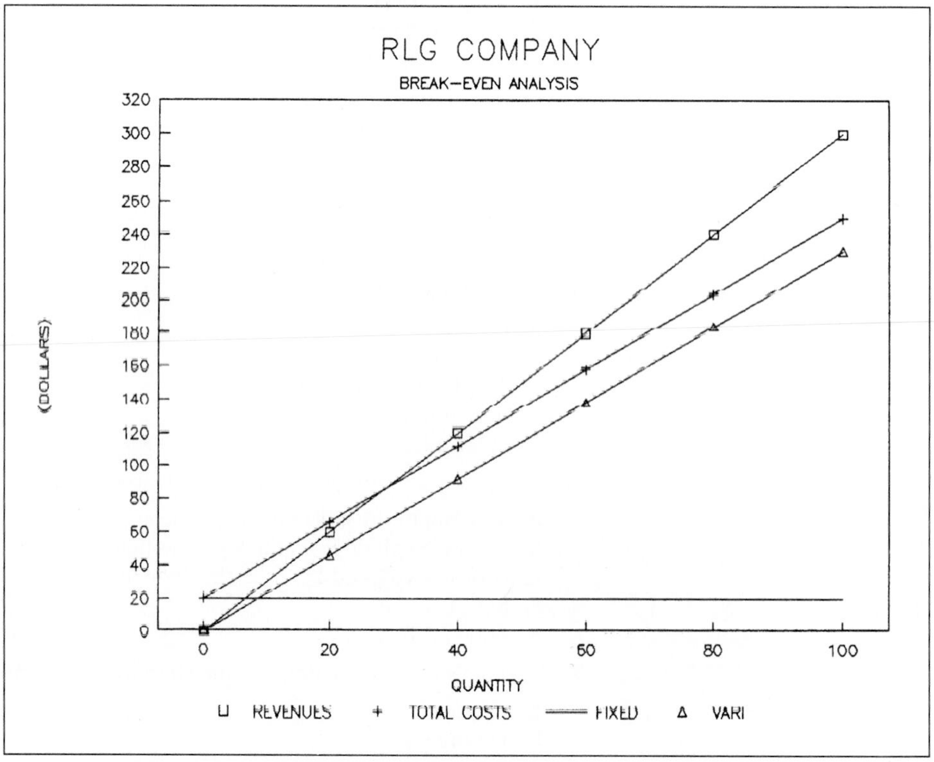

Figure 8–17
Sample graph.

4. One worksheet can generate only one graph.
5. Only one segment of a pie chart can be exploded.
6. 1-2-3 can generate up to eight different crosshatch patterns.
7. You can have up to two title lines in a graph.
8. There are two types of grids available in line graphs.
9. To draw a line graph, you can use either lines or symbols but not both.
10. In an XY graph, one of the data ranges must be the X range.

ANSWERS

Multiple Choice		True/False	
1.	d	1.	T
2.	c	2.	T
3.	b	3.	F
4.	d	4.	F
5.	e	5.	F
6.	a	6.	T
7.	c	7.	T
8.	e	8.	T
9.	d	9.	F
10.	a	10.	T

1-2-3 and WYSIWYG

9

9–1 INTRODUCTION

This chapter provides comprehensive coverage of the WYSIWYG add-in program included in 1-2-3 Release 2.4. Using this program, you can create pleasant-looking reports with a variety of formats. Most of the commonly used commands are described.

9–2 WHAT IS WYSIWYG?

WYSIWYG stands for what you see is what you get: what you see on the computer screen is exactly what you get on your printout. It is also the name of a 1-2-3 spreadsheet publishing add-in program that is included in Release 2.4. The WYSIWYG program formats and prints the output generated by 1-2-3 in presentation-quality form.

The WYSIWYG program enables you to boldface, underline, double underline, draw lines, draw boxes, and most important of all, integrate graphs in the same printout with your worksheet data. With WYSIWYG you can use up to eight fonts with any printer. A **font** is a typeface in a particular point size, for example, Bitstream Swiss 24 point. A point is a unit of measurement that determines the height of a character.

To see the power of WYSIWYG, compare Figures 9–1 and 9–2. (The spreadsheet is displayed in Figure 9–3.) The first figure was generated by 1-2-3's Print command and the second figure was generated by WYSIWYG. To create Figure 9–2, we got WYSIWYG started and did the following:

- :Format, Font, 2, A1..B1, Enter
- :Format, Shade, Dark, A2..B2, Enter
- :Format, Font, 1, B4..E4, Enter
- :Format, Font, 2, A6..A6, Enter
- :Format, Font, 2, A12..A12, Enter
- :Format, Lines, Outline, B6..E19, Enter
- :Graph, Add, Current, B21..E34, Enter, Quit
- :Print, Range, Set, A1..E34, Enter, Go

This chapter describes these features for producing great looking reports. Note that in this example we first created a bar graph, then integrated it into the printout.

Figure 9–1
Report directly printed by 1-2-3's Print command.

OCEAN CITY TOURIST ATTRACTION
(1993 Figures in thousands of dollars)

	Spring	Summer	Fall	Winter
Current Assets				
Cash	$36,249	$42,495	$58,761	$72,300
Accounts Receivable	26,700	23,821	22,545	22,768
	-------	-------	-------	-------
Total Current Assets	62,949	66,316	81,306	95,068
Fixed Assets				
Property, and Plant				
Land	49,121	48,700	45,600	40,410
Building	82,212	82,212	79,100	78,275
Gross P, and P	131,333	130,912	124,700	118,685
Accumulated Depreciation	(48,814)	(37,600)	(36,945)	(29,725)
	-------	-------	-------	-------
Net P, and P	82,519	93,312	87,755	88,960

Figure 9–2
Report generated by WYSIWYG.

OCEAN CITY TOURIST ATTRACTION
(1992 Figures in thousands of dollars)

	Spring	Summer	Fall	Winter
Current Assets				
Cash	$36,249	$42,495	$58,761	$72,300
Accounts Receivable	26,700	23,821	22,545	22,768
Total Current Assets	62,949	66,316	81,306	95,068
Fixed Assets				
Property, and Plant				
Land	49,121	48,700	45,600	40,410
Building	82,212	82,212	79,100	78,275
Gross P, and P	131,333	130,912	124,700	118,685
Accumulated Depreciation	(48,814)	(37,600)	(36,945)	(29,725)
Net P, and P	82,519	93,312	87,755	88,960

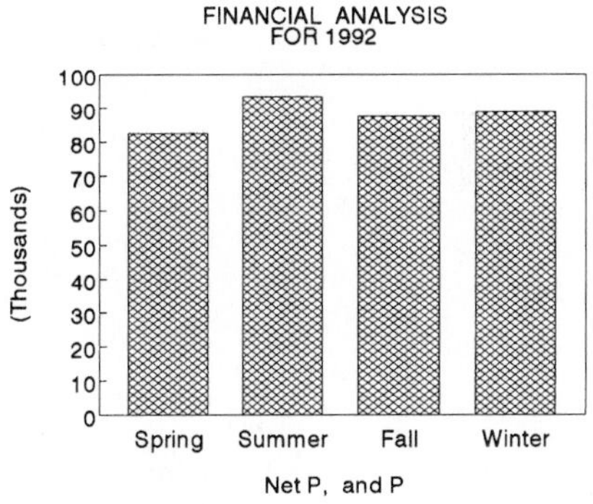

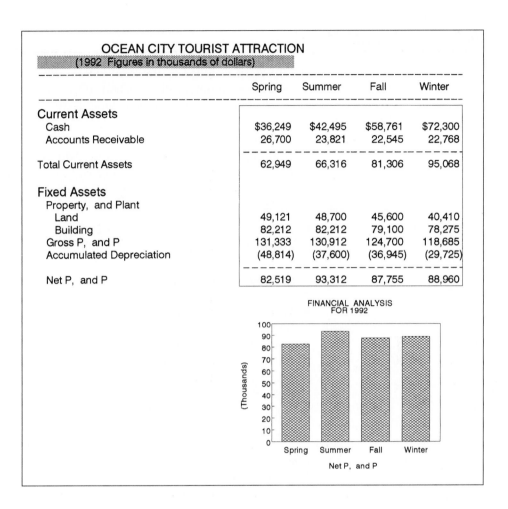

Figure 9–3
Sample worksheet with WYSIWYG main menu displayed.

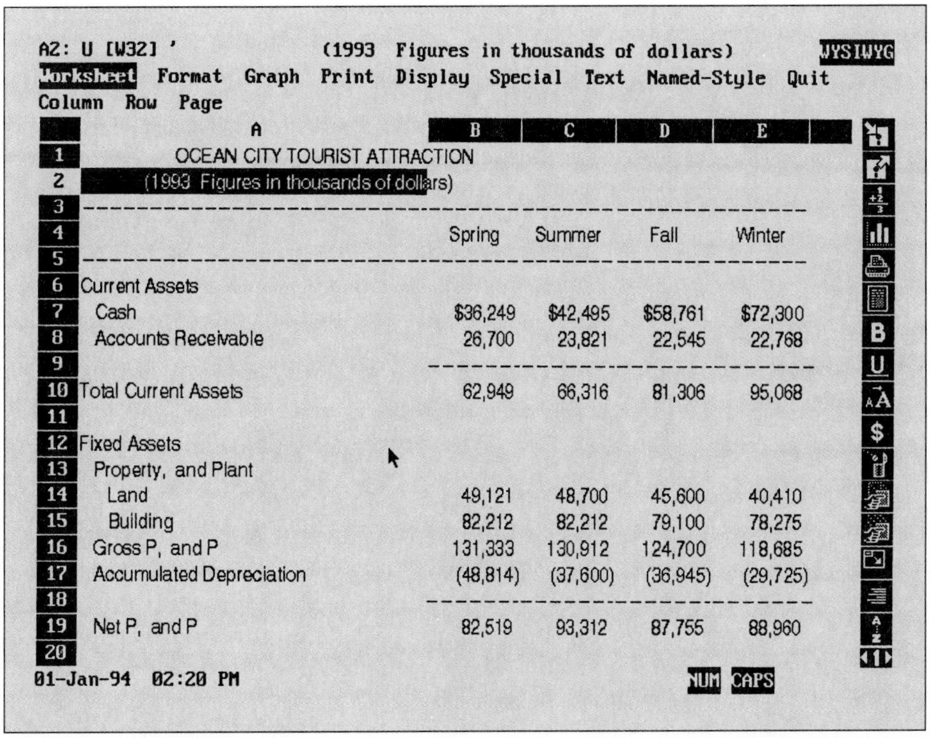

9–3 GETTING STARTED

WYSIWYG is installed at the same time 1-2-3 is installed. In 1-2-3 Release 2.4, WYSIWYG is automatically attached to the worksheet. If for any reason it is not attached after installation, follow these steps:

- Get 1-2-3 started.
- From the main menu select Add-In. Add-in programs are additional software that can be added to the current software in order to improve its features. WYSIWYG is one example of such a program.
- From this menu select Attach.
- From the Attach menu select WYSIWYG.ADN and press Enter. You will be prompted with:

```
No-Key    8    9    10
```

- Make a selection. For example, if you select 10, later you can invoke the WYSIWYG menu by pressing Alt+F10. If you select No-Key, you will not be able to invoke WYSIWYG by pressing Alt and one of the function keys. In this case you must activate WYSIWYG by pressing the : key (colon). This is what we did.
- Press Q (for Quit) to exit this menu. This will take you back to WYSIWYG's READY mode. Now the WYSIWYG program is residing in RAM. You can invoke it by pressing : (colon).

WYSIWYG occupies a considerable amount of RAM memory. Therefore, when you no longer need the program, detach it from RAM by selecting Detach from the Add-In menu.

To automate the attaching processes, use these commands:

/Worksheet Global Default Other Add-In Set

You can have up to eight add-ins attached to 1-2-3 at a time. Select 1, then specify WYSIWYG.ADN as your add-in to attach automatically. To finalize this you must also use the /Worksheet Global Default Update command to save the new add-in settings.

After WYSIWYG is attached, press the : (colon) to get into its main menu. You can also invoke the menu by using a mouse. If you move the mouse cursor to the control panel and press the right mouse button, each press of the right mouse button alternatively activates either the 1-2-3 or WYSIWYG menu. Similar to 1-2-3, WYSIWYG includes three distinct areas: the worksheet area, the control panel, and the status line. Figure 9–3 illustrates a sample worksheet. Depending on the type of font you select, the worksheet on your computer may be displayed slightly differently.

When the WYSIWYG menu is activated, as usual the control panel includes three lines. The first line shows the type of font (if used) and the format of the cell, for example, boldface, underline, or shading. The second line displays the WYSIWYG main menu. If the main menu is not displayed, only one line appears in the control panel. The line tells you about the type of font and the present position (cell reference) of the cursor. At the upper right of the control panel are the mode indicators of WYSIWYG. At the bottom of the screen the status line displays valuable information such as CAPS, END, SCROLL, or NUM as in Figure 9–3.

For different data entry purposes, you may want to exit the WYSIWYG menu by pressing the Esc key, for example.

9–4 HOW 1-2-3 AND WYSIWYG WORK TOGETHER

The 1-2-3 and WYSIWYG programs work in harmony. This means that as long as WYSIWYG is attached, saving your 1-2-3 files automatically saves the WYSIWYG formatting. All the formatting done to a worksheet becomes part of the worksheet file. However, these formatting features are stored in *another file* with the .FMT extension. Don't worry though, the next time you retrieve a spreadsheet that has been formatted with WYSIWYG, 1-2-3 will "remember" to format the spreadsheet using settings from the corresponding .FMT file.

Whatever changes are made to the worksheet in 1-2-3 are reflected in WYSIWYG. For example, if you erase a cell or change its format, the changes are automatic and they are reflected in WYSIWYG.

To maintain all of your formatting features make sure that the WYSIWYG add-in is attached. Also make sure to save your work in 1-2-3 by using the /File Save command. If you forget to save your worksheet, all your changes will be lost.

Remember that any formatting you perform in 1-2-3 carries over to WYSIWYG. For example, a cell formatted as Comma option with four decimal places is displayed as such in WYSIWYG. However, the changes made through WYSIWYG do not modify the worksheet. All the formatting done through WYSIWYG is saved in a file with the same name as the original file but with the extension FMT. For example, file FIRST will be saved as FIRST.WK1 in 1-2-3 and FIRST.FMT in WYSIWYG.

WYSIWYG allows you to adjust column widths and row heights more finely than 1-2-3. For example, a column width can be set to 8.2 or 14.57 characters. Column width and row height adjustments can be done by using the :Worksheet Column command. We will talk about worksheet commands in detail later. In WYSIWYG one character width is equal to the width of a number such as 1, 2, or 9 formatted in Font 1.

Row heights are set to Auto, meaning that WYSIWYG adjusts the height of a row automatically. This is done to accommodate the largest font in a given row. Row heights are measured in points. By using the :Worksheet Row Set-Height command you can change the automatic feature to your own format.

9–5 A QUICK REVIEW OF THE WYSIWYG COMMAND MENU

The main menu of WYSIWYG includes nine options:

Worksheet	Sets column widths, row heights, and page breaks.
Format	Changes the format of a cell or a range, including boldfacing, underlining, shading, and drawing lines.
Graph	Changes graph settings and adds or removes graphs to and from the worksheet.
Print	Prints the worksheet and specifies print settings.
Display	Changes the display mode and enlarges and reduces the worksheet display.
Special	Copies, moves, imports, and exports formats from one worksheet to another worksheet.
Text	Performs editing, aligning, and reformatting tasks on a text range.

Named-Style	Defines a named style, which is a collection of WYSIWYG formats taken from a single cell. (The format of a cell includes all the attributes assigned to it with Format commands. You can apply a named style to a range in a worksheet. Every worksheet can include up to eight named styles.)
Quit	Returns to READY mode.

These commands are discussed in detail throughout the chapter.

9–6 DEFINING A RANGE IN WYSIWYG

Defining a range in WYSIWYG is similar to the same task in 1-2-3. Use any of the following procedures:

- Type the range address, for example, *A1..A10.*
- Use a range name, for example, ASSET or LIABILITY. You can also press F3 then choose the name from a list (if you have any).
- Highlight the range.
- Use the mouse to highlight the range.

To format a range, you can either issue the command first, then specify the range, or vice versa. Each method has its own application. For example, defining the range first then issuing the command is helpful if a given range requires several formatting features. To specify a range before issuing the command, follow these steps:

1. Put the cursor in the upper left corner of the range.
2. Press the F4 function key. This anchors the cellpointer. At this point you will see POINT as the mode indicator.
3. Highlight the range by using the arrow keys.
4. Press Enter.
5. Issue your desired command, for example, :Format Shade.

Moving the cursor to another area or pressing the Esc key will "deselect" the selected range.

9–7 FORMATTING

9–7–1 Format Lines Command

The :Format lines command lets you generate horizontal and vertical lines, draw boxes around cells, and create outlines around ranges. Each cell on your worksheet can have a line along any of its four edges. When you invoke the :Format lines command, the following options are presented:

```
Outline  Left  Right  Top  Bottom  All  Double  Wide  Clear  Shadow
```

The Outline option draws an outline around a range. The Left option draws a line at the left side of each cell in a range. The Right option draws a line at the right side of each cell in a range. The Top option draws a line at the top of each cell in a range. The Bottom option draws a line at the bottom of each cell in a range. The All option draws a box around each cell in a range. The Double option draws double lines along the edges of each cell in a range or around the edge of a range. The Wide option draws wide horizontal or vertical lines along the edges of each cell in a range or around the edge of a range. The Clear option removes all the lines (you must specify the desired range). The Shadow option adds a drop shadow to a range or removes a drop shadow from a range.

You can choose any of these options and then specify the range. To make this clearer, consider Figures 9–4 and 9–5. Figure 9–5 was created as follows:

Figure 9–4
Sample worksheet.

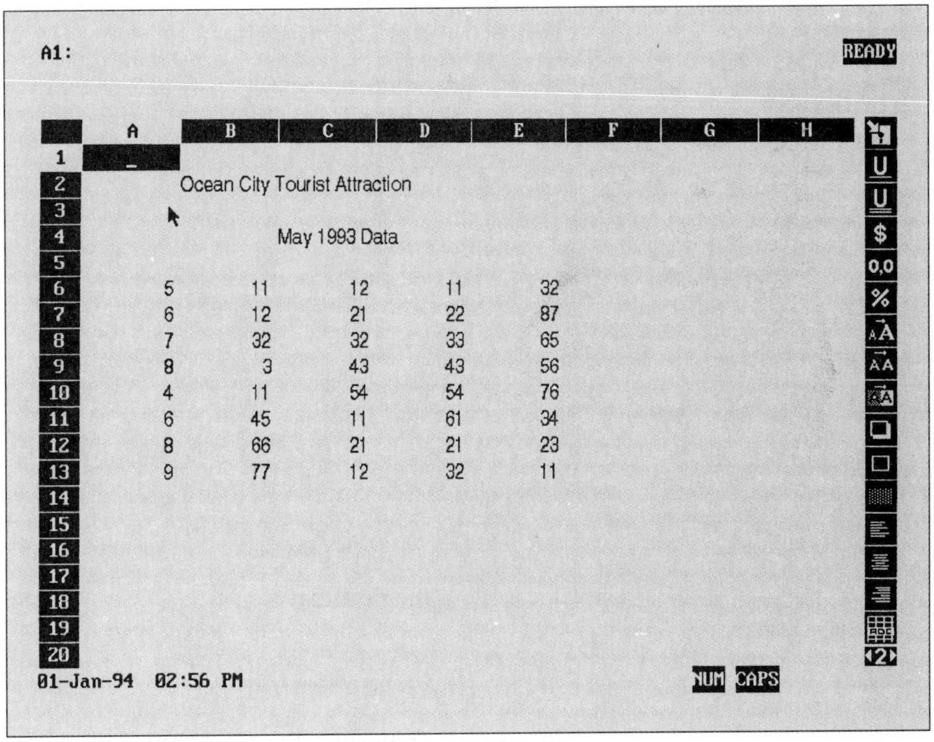

Figure 9–5
Example of a worksheet with outlines, lines, and boxes.

Ocean City Tourist Attraction

May 1993 Data

5	11	12	11	32
6	12	21	22	87
7	32	32	33	65
8	3	43	43	56
4	11	54	54	76
6	45	11	61	34
8	66	21	21	23
9	77	12	32	11

- Start WYSIWYG (if it is not already started)
- :Format, Lines, Outlines, B2..D2, Enter
- :Format, Lines, Bottom, A4..F4, Enter
- :Format, Lines, All, A6..E13, Enter
- :Print, Range, Set, Al..F13, Enter, Go

If you change your mind, selecting :Format Lines Clear allows you to remove the lines from your worksheet. Also see Table 9–3 at the end of the chapter for SmartIcons for enhancing the 1-2-3 output.

9–7–2 Format Shade Command

The :Format Shade command allows three types of shading: light, dark, and solid black. Shades help to emphasize the data on the worksheet. If you invoke the :Format Shade command, you see:

```
Light      Dark      Solid      Clear
```

Say that in the previous example you decide to put the title in dark shading, the first column in light, and the last column in solid. Do the following:

- Get WYSIWYG started and load the previous figure (Figure 9–5).
- :Format, Shade, Dark, B2..D2, Enter
- :Format, Shade, Light, A6..A13, Enter
- :Format, Shade, Solid, F6..F13, Enter
- :Print, Range, Set, A1..F13, Enter, Go

Figure 9–6 is the result.

9–7–3 Format Underline Command

The :Format Underline command allows three types of underlining: single, double, and wide. Single underlining applies only to data contained in the cell that

Figure 9–6
Example of dark, light, and solid shading.

Ocean City Tourist Attraction

May 1993 Data

5	11	12	11	32	
6	12	21	22	87	
7	32	32	33	65	
8	3	43	43	56	
4	11	54	54	76	
6	45	11	61	34	
8	66	21	21	23	
9	77	12	32	11	

Figure 9–7
Example of single and double underlining.

Ocean City Tourist Attraction

May 1993 Data

5	11	12	11	32
6	12	21	22	87
7	32	32	33	65
8	3	43	43	56
4	11	54	54	76
6	45	11	61	34
8	66	21	21	23
9	77	12	32	11

you specify and appears only if there is data in the cell. Double underlining results in a double bar at the base of the cell. It extends across the entire cell width regardless of whether that cell has data in it or not. We used the sample worksheet in Figure 9–4 to create Figure 9–7 as follows:

- :Format, Underline, Single, A6..E6, Enter
- :Format, Underline, Double, A13..E13, Enter
- :Format, Underline, Wide, A10..E10, Enter
- :Print, Range, Set, A1..F13, Enter, Go

9–7–4 Formatting Sequences

The :Format command enables you to format a cell or a range. To format individual characters within a cell or a range, you have to use **formatting sequences.** By means of formatting sequences you can boldface, italicize, make subscripts, and so forth (see Table 9–1). To format a character within a cell, follow these steps:

1. Press Ctrl+A to invoke the attribute. A solid triangle symbol appears.
2. Type in the one-character or two-character code for the attribute (see Table 9–1), for example, type *b.* Remember to type the code exactly as listed in Table 9–1. Uppercase and lowercase are considered different.
3. Type in the character(s) or words that you want to format.
4. Press Ctrl+N to end the formatting sequences. At this time an upside down solid triangle appears. This means you have completed formatting.

You can also specify multiple attributes by following these steps:

1. Press Ctrl+A and the first attribute code followed by Ctrl+A and the second code, and so forth. Then type the word or character(s) to be formatted.
2. To end the process, press Ctrl+A or Ctrl+N.

If you decide to conceal all formatting sequences, press Ctrl+N. To cancel one of the attributes, press Ctrl+E followed by the attribute code.

Table 9–1
Character Codes for Attributes

Code	Description
b	Bold
i	Italic
u	Superscript
d	Subscript
o	Outline
f	Flashing
x	Flip x-axis
y	Flip y-axis
1_	Single underline
2_	Double underline
3_	Wide underline
4_	Box around characters
5_	Strike through characters
1c	Default color
2c	Red
3c	Green
4c	Dark Blue
5c	Cyan
6c	Yellow
7c	Magenta
8c	Reverse colors
1F	Font 1
2F	Font 2
3F	Font 3
4F	Font 4
5F	Font 5
6F	Font 6
7F	Font 7
8F	Font 8

9–8 WYSIWYG TEXT COMMANDS

By use of the :Text command 1-2-3 becomes a limited word processor. When you invoke the :Text command, the following options are displayed:

```
Edit    Align    Reformat    Set    Clear
```

The Edit command enters and edits labels in a text range directly in a worksheet. When you enter labels in a text range, the formatting description appears in the control panel. The mode indicator indicates TEXT (see Figure 9–8). If you enter numbers with :Text Edit, 1-2-3 enters the numbers as labels. Remember that when you issue the :Text Edit command, you must first specify text range. As an example we issued :Text Edit, then specified A10..C15 as the text range. As you can see in Figure 9–8, 1-2-3 indicates that A10 is row 1. It presents the column as column 0 and is left aligned. You will see A10 row: 1 Col: 0 Left-Aligned on the control panel.

When you are typing and reach the end of the range, the words wrap to the next line. Notice that while you are working with the Text command, the mode indicator displays TEXT. To start a new paragraph (1) press Enter twice to leave a blank line between paragraphs, (2) press Ctrl+Enter to insert a paragraph symbol, or (3) press Enter once and press the space bar several times at the beginning of the paragraph. To skip the EDIT mode, press Esc.

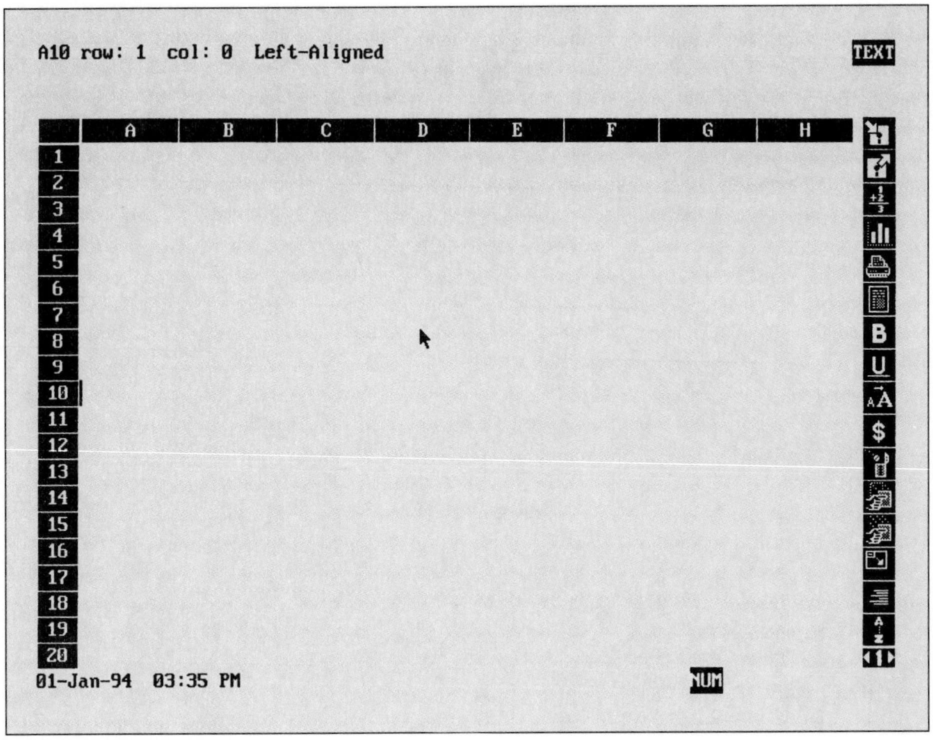

Figure 9–8
Example of :Text Edit.

The Align option allows you to place text left, right, center, or even aligned. When you select this option, and others, 1-2-3 requests a range. Specify the range, then press Enter.

The Reformat option rearranges a column of labels so the labels fit within a text range. Note that /Worksheet Global Protection Disable must be used.

The Set command specifies a text range so you can use the Text commands with labels in that range.

The Clear option removes the {Text} attribute from cells in the range. This means that after using :Text Clear, the formatting description {Text} no longer appears in the control panel when the cellpointer is in a text range. Table 9–2 provides a summary of the keys used with the :Text Edit command.

To get out of the TEXT mode, press Esc.

9–9 PRINT COMMAND

The Print command allows you to control the printing process. When you invoke the Print command from the WYSIWYG main menu, the following options are displayed:

```
Go  File  Background  Range  Configuration  Settings  Layout  Preview  Info  Quit
```

A brief description of each option follows.

Go prints the specified range. File sends the output to a file on disk. Background selects an encoded file as the print destination. 1-2-3 prints as you continue to work. Range specifies or clears the print range. Configuration specifies printer, interface, and printer options. Settings controls page numbers and the appearance of a report.

Table 9–2
Cursor Movement and Editing Features in :Text Edit Mode

Key	Function
↑ (up arrow)	Moves to character above.
↓ (down arrow)	Moves to character below.
→ (right arrow)	Moves one character to right.
← (left arrow)	Moves one character to left.
Ctrl+←	Moves to beginning of preceding word.
Ctrl+→	Moves to end of next word.
PgDn	Moves to next screen.
PgUp	Moves to preceding screen.
Home	Moves to beginning of line.
Home, Home	Moves to beginning of paragraph.
End	Moves to end of line.
End, End	Moves to end of paragraph.
Backspace	Deletes character to left of cursor.
Del	Deletes character to right of cursor.
Ins	Toggles between INSERT mode (the default) and TYPEOVER mode.
Enter	Begins a new line.
Ctrl+Enter	Begins a new paragraph.
F3	Displays a format menu.
Esc	Returns to READY mode.

The Settings option leads to these choices:

```
Begin   End   Start-Number   Copies   Wait   Grid   Frame   Reset   Quit
```

The Begin option starts printing on page 1 and ends printing on page 9,999. The End option allows you to specify a number between 1 and 9,999. The Start-Number option allows you to specify the page number for the first page. The Copies option allows you to request between 1 and 99 copies. The Wait option waits for paper before printing each page. The Grid option specifies whether to print grid lines in the print range. The Frame option specifies whether to print the worksheet frame with the print range. The Reset option restores the default print settings. The Quit option exits the Print menu.

To print wide worksheets use the :Print Configuration Orientation command and select Landscape mode, which prints your worksheet sideways. The default is Portrait mode. Wide worksheets can also be printed in a compressed manner, which allows more characters to be printed in an 80-column page.

The Layout option from the main menu controls the overall positioning and appearance of the page. The Preview option lets you preview a report before printing it. The Info option removes or displays the WYSIWYG print setting dialog box. A shortcut is pressing F6 to remove or display the WYSIWYG print settings dialog.

The :Print File command allows you to save WYSIWYG output in an encoded file on disk. Such a file receives .ENC as its extension. This feature is useful if you want to print a number of files at once. To print an encoded file you must end the 1-2-3 session and use the DOS COPY command with the /B switch. For example, if you want to print EXAMPLE.ENC using the LPT1 interface port, at the DOS prompt you must type

COPY EXAMPLE.ENC/B LPT1   Enter

9–10 CREATING THICK HORIZONTAL AND VERTICAL LINES

To highlight certain portions of a worksheet you can draw thick lines in any location. Figure 9–9 is a sample worksheet. We created Figure 9–10 as follows. For the horizontal line we used the commands :Format, Shade, Solid, B5..E5, Enter. For the vertical lines we used :Format, Shade, Solid, E5..E19, Enter. To print this worksheet we used :Print, Range, Set, A1..E19, Enter, Go. The final work is displayed in Figure 9–10.

Figure 9–9
Sample worksheet.

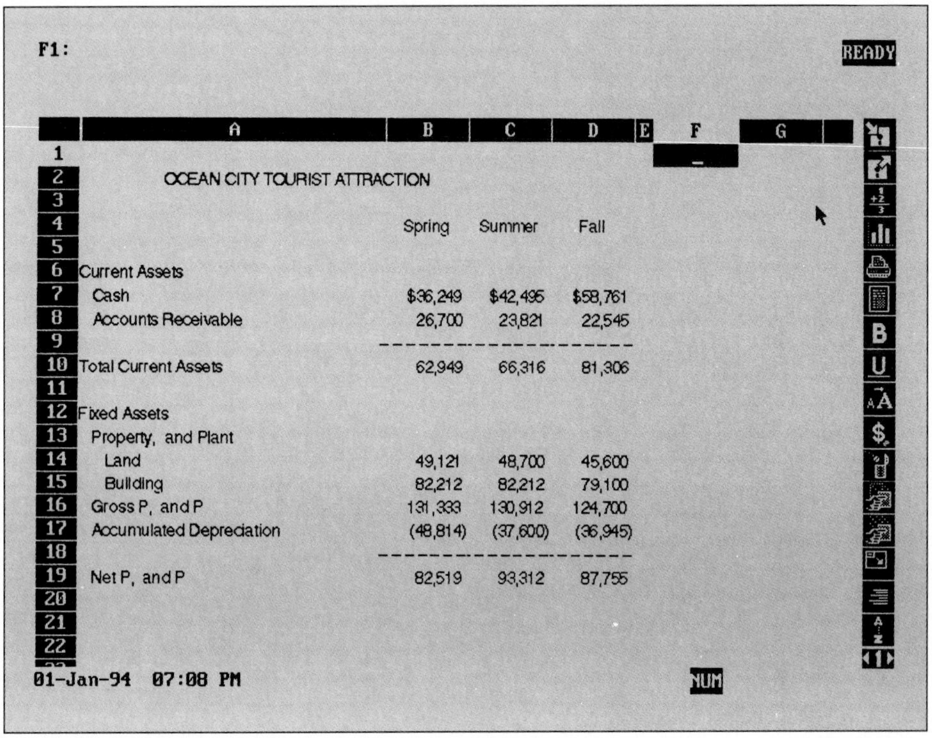

Figure 9–10
Sample worksheet with thick horizontal and vertical lines.

OCEAN CITY TOURIST ATTRACTION			
	Spring	Summer	Fall
Current Assets			
Cash	$36,249	$42,495	$58,761
Accounts Receivable	26,700	23,821	22,545
	-------	-------	-------
Total Current Assets	62,949	66,316	81,306
Fixed Assets			
Property, and Plant			
Land	49,121	48,700	45,600
Building	82,212	82,212	79,100
Gross P, and P	131,333	130,912	124,700
Accumulated Depreciation	(48,814)	(37,600)	(36,945)
	-------	-------	-------
Net P, and P	82,519	93,312	87,755

9–11 CREATING A SHADOW BOX

Shadow boxes are useful in highlighting a certain portion of a worksheet. Figure 9–11 is a sample worksheet. Figure 9–12 was created as follows:

- :Format, Lines, Outline, B3..E18, Enter (this draws a box around the specified range)

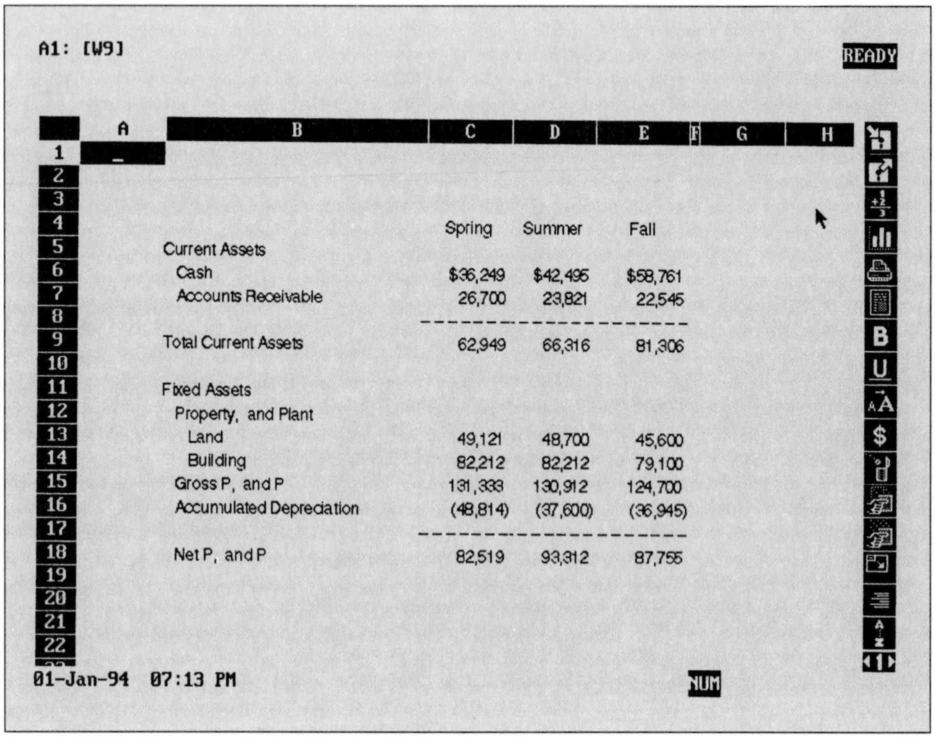

Figure 9–11
Sample worksheet.

Figure 9–12
Shadow box.

	Spring	Summer	Fall
Current Assets			
Cash	$36,249	$42,495	$58,761
Accounts Receivable	26,700	23,821	22,545
	----------	----------	----------
Total Current Assets	62,949	66,316	81,306
Fixed Assets			
Property, and Plant			
Land	49,121	48,700	45,600
Building	82,212	82,212	79,100
Gross P, and P	131,333	130,912	124,700
Accumulated Depreciation	(48,814)	(37,600)	(36,945)
	----------	----------	----------
Net P, and P	82,519	93,312	87,755

- :Format, Shade, Solid, B2..E2, Enter (this draws a solid shade in row 2 of the worksheet)
- :Format, Shade, Solid, F3..F18, Enter (this draws a solid shade in column F)

9–12 FONTS AND THE FORMAT FONT COMMAND

Recall that a font is a typeface of a particular size. A typeface is the overall design of the screen or printed characters. The size of a font is usually measured by its height in points, and a point is approximately 1/72 of an inch. Thus, a 20-point font called Triumvirate is approximately .27 of an inch.

WYSIWYG allows a combination of up to eight fonts in a given output. Figure 9–13 illustrates the available **font set.** This figure was generated by :Format Font. In addition to the choices in the font set, soft fonts can also be used. Soft fonts are fonts on diskettes that you transfer to your printer from your computer's disk drive or font cartridges that you install in your printer. These fonts can be printed by downloading the fonts to the printer or by using the printer's GRAPHICS mode. Figure 9–14 illustrates a sample worksheet for different typefaces in different point sizes.

When you invoke the :Format Font command, you receive the following options (see also Figure 9–13):

```
1  2  3  4  5  6  7  8    Replace  Default  Library  Quit
```

Options 1 through 8 apply the highlighted font to a specified range. The Replace option replaces the highlighted font in the current font set with one of the fonts that you generated or added in the Install program. When you select this option, another menu is presented (see Figure 9–15). The Default option saves the current font set as default or replaces the current font set with the default set. The

Figure 9–13
WYSIWYG font set.

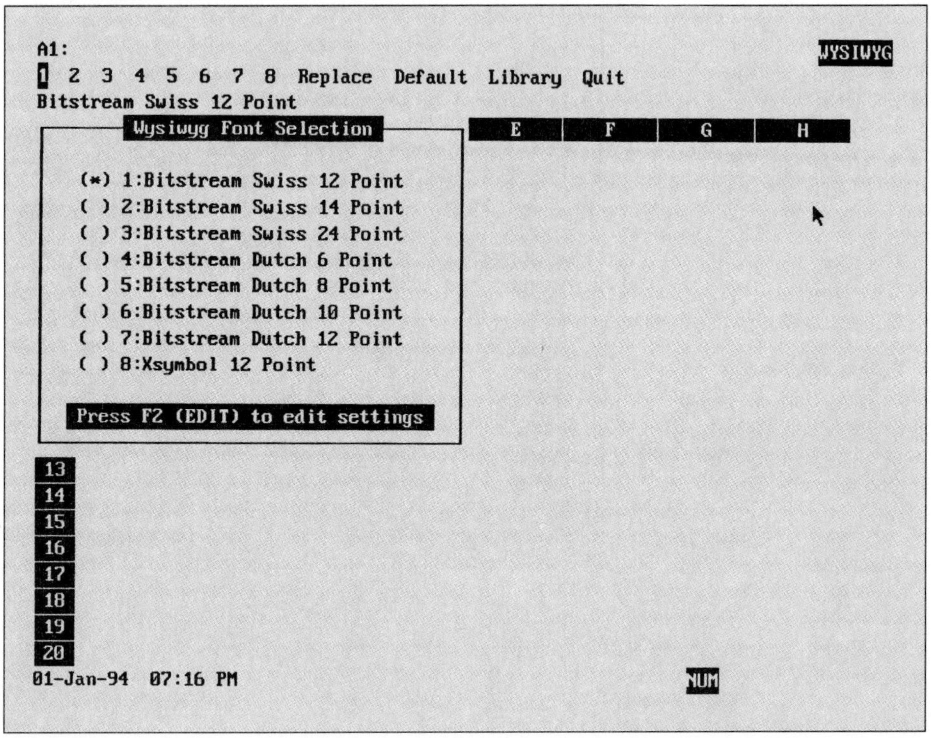

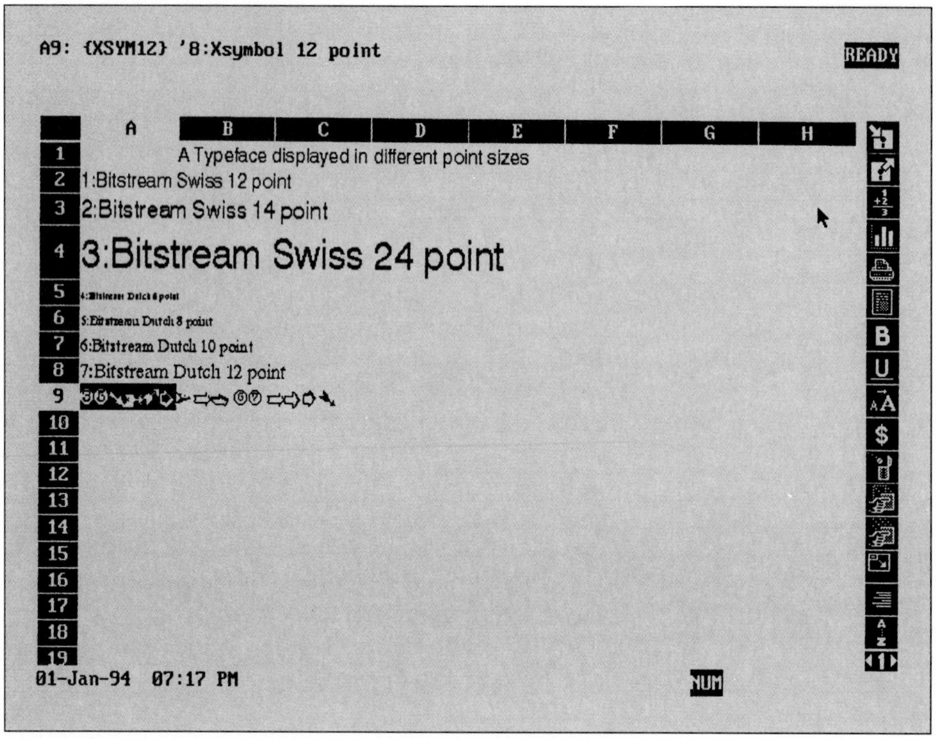

Figure 9–14
Sample worksheet with typeface in different point sizes.

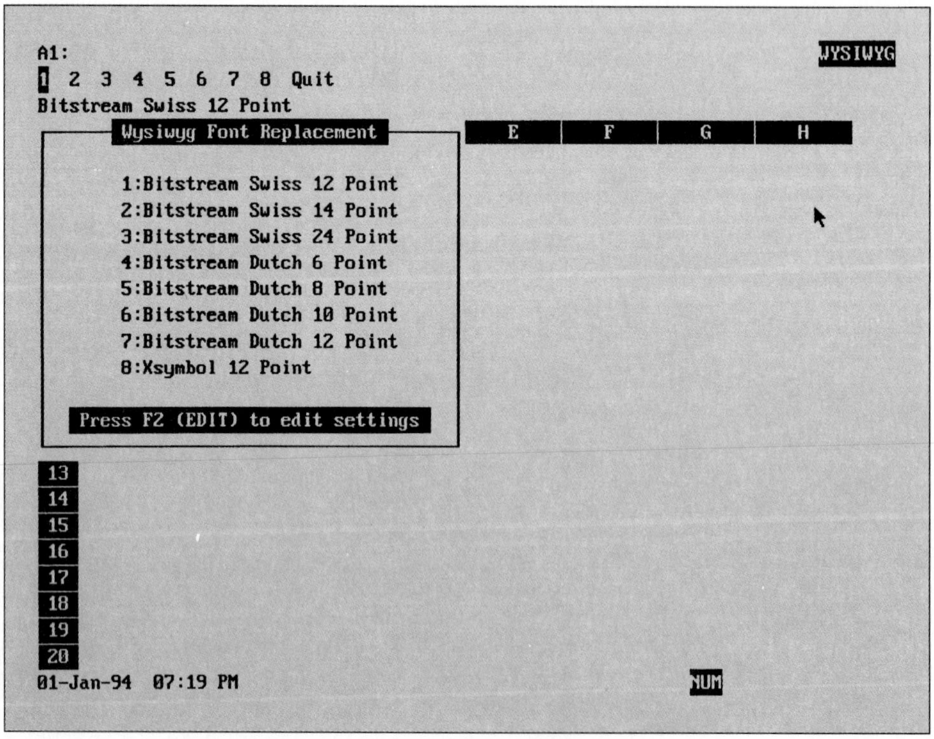

Figure 9–15
WYSIWYG additional typefaces.

Library option retrieves, saves, or erases a font set library file on disk. The font sets saved in library files have the extension .AFS.

9–13 GRAPH COMMAND

The Graph command allows you to include graphs in a worksheet. By means of this feature you can change the size of text in a graph, add white space around the graph, and place a graph alongside data.

WYSIWYG lets you print the worksheet and graphs together. You can have up to 20 graphs in the worksheet, and you can position them however you like. To export a graph from 1-2-3 to WYSIWYG, you must first save the graph in 1-2-3 by using the /Graph Save command. This generates a file with the extension .PIC. (Refer to Chapter 8 for detailed discussion of 1-2-3 graphs.) When you choose Graph from the WYSIWYG main menu, you receive the following options:

```
Add  Remove  Goto  Settings  Move  Zoom  Compute  View  Edit  Quit
```

Add	Adds a graph to the current worksheet.
Remove	Removes a graph from the current worksheet.
Goto	Moves the cell pointer to a graph.
Settings	Replaces a graph, resizes or moves a graph, turns the automatic recalculation of a graph on or off.
Move	Moves a graph to another range in the worksheet.
Zoom	Displays a full-screen view of a graph.
Compute	Recalculates and redraws a graph.
View	Views a .PIC or a .CGM file.
Edit	Allows editing of a graph.
Quit	Returns to READY mode.

9–13–1 Inserting a Graph into a Worksheet

To insert a graph into a worksheet, you must first select the range that indicates the position of the graph. WYSIWYG automatically sizes the graph to fit within the selected range. After the graph is exported to your worksheet you can view the graph in TEXT or GRAPHICS mode. Let us walk through a simple example. We want to export the graph presented in Figure 9–16 to the worksheet presented in Figure 9–17. Remember that the graph in Figure 9–16 is saved as CH9-16.PIC. Do the following:

- Get the WYSIWYG program started.
- Graph, Add, PIC, CH9-16.PIC, Enter, B19..D30, Enter, Quit

At this point if you are in the GRAPHICS mode, you will see the graph (see Figure 9–18). In TEXT mode you will not see the graph. Remember that when you specify your PIC file you must specify the drive and/or directory (if the graphics file is not in your default drive and/or directory).

9–13–2 Integrating Two Graphs into a Worksheet

We want to export the graph presented in Figure 9–19 into our previous worksheet (Figure 9–18). Do the following:

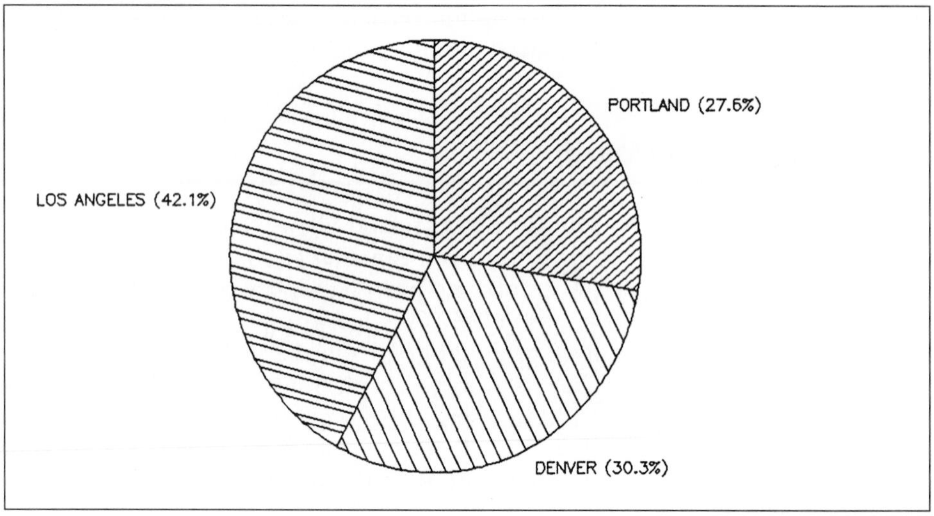

Figure 9–16
Sample graph.

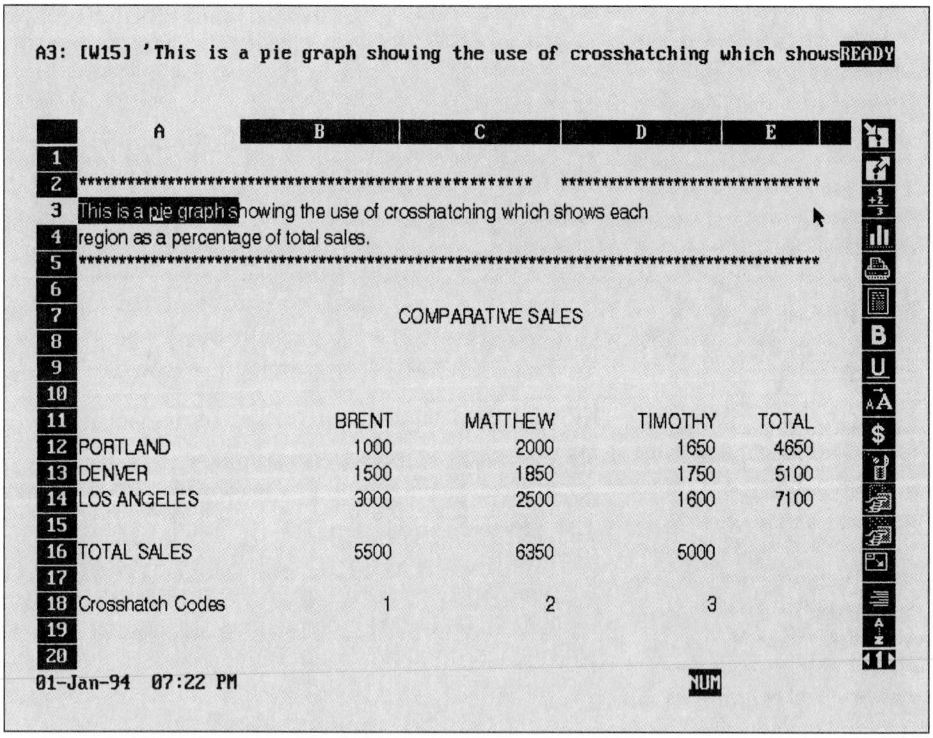

Figure 9–17
Sample worksheet.

- Get WYSIWYG started.
- Load the previous Figure 9–18 by using /File, Retrieve, CH9-18, Enter (in 1-2-3).
- Remove the previous graph from the worksheet by doing :Graph, Remove, B19..D30, Enter (now you can add the two graphs in more appropriate places).
- Add, PIC, CH9-16.PC, Enter, A20..B30, Enter
- Add, PIC, CH9-19.PIC, Enter, C20..E30, Enter, Quit

If you print this worksheet you should see something similar to Figure 9–20.

Figure 9–18
Worksheet and graph integrated.

** ********************************
This is a pie graph showing the use of crosshatching which shows each
region as a percentage of total sales.
****

COMPARATIVE SALES

	BRENT	MATTHEW	TIMOTHY	TOTAL
PORTLAND	1000	2000	1650	4650
DENVER	1500	1850	1750	5100
LOS ANGELES	3000	2500	1600	7100
TOTAL SALES	5500	6350	5000	
Crosshatch Codes	1	2	3	

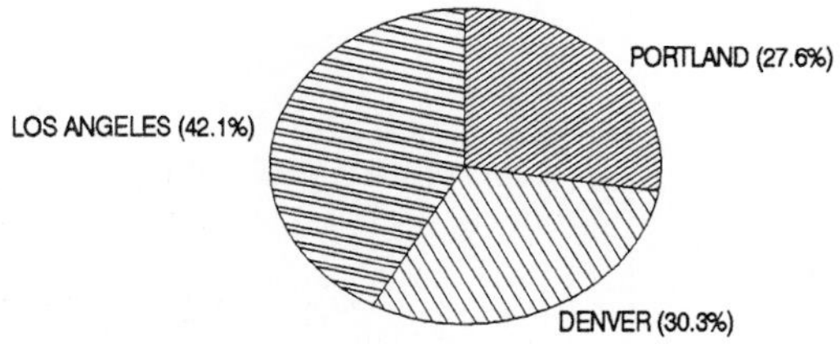

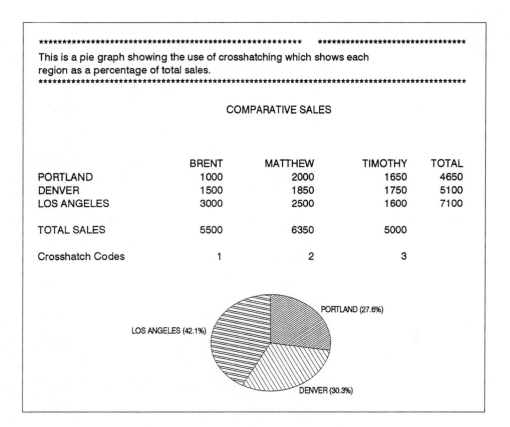

Figure 9–19
Sample graph.

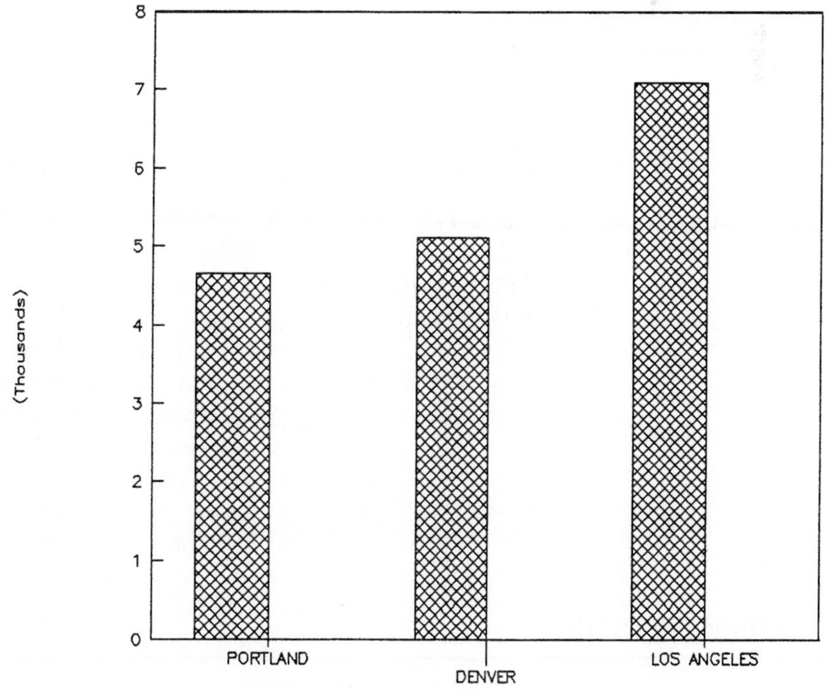

Figure 9–20
Two graphs integrated with the worksheet.

** *********************************

This is a pie graph showing the use of crosshatching which shows each region as a percentage of total sales.

****

COMPARATIVE SALES

	BRENT	MATTHEW	TIMOTHY	TOTAL
PORTLAND	1000	2000	1650	4650
DENVER	1500	1850	1750	5100
LOS ANGELES	3000	2500	1600	7100
TOTAL SALES	5500	6350	5000	
Crosshatch Codes	1	2	3	

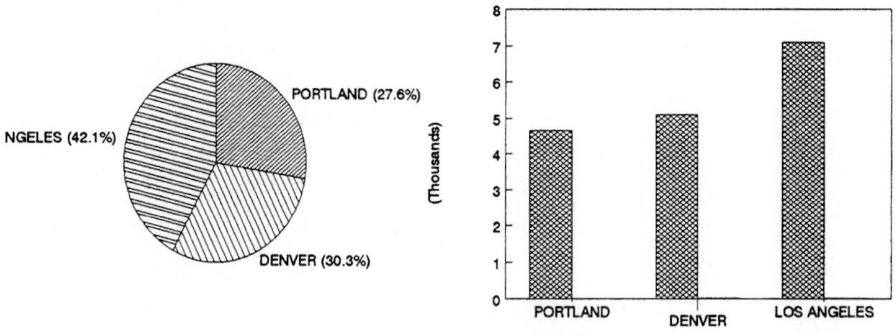

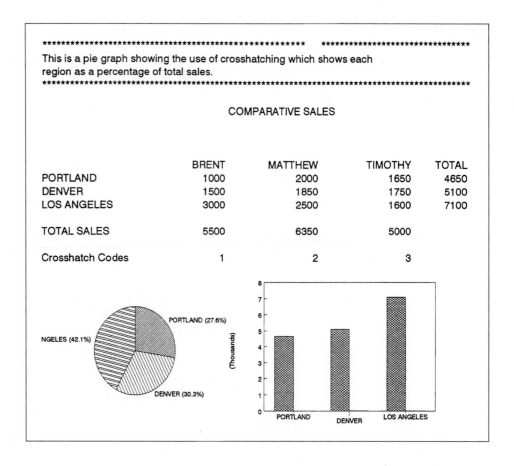

9–14 DISPLAY COLORS

If you have a color monitor and a color display card, you can use the :Display Colors command to change the colors that WYSIWYG uses. When you invoke :Display Colors, the following menu is presented:

```
Background  Text  Unprot  Cell-Pointer  Grid  Frame  Neg  Lines  Shadow  Replace  Quit
```

The Background option allows you to select the background screen color. For all these options there are eight colors from which you can choose. The Text option allows you to select the color of the text in the worksheet. Unprot specifies the color of data in unprotected ranges. The Cell-Pointer option selects the color of the cell pointer. The Grid option specifies the grid color. The Frame option specifies the color of the worksheet frame. The Neg option specifies the default color of negative numbers. The Lines option specifies the color of cell borders. The Shadow option specifies the color of drop shadows. The Replace option replaces colors in the color palette. The Quit option puts you back in the Display menu.

9–15 FORMAT COLOR

The :Format Color command allows you to view or print text and numbers in eight different colors on monitors or printers that support this feature. When you invoke :Format Color, you receive the following options:

```
Text     Background     Negative     Reverse     Quit
```

As discussed earlier, you can select any of these options for choosing different colors.

9–16 DISPLAY ZOOM

The :Display Zoom command allows you to select from a number of different worksheet font size attributes when you are working in the GRAPHICS mode. When you invoke :Display Zoom, the following options are displayed:

```
Tiny     Small     Normal     Large     Huge     Manual
```

The Tiny option reduces cells to 63 percent of their normal size. The Small option reduces cells to 87 percent of their normal size. The Normal option displays cells in their normal size. The Large option enlarges cells to 125 percent of their normal size. The Huge option enlarges cells to 150 percent of their normal size. Remember that enlarging or reducing has no effect on printouts—it only affects the presentation of the worksheet on the screen. Remember also that to see the enlarged or reduced worksheet you must be in the GRAPHICS mode. The Manual option manually enlarges or reduces the size of cells.

Enlarging the display is useful if you are working with very small fonts. Reducing the display is useful if you are working with very large fonts.

9–17 WORKSHEET COMMANDS

When you invoke the Worksheet command from the WYSIWYG main menu, you receive the following options:

```
Column     Row     Page
```

The Column option gives you two alternatives: Set-Width and Reset-Width. If you choose Set-Width, you can specify any number between 1 to 240 with up to two decimals. You can either type the number or use the left and right arrow to visually adjust the column width.

The Row option allows you to set the height of a row. The default row height is 14 points. You can specify any number between 1 and 255. Use :Worksheet Row Auto to automatically adjust row heights to accommodate the largest font in a row. If you want to adjust the height of one row, move the cell pointer to that row and invoke :Worksheet Row Auto.

The Page command allows you to manually insert row and column page breaks. If you do not invoke this feature, WYSIWYG automatically breaks the range up into page-sized segments. A dashed line appears within the print range wherever WYSIWYG has determined that a page break is necessary. WYSIWYG breaks a page in two ways:

1. A column page break occurs when the range specified exceeds the paper width.
2. A row page break occurs when the range specified exceeds the paper length.

For printing worksheets that are too long or too wide, WYSIWYG proceeds vertically, as does 1-2-3. It starts from top to bottom then left to right. This

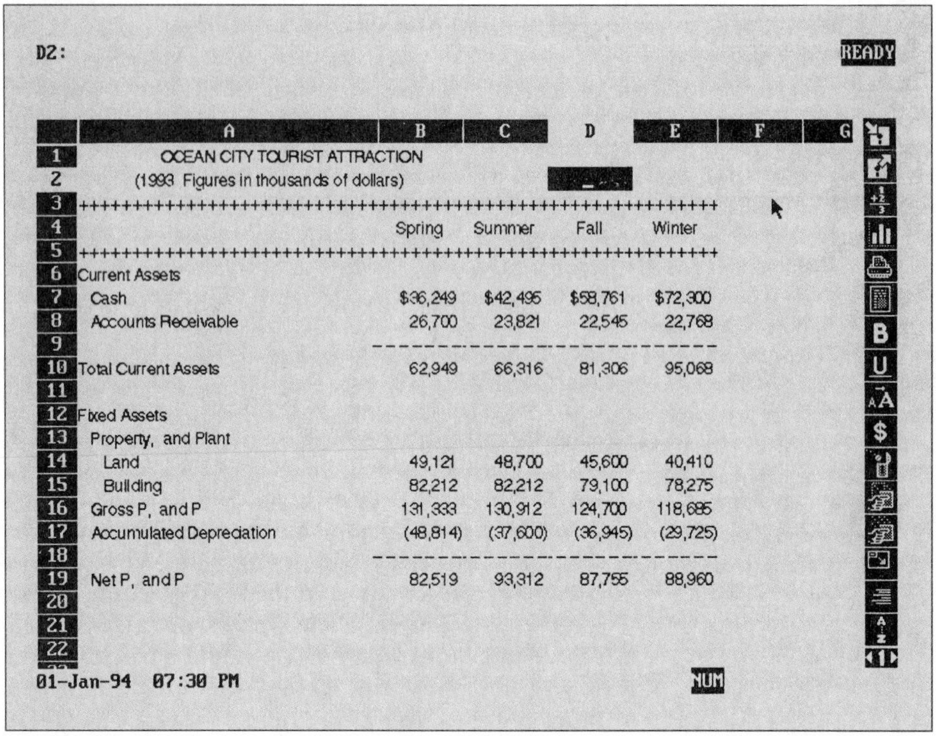

Figure 9–21
Sample worksheet.

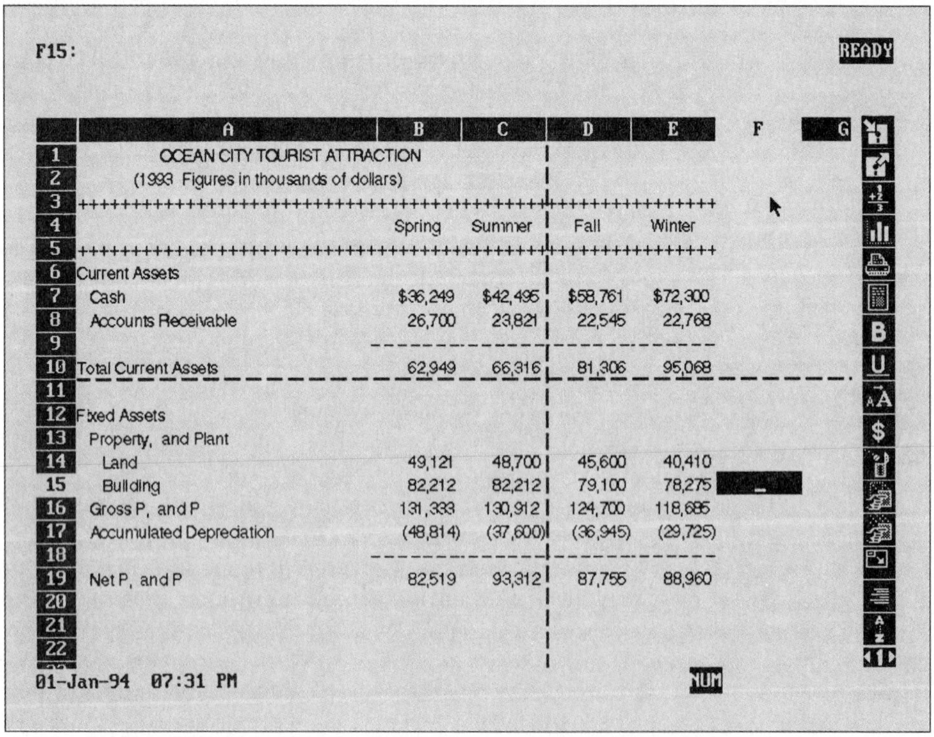

Figure 9–22
Sample worksheet with vertical and horizontal page breaks.

means it prints the length of the worksheet page-by-page, then it proceeds with the width. To use the page break feature, all you have to do is to invoke :Worksheet Page then select Row, Column, or Delete. After this selection, you must specify the first column or the first row of the range. Figure 9–21 illustrates a sample worksheet. Figure 9–22 illustrates a vertical and a horizontal page break. For the column page break, move the cursor to column D then select :Worksheet, Page, Column, Quit; for the row page break, move to row 11 then select :Worksheet, Page, Row, Quit.

9–18 SPECIAL COMMANDS

If you invoke Special from the WYSIWYG main menu, you receive the following options:

```
Copy       Move        Import      Export
```

The Copy option allows you to copy the format of a cell or a range to another cell or range. Remember this command only copies the format of the cell, not the data. Also, you cannot copy graphs with :Special Copy. The Copy command can save you a lot of time if you are dealing with identical worksheets, tables, or ranges. You can format one of these worksheets, tables, or ranges, then copy it to another worksheet, table, or range. The format attributes of a cell include font, boldface, color, lines, underlining, and shading.

The Move command allows you to move the format of a cell or a range to another cell or range. Remember when you use the Move command the format of the original cell or range is set to default. The destination cell or range adopts the format of the original cell or range. This command is useful if you import the format of a different worksheet and the cell locations do not quite match. By using :Special Move you can correct the problem.

The Import command is used to import the format of an existing worksheet to a new worksheet. Remember that all the formats in the receiving worksheet are replaced by the incoming worksheet. This command can save you considerable time when you work with identical worksheets. You can format one of them, then import it to all the new ones.

The Export option replaces the font set, formats, named styles, and graphics in WYSIWYG (.FMT) format file on disk with the font set, formats, named styles, and graphs from the current file.

SUMMARY

This chapter focused on WYSIWYG, an add-in program included in 1-2-3 Release 2.4. WYSIWYG allows you to generate pleasant-looking reports, integrate graphs into 1-2-3 output, and incorporate various types of fonts. See Table 9–3 for output enhancement SmartIcons.

REVIEW QUESTIONS

*These questions are answered in Appendix A.

1. What is the WYSIWYG program? What are the unique advantages of WYSIWYG for printing worksheets?
*2. How do you get WYSIWYG started? What keys can be assigned to WYSIWYG as the start-up key?

Table 9–3
Output Enhancement Icons

WYSIWYG Mode	Text Mode	Description
U	U	**W** Adds a single underline to data in a range or removes a single underline.
U	U	**W** Adds a double underline to data in a range or removes a double underline.
	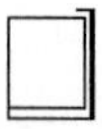	**W** Draws an outline around a range and draws a drop shadow below and to the right of the range or removes an existing drop shadow and outline.
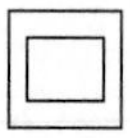		**W** Draws a single-line, double-line, or wide outline around a range or clears the outline, depending on the current type of outline.
	###	**W** Adds light, dark, or solid shading to a range or removes the shading, depending on the current type of shading in the range.
B	B	**W** Displays data in a range in bold or clears bold from a previously formatted range.
I	I	**W** Displays data in a range in italic or clears italic from a previously formatted range.
N	N	**W** Clears all WYSIWYG formatting from a range and restores the default font.

Column 1 shows icons if WYSIWYG is attached. Column 2 shows icons as they appear when WYSIWYG is either not attached or is set to: Display Mode Text.
The icons identified by **W** work only when WYSIWYG is attached.

3. Can you make the WYSIWYG start-up an automatic process? If yes, how?
4. If you assign the No-Key option to WYSIWYG, then how do you get it started?
5. What are the three distinct areas of a WYSIWYG worksheet?
6. What are status indicators? Give two examples.
7. Can you save a file from the WYSIWYG menu? If no, then how can you save your work?
8. How are WYSIWYG files identified?
*9. What are the two modes of WYSIWYG? How do you switch between them?
10. How many options are there in the WYSIWYG main menu? Briefly explain them.
11. How do you define a range in WYSIWYG? Do you define a range first, then invoke the desired command, or vice versa?
12. What are the options under :Format lines? What is the difference between the Outline option and the All option?
13. What are the options under :Format shade?
*14. How many underlining features are supported by WYSIWYG?
15. What are the options under the :Print command?
16. What are the options under :Print Settings?
*17. What are the applications of :Print File command?
18. What is a font? How many fonts are supported by WYSIWYG?
19. What is a font library? Can you transfer a font from one worksheet to another one? If yes, how?

*20. What is the application of Goto in the :Graph command?
21. How do you remove a graph from a worksheet?
22. How many graphs can be included in a worksheet?
23. What are the applications of :Graph Settings?
24. How many colors are supported by WYSIWYG? What does :Display Colors do?
*25. What are the applications of :Display Zoom command? Does this command have any effect on the printout?
26. What are the applications of the Worksheet command?
27. How does WYSIWYG perform a page break? What are the differences between column and row commands in 1-2-3 and their counterparts in WYSIWYG?
28. What are the applications of Special commands? What is the difference between the WYSIWYG Copy command and the 1-2-3 Copy command?

HANDS-ON EXPERIENCE

1. Get WYSIWYG started. By pressing the F1 function key, invoke online help. What type of help is available?
2. Using Figure 9–23 do the following:
   a. Draw an outline around the title of the worksheet.
   b. Using :Format Lines Left draw a line on the first column.
   c. Using :Format Lines Right draw a line on the last column.
   d. Using :Format Lines Top draw a line on the top of the first row.
   e. Using :Format Lines Bottom draw a line on the bottom of the last row.
3. Using Figure 9–23 draw a line around each cell in the worksheet (Hint: use :Format Lines All). Do the following:
   a. Using :Format Shade draw a dark shade for the worksheet title.
   b. Draw a dark shade for the last row.

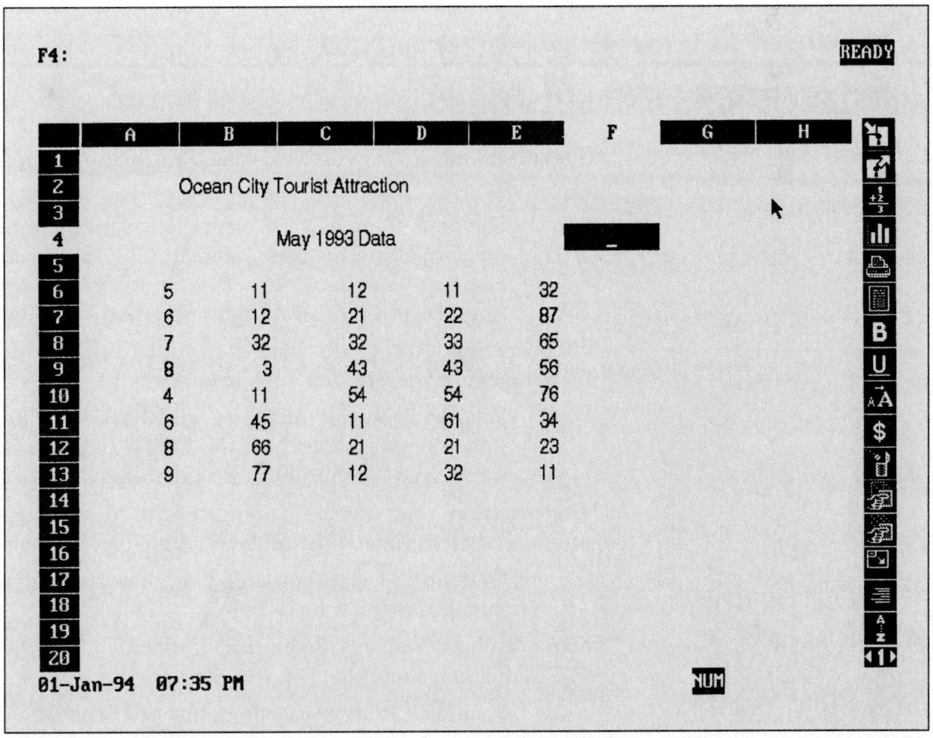
F4:
READY
A B C D E F G H
Ocean City Tourist Attraction
May 1993 Data
5 11 12 11 32
6 12 21 22 87
7 32 32 33 65
8 3 43 43 56
4 11 54 54 76
6 45 11 61 34
8 66 21 21 23
9 77 12 32 11
01-Jan-94 07:35 PM
NUM

Figure 9–23
Sample worksheet.

   c. Using :Format Underline, draw a double underline for the first row.
   d. Print the final work.
4. Using Figure 9–23 do the following:
   a. Create a thick horizontal and vertical line for this worksheet.
   b. Create a shadow box for this worksheet.
   c. Print the worksheet.
5. Load the worksheet presented in Figure 9–21 and do the following:
   a. Change the title to Bitstream 14 point.
   b. Change the last row to Bitstream Dutch 12 point.
   c. Change the first row to Bitstream 12 point.
   d. Print the final result.
6. Load Figure 9–21 and print grid lines in the worksheet. Add the graph presented in Figure 9–19 to this worksheet.
7. Load the worksheet in Figure 9–21 and do the following:
   a. Add the graph presented in Figure 9–16 to this worksheet.
   b. Remove this graph and replace it with the graph in Figure 9–19.
   c. Using the settings option, change the font on this graph to a font of your choice.
   d. Print the final work.

KEY TERMS

font	formatting sequence
font set	WYSIWYG

KEY COMMANDS

Display	Named-Style	Special
Format	Print	Worksheet
Graph		

MISCONCEPTIONS AND SOLUTIONS

Misconception You performed several formatting features but they are not presented in your worksheet.

> **Solution** Probably you forgot to save your worksheet. WYSIWYG does not save the formatting features automatically. You must exit WYSIWYG and use 1-2-3's File Save command to save your worksheet before you terminate the session. Another possibility is that you detached WYSIWYG before saving your work.

Misconception You made changes to your worksheet during the WYSIWYG session but the changes are not reflected in your worksheet.

> **Solution** Changes made to your worksheet are saved on a different worksheet with the same name and the FMT extension. Also, changes made in 1-2-3 are transferred to WYSIWYG not vice versa.

Misconception You are performing several formatting features to a range. Issuing the command then specifying the range is a time-consuming process.

> **Solution** Define the range first, then apply all the formatting commands to this range. You save a lot of time.

Misconception You specified a print range in 1-2-3 but the actual printout from WYSIWYG is different from what you specified.

> **Solution** Print ranges do not transfer from 1-2-3 to WYSIWYG.

Misconception Creating a set of fonts from worksheet to worksheet is time consuming.

Solution Save such fonts in a font library, then import them to your desired worksheet.

Misconception Specifying the width of columns in WYSIWYG by typing numbers may be misleading.

Solution Use right and left arrows to define the width of a column as finely as required or desired.

Misconception Repeating the same format from cell to cell is time consuming.

Solution Use :Special Copy command to easily duplicate formatting features from a cell to any other cell(s).

ARE YOU READY TO MOVE ON?

Multiple Choice

1. Using WYSIWYG, you can do all of the following except
   a. adding a graph to your reports
   b. adding two graphs to your reports
   c. boldfacing the title
   d. drawing lines around data ranges
   e. you can do all of the above
2. You can assign all of the following keys to WYSIWYG except
   a. F7
   b. F8
   c. F9
   d. F5
   e. F10
3. To invoke the WYSIWYG menu, you must press
   a. : key
   b. / key
   c. ? key
   d. F10 key
   e. none of the above
4. Files created by WYSIWYG have the extension
   a. PRT
   b. FMT
   c. WK1
   d. PIC
   e. none of the above
5. All of the following options are included in WYSIWYG menu except
   a. Worksheet
   b. Format
   c. Graph
   d. Special
   e. they are all included
6. Using the WYSIWYG Format Lines command you can do all of the following except
   a. draw outlines
   b. draw double lines
   c. draw triangles around cells
   d. draw wide lines
   e. draw shadow boxes

7. Formatting sequences are used to format
   a. individual character(s) within a cell
   b. a cell
   c. a range
   d. a graph
   e. none of the above
8. How many fonts does WYSIWYG support directly?
   a. 6
   b. 7
   c. 8
   d. 5
   e. 4
9. Using the Text command, you can do all of the following except
   a. edit text
   b. perform a search and replace operation
   c. reformat text
   d. align text
   e. start a new paragraph
10. The Print command includes all of the following options except
    a. Go
    b. Background
    c. Range
    d. Move
    e. Configuration

True/False

1. When you print into a file using WYSIWYG, the file extension generated is ENC.
2. The ENC file can be printed through DOS COPY command.
3. You can create a shadow box with WYSIWYG.
4. WYSIWYG does not support any font other than the original eight default fonts.
5. Only a PIC graph can be inserted into your worksheet using WYSIWYG.
6. By means of the Remove command, you can remove a graph from your worksheet.
7. The :Display Zoom command always changes your printed output.
8. :Worksheet commands allow you to change the column widths or row heights.
9. A format generated in one cell cannot be transferred to another cell.
10. WYSIWYG does not include the Print command.

ANSWERS

Multiple Choice		True/False	
1.	e	1.	T
2.	d	2.	T
3.	a	3.	T
4.	b	4.	F
5.	e	5.	F
6.	c	6.	T
7.	a	7.	F
8.	c	8.	T
9.	b	9.	F
10.	d	10.	F

Using 1-2-3 for Database Operations

10

10–1 INTRODUCTION

In this chapter we discuss the principles of database and database management using 1-2-3. Major database operations—file creation, update, sort, and search—are illustrated through several examples. Some advanced features of 1-2-3 database operations such as database statistical functions, the Data Fill command, the Data Table 1 command, the Data Table 2 command, and distribution analysis are highlighted.

10–2 BASIC DATABASE OPERATIONS

If you use 1-2-3 as a **database,** you can have 8,192 records (rows) and 256 fields (columns). Major database operations include database creation, updating, sorting, and searching.

When you create a database, you enter labels, formulas, or values in different cells. You can widen the cells from the default width of nine by using the /Worksheet Global Column-Width command, the /Worksheet Column Set-Width command, or the /Worksheet Column Column-Range command.

You update a database by changing the contents of a field (editing); inserting a new record or field with /Worksheet Insert Row or /Worksheet Insert Column, respectively; deleting a record or field with /Worksheet Delete Row or /Worksheet Delete Column, respectively; deleting an entire database with /Worksheet Erase Yes; or deleting a portion of a database with /Range Erase.

You can sort your database in either ascending or descending order, using a primary key and a secondary key. The primary key is the first field chosen for a sort operation; the secondary key is the second field chosen for a sort operation. You can perform any type of search by using different criteria.

1-2-3 has facilities for other complex database operations, such as Join (joining two databases) and Merge (adding one database to the bottom of another). These features can be implemented with macros, which are discussed in Chapter 11.

10–3 A DATABASE EXAMPLE

Figure 10–1 is an example of a database. This database has 15 records, and each record contains six fields. Each field begins with a field name, which must be unique. The field name must be a label, but the label can be numeric, such as 5 or 9. The field name can be more than one line long; only the last row will be considered the field name, however. The example database shown in Figure 10–1 was created in the same way as our other worksheets. Numbers and figures are right justified and labels are left justified.

10–4 SORTING A DATABASE

You can **sort** a database in ascending or descending order by any field. To access the Sort command, choose Data from the Main menu of 1-2-3, then select Sort. You are presented with the following options:

```
Data-Range Primary-Key Secondary-Key Reset Go Quit
```

Figure 10–1
A 1-2-3 database.

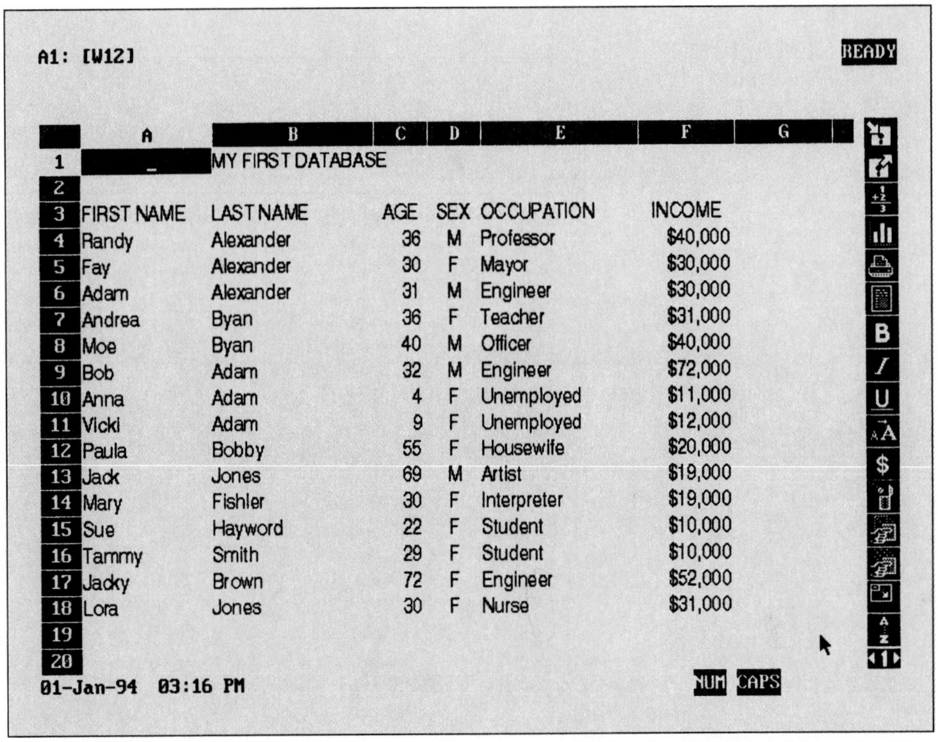

Choose Data-Range to specify the data to be sorted. This usually includes all data items in your database, although you may include just a portion of your database. The field names must not be included in the data range or they will be considered part of the database and will be sorted along with your data items.

You use the Primary-Key option to specify the first key to be used in the sort operation. You can choose any field in your database as the primary key. The Secondary-Key option specifies the second key on which the database will be sorted.

You use the Reset option to change the parameters of your database. When you choose Reset again, all your settings will return to their defaults.

The Go option executes the Sort operation, and Quit lets you escape from this menu. Also see Table 10–1 presented at the end of the chapter for sort SmartIcons.

Figure 10–2 shows the information from Figure 10–1 after we sorted it using range B4..B18 as the primary key. This figure was generated with the following keystrokes:

> /Data, Sort, Data-Range, A4..F18, Enter, Primary-Key, B4..B18, Enter, A, Enter, Go

1-2-3, by default, sorts in descending order. If you don't want this default setting, press A (ascending) when prompted for the sort sequence and press Enter.

The order in which 1-2-3 performs a sort is determined by a collating sequence. You may choose one of three collating sequences during the install operations:

- Numbers last. Ignoring capitalization and most accent marks, this option sorts information in the following order:

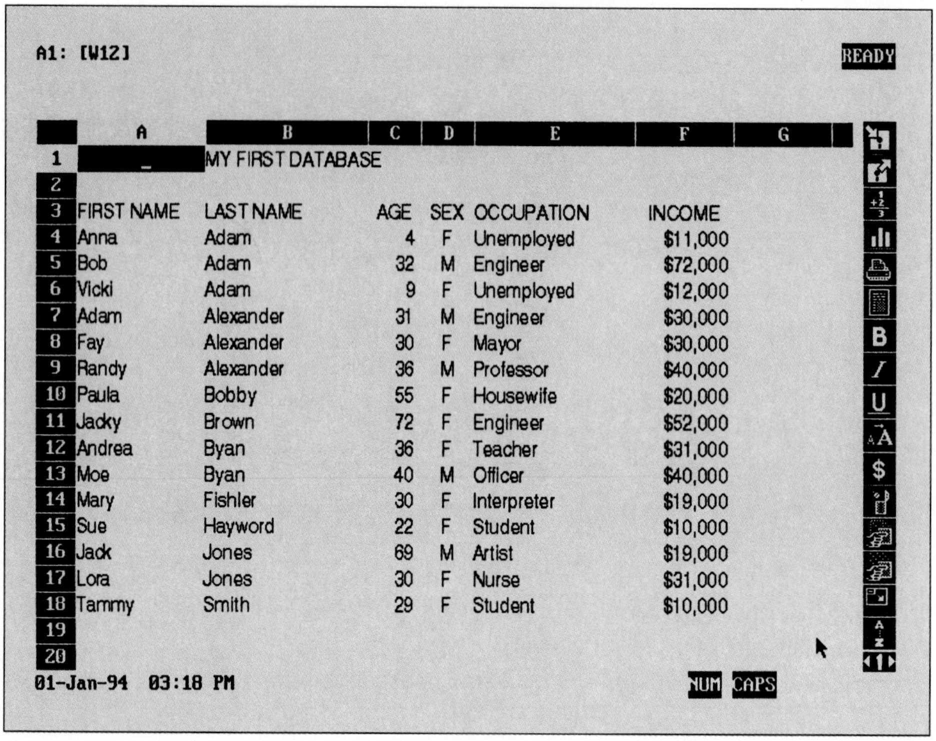

A1: [W12] READY

	A	B	C	D	E	F
1	_	MY FIRST DATABASE				
2						
3	FIRST NAME	LAST NAME	AGE	SEX	OCCUPATION	INCOME
4	Anna	Adam	4	F	Unemployed	$11,000
5	Bob	Adam	32	M	Engineer	$72,000
6	Vicki	Adam	9	F	Unemployed	$12,000
7	Adam	Alexander	31	M	Engineer	$30,000
8	Fay	Alexander	30	F	Mayor	$30,000
9	Randy	Alexander	36	M	Professor	$40,000
10	Paula	Bobby	55	F	Housewife	$20,000
11	Jacky	Brown	72	F	Engineer	$52,000
12	Andrea	Byan	36	F	Teacher	$31,000
13	Moe	Byan	40	M	Officer	$40,000
14	Mary	Fishler	30	F	Interpreter	$19,000
15	Sue	Hayword	22	F	Student	$10,000
16	Jack	Jones	69	M	Artist	$19,000
17	Lora	Jones	30	F	Nurse	$31,000
18	Tammy	Smith	29	F	Student	$10,000
19						
20						

01-Jan-94 03:18 PM NUM CAPS

Figure 10–2
Database sorted by last name.

1. Blank cells
2. Labels beginning with letters in alphabetical order
3. Labels beginning with numbers in numeric order
4. Labels beginning with other characters

- Numbers first. Ignoring capitalization and most accent marks, this option sorts information in the following order:
  1. Blank cells
  2. Labels beginning with numbers in numeric order
  3. Labels beginning with letters in alphabetical order
  4. Labels beginning with other characters
- ASCII. This option sorts information in the following order:
  1. Blank cells
  2. All labels, using their ASCII values

You can choose Numbers First or Numbers Last as the collating sequence. Uppercase and lowercase letters have the same values. As a general rule, nonlabel, nonnumeric, and composed characters (characters created with the F1+Alt key combination) come at the end of the listing.

10–5 SEARCH OPERATIONS

When you perform a **Search** operation, you are interested in a specific record or records that meet certain criteria. For example, in a student grade file, you might want to search for all students who have a GPA greater than 3.60, or in an employee file, for all employees who hold a master's degree. To conduct a search operation, choose Data from the Main menu, then choose Query. The Query menu is as follows:

```
Input Criterion Output Find Extract Unique Delete Reset Quit
```

Choose Input to specify your data. This should be the entire database including the field names. For example, in Figure 10–1 the Input range is A3..F18.

The Criterion range is outside the database range and includes the name of the field(s) and the criterion for which you are searching. The field names in Criterion range must be identical to those used in the database. For example, in the database shown in Figure 10–1, the Criterion range for all the engineers would be

OCCUPATION
Engineer

OCCUPATION is the field name; Engineer is contained in this field. Up to 32 fields can be considered for a search.

The Output range is a portion of a worksheet outside the database range; it contains the names of fields in the database that you want to extract (uppercase or lowercase does not matter, but it is a good practice to be consistent). Field names constitute the first line in the Output range.

The Find option is used to choose a record, or series of records, based on the Criterion range (an Output range is not needed with the Find option). To use the Find option, define the Input range and the Criterion range and choose Find. The selected record(s) will be highlighted.

With the Extract option, a portion of a database can be copied to the Output range, based on the Criterion range (assuming you have already defined the Output range).

Use the Unique option to extract only a unique portion of a database. In this case, duplicate records are not chosen. For example, if you want to choose just one representative of each occupation, only one engineer will be selected, one professor, and so on. A good application for the Unique option is the generation of mailing lists. The Unique option eliminates duplicate labels.

Use the Delete option to erase a portion of a database based on the Criterion range.

10–5–1 Search with a Single Criterion

In Figure 10–3, the database on the left side was searched for all engineers—a search with a **single criterion.** First, establish the criterion range as we did in cells F6..F7. The title "CRITERION RANGE" is optional. This figure was generated with the following keystrokes:

/Data, Query, Input, A5..D13, Enter, Criterion, F6..F7, Enter, Find

When you choose the Find option, the cursor points to the first record that meets a particular criterion. If you move the cursor to the records below the first one selected, the cursor points to the next selected record (if there is any). This continues until all the candidates are highlighted. If you try to move the cursor further, 1-2-3 beeps, indicating that there are no more matches to be highlighted.

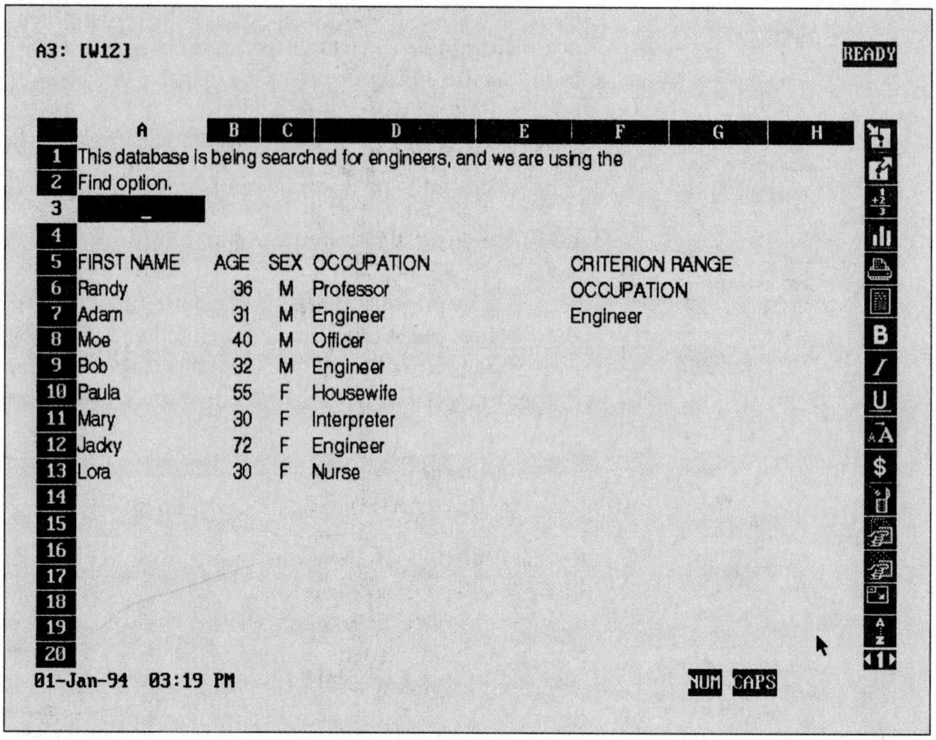

Figure 10–3
Example of Find with a single criterion.

To demonstrate the actual output, we used the Extract option. Before you do the Extract operation, you must generate an output area. To do this, copy your database field names to a blank area of your worksheet and specify this area as the Output range. So the first line of your output range must start with the field names of your database. In Figure 10–4, we first copied the database field

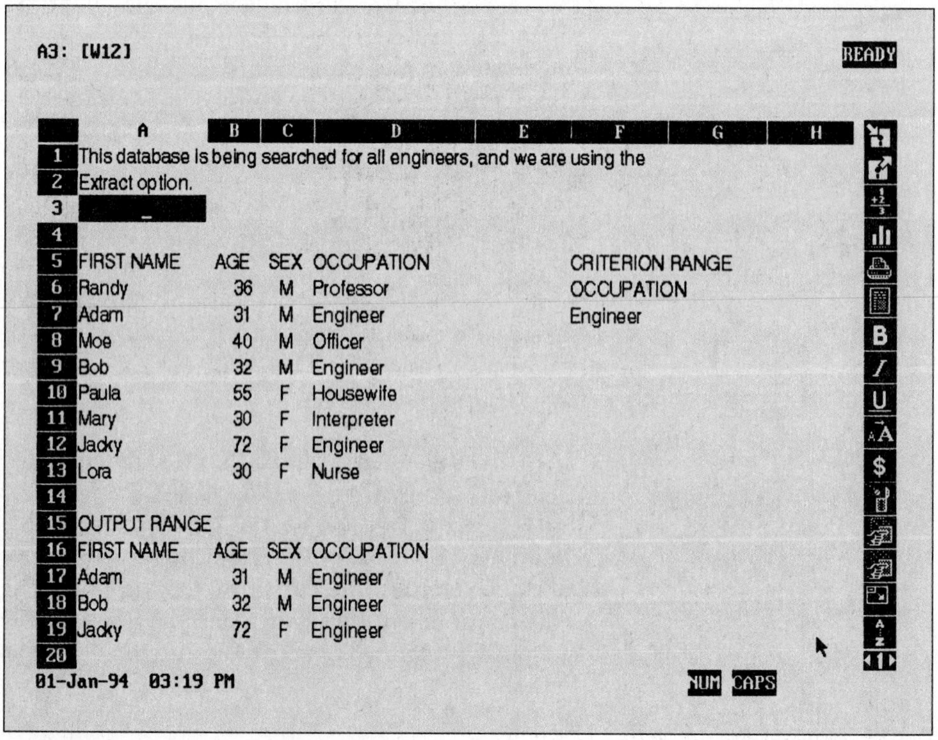

Figure 10–4
Example of Extract with a single criterion.

titles in cells A16..D16. We generated the information shown in Figure 10–4 by selecting /Data Query Input. We indicated range A5..D13 and pressed Enter. Next, we selected Criterion, indicated range F6..F7, and pressed Enter. Finally, we chose Output, indicated range A16..D20, pressed Enter, and selected Extract.

The Output range does not need to include the entire range for the extracted output. You only need to copy the names of the fields from the database and specify the first line of the Output range. The first line of the Output range is always the row that contains the names of the fields for the extracted output.

10–5–2 Search with Two Criteria

On many occasions you are interested in two criteria and either one is acceptable, for example, an employee with either a bachelor's degree or 17 years of experience, or students who are majoring in either MIS or computer science. In computer terminology, this is called an OR condition. In Figure 10–5, we first established the criterion and output ranges, then searched the database for people who are either engineers or teachers by choosing /Data Query Input. We indicated range A3..E11 (as the Input range) and pressed Enter. Next, we selected Criterion, indicated range G4..G6, and pressed Enter. Finally, we chose Output, indicated range A15..E20, pressed Enter, and chose Extract.

To perform the OR Search in 1-2-3, the criteria must be in a vertical line (a column).

10–5–3 Search with Multiple Criteria

The opposite of the OR condition is the AND condition. You use this condition when you are interested in searching for records meeting **multiple criteria.** For example, you may want to search for all the students who have a GPA of 3.6 or better and are MIS majors, or for all the employees who have 10 years of experi-

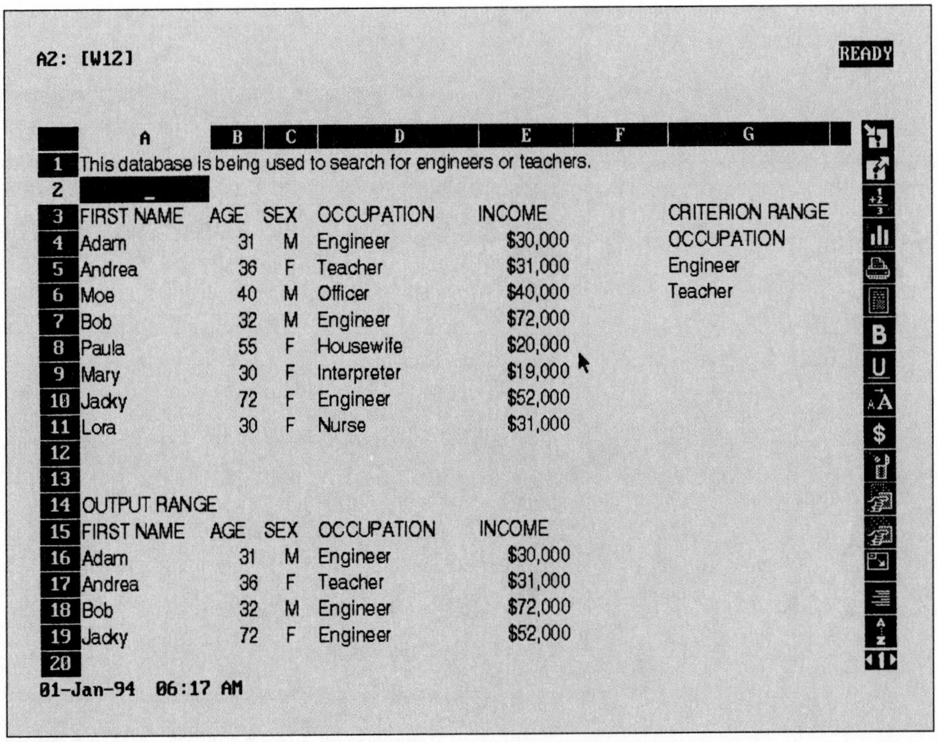

Figure 10–5
Searching with two criteria.

ence and a bachelor's degree and who speak Spanish. An employee must meet all of these criteria to be selected.

To perform the AND Search, the criteria must be in a horizontal line. Using the database shown in Figure 10–6 (this worksheet is also saved on the left

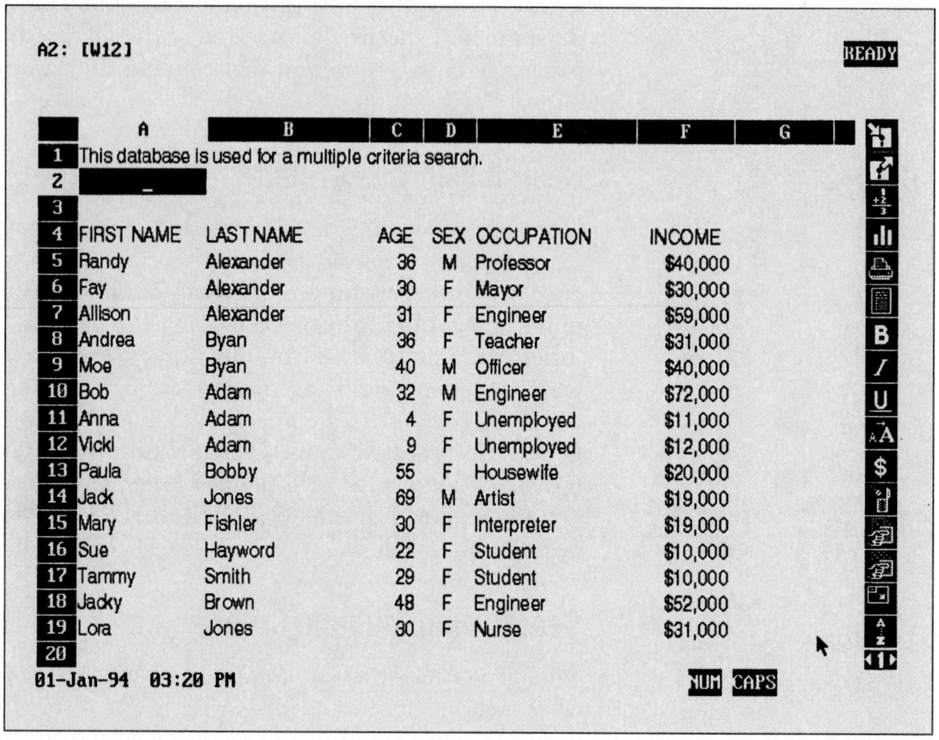

A2: [W12] READY

This database is used for a multiple criteria search.

FIRST NAME	LAST NAME	AGE	SEX	OCCUPATION	INCOME
Randy	Alexander	36	M	Professor	$40,000
Fay	Alexander	30	F	Mayor	$30,000
Allison	Alexander	31	F	Engineer	$59,000
Andrea	Byan	36	F	Teacher	$31,000
Moe	Byan	40	M	Officer	$40,000
Bob	Adam	32	M	Engineer	$72,000
Anna	Adam	4	F	Unemployed	$11,000
Vicki	Adam	9	F	Unemployed	$12,000
Paula	Bobby	55	F	Housewife	$20,000
Jack	Jones	69	M	Artist	$19,000
Mary	Fishler	30	F	Interpreter	$19,000
Sue	Hayword	22	F	Student	$10,000
Tammy	Smith	29	F	Student	$10,000
Jacky	Brown	48	F	Engineer	$52,000
Lora	Jones	30	F	Nurse	$31,000

01-Jan-94 03:20 PM NUM CAPS

Figure 10–6
Database used for the multiple criteria search.

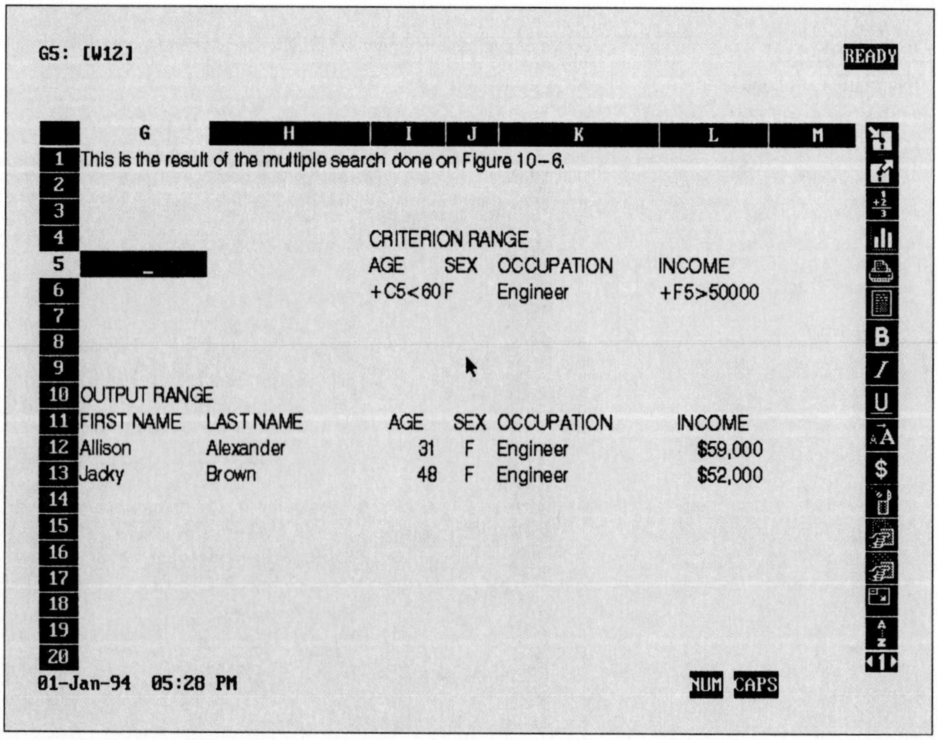

G5: [W12] READY

This is the result of the multiple search done on Figure 10–6.

CRITERION RANGE

AGE	SEX	OCCUPATION	INCOME
+C5<60	F	Engineer	+F5>50000

OUTPUT RANGE

FIRST NAME	LAST NAME	AGE	SEX	OCCUPATION	INCOME
Allison	Alexander	31	F	Engineer	$59,000
Jacky	Brown	48	F	Engineer	$52,000

01-Jan-94 05:28 PM NUM CAPS

Figure 10–7
Using the AND option with a multiple criteria search.

side of Figure 10–7—you do not need to see this!), we created Figure 10–7, which illustrates an AND condition for all female engineers who make more than $50,000 and are less than 60 years old. We first established the criterion and output ranges. Figure 10–7 was generated with the following keystrokes:

> /Data, Query, Input, A4..F19, Enter, Criterion, I5..L6, Enter, Output, G11..L30, Enter, Extract

You can include up to 32 fields in your Criterion range. You also can combine AND and OR conditions. When you combine AND and OR, 1-2-3 starts from the top of the database and compares each record to the criteria established in the Criterion range. If there is a match, that record is selected. Otherwise the record is skipped.

Another interesting search is to apply AND and OR choices to one particular field. An example of this is shown in Figure 10–8. In this figure, we searched for people who are between 30 and 40 years old. As usual, we first established the criterion and output ranges. This figure was generated with the following keystrokes:

> /Data, Query, Input, A3..B18, Enter, Criterion, E4..E5, Enter, Output, E9..F18, Enter, Extract

In Figure 10–9, we searched for people who are under 10 or over 70 years old. First, establish the criterion and output ranges. This figure was generated with the following keystrokes:

> /Data, Query, Input, A3..B18, Enter, Criterion, E4..E5, Enter, Output, E9..F18, Enter, Extract

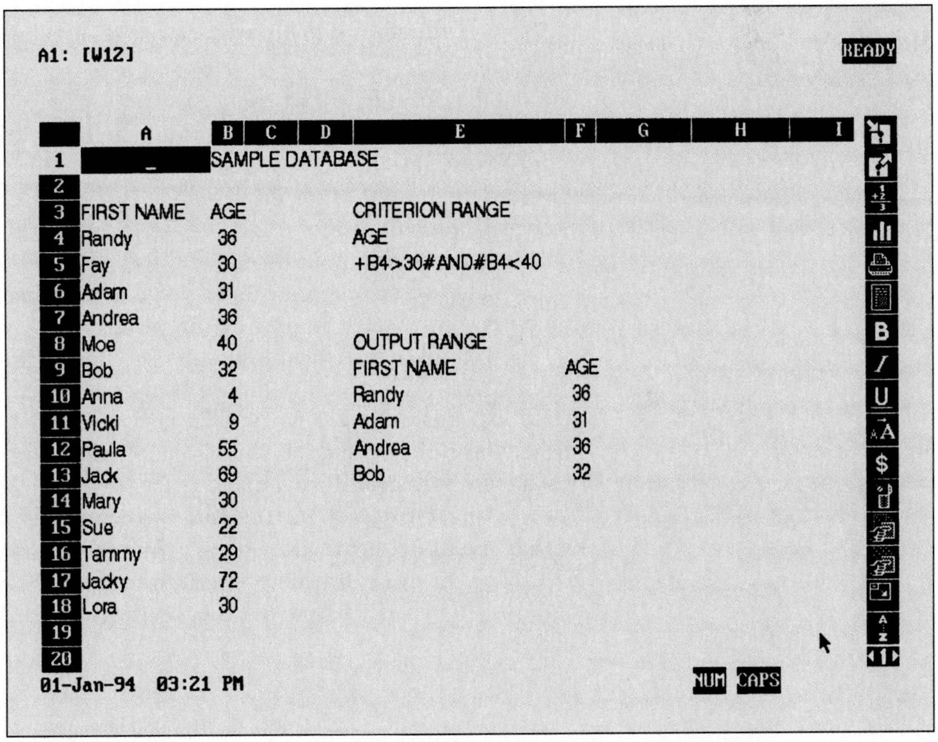

Figure 10–8
Search using AND in one field.

Figure 10–9
Search with OR within one field.

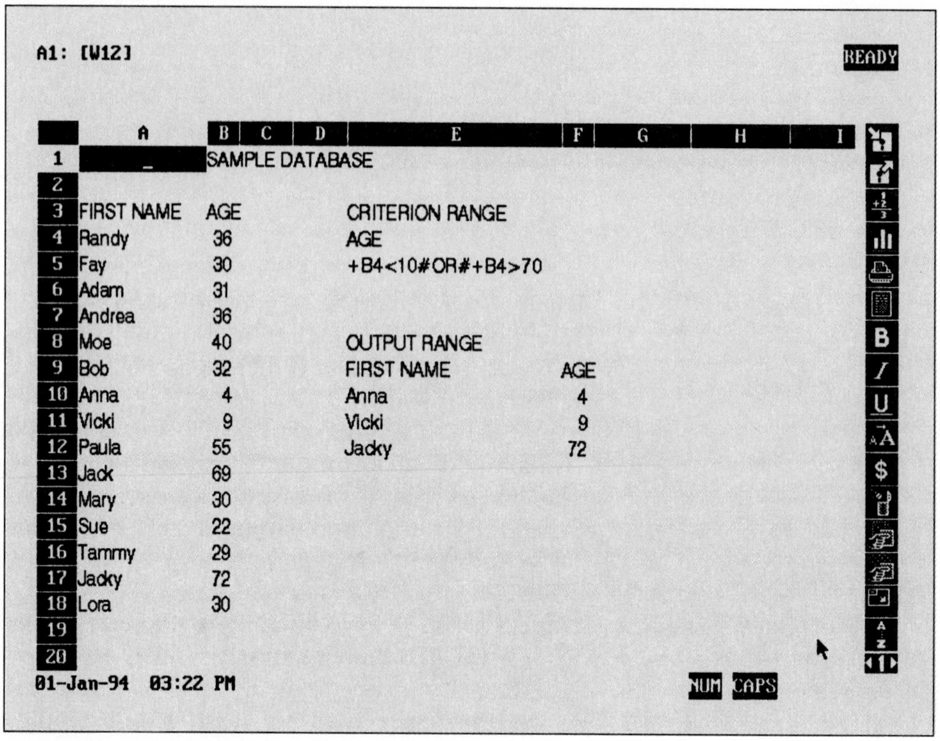

10–6 DATABASE STATISTICAL FUNCTIONS

The statistical functions discussed in Chapter 7 can be used with database data with minor variations. A **database statistical function** follows this format:

@Dfunction name(database range,offset value,criterion range)

The database range (input range) is usually the entire database or a selected portion of the database. The offset value defines which column of the database is under investigation. This value must be between 0 and the maximum number of columns in the database minus one. If the offset value is 2, it means you are interested in column 3 of the database or field 3; if the offset value is 10, it means you are interested in column 11, and so on.

The criterion range must have a field heading. Below it you can define any criteria in which you may be interested.

Database statistical functions provide more flexibility than their statistical counterparts. The seven database statistical functions are @DAVG, @DCOUNT, @DMAX, @DMIN, @DSTD, @DSUM, and @DVAR. By changing the criterion range, you can perform all sorts of analyses. Figure 10–10 shows some examples of database statistical functions.

In Figure 10–10, the database range is A3..C18, the offset value is 1 (which means column 2 is under investigation), and the criterion range is H19..H20. In this example, we are interested in only those people who are older than 10. (In cell H20, we used the Text format to show the actual contents of this cell.)

Figure 10–10
Database statistical functions.

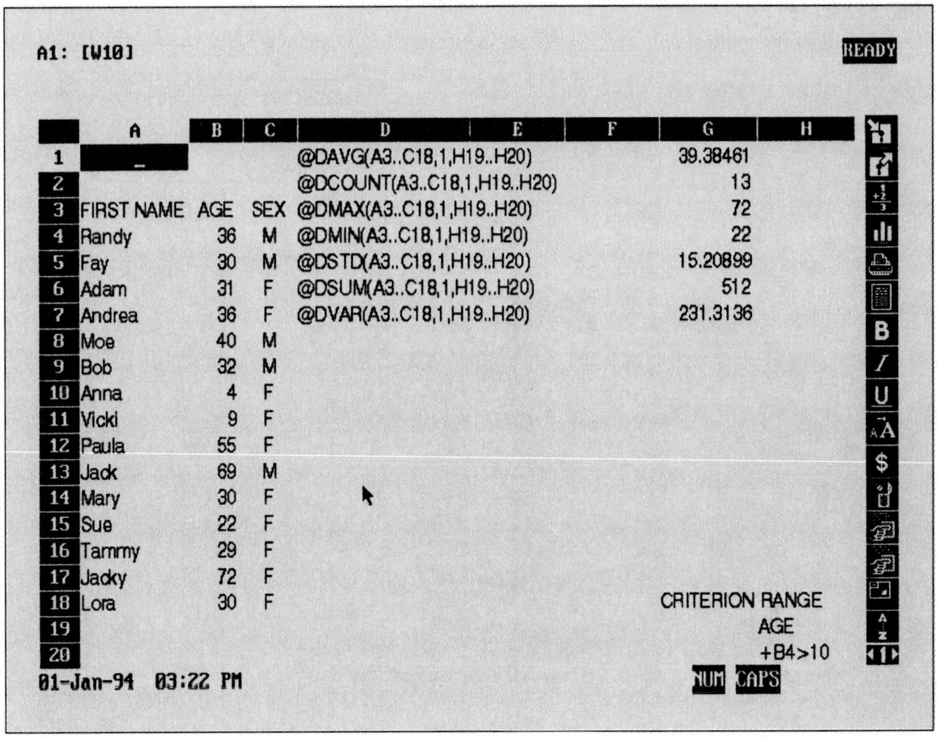
A1: [W10]
READY
A B C D E F G H
1 @DAVG(A3..C18,1,H19..H20) 39.38461
2 @DCOUNT(A3..C18,1,H19..H20) 13
3 FIRST NAME AGE SEX @DMAX(A3..C18,1,H19..H20) 72
4 Randy 36 M @DMIN(A3..C18,1,H19..H20) 22
5 Fay 30 M @DSTD(A3..C18,1,H19..H20) 15.20899
6 Adam 31 F @DSUM(A3..C18,1,H19..H20) 512
7 Andrea 36 F @DVAR(A3..C18,1,H19..H20) 231.3136
8 Moe 40 M
9 Bob 32 M
10 Anna 4 F
11 Vicki 9 F
12 Paula 55 F
13 Jack 69 M
14 Mary 30 F
15 Sue 22 F
16 Tammy 29 F
17 Jacky 72 F
18 Lora 30 F
CRITERION RANGE
19 AGE
20 +B4>10
01-Jan-94 03:22 PM
NUM CAPS

10–7 BUILDING A TABLE USING THE DATA FILL COMMAND

You can use the /Data Fill command to build tables. You must define a range (which becomes the table) and the Start, Step, and Stop values. These values fill in the table from top to bottom and from left to right. If you don't specify any values, 1-2-3 uses default values for Start (0), Step (1), and Stop (8191).

Table building continues until either the range is filled or the Stop value has been reached. Any of the three values can be a formula if the formula is defined at the time it is needed by the /Data Fill command.

An excellent application of the /Data Fill command is to return a sorted database to its original unsorted form. Before you sort the database, in a separate column, use the /Data Fill command to number all the records in the database. Then, when you sort your database, this column will also be sorted. When you have finished with the database, you can return it to its original form by choosing the record number as the primary key and sorting the database again.

Figure 10–11 shows an example of the /Data Fill command. In the upper portion of the figure, we defined a high value for Stop (5000), but 1-2-3 stopped when range A1..D1 was filled. In the lower portion of the figure, 1-2-3 stopped when the Stop value was reached (19,000) even though the specified table was not filled. We generated the upper portion by selecting /Data Fill, A1..D1, Enter, 1, Enter, 2, Enter, 5000, Enter. The lower portion was generated by selecting /Data Fill, A10..A20, Enter, 10000, Enter, 1000, Enter, 19000, Enter.

Also see Table 10–1 presented at the end of the chapter for the Fill SmartIcon.

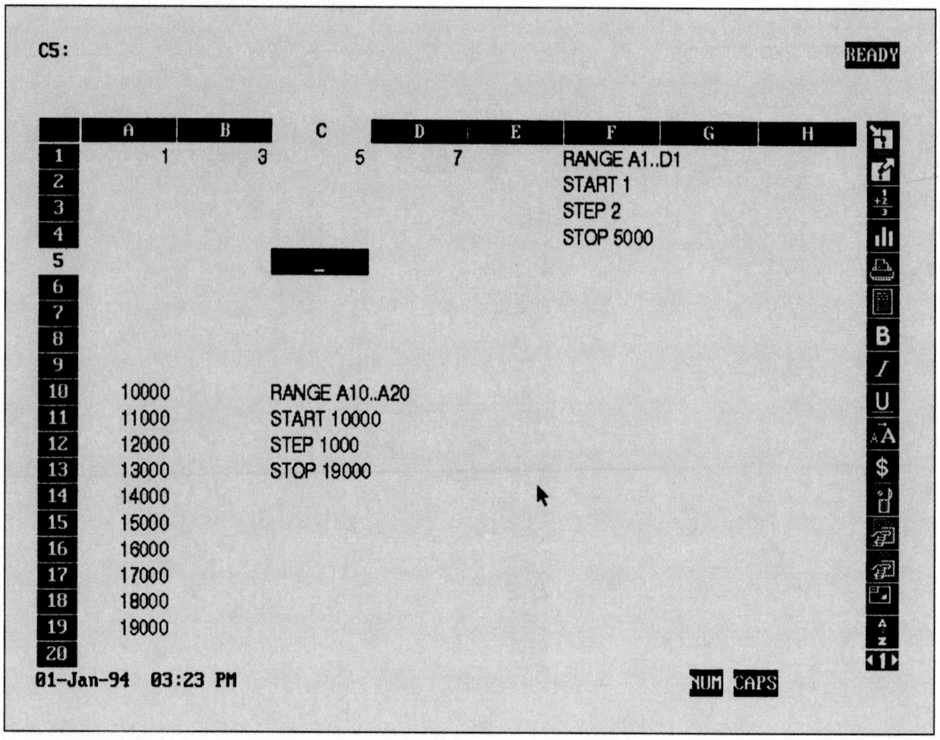

Figure 10–11
Using the Data Fill command.

10–8 WHAT-IF ANALYSIS USING DATA TABLE 1

The /Data Table 1 command can be used to determine the effect of one variable on a formula or an entire worksheet—a **what-if analysis.** There are many areas where this command can be useful. The effect of different interest rates on an IRA plan, the effect of different interest rates on a loan, or the effect of different commission percentages on the total commission generated by a salesperson, are just a few examples of how you can use this command. Figure 10–12 illustrates /Data Table 1 in graphic format.

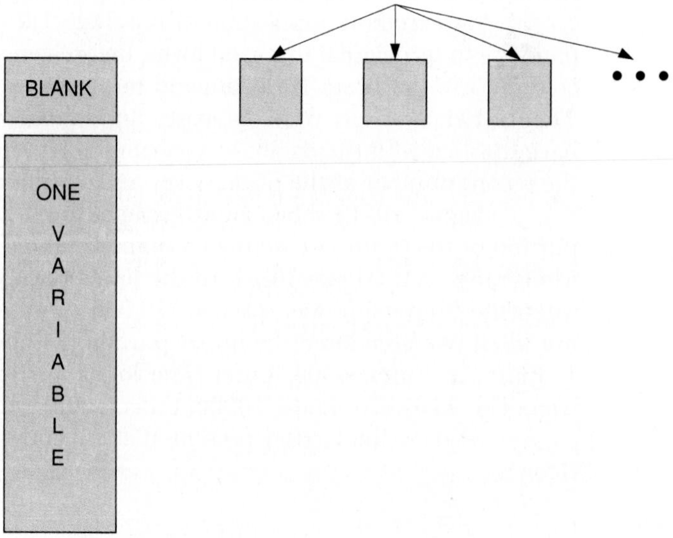

Figure 10–12
/Data Table 1 in graphic format.

To use /Data Table 1, you first must establish a table range. In Figure 10–13, C4..E15 is the table range. The table range can be anywhere in the worksheet.

Next, you must choose an empty cell outside the table range as the input cell. The address of this cell will be used to change values in a formula and is used in 1-2-3's internal calculations. Don't be concerned about its role. In this example, the input cell is A5.

Now fill in the changing values in a column, in this case, cells C5..C15. Above and to the right of these values in cell D4 is the formula, in this case, the future value, @FV(2000,A5,20). This function calculates the future value of an IRA plan to which you contribute $2,000 each year for 20 years with a variable interest rate.

We copied the @FV formula to cell E4, but we changed the number of years to 30. The intersection of these values (interest rates and formulas) is empty—this empty cell will be used by /Data Table 2.

When you have defined the parameters, the future value of the IRA plan will be calculated for the different interest rates and numbers of years. Figure 10–13 shows an application of the /Data Table 1 command. After building the table, the following keystrokes were used to fill in the table:

/Data, Table, 1, C4..E15, Enter, A5, Enter

If you change some of the input values, press F8 while in the READY mode to recalculate the entire table. Of course, this table can be much more complicated. For example, you could perform this calculation for several annuity periods. All you have to do is define these periods and leave the rest to the amazing power and accuracy of 1-2-3.

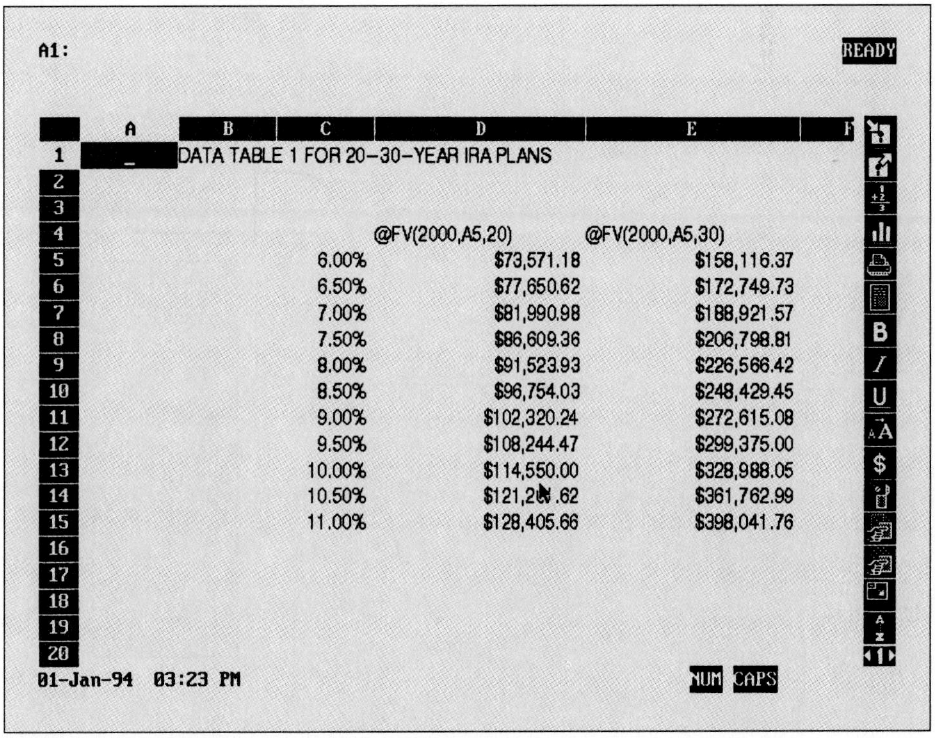
A1: READY

	A	B	C	D	E
1		DATA TABLE 1 FOR 20–30–YEAR IRA PLANS			
2					
3					
4				@FV(2000,A5,20)	@FV(2000,A5,30)
5			6.00%	$73,571.18	$158,116.37
6			6.50%	$77,650.62	$172,749.73
7			7.00%	$81,990.98	$188,921.57
8			7.50%	$86,609.36	$206,798.81
9			8.00%	$91,523.93	$226,566.42
10			8.50%	$96,754.03	$248,429.45
11			9.00%	$102,320.24	$272,615.08
12			9.50%	$108,244.47	$299,375.00
13			10.00%	$114,550.00	$328,988.05
14			10.50%	$121,2[illegible].62	$361,762.99
15			11.00%	$128,405.66	$398,041.76
16					
17					
18					
19					
20					

01-Jan-94 03:23 PM NUM CAPS

Figure 10–13
Using /Data Table 1 to show the effects of different interest rates on two IRA plans.

10–9 WHAT-IF ANALYSIS USING DATA TABLE 2

You can use the /Data Table 2 command to calculate the effects of two variables over the entire worksheet or specified range. Figure 10–14 illustrates /Data Table 2 in graphic format.

Suppose that Sunrise Electronics Firm has designed a formula for calculating the total salary of each employee. The total salary is calculated based on the years of education and number of years of experience. In every case, $2,000 is the base salary. The formula is

2000+50*A1+75*B1

where A1 is the number of years of experience and B1 is the number of years of education. These are the input cells.

In Figure 10–15, we used the /Data Table 2 command to calculate the entire table for the Sunrise Electronics Firm. The table range is D3..H18, input cell 1 is A5, input cell 2 is B5. The formula

2000+50*A5+75*B5

was copied into cell D3, which is the intersection of row 3 (years of education) and column D (years of experience). Enter numbers 1 through 15 in cells D4..D18 and numbers 12, 16, 18, and 21 in cells E3..H3. If you want, you can change any of these values and press F8. The entire table will be recalculated immediately. After the table was built, the following key strokes were used to fill in the table:

/Data, Table, 2, D3..H18, Enter, A5, Enter, B5, Enter

Figure 10–14
/Data Table 2 in graphic format.

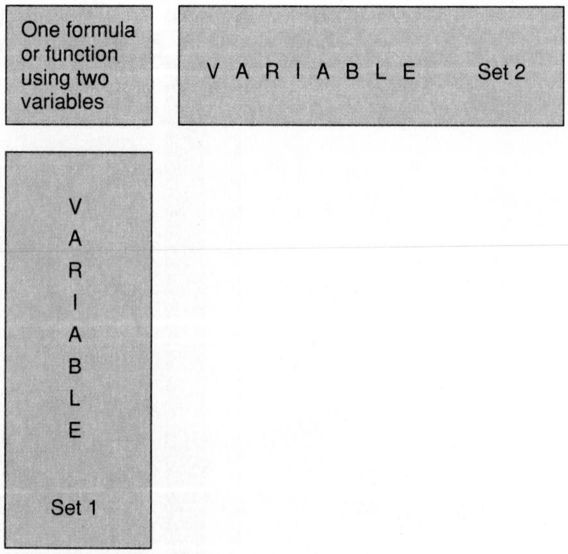

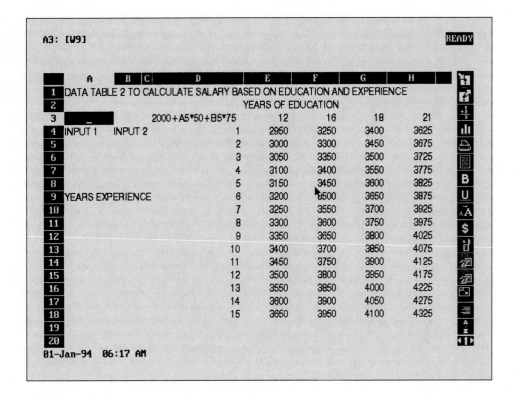

Figure 10–15
Using /Data Table 2 to show the effect of years of experience and education on salary.

A3: [W9] READY

	A	B	C	D	E	F	G	H
1	DATA TABLE 2 TO CALCULATE SALARY BASED ON EDUCATION AND EXPERIENCE							
2					YEARS OF EDUCATION			
3				2000+A5*50+B5*75	12	16	18	21
4	INPUT 1	INPUT 2		1	2950	3250	3400	3625
5				2	3000	3300	3450	3675
6				3	3050	3350	3500	3725
7				4	3100	3400	3550	3775
8				5	3150	3450	3600	3825
9	YEARS EXPERIENCE			6	3200	3500	3650	3875
10				7	3250	3550	3700	3925
11				8	3300	3600	3750	3975
12				9	3350	3650	3800	4025
13				10	3400	3700	3850	4075
14				11	3450	3750	3900	4125
15				12	3500	3800	3950	4175
16				13	3550	3850	4000	4225
17				14	3600	3900	4050	4275
18				15	3650	3950	4100	4325
19								
20								

01-Jan-94 06:17 AM

10–10 DISTRIBUTION ANALYSIS

There are many times when you may be interested in classifying data into an orderly group. For example, you may want to classify the salaries of all the employees of Jack's Manufacturing into nine groups or classify your customers into eight sales groups. The /Data Distribution command will perform this **distribution analysis** for you.

Figure 10–16 shows an example of the /Data Distribution command. To use this command, you first must define the range of values you want to classify. Then select two empty columns. The first one is used for your Bin range. The bin range contains the numeric intervals you want to use for the analysis. When you enter the intervals, 1-2-3 shows how many values are less than or equal to a particular interval but greater than the preceding interval. The column to the right of the bin range must be blank—for the results. In our example, the empty column adjacent to the bin range column will be used by 1-2-3 in calculating the frequency distribution.

In Figure 10–16, we invoked the /Data Distribution command. The values range is B4..B17 and the Bin range is D4..D8 (we have organized salaries into five groups in ascending order). As you can see, the first frequency value is 6. This means there are six people with incomes between $0 and $20,000. There are four people with incomes between $20,001 and $40,000, and so forth. The last frequency value is 0, which indicates that nobody is making more than $100,000.

Figure 10–16
Example of /Data Distribution.

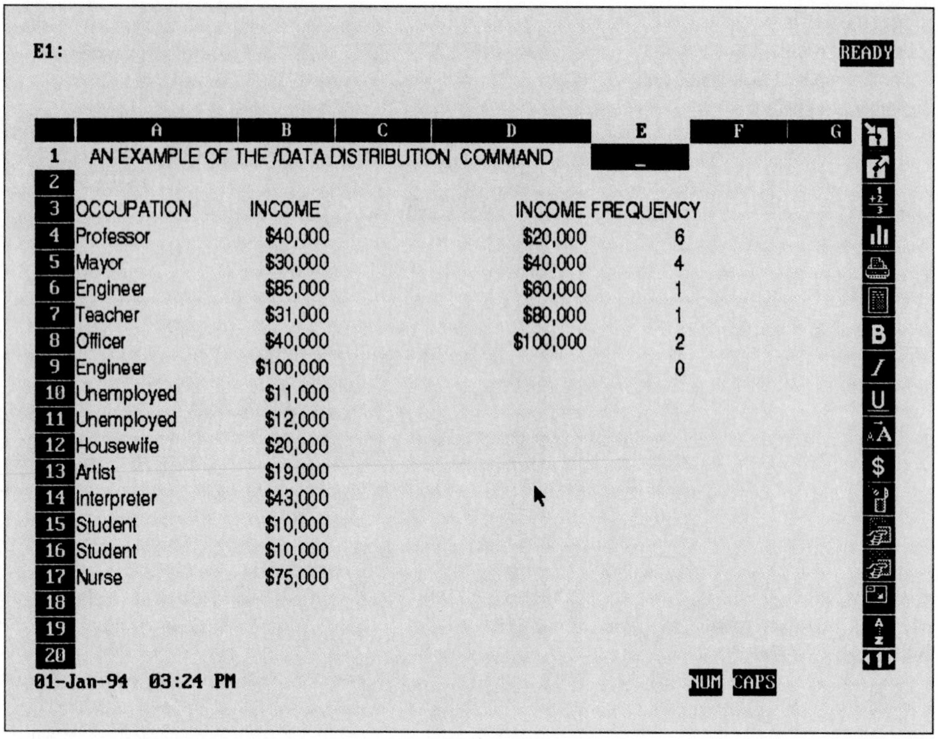

SUMMARY

This chapter reviewed database operations using 1-2-3. We discussed Sort and Search operations, and we touched on the AND and OR search criteria. We also reviewed database statistical functions. The chapter concluded with a discussion of the Data Fill, Data Table, and Data Distribution commands. See Table 10–1 for database SmartIcons.

REVIEW QUESTIONS

*These questions are answered in Appendix A.

1. What is a database?
2. How do you create a database using 1-2-3?
3. What is the difference between numeric and nonnumeric data in a database?
*4. How do you erase a record in a database?
5. How do you erase a field in a database?
*6. How many fields can you have in a database?
7. How many records can you have in a database?
8. How do you perform editing in a database?
9. How do you sort a database?
*10. What is the difference between the Primary-Key and Secondary-Key options?
11. What is the difference between the AND condition and the OR condition in the Criterion range?
*12. How many fields can be included in your Criterion range?
13. What is the difference between a Sort and a Search range?

Table 10–1
Database Icons

WYSIWYG Mode	Text Mode	Description
A Z	A→Z	Sorts a database in ascending order (A through Z and smallest to largest values), using the selected column as the sort key.
Z A	Z→A	Sorts a database in descending order (Z through A and largest to smallest values), using the selected column as the sort key.
	FILL	Fills the highlighted range with a sequence of values.

Column 1 shows icons if WYSIWYG is attached. Column 2 shows icons as they appear when WYSIWYG is either not attached or is set to: Display Mode Text.
The icons identified by **W** work only when WYSIWYG is attached.

14. How many database statistical functions does 1-2-3 have?

15. What is the major difference between these functions and their statistical counterparts?

16. What are two applications of the /Data Fill command?

17. What are the default values for the /Data Fill command?

***18.** When does the /Data Fill command stop building tables?

19. Why, and how, can /Data Table 1 and /Data Table 2 be used as tools for decision support systems?

20. Give two applications of /Data Table 1 and /Data Table 2.

21. What are some of the applications of the /Data Distribution command?

22. Why must the bin range in /Data Distribution be in ascending order?

***23.** What will happen in /Data Distribution if one of your data items falls outside the bin range?

HANDS-ON EXPERIENCE

1. Generate the following database for a 1-2-3 class:

First Name	Last Name	Major	Age	Sex	GPA
Cora	Barnes	CS	22	F	3.20
Sue	Jones	MIS	29	F	2.80
Bobby	Trana	CS	30	F	3.70
Tammy	Smith	Marketing	22	F	3.85
John	Porsche	Management	36	M	3.60
Brian	Raban	Accounting	19	M	2.20
Adam	Vigen	MIS	21	M	3.70
Clark	Standard	CS	28	M	3.00
Stanley	Jones	Personnel	24	M	2.90
Harry	Mohan	Management	26	M	2.75

a. Add two more students to this list.
b. Sort this list by GPA.
c. Sort this list by age.
d. Sort first by sex, then by age.
e. Extract all MIS majors.
f. Extract all MIS majors who have a GPA greater than 3.70.
g. Extract students majoring in either MIS or accounting.

h. Extract students older than 25 years who have a GPA greater than 3.50 and who are female.
i. Extract students who are between 30 and 20 years old.
j. Extract students who are either under 20 or above 30 years old.

2. Using the /Data Fill command, build a table with a Start value of 10, a Step value of 5, and a Stop value of 200. Define your own fill range.
3. Using /Data Table 1, construct a table for the different loan payments for an automobile costing \$30,000 with a 5-year loan with interest rates of 6, 7, 8, 9, 10, 11, 12, 13, and 14 percent.
4. Using /Data Table 2, construct a table for the different loan payments for an automobile costing \$30,000 with 3-, 4-, 5-, and 6-year loans with interest rates of 6, 7, 8, 9, 10, 11, 12, 13, and 14 percent.
5. Using the /Data Distribution command, classify the following sales data into six groups. The interval between each group is 20,000:

100,000
150,000
135,000
200,000
164,000
169,000
220,000
300,000
250,000

6. Retrieve CHAPT8 and perform the following:
   a. Sort the existing database by age.
   b. Sort the existing database by total score.
   c. Sort the existing database by sex and major.
   d. Extract all the MIS majors.
   e. Extract all the MIS majors who are female.
   f. Extract all the MIS majors who are female and are graduate students.
   g. Extract all the students who have a total score greater than 92.
   h. Extract all the students who are MIS or CS majors.
   i. Using the Unique option, print one representative of each major.
   j. Save this worksheet as CHAPT10.
   k. Using the Delete option, delete all the students who are majoring in CS and are freshmen.
7. Retrieve CHAPT8 and perform the following:
   a. Using /Data Fill, number all students from 1 to 10 in column K.
   b. Sort this new database by age.
   c. Using column K as the primary key, return the worksheet to its original form.
   d. Using database statistical functions, generate the seven statistics for male and female students.
   e. Using /Data Distribution, generate a distribution analysis for the total scores. Save this final worksheet as CHAPT10 (use the Replace option).
8. Using the database presented in Figure 10–17, do the following:
   a. Extract all the employees whose phone number starts with the digits 58.
   b. Extract all the employees who are on the fourth floor and whose phone number starts with the digits 58.
   c. Extract all the employees who are on the fourth floor, whose phone number starts with the digits 58, and who are in office 16.
   d. Extract all of the R&D employees.
   e. Sort the database by phone number in descending order.
   f. Sort all the employees by department in descending order, then by floor in ascending order.

Figure 10–17
A sample database.

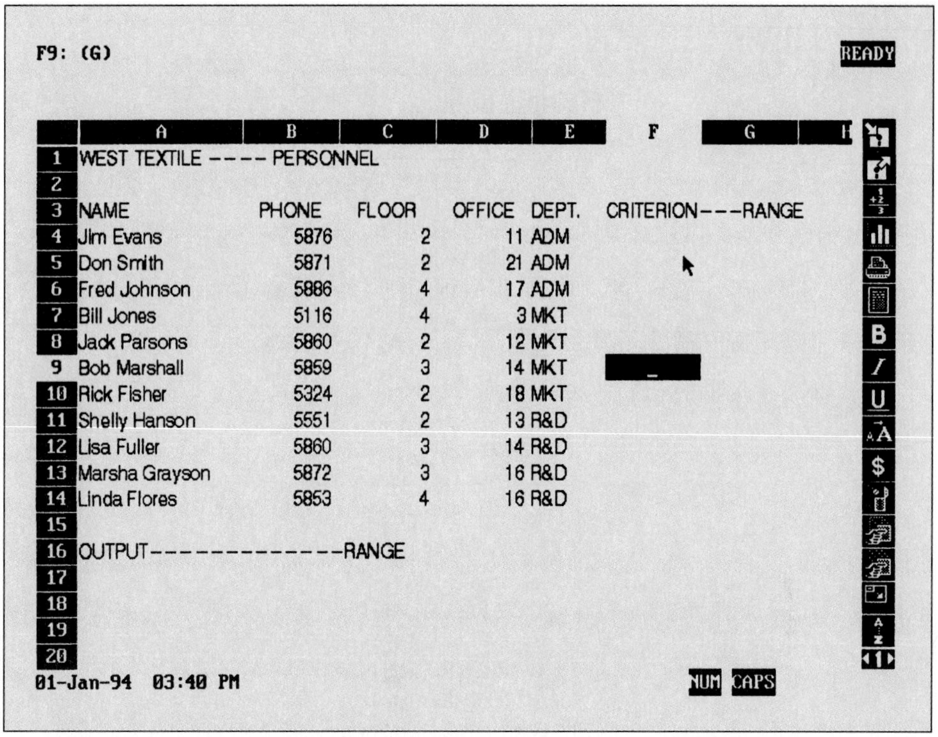

KEY TERMS

- Database
- Database statistical function
- Distribution analysis
- Multiple criteria
- Search
- Single criterion
- Sort
- What-if analysis

KEY COMMANDS

- Delete
- Distribution
- Extract
- Find
- Query
- Sort
- Unique

MISCONCEPTIONS AND SOLUTIONS

Misconception You try to sort a worksheet and you leave out a portion of the worksheet in your data range. There is no way to return to the original database (except by retyping it).

> **Solution** Either save the original database in a file or make sure that you have included the entire database in your data range.

Misconception You used the Extract option but not all the appropriate data have been extracted.

> **Solution** Check to see whether your Output range is large enough.

Misconception If you perform different types of sort operations with the same worksheet, you may end up with erroneous results.

> **Solution** After each sort use the Reset option to clear the sort range as well as the sort keys. Then you can start fresh with the next sort.

ARE YOU READY TO MOVE ON?

Multiple Choice

1. When using 1-2-3 as a database, you can include up to
   a. 256 fields
   b. 8,192 records
   c. 128 fields
   d. 256 records
   e. both a and b
2. 1-2-3 allows
   a. one key as a sort key
   b. two keys as sort keys
   c. three keys as sort keys
   d. four keys as sort keys
   e. five keys as sort keys
3. The size of each field in a 1-2-3 database can be up to
   a. 120 characters
   b. 200 characters
   c. 240 characters
   d. 260 characters
   e. 210 characters
4. Field names must be
   a. included in the data range in a Sort operation
   b. included in the data range in a Search operation
   c. excluded from the data range in a Sort operation
   d. included in both Search and Sort operations
   e. both b and c
5. 1-2-3 allows up to
   a. 10 fields in an AND Search operation
   b. 20 fields in an AND Search operation
   c. 30 fields in an AND Search operation
   d. 32 fields in an AND Search operation
   e. none of the above
6. When you perform an OR Search, your desired data item(s)
   a. must be organized horizontally
   b. must be organized vertically
   c. can be organized either horizontally or vertically
   d. must be organized in column AA
   e. none of the above
7. When searching for a numeric field, the address of the field must be preceded by a(n)
   a. plus sign (+)
   b. slash (/)
   c. asterisk (*)
   d. question mark (?)
   e. none of the above
8. The offset value in 1-2-3 statistical functions defines
   a. which row is under investigation
   b. which cell is under investigation
   c. which column is under investigation
   d. which formula is under investigation
   e. none of the above

9. In the /Data Fill command, the default value for Stop is
   a. 0
   b. 1
   c. 2000
   d. 8191
   e. 9182
10. In the /Data Distribution command, if a particular data item doesn't fall within the identified range, you will receive
    a. a number that tells you how many of such data you have
    b. an error
    c. 0
    d. 8192
    e. none of the above

True/False

1. When using 1-2-3 as a database, you can have only 128 fields.
2. 1-2-3 allows five keys for sort operations.
3. The names of the fields in a database must be included as part of the data range in Sort operations.
4. The size of each field can be from 1 to 240 characters long in 1-2-3.
5. 1-2-3 allows only 20 fields to be considered in an AND Search (horizontal search).
6. To search for either criterion (OR Search), your desired items must be in a horizontal line.
7. When you use the Extract option, you must specify an Output range.
8. Editing in a 1-2-3 database is different from editing in a 1-2-3 worksheet.
9. Usually, 1-2-3 database statistical functions provide more flexibility than their worksheet counterparts.
10. In the /Data Fill command, the default value for Step is 0.

ANSWERS

Multiple Choice		True/False	
1.	e	1.	F
2.	b	2.	F
3.	c	3.	F
4.	e	4.	T
5.	d	5.	F
6.	b	6.	F
7.	a	7.	T
8.	c	8.	F
9.	d	9.	T
10.	a	10.	F

1-2-3 Macros

11

11–1 INTRODUCTION

In this chapter we discuss the principles of macro design and use. Guidelines for naming, debugging, and documenting macros are provided. The chapter introduces over 20 of the most commonly used macros.

11–2 DEFINING A MACRO

In simple terms, a **macro** is a collection of keystrokes. As you have learned, all commands in 1-2-3 are executed with a series of keystrokes; therefore, everything in 1-2-3 can be done by using a macro.

Suppose that you have to type a statement in many different locations of your worksheet. You have two alternatives: either type this statement over and over or create a macro. Whenever you are issuing the same commands or statements again and again, consider using macros. Macros increase the speed and accuracy of your operations.

11–3 CREATING A MACRO

The first question asked by novice macro users is, "Where do I put the macro?" You can put a macro in any of the empty cells in your worksheet. It is a good practice to put a macro in a location that is easy to reach but out of your way. Most macro users put the names of their macros in column AA—close enough for easy access. You must be careful, however, if you use the /Worksheet Insert Row or /Worksheet Delete Row command. You may insert a blank row into your macro or delete one of your macro lines. Putting your macros outside your active area is also a good practice. In this case, /WDR or /WIR will not affect your macros.

Move the cellpointer to cell AB1 and type the following label:

THE TOTAL COSTS OF PRODUCTION FOR THIS PERIOD

Next, you must name your macro. A macro name can be any letter of the alphabet, uppercase or lowercase. The name must be preceded by a back slash (\), and you must enter the name as a label using one of the label prefixes. To name your macro \A, in cell AA1, enter

'\A

Next, you must name the cell in which the macro is residing. Move the cellpointer to cell AB1 and select /Range Name Create. Type *\A* for the name and press Enter. Next, 1-2-3 prompts you for the range. Because your cellpointer is already in cell AB1, you just have to press Enter. You can name a macro with up to 15 characters using the same procedure. To execute a macro with a name longer than 1 character, you must press Alt+F3, then type the macro name or point to it.

Figure 11–1 shows your first macro. You can execute this macro from any location in the worksheet. Move the cellpointer to cell A1. Press the Alt and the A keys at the same time. The phrase "THE TOTAL COSTS OF PRODUCTION FOR THIS PERIOD" appears in the control panel. Just press Enter to enter this label into cell A1.

The next question you may ask is, "Can I include Enter in a macro?" Yes, you can. Each key on your keyboard has a macro **key representative.** Table 11–1 shows most of the key representatives and commands.

Figure 11–1
Sample macro.

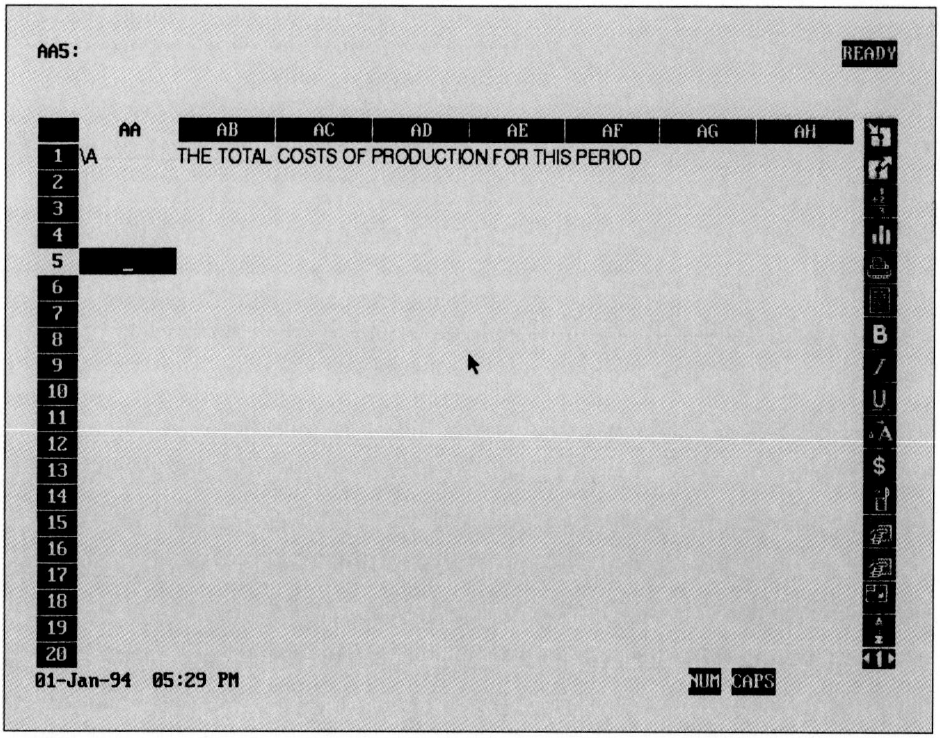

Table 11–1
Key Representatives

Description	Macro Keyboard
Absolute	{ABS}
Backspace	{BACKSPACE} or {BS}
Shift+Tab (one screen left)	{BIGLEFT}
Tab (one screen right)	{BIGRIGHT}
Calc (F9)	{CALC}
Delete (only in EDIT mode)	{DELETE} or {DEL}
Down arrow	{DOWN}
Edit (F2)	{EDIT}
End	{END}
Escape	{ESCAPE} or {ESC}
Goto (F5)	{GOTO}
Graph (F10)	{GRAPH}
Home	{HOME}
Left arrow	{LEFT}
Name (F3)	{NAME}
PgDn	{PGDN}
PgUp	{PGUP}
Query (F7)	{QUERY}
Enter	~
Right arrow	{RIGHT}
Table (F8)	{TABLE}
To enter braces	{{{entry}}}
To enter tilde as ~	{~}
Up arrow	{UP}
Window	{WINDOW}

To specify two or more consecutive uses of the same key, you can include a repetition factor within the braces. For example, {DOWN 6} tells 1-2-3 to move the cellpointer down six cells.

As you can see, the representative for the Enter key is the tilde (~). Move to cell AB1 and edit the content of this cell by pressing F2. Add a tilde to the end of the label. Now the content of AB1 is as follows:

THE TOTAL COSTS OF PRODUCTION FOR THIS PERIOD~

Move the cursor to cell A2 and invoke your macro by pressing Alt+A. This time the phrase is entered directly into cell A2—you don't have to press Enter.

The macro you just created contains only a label. You also can use macros to automate commands. To create this kind of macro, first you must record all the steps that you follow for performing a command. Suppose that you want to format a number with the Currency format and two decimal places. The keys you press to do this are as follows:

/ (to display the Main menu)
R (to choose Range)
F (to select Format)
C (to choose Currency)
2 (to select 2 decimal places)
Enter (to enter the 2)
Enter (to enter the cell as the range to be formatted)

To create this macro, move the cellpointer to cell AA3 and enter

'\B

In cell AB3, enter

'/RFC2~~

Use /Range Name Create to name cell AB3 as \B. Now, move the cellpointer to the cell that contains the number you want to format and invoke your macro. The number will be formatted as you wanted. Figure 11–2 shows this process (the column width has been set to 12, otherwise you will receive a series of asterisks).

11–4 CREATING AN INTERACTIVE MACRO

In the formatting example, you used a macro to format numbers that are already entered into your worksheet. You also can create an **interactive macro** so that when you execute it, the macro process will stop and wait for you to enter a number, and then continue. You use a question mark (?) to accomplish this.

To show how this feature works, move your cellpointer to column AB1 (in a blank worksheet) and type the following:

YOU TELL ME A NUMBER
{DOWN}
{?}~
'/RFC2~~

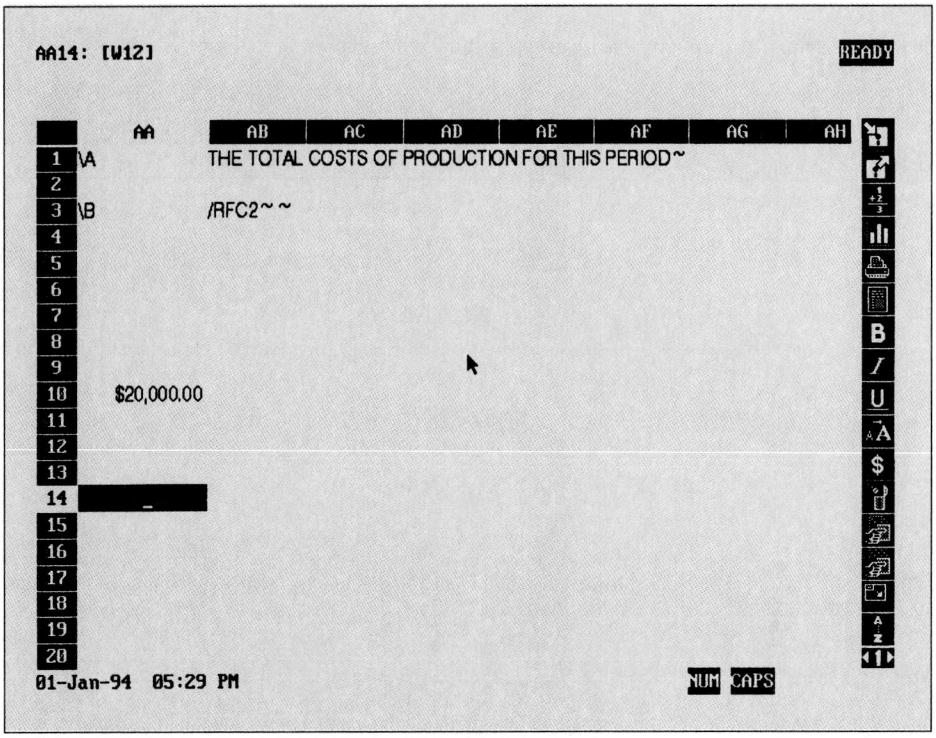

Figure 11–2
Formatting macro.

Name this macro \C. Move the cellpointer to cell AA6 (be sure the cell width is 12) and invoke the macro. 1-2-3 displays the label

YOU TELL ME A NUMBER

in cell AA6. The mode indicator CMD is displayed at the bottom of the screen, meaning that the macro is in progress. The macro is waiting for you to enter a number. Type *36000* and press Enter. The number will be entered and formatted. Figure 11–3 shows this process.

You can enhance the macro by including the statement

'/WCS {?}

(Worksheet Column Set-Width) to enable you to set the column width. You also could include a question mark in place of the number of decimal places, so that you can enter the number of decimal places yourself. Figure 11–4 shows these variations of the original macro. To stop a macro, press Ctrl+Break.

11–5 EXECUTING A MACRO

A macro can contain up to 240 keystrokes. The macro is executed from left to right and top to bottom. As soon as the macro encounters a blank cell, it halts the execution. Therefore, if you are putting more than one macro in a worksheet, make sure there is at least one empty line between macros.

It is also a good idea to document your macro. Because the name of your macro is only one letter long, there is no way to remember what each macro does. To the right of the macro, you should skip one cell, then type a description of what task a particular macro performs. Figure 11–5 shows an example of a macro.

Figure 11–3
Interactive macro.

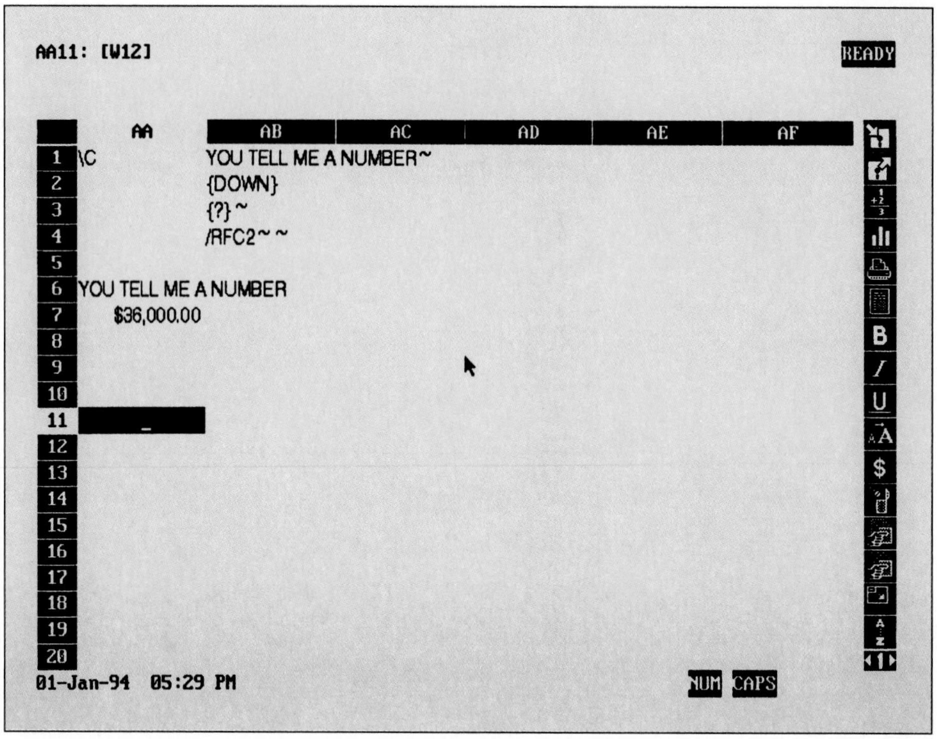

Figure 11–4
Variations of interactive macro.

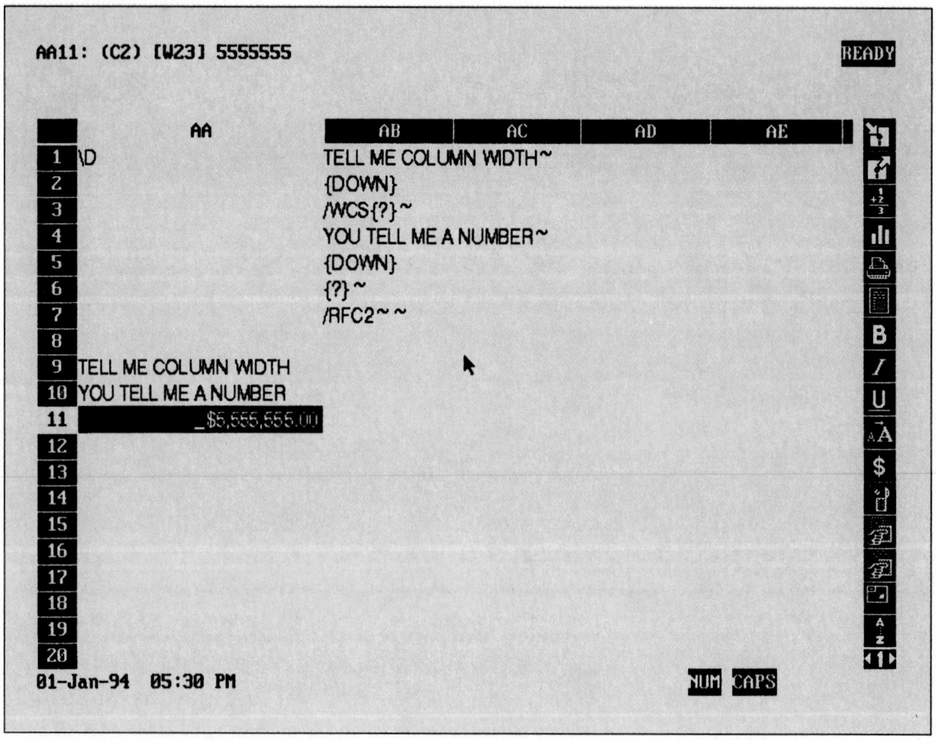

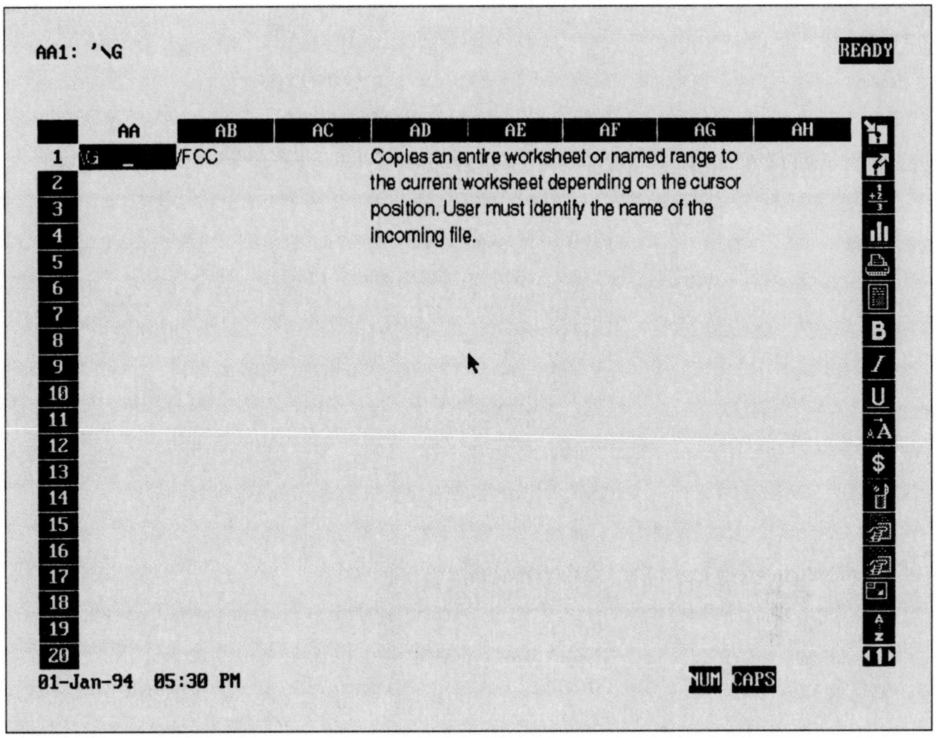

Figure 11–5
Example of a documented macro.

In cell AA1, the letter \G is the name of the macro. In cell AB1 is the macro itself. And, finally, in cell AD1 the function of the macro is described.

11–6 DEBUGGING A MACRO

Of course, you can always make a mistake when you are typing a macro. However, it is hard to **debug** (edit) macros because they are executed so fast. 1-2-3 provides a facility for slowing down the execution so that you can step through your macro a keystroke at a time. Press Alt+F2. (Also see Table 11–2 presented at the end of the chapter for macro SmartIcons.) The status indicator will display

STEP

Next, invoke your macro, the STEP indicator disappears, and your macro is displayed on the lower left corner of the screen. In this mode, 1-2-3 pauses after the execution of each keystroke. To continue, press any key. If you see the problem, you can press Ctrl+Break to abort the execution of the macro. Then you can edit your macro.

If you continue through your macro step by step (by pressing a key) until the macro is fully executed, the macro display on the lower left corner of the screen disappears and the STEP will be back, which means the macro is fully executed. To get out of STEP mode, press Alt+F2, and the STEP indicator disappears.

11–7 CREATING AN AUTOMATIC MACRO

If you name your macro \0 (zero), it will execute automatically when the worksheet containing this macro is loaded. This **automatic macro** feature is very useful for designing menus. If you save your worksheet containing the \0 macro as AUTO123.WK1, it will be loaded into RAM automatically when you start 1-2-3. Figure 11–6 shows a \0 macro.

11–8 CREATING A MACRO LIBRARY

When you get used to designing and using macros, you may want to copy some of your macros from worksheet to worksheet. If you put all your macros in a remote location of your worksheet, such as column AA, and if you document these macros properly, you can use these macros again and again. This is called a **macro library.** Be aware, however, that if you transfer your macros to a different worksheet, you must rename them. Figure 11–7 presents some commonly used macros. The best way to transfer your macros from worksheet to worksheet is to use the /File Xtract command first. Then, by using /File Combine Copy, you can enter these macros into a new worksheet.

11–9 SELECTED MACRO COMMANDS

1-2-3 macro commands perform specific tasks. Because these commands are very similar to programming language commands, they make 1-2-3 a powerful programming language. Some of the most commonly used macro commands are discussed next.

11–9–1 {BRANCH address}

The {BRANCH} command continues macro execution at a specified cell. The specified location or address can be either a single cell or a range. This command

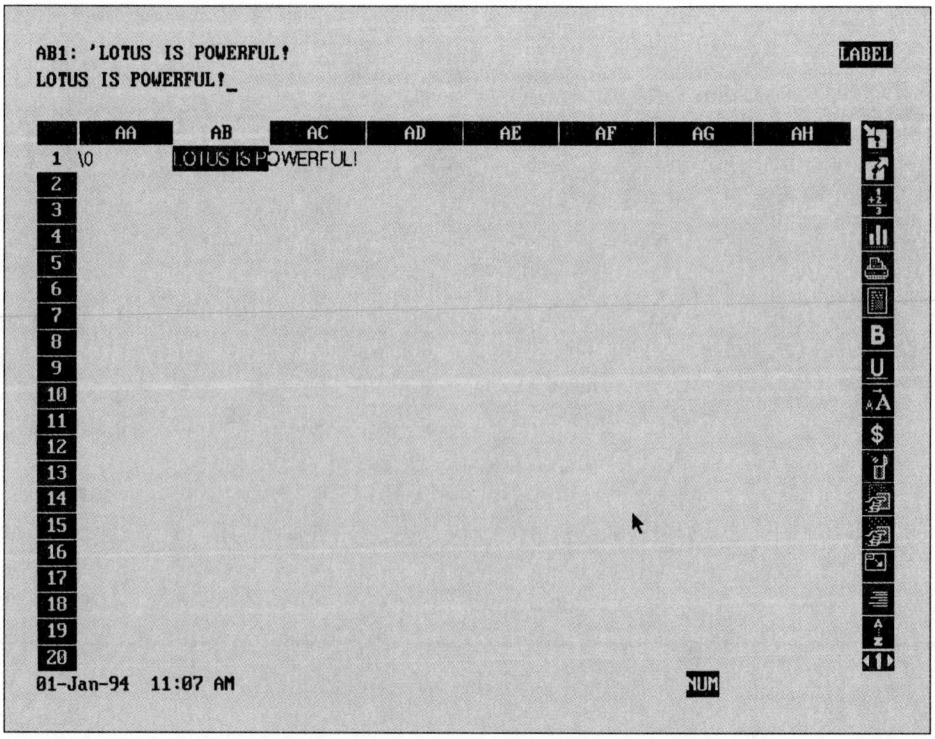

Figure 11–6
Automatic worksheet and automatic macro.

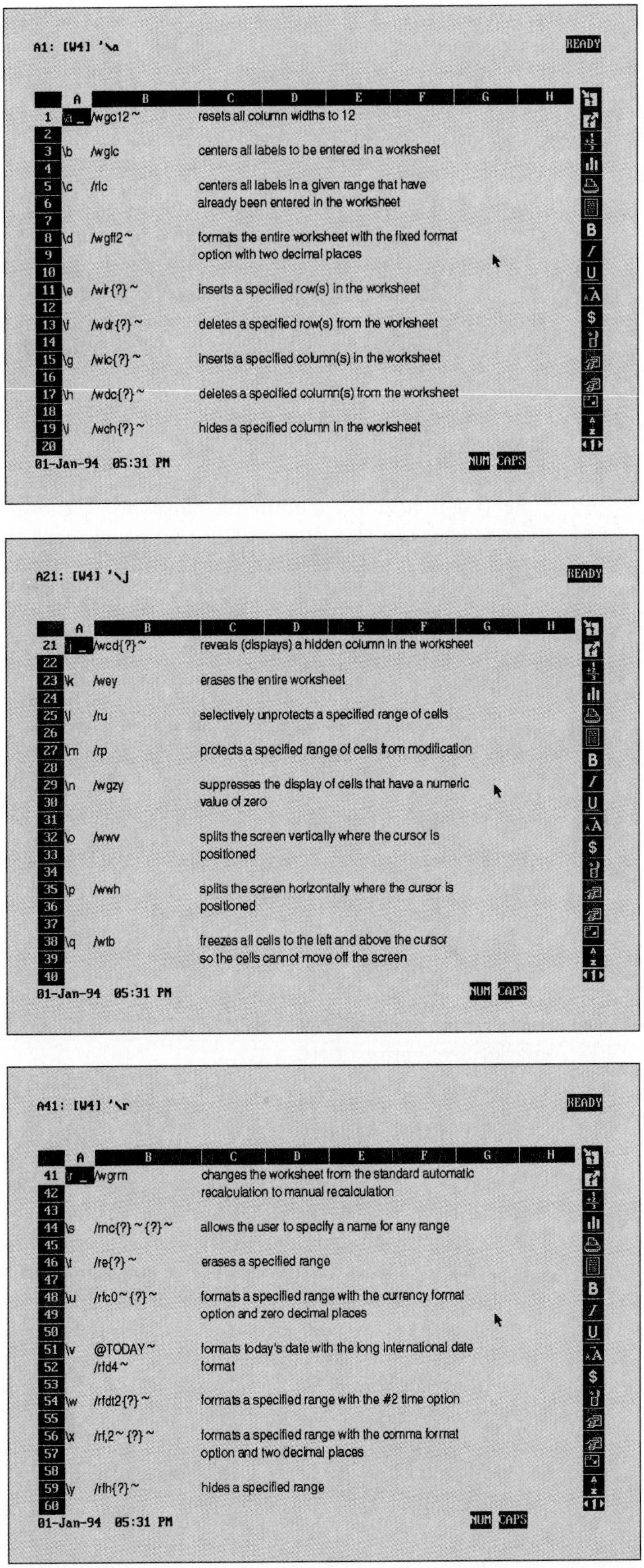

Figure 11–7
Commonly used macros.

is the same as a GOTO command; however, there is a difference between the two. The 1-2-3 Goto command moves the cellpointer. The command {BRANCH} transfers control (or macro execution) to a specified location. See Figure 11–8.

11–9–2 {IF}

The command {IF} executes a macro conditionally. This command is similar to the IF-THEN-ELSE command available in many programming languages. The instructions in the cell after the IF are the THEN part, and those below the cell are the ELSE part. If the expression does not have a value of zero, 1-2-3 considers it true and the statement in the same cell (the cell that includes IF) will be executed; otherwise, the statement in the cell below will be executed. See Figure 11–8.

11–9–3 {GET address}

The {GET address} command pauses for the user to input a single character, then stores it in an address. The single character can be either a standard typewriter key or a 1-2-3 standard key (TABLE, QUERY, etc.). See Figure 11–8.

11–9–4 {LET address, number, or string}

The {LET} command stores a number or string in an address or location. It can be used to generate a label or numeric entry. For example, {LET R10, 2+3: value} stores the number 5 and {LET R11, 2+3: string} stores the label 2+3. See Figure 11–9.

11–9–5 {GETLABEL prompt, address} and {GETNUMBER}

The {GETLABEL} command pauses for the user to type a character string, then stores it as a label in the specified address. {GETNUMBER} does the same thing but stores the data as a number. Your prompt (your message or statement) must be short enough to fit into the control panel. Also, if your prompt includes separators (commas or semicolons), you must enclose the prompt within quotation marks. See Figure 11–10.

11–9–6 {FOR Counter, Start, Stop, Starting address}

The {FOR} command executes a macro a specified number of times. This is equivalent to the FOR-NEXT loop in BASIC or the DO loop in FORTRAN. Other programming languages have something similar to this command. The Counter keeps track of the number of times the macro has been executed. Start is the starting value stored in the counter location. Stop marks the terminal value that the counter variable can achieve. Step tells the counter how to increment the counter. The Starting address is the cell address or range in which the macro starts the execution. 1-2-3 always checks the condition of Start, Stop, and Step before executing the macro. If the value of step is 0, an endless loop is generated (a loop that never stops). If the start value exceeds the stop value, the macro will not be executed at all. See Figure 11–11.

Figure 11–8
Example of GET, Goto, IF, and BRANCH.

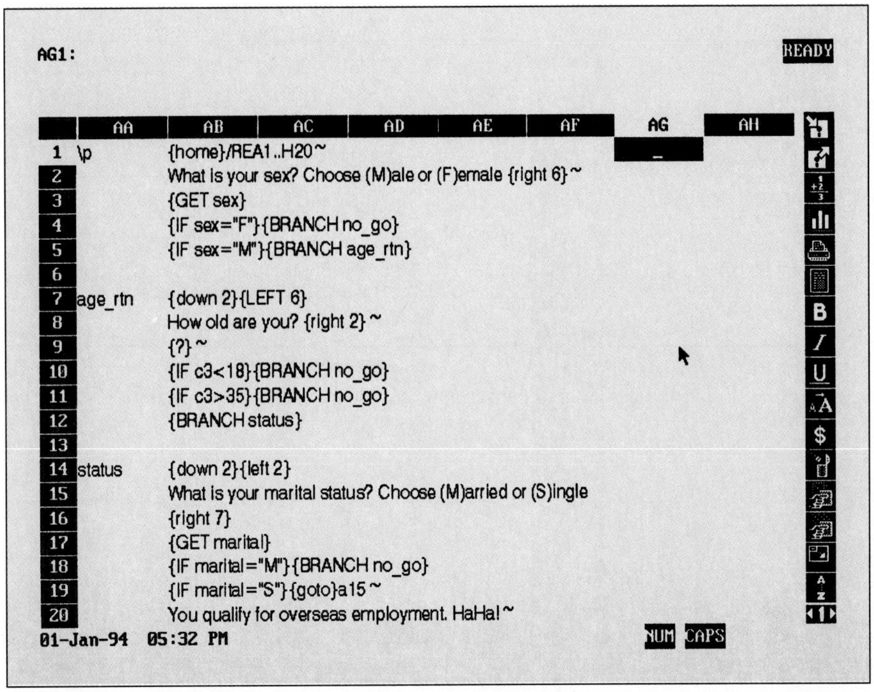

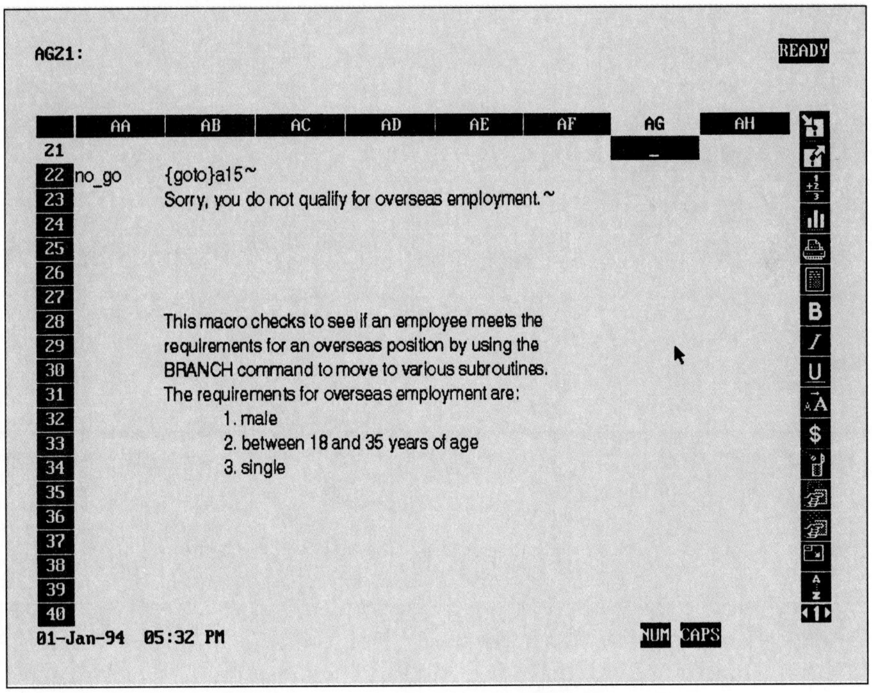

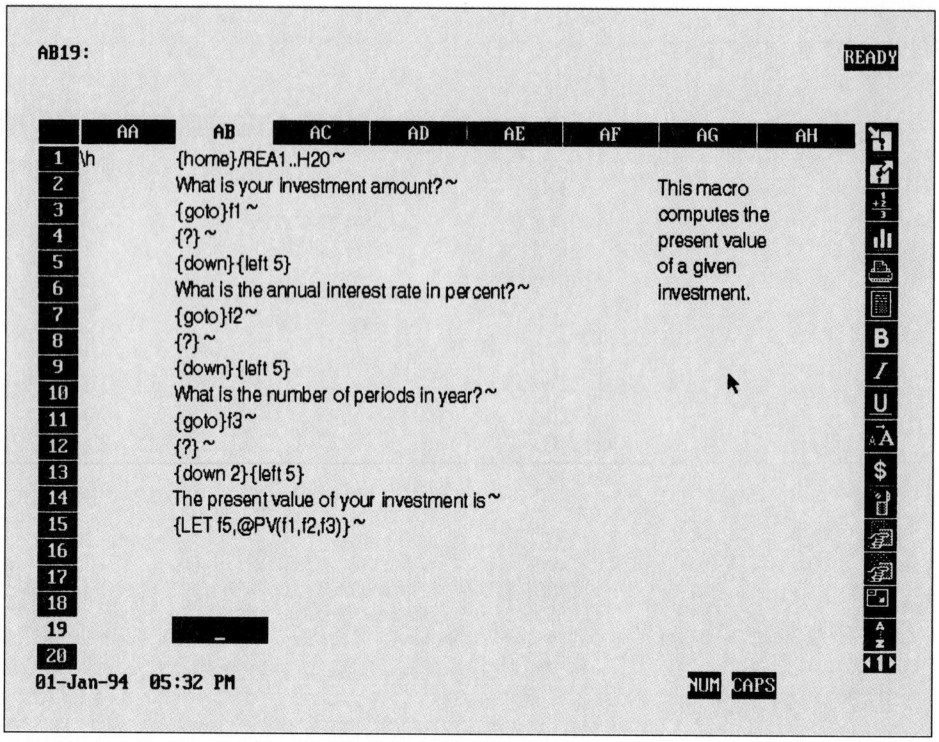

Figure 11–9
Example of LET command.

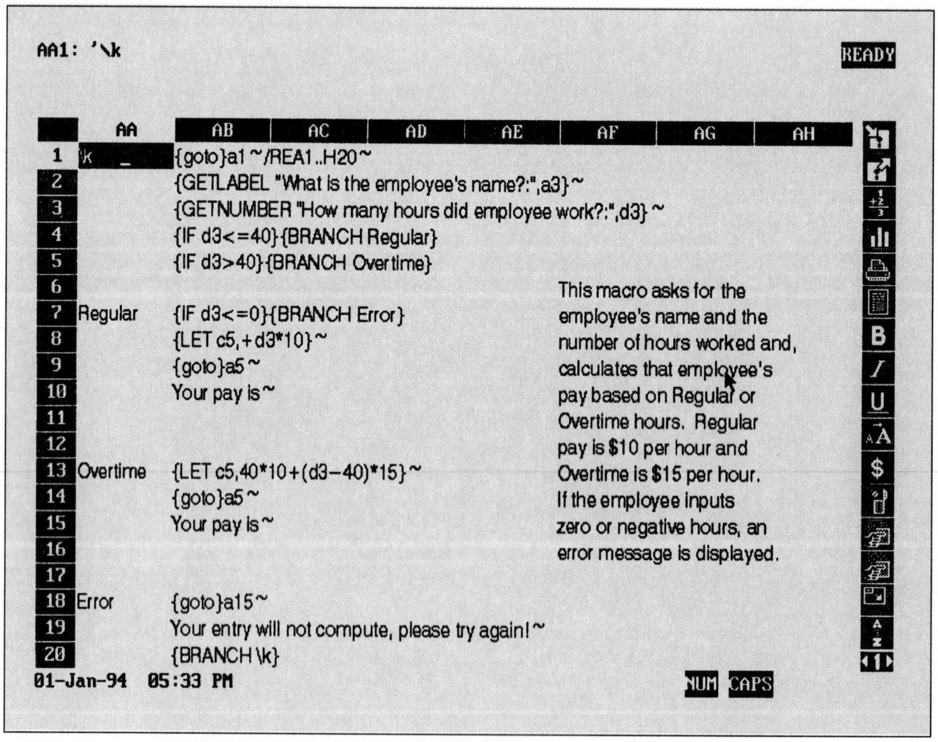

Figure 11–10
Example of GETLABEL and GET-NUMBER.

Figure 11–11
Example of the FOR command.

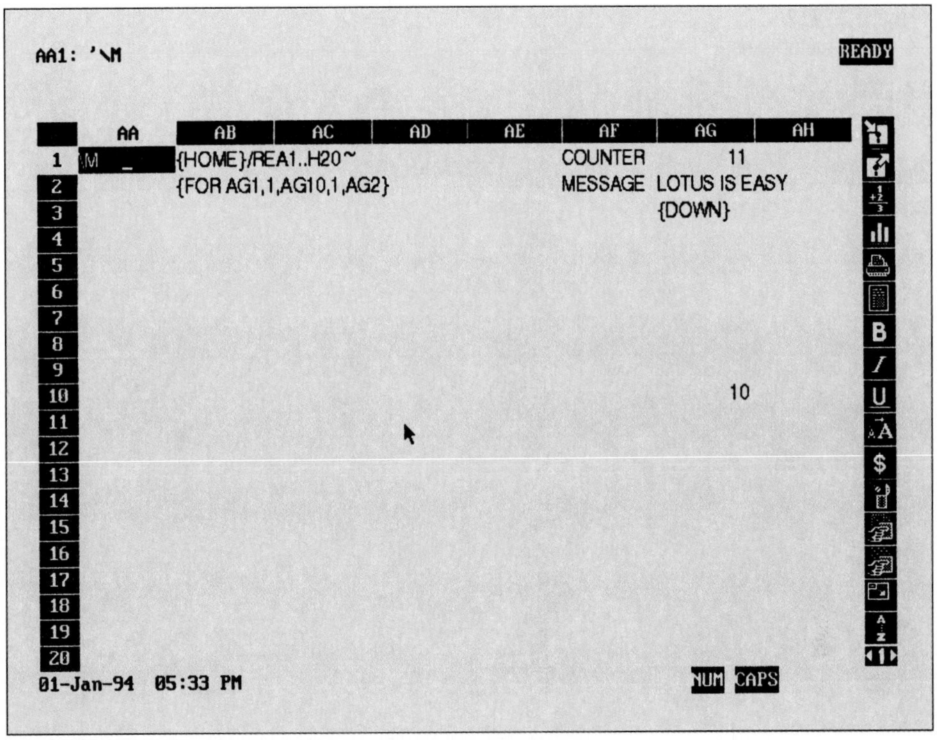

11–10 ASSIGNING A MACRO TO A USER ICON

To assign a macro to a user icon, do the following:

1. Select the user icon (the last icon in the palette next to the last palette, see Figure 11–12). The user icon descriptions dialog box appears (see Figure 11–13).
2. Select the user icon to which you want to assign a macro. We selected U1.
3. Select Assign Macro to Icon. The user-defined icon dialog box appears (see Figure 11–14).
4. In the Icon Description box, type a description of the macro. The limit is 72 characters. We typed *FORMAT*. This description appears in the control panel when you highlight the icon.
5. In the Macro Text box, type the macro instruction. The limit is 240 characters. We typed */RFC2~~*. You can also use an existing set of macro instructions in the current worksheet as the text for the macro.
6. Select OK, OK.

Now if you execute this macro (the FORMAT macro), the highlighted range will be formatted with the currency option and two decimals.

To assign one of the macros in the current worksheet to one of these icons, type the macro name in the Source Range box. For example, type \A and then select the Get Macro from Sheet option in order to guide 1-2-3 to the macro text position.

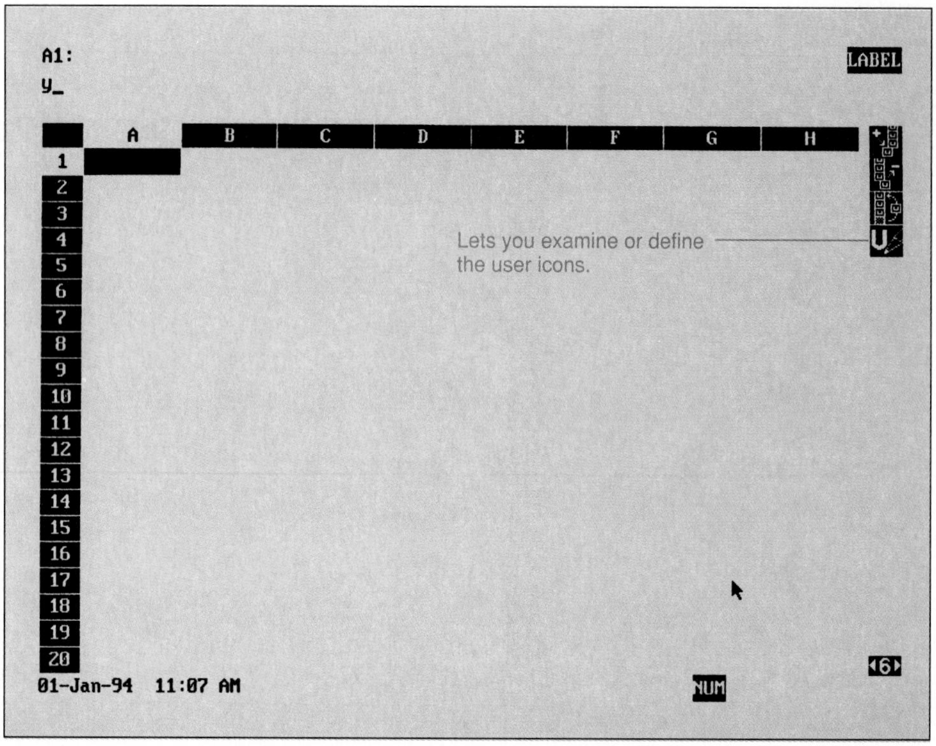

Figure 11–12
Icons for customizing.

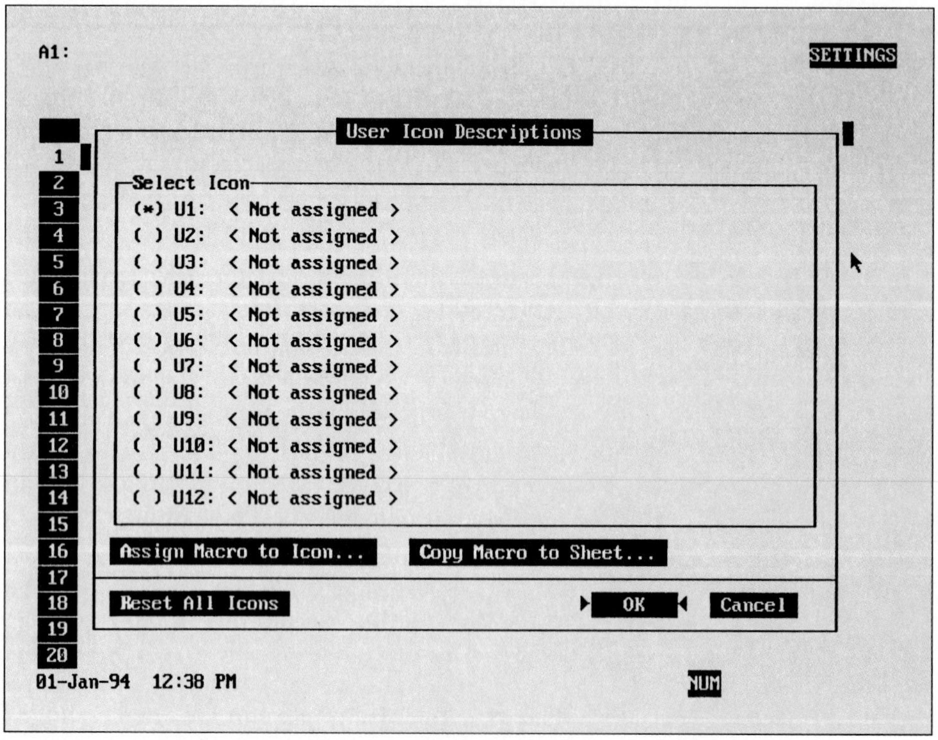

Figure 11–13
User icon descriptions.

Figure 11–14
User-defined icon.

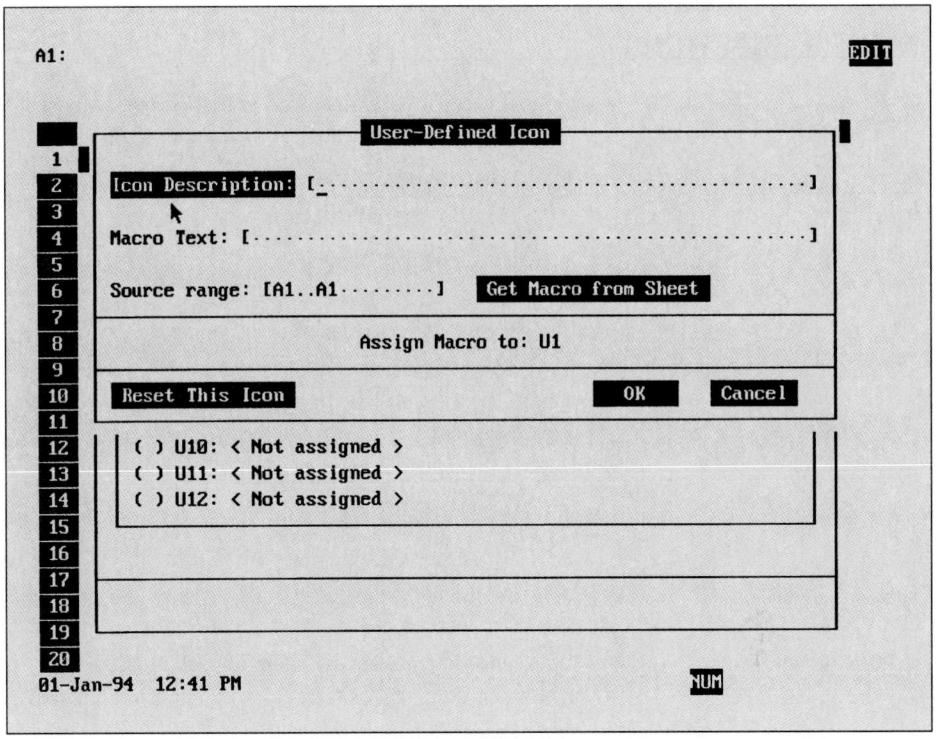

SUMMARY

This chapter covered the principles of macro design and macro use, as well as macro creation, documentation, and execution. We also discussed debugging a macro and the automatic macro. More than 20 commonly used macros we discussed should provide you with a good background for getting started with macros. Also, selected macro commands were introduced. We concluded with a discussion on assigning a macro to a user icon. See Table 11–2 for macro SmartIcons.

Table 11–2
Macro Icons

WYSIWYG Mode	Text Mode	Description
	STEP	Turns on STEP mode, which executes macros one step at a time for debugging. Equivalent to pressing Alt+F2.
	RUN	Runs the macro you assigned to user icon U1. The SmartIcons add-in includes 12 user icons, labeled U1, U2, and so on through U12.
	U1	Lets you select and run a macro.

Column 1 shows icons if WYSIWYG is attached. Column 2 shows icons as they appear when WYSIWYG is either not attached or is set to: Display Mode Text.
The icons identified by **W** work only when WYSIWYG is attached.

REVIEW QUESTIONS

*These questions are answered in Appendix A.

1. What is a macro?
2. What are some of the advantages of using a macro?
3. How do you name a macro?
*4. How do you invoke a macro?
5. How do you document a macro?
*6. What is the function of a \0 macro?
7. How many macros can you have in a worksheet?
8. What is a self-booting worksheet?
*9. What are some of the applications of a self-booting worksheet?
10. How do you debug a macro?
11. What is the STEP indicator?
12. When you start debugging, what is displayed on the lower left corner of the screen?
*13. What is the CMD indicator?
14. How do you get out of the STEP mode?
*15. How do you halt the execution of a macro?
*16. How many keystrokes can be included in a macro?
17. How is a macro executed?
18. What are some examples of macro commands? What are some applications of each command?
19. How do you assign a macro to a user icon?
20. Can you assign a pre-existing macro to one of these icons?

HANDS-ON EXPERIENCE

1. Design a macro to generate a pie chart using the following data:

Sue	2,000
Sam	18,000
Sara	15,000

2. Design a macro to load a file from disk to worksheet and then erase the worksheet.
3. Design a macro to print the following message and then exit the 1-2-3 worksheet:

   IT WAS A PRODUCTIVE SESSION!

4. Design an interactive macro that accepts any three numbers and then calculates their average.
5. Design a macro that accepts any number up to eight digits long and then formats it using the Comma option with three decimal places.
6. Design a macro that prints any portion of a worksheet using default settings.
7. Retrieve CHAPT10 and perform the following:
   a. Erase the current title of this worksheet.
   b. Move the cursor to cell AA1.

c. Generate a macro that automatically prints the old title for this worksheet.
d. Generate a macro that automatically formats all the test scores to a fixed format with two decimal places.

8. Using the FOR command, design a macro that displays the message COMPUTERS ARE POWERFUL 20 times.

KEY TERMS

Automatic macro	Key representative	Macro
Debug	Interactive macro	Macro library

KEY COMMANDS

Alt+F3 (to execute a macro that has a name longer than one character)

BRANCH (to transfer control to a different location)

Create an interactive macro (?)

FOR (to execute a task a number of times)

GET (to store a value in an address)

GETLABEL (to receive nonnumeric data from the keyboard)

GETNUMBER (to receive numeric data from the keyboard)

IF (to compare against a value or an address)

Turn on SINGLE STEP mode (Alt+F2)

MISCONCEPTIONS AND SOLUTIONS

Misconception 1-2-3 handles macros and functions differently. 1-2-3 does not adjust cell addresses when you use the Move, Copy, Worksheet Delete, and Worksheet Insert commands. If your macro uses cell addresses and you have rearranged your worksheet, your macro may no longer work.

Solution To avoid this, use range names to refer to cells.

ARE YOU READY TO MOVE ON?

Multiple Choice

1. The maximum number of keyboard macros that 1-2-3 allows is
   a. 23 macros
   b. 24 macros
   c. 25 macros
   d. 26 macros
   e. 27 macros
2. To get out of the STEP mode, you have to press
   a. Break
   b. Alt
   c. Del
   d. Alt+F2
   e. none of the above
3. To start the debugging facility in a macro operation, you have to press
   a. Alt+F2
   b. Alt+F1

c. Alt+F3
d. Ctrl+Del
e. Ctrl+Del+Alt

4. You can include up to __________ in a macro
   a. 200 keystrokes
   b. 210 keystrokes
   c. 240 keystrokes
   d. 190 keystrokes
   e. 180 keystrokes
5. A macro can only be in
   a. cell A1
   b. cell AA1
   c. cell AB1
   d. cell AC1
   e. none of the above
6. The equivalent of the Enter key in macro design is the
   a. question mark (?)
   b. tilde (~)
   c. asterisk (*)
   d. slash (/)
   e. none of the above
7. The CMD status indicator is displayed whenever
   a. a macro execution is over
   b. a macro execution is in progress
   c. a macro is being debugged
   d. a macro has caused an error
   e. none of the above
8. To design an interactive macro, you must use
   a. an asterisk (*)
   b. a tilde (~)
   c. a slash (/)
   d. a question mark (?)
   e. none of the above
9. To document a macro, you must
   a. use a special command
   b. move the cursor to cell A1
   c. skip one column then start typing
   d. use the F6 key
   e. none of the above
10. Which one of the following is not a valid 1-2-3 macro command?
    a. FOR
    b. LET
    c. GET
    d. BRANCH
    e. all of the above

True/False

1. Using 1-2-3 macros, you can automate the keyboard.
2. Assigning a name to a macro is like naming any other cell(s) in the worksheet.
3. To invoke a macro, you only have to type the macro name on the keyboard.
4. You can have only 26 macros in a worksheet.
5. 1-2-3 has a self-booting macro. This macro must be named with the letter "S."

6. A macro, after being designed, can be debugged.
7. The CMD indicator is displayed whenever the execution of the macro is finished.
8. To get out of the STEP mode, you have to press the Break key.
9. Only 10 keystrokes can be included in a macro.
10. You can include a repetition factor within the braces when you design a macro.

ANSWERS

Multiple Choice		True/False	
1.	e	1.	T
2.	d	2.	T
3.	a	3.	F
4.	c	4.	F
5.	e	5.	F
6.	b	6.	T
7.	b	7.	F
8.	d	8.	F
9.	c	9.	F
10.	e	10.	T

Appendix A
Lotus 1-2-3

A

A–1 INTRODUCTION

This appendix provides a summary of Lotus 1-2-3 features not covered or briefly covered in the previous chapters. It summarizes the different types of indicators and function keys, lists 1-2-3 functions, and gives answers to selected review questions. At the end of the appendix, complete 1-2-3 and WYSIWYG command maps are displayed.

A–2 SPECIAL FEATURES

Some of the most important features of 1-2-3 Release 2.4 are listed next.

1. The UNDO feature lets you recover from errors (Alt+F4).
2. The minimal recalculation feature recalculates only cells that depend on the most recent change to the worksheet.
3. The file-linking feature lets you create formulas that rely on values in other worksheets. To link cells from different files, the format is

    +<<file name> >cell reference

    For example, if you want to enter the contents of cell A5 from the worksheet named SAMPLE into cell A1 in your current worksheet, you would enter

    +<<SAMPLE> >A5

    in cell A1.
4. Using the /Graph Name Table command, you can create a table of named graphs. Using /Graph Group (specify the range) Columnwise or Rowwise, you can specify all graph ranges at once. Using /Graph Options Legend Range, you can set legends for all ranges.
5. Using /Worksheet Column Column-Range, you can change the width of one or several columns.
6. The Search/Replace (/Range Search) feature allows you to perform search and replace operations in a range.
7. Network compatibility recognizes a network's built-in file security and ensures that users who save files do not write over each other's changes.
8. The /File Save Backup command renames the previous disk copy of the current file with the extension BAK and saves the new version under the original file name. You do this by using /File Save (for an existing file) and selecting the Backup option instead of the Replace option.
9. The Learn feature records your keystrokes to be used later as macros.

A–3 INDICATORS

In the upper right, lower right, and lower left of a 1-2-3 worksheet, you see information called indicators. There are four types of indicators: mode, status, date, and time.

A–3–1

Mode Indicators

The mode indicator appears in the upper right corner of the worksheet. The important mode indicators include the following:

- WAIT Indicates that 1-2-3 is executing or processing a command. Wait until this indicator goes off before performing another task. WAIT is displayed, for example, when Lotus is recalculating a balance sheet after you have changed one of the values.
- VALUE Indicates that you are entering a number or a formula.
- READY Indicates that 1-2-3 is ready to accept the next command or the next action. For example, in this mode you can enter data into the worksheet, call the menu, and so forth.
- POINT Indicates that the cellpointer is pointing to a cell or a range.
- MENU Indicates that the 1-2-3 menu is being displayed. For example, when you press the / key (the forward slash key) to invoke the main menu, the indicator is MENU.
- LABEL Indicates that you are entering a label. A label is any nonnumeric data item. If you type *I am busy,* you will see LABEL as the indicator.
- HELP Indicates that you have invoked the help facility.
- FIND This indicator is displayed when the /Data Query Find operation is in progress. For more detail, see Chapter 10.
- FILES This indicator appears whenever a File menu is invoked, such as /File Save or /File Retrieve (see Chapter 5).
- ERROR This indicator appears whenever an error occurs. For example, if you try to save a file in drive A and it doesn't contain a disk, you will receive the ERROR indicator. To clear the error indicator, press either Enter or Esc.
- EDIT This indicator appears when you are performing any kind of editing.

A–3–2

Status Indicators

Status indicators appear in the lower right corner of the worksheet. The important status indicators are as follows:

- STEP When this indicator appears, it means the STEP mode has been turned on. To do this you must press Alt and F2 together. To get out of the STEP mode, press Alt and F2 again.
- SCROLL Indicates that the Scroll Lock Key is on. If you move the cellpointer, the worksheet will move while the cellpointer stays in the same position.
- OVR This indicator appears if the Ins key is on. This is used when you perform some editing tasks.
- NUM Indicates that the Num Lock Key is on. When Num Lock is on, the arrow keys serve as a numeric pad (like a calculator). The arrow keys cannot be used for moving the cellpointer around the worksheet while in this mode.
- END Indicates that the End key has been pressed. This is used in combination with one of the arrow keys for moving to the last location in a worksheet.
- CMD Appears during the execution of a macro. As soon as macro execution is over, the indicator disappears.

- CIRC This indicator appears if a cell is referring to itself. For example, if you enter *+A11* in cell A11, you will see the CIRC indicator. This happens only when the recalculation order is natural. A circular reference may or may not be an error. Many times a circular reference can be resolved by recalculating the worksheet several times, which you can do automatically with the /Worksheet Global Recalculation Iteration command. However, if an error has produced the CIRC indicator, you must find the error and correct it. Use /Worksheet Status to find the location of the error.
- CAPS Indicates that the Caps Lock key is on. To turn it off, press the key again.
- CALC Indicates that the worksheet needs to be recalculated. If you press F9, this indicator will disappear.
- UNDO Indicates that the UNDO feature is on. This means you can reverse (cancel) the last action.

A–3–3 Date and Time Indicators

These indicators appear in the lower left corner of the screen. You can change this format by using /Worksheet Global Default Other or you can delete the indicator with /Worksheet Global Default Other Clock None.

A–4 FUNCTION KEYS

1-2-3 uses the IBM-type keyboard function keys very effectively. These keys make the user's job much easier by performing different tasks. Some of these keys are used individually, such as F1 through F10, and some of them are used in conjunction with other keys, for example, Alt+F2 for STEP mode. Descriptions of these keys follow:

- F1(HELP) Accesses the Lotus online help facility.
- F2(EDIT) Shifts 1-2-3 into EDIT mode. The contents of the current cell are displayed on the control panel and the edit cursor is positioned at the end of the cell's contents. You can perform any editing necessary. When you are finished, press Enter.
- F3(NAME) Displays all the range names while in POINT mode. If you press this key a second time, you will receive a full-screen listing of all the range names. This is helpful if you want to know all the range names before assigning another name.
- F4(ABS) While in the POINT mode, changes the addressing assignment of a cell address. You press this key to cycle through the choices of absolute, mixed, and relative. (See Chapter 6.)
- F5(GOTO) Used to move to any location in the worksheet.
- F6(WINDOW) Moves the cellpointer between two split screens (discussed in Chapter 6).
- F7(QUERY) Performs the most recent /Data Query operation (discussed in Chapter 10).
- F8(TABLE) Repeats the last /Data Table command, for example, recalculates the present table (discussed in Chapter 10).
- F9(CALC) Recalculates the worksheet.

- F10(GRAPH) In the READY mode, redraws the most recent graph. This is very handy when you are performing what-if analysis. (See Chapter 8.)
- ALT+F1(Compose) In conjunction with other keys, ALT+F1 is used to generate international characters.
- ALT+F2(Step) Switches 1-2-3 into STEP mode for debugging a macro.
- ALT+F4(Undo) Reverses the last action.

A–5 SPECIAL KEYS

Besides function keys, some other useful keys to remember include the following:

- Backspace Erases a character or a range to the left of the cursor.
- Backtab (Shift+←) In the READY mode, moves the cellpointer one screen to the left. In the EDIT mode, moves the edit cursor five positions to the left.
- Tab (→) In the READY mode, moves the cellpointer one screen to the right. In the EDIT mode, it moves the edit cursor five positions to the right.
- Break Cancels the current operation. To use this feature, you must press Ctrl+Break.
- Del In the EDIT mode, erases the current character.
- Esc Cancels the current operation, for example, gets you out of the Lotus menu, erases a line, and so forth.
- Alt In conjunction with a macro name, invokes a particular macro.
- Period (.) When you try to enter a range, it anchors the cellpointer (discussed in Chapter 6).
- Enter Finalizes the operation. This can be entering data, issuing a command, and so forth.

A–6 SUMMARY OF LOTUS FUNCTIONS

A–6–1 Mathematical Functions

Function	Result
@ABS(A)	Absolute value of A
@ACOS(A)	Arc cosine of A
@ASIN(A)	Arc sine of A
@ATAN(A)	2-quadrant arc tangent of A
@ATAN2(A,B)	4-quadrant arc tangent of B/A
@COS(A)	Cosine of A
@EXP(A)	E(2.718282) raised to the power A
@INT(A)	Integer part of A
@LN(A)	Log of A base E
@LOG(A)	Log of A base 10
@MOD(A,B)	Remainder of A/B
@PI	Pi (3.14159 . . .)

@RAND	Random number between 0 and 1
@ROUND(A,n)	A rounded to n places
@SIN(A)	Sine of A
@SQRT(A)	Square root of A
@TAN(A)	Tangent of A

A–6–2 Financial Functions

Function	Result
@FV(payment,interest rate,term)	Future value of annuity invested at a certain interest rate for a number of periods
@PV(payment,interest rate,term)	Present value of annuity invested at a certain interest rate for a number of periods
@IRR(estimate,range)	Internal rate of return for range of cash flows—supply estimate interest rate between 0 and 1
@NPV(interest rate,range)	Net present value of future cash flows at constant interest rate
@PMT(principal,interest rate,term)	Loan payment based on principal, at a certain interest rate over a number of periods
@CTERM(interest rate,future value,present value)	Compounded term of an investment reaches from a given present value to a given future value with a given fixed interest rate
@TERM(payment,interest rate,future value)	Number of payment periods necessary to accumulate a given future value
@RATE(future value,present value,term)	Interest rate necessary for a present value to reach a given future value
@SLN(cost,salvage value,life)	Straight-line depreciation
@SYD(cost,salvage value,life,period)	Sum-of-years'-digits depreciation
@DDB(cost,salvage value,life,period)	Double-declining-balance depreciation

A–6–3 Statistical Functions

Function	Result
@AVG(range)	Average of values in the range
@COUNT(range)	Number of nonblank entries in the range
@MAX(range)	Maximum value in the range
@MIN(range)	Minimum value in the range
@STD(range)	Population standard deviation of items in the range
@SUM(range)	Sum of the values in the range
@VAR(range)	Population variance of values in the range

A–6–4 Logical Functions

Function	Result
@FALSE	Returns the logical value 0
@IF(condition,A,B)	Returns A if condition is True, and B if condition is False
@ISAAF	Checks the status of an add-in function
@ISAPP	Checks whether a particular program has been installed or attached with the add-in manager
@ISERR(A)	Returns True (1) if A contains the value ERR; otherwise returns False (0)
@ISNA(A)	Returns True (1) if A contains the value NA; otherwise returns False (0)
@ISNUMBER(A)	Returns True (1) if A contains a numeric value; otherwise returns False (0)
@ISSTRING(A)	Returns True (1) if A contains a string value; otherwise returns False (0)
@TRUE	Returns the logical value 1

A–6–5 String Functions

Function	Result
@CHAR(A)	Returns the ASCII/LICS (Lotus International Character Set) character represented by A
@CODE(string)	Returns the ASCII/LICS code for the first character in the string
@CLEAN(string)	Eliminates nonprintable characters from the string
@EXACT(string1,string2)	Compares two strings
@FIND(search string,string,start number)	Position at which the first occurrence of the search string begins in the string
@LEFT(string,m)	Returns the m leftmost characters in the string
@LENGTH(string)	Returns the length of the string
@LOWER(string)	Changes the string to lowercase
@MID(string,start number,m)	Returns m characters of the string, beginning with the character at start number
@N(range)	Returns the numeric value in the upper left corner cell in the range
@PROPER(string)	Capitalizes the first letter of every word in the string
@REPEAT(string,m)	Duplicates the string m times
@REPLACE(original string,start number,m,new string)	m characters are removed from the original string and replaced with the new string at start number
@RIGHT(string,m)	Returns the m rightmost characters in the string
@S(range)	Returns the string value of a cell in the range
@STRING(y,m)	Returns numeric value y as a string, with m decimal places
@TRIM(string)	Removes leading/trailing spaces from the string
@UPPER(string)	Changes the string to uppercase
@VALUE(string)	Converts the string to a numeric value

A–6–6 Date and Time Functions

Functions that generate serial numbers:

Function	Result
@DATE(year,month,day)	Serial number of year, month, day
@DATEVALUE(date string)	Serial number of date
@NOW	Serial number of current date and time
@TIME(hour,minute,second)	Serial number of time between 0 and 1
@TIMEVALUE(time string)	Serial number of time

Functions that accept serial numbers as input:

Function	Result
@DAY(date number)	Returns day number (1–31) of date number
@HOUR(time number)	Returns hour number (0–23) of time number
@MINUTE(time number)	Returns minute number (0–59) of time number
@MONTH(date number)	Returns month number (1–12) of date number
@SECOND(time number)	Returns second number (0–59) of time number
@YEAR(date number)	Returns year number (0–199) of date number

A–6–7 Special Functions

Function	Result
@@(cell address)	Returns the contents of the cell referenced by cell address
@CELL(attribute,*range)	Returns information about the attribute in the upper left corner cell of range** (see attribute table).
@CELLPOINTER(attribute*)	Returns information about the attribute in the highlighted cell
@CHOOSE(y,v0,v1, . . ., vn)	Returns the yth argument in list v0, v1, . . ., vn
@COLS(range)	Returns the number of columns in range
@ERR	Returns the value of ERR (error)
@HLOOKUP(y,range,row number)	Performs horizontal table lookup
@INDEX(range,column number,row number)	Returns the value of the cell in the range at the intersection of column and row
@NA	Returns the value NA (NOT AVAILABLE)
@ROWS(range)	Returns the number of rows in the range
@VLOOKUP(y,range,column)	Performs vertical table lookup

A–6–8 Attribute Table for the @CELL Function

Attribute	Result
"ADDRESS"	Returns the current cell address, e.g., A1
"COL"	Returns the current column number (1 to 256)

* The string argument for the @CELLPOINTER function can be "ROW", "COL", "WIDTH", "PREFIX", "ADDRESS", "TYPE", "FORMAT", "CONTENTS".

** Specify a single cell as a range, for example, A2..A2 or !A2.

"CONTENTS"	Returns the contents of the current cell
"FORMAT"	Returns the current numeric formula of a given address: • F0 to F15 for Fixed, 0 to 15 decimal places • S0 to S15 for Scientific, 0 to 15 decimal places • C0 to C15 for Currency, 0 to 15 decimal places • G for general • P0 to P15 for Present • D1 to D5 for Date 1 to Date 5, and D6 to D9 for Time 1 to Time 4 format (see Chapter 6) • T for Text • A blank if the cell contains an empty string
"PREFIX"	Returns the current label prefix: ' (apostrophe) for left justified " (double quotations) for right justified ^ (caret) for centered
"PROTECT"	Returns the protection status: 1 if it is protected 0 if it is not protected
"ROW"	Returns the current row number (1 to 8,192)
"TYPE"	Returns the data type in a cell: b for blank v for numeric value or formula L for label or string
"WIDTH"	Returns the current column width (1 to 240)

A–7 ANSWERS TO SELECTED REVIEW QUESTIONS

Chapter 1

2. Disk drive and keyboard.
6. Floppy and hard disks.
13. It varies. It starts at 1 to 4 megabytes, or higher.
17. Keep it in a dust-free environment. Protect it against excessive heat and humidity. Provide a constant electrical current.
22. Every application program provides an editing feature so you can edit your mistakes. Or, in the worst case, you can retype your mistakes.
27. Priority of operations, or precedence of operations, refers to the order in which a computer handles calculations. The order is as follows:
    - Expressions inside parentheses have the highest priority.
    - Exponentiation (raising to power) has the next highest priority.
    - Multiplication and division have the third highest priority.
    - Addition and subtraction have the fourth highest priority.
    - When there are two or more operations with the same priority, operations proceed from left to right.

Chapter 2

3. Because all your programs and data files will be saved with that information. Later, you can determine when a document was created, which version of a document is the most recent one, and so on.
7. Type *A:* and press Enter.

15. A batch file is a disk file that includes a series of commands and statements. To execute this file you must type the file name. An autoexec file starts execution as soon as you get your computer started.
16. Internal: COPY, DATE, TIME; external: FORMAT, DISKCOPY, DISKCOMP

Chapter 3

1. Lotus 1-2-3 is much faster and more accurate than a manual accounting spread- sheet.
4. Select Q (for Quit) from the Main menu then press Y (for Yes).
11. You can either retype your entry or edit the contents of a cell by using the F2 function key.
15. The Esc key allows you to change your mind when you are entering data or accessing a command.

Chapter 4

4. Change the directory to the directory that includes your 1-2-3 files by using the DOS CD command, then type *123* and press Enter.
7. Not really. However, your numbers will be right justified and your labels will be left justified.
8. After invoking the menu by pressing the / (forward slash) key, either move the cursor to the option and press Enter or just type the first letter of the option.
12. Press the Print Screen key (in enhanced keyboards) or press Shift and PrtSc (in standard keyboards) or use the Print command.
14. Choose the /File Save command, erase the current drive/directory by using the backspace key, then type *C:* followed by a file name, then press Enter. For example: */FSC:TRY* (Enter).
20. The minus sign (–) is a numeric character. Because you are using it as a label, you must start with one of the label prefixes.

Chapter 5

3. Yes. Just invoke the file with the password, then when you want to save the file again, invoke /File Save then press Enter.
9. There are three options: Copy, Add, and Subtract.
11. The File Xtract command copies your entire current file or a portion of it onto a disk.
23. By issuing /File Import.

Chapter 6

3. The default is nine characters long.
4. The data must be entered later. The /Worksheet Global Label-Prefix command does not have any effect on existing data.
13. The /Worksheet Page command creates a page break. The cellpointer must be in column A.
15. Yes. Range A1..IV8192 is equal to the worksheet itself.
19. Press the F3 function key. You will see all your range names. You can also issue the /Range Name Table command to generate an alphabetical listing of all your range names.
24. You will see the effect of /Range Protect if you first issue /Worksheet Global Protection Enable.
28. Start the range name with a $ (a dollar sign). For example, $ASSET is absolute.

33. There are five date options. Choosing a format is a matter of style.
39. Yes.

Chapter 7

2. A 1-2-3 function dynamically calculates various operations without any additional effort by the user. All that is needed is the input data for the function. The rest is done automatically.
6. An invalid argument is a type of argument that does not conform to 1-2-3 or standard mathematical conventions. For example, in the function @SQRT(–25), the argument is not valid because negative numbers do not have square roots.
8. The @ABS function returns the positive value of an argument. It is used when only positive values make sense. For example, number of employees, number of machineries, and so on.
10. Yes. Add .50 to the argument of the function. For example, @INT(9.6+.50).
13. +B10^.50.
14. @FV is used for future value calculations; for example, the future value of a 30-year IRA. @NPV is used to discount a series of future values to today's value.
22. The argument of @DATE is always a standard date; for example, @DATE(90,7,1). It returns a serial number corresponding to a certain year, month, or day. The @DATEVALUE function is similar to @DATE, and it returns the serial number of a date. However, the date is written as a string; for example, @DATEVALUE("01-Jul-91").
23. The @HLOOKUP function performs a horizontal search. The @VLOOKUP function performs a vertical search.
24. General table search, commission table search, tax table search, inventory management, and so forth.

Chapter 8

3. There are only seven types. There can be only six data ranges.
6. The X range is used in an XY graph as a data range; it is used to label the x-axis in other graphs. Also, it is used to label the pieces of pie charts.
8. Yes. /File Save generates WK1 as its extension. /Graph Save generates PIC as its extension.
11. There is no limit.
21. Yes, by pressing the F10 function key.
23. You cannot modify a graph within the PrintGraph program. You must exit the PrintGraph program and enter the 1-2-3 worksheet, perform the modifications, save your work, and then reenter the PrintGraph program.

Chapter 9

2. To get WYSIWYG started, choose Add-In from the main menu then choose Attach then choose WYSIWYG.ADN and press Enter. Assign a key to it. Later to invoke it, either press Alt and the assigned key or press the : (colon) key.
9. TEXT mode and GRAPHICS mode. You can switch between these two modes by selecting :Display Mode command.
14. Three types of underlinings: single, double, and wide.
17. The :Print File command allows you to print your worksheet to a file for later printing.
20. The Goto command allows you to move to a specific graph.
25. The :Display Zoom command allows you to change the on-screen display of your worksheet.

Chapter 10

4. You can erase a record with the /Worksheet Delete Row command.
6. You can have up to 256 fields.
10. There is no difference between these two keys. However, the primary key is the first key and the secondary key is the second key.
12. Up to 32 for the AND search. For OR, the limit is the number of fields in the database.
18. It stops whenever the data range is fully occupied or whenever the upper limit (Stop value) has been reached.
23. The frequency of this data will be displayed at the bottom of the bin range.

Chapter 11

4. Press and hold down the Alt key and enter the name of the macro. You can also use the Run command (Alt+F3).
6. The \0 (zero macro) is a self-booting macro—as soon as the worksheet that includes this macro is loaded, the zero macro is executed automatically.
9. In menu design, the self-booting worksheet is useful for users with minimum computer knowledge.
13. The CMD indicator is displayed whenever a macro is being executed.
15. Press Ctrl+Break.
16. There can be up to 240 keystrokes.

A–8 LOTUS COMMAND MAP

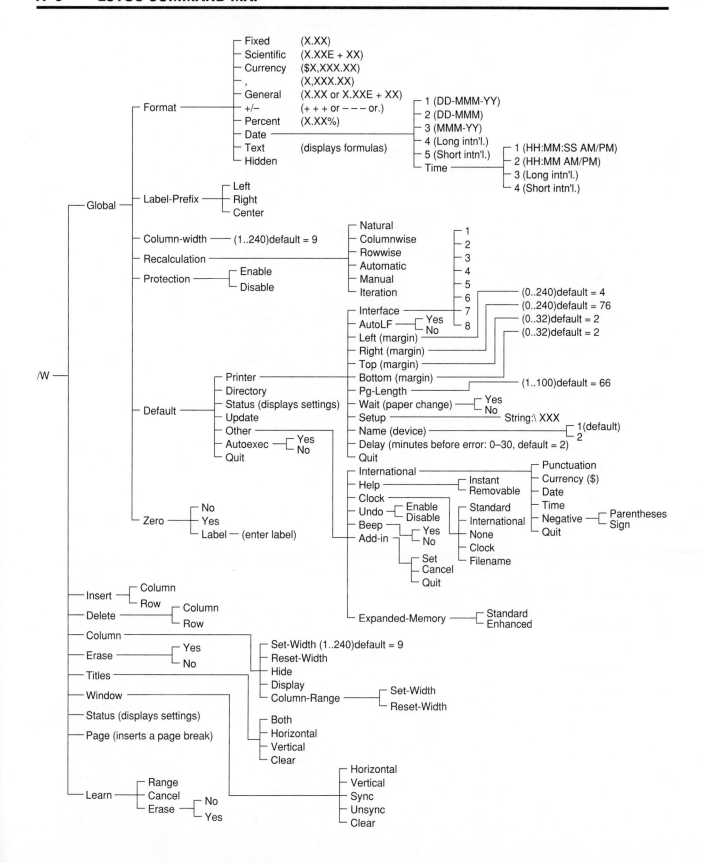

- /W
  - Global
    - Format
      - Fixed (X.XX)
      - Scientific (X.XXE + XX)
      - Currency ($X,XXX.XX)
      - , (X,XXX.XX)
      - General (X.XX or X.XXE + XX)
      - +/– (+ + + or – – – or.)
      - Percent (X.XX%)
      - Date
        - 1 (DD-MMM-YY)
        - 2 (DD-MMM)
        - 3 (MMM-YY)
        - 4 (Long intn'l.)
        - 5 (Short intn'l.)
        - Time
          - 1 (HH:MM:SS AM/PM)
          - 2 (HH:MM AM/PM)
          - 3 (Long intn'l.)
          - 4 (Short intn'l.)
      - Text (displays formulas)
      - Hidden
    - Label-Prefix
      - Left
      - Right
      - Center
    - Column-width — (1..240)default = 9
    - Recalculation
      - Natural
      - Columnwise
      - Rowwise
      - Automatic
      - Manual
      - Iteration
    - Protection
      - Enable
      - Disable
    - Default
      - Printer
        - Interface
          - 1
          - 2
          - 3
          - 4
          - 5
          - 6
          - 7
          - 8
        - AutoLF
          - Yes
          - No
        - Left (margin) — (0..240)default = 4
        - Right (margin) — (0..240)default = 76
        - Top (margin) — (0..32)default = 2
        - Bottom (margin) — (0..32)default = 2
        - Pg-Length — (1..100)default = 66
        - Wait (paper change)
          - Yes
          - No
        - Setup — String:\ XXX
        - Name (device)
          - 1(default)
          - 2
        - Delay (minutes before error: 0–30, default = 2)
        - Quit
      - Directory
      - Status (displays settings)
      - Update
      - Other
        - International
          - Punctuation
          - Currency ($)
          - Date
          - Time
          - Negative
            - Parentheses
            - Sign
          - Quit
        - Help
          - Instant
          - Removable
        - Clock
          - Standard
          - International
          - None
          - Clock
          - Filename
        - Undo
          - Enable
          - Disable
        - Beep
          - Yes
          - No
        - Add-in
          - Set
          - Cancel
          - Quit
        - Expanded-Memory
          - Standard
          - Enhanced
      - Autoexec
        - Yes
        - No
      - Quit
    - Zero
      - No
      - Yes
      - Label — (enter label)
  - Insert
    - Column
    - Row
  - Delete
    - Column
    - Row
  - Column
    - Set-Width (1..240)default = 9
    - Reset-Width
    - Hide
    - Display
    - Column-Range
      - Set-Width
      - Reset-Width
  - Erase
    - Yes
    - No
  - Titles
    - Both
    - Horizontal
    - Vertical
    - Clear
  - Window
    - Horizontal
    - Vertical
    - Sync
    - Unsync
    - Clear
  - Status (displays settings)
  - Page (inserts a page break)
  - Learn
    - Range
    - Cancel
    - Erase
      - No
      - Yes

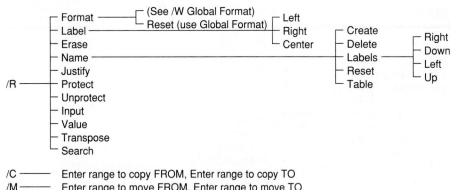

- /R
  - Format
    - (See /W Global Format)
    - Reset (use Global Format)
  - Label
    - Left
    - Right
    - Center
  - Erase
  - Name
    - Create
    - Delete
    - Labels
      - Right
      - Down
      - Left
      - Up
    - Reset
    - Table
  - Justify
  - Protect
  - Unprotect
  - Input
  - Value
  - Transpose
  - Search

- /C — Enter range to copy FROM, Enter range to copy TO
- /M — Enter range to move FROM, Enter range to move TO

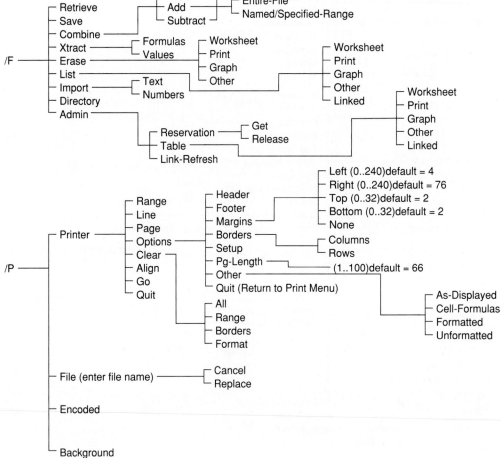

- /F
  - Retrieve
  - Save
  - Combine
    - Copy / Add / Subtract
      - Entire-File
      - Named/Specified-Range
  - Xtract
    - Formulas
    - Values
  - Erase
    - Worksheet
    - Print
    - Graph
    - Other
  - List
    - Worksheet
    - Print
    - Graph
    - Other
    - Linked
  - Import
    - Text
    - Numbers
  - Directory
  - Admin
    - Reservation
      - Get
      - Release
    - Table
      - Worksheet
      - Print
      - Graph
      - Other
      - Linked
    - Link-Refresh

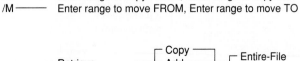

- /P
  - Printer
    - Range
    - Line
    - Page
    - Options
      - Header
      - Footer
      - Margins
        - Left (0..240)default = 4
        - Right (0..240)default = 76
        - Top (0..32)default = 2
        - Bottom (0..32)default = 2
        - None
      - Borders
        - Columns
        - Rows
      - Setup
      - Pg-Length — (1..100)default = 66
      - Other
        - As-Displayed
        - Cell-Formulas
        - Formatted
        - Unformatted
      - Quit (Return to Print Menu)
    - Clear
      - All
      - Range
      - Borders
      - Format
    - Align
    - Go
    - Quit
  - File (enter file name)
    - Cancel
    - Replace
  - Encoded
  - Background

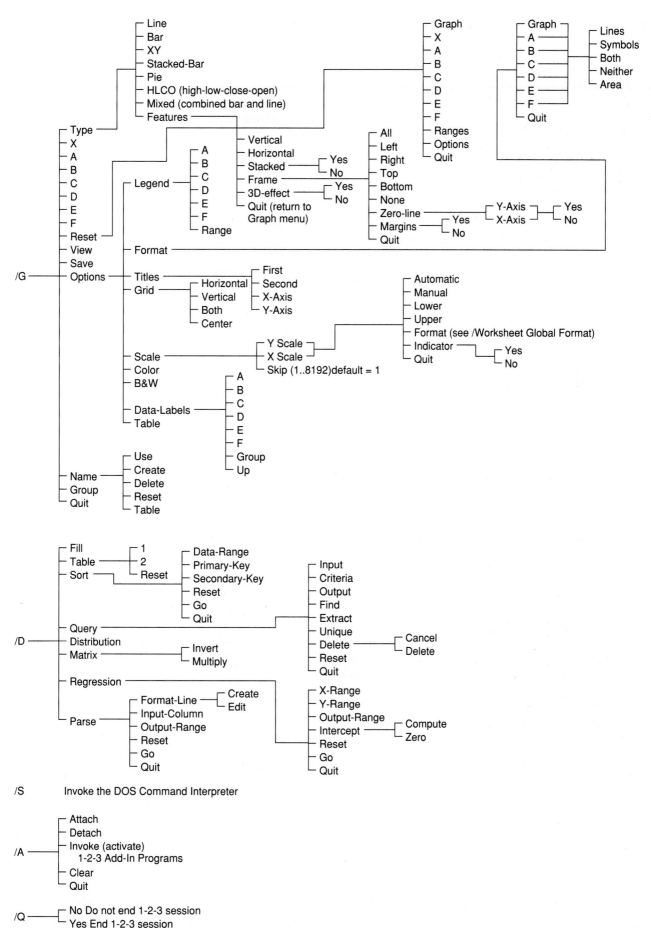

- /G
  - Type
    - Line
    - Bar
    - XY
    - Stacked-Bar
    - Pie
    - HLCO (high-low-close-open)
    - Mixed (combined bar and line)
    - Features
      - Vertical
      - Horizontal
      - Stacked
        - Yes
        - No
      - Frame
        - All
        - Left
        - Right
        - Top
        - Bottom
        - None
        - Zero-line
          - Y-Axis
          - X-Axis
            - Yes
            - No
        - Margins
          - Yes
          - No
        - Quit
      - 3D-effect
        - Yes
        - No
      - Quit (return to Graph menu)
  - X
  - A
  - B
  - C
  - D
  - E
  - F
  - Reset
    - Graph
    - X
    - A
    - B
    - C
    - D
    - E
    - F
    - Ranges
    - Options
    - Quit
  - View
  - Save
  - Options
    - Legend
      - A
      - B
      - C
      - D
      - E
      - F
      - Range
    - Format
      - Graph
      - A
      - B
      - C
      - D
      - E
      - F
        - Lines
        - Symbols
        - Both
        - Neither
        - Area
      - Quit
    - Titles
      - First
      - Second
      - X-Axis
      - Y-Axis
    - Grid
      - Horizontal
      - Vertical
      - Both
      - Center
    - Scale
      - Y Scale
      - X Scale
        - Automatic
        - Manual
        - Lower
        - Upper
        - Format (see /Worksheet Global Format)
        - Indicator
          - Yes
          - No
        - Quit
      - Skip (1..8192)default = 1
    - Color
    - B&W
    - Data-Labels
      - A
      - B
      - C
      - D
      - E
      - F
      - Group
      - Up
    - Table
  - Name
    - Use
    - Create
    - Delete
    - Reset
    - Table
  - Group
  - Quit

- /D
  - Fill
  - Table
    - 1
    - 2
    - Reset
  - Sort
    - Data-Range
    - Primary-Key
    - Secondary-Key
    - Reset
    - Go
    - Quit
  - Query
    - Input
    - Criteria
    - Output
    - Find
    - Extract
    - Unique
    - Delete
      - Cancel
      - Delete
    - Reset
    - Quit
  - Distribution
  - Matrix
    - Invert
    - Multiply
  - Regression
    - X-Range
    - Y-Range
    - Output-Range
    - Intercept
      - Compute
      - Zero
    - Reset
    - Go
    - Quit
  - Parse
    - Format-Line
      - Create
      - Edit
    - Input-Column
    - Output-Range
    - Reset
    - Go
    - Quit

/S Invoke the DOS Command Interpreter

- /A
  - Attach
  - Detach
  - Invoke (activate) 1-2-3 Add-In Programs
  - Clear
  - Quit

- /Q
  - No Do not end 1-2-3 session
  - Yes End 1-2-3 session

A–9 WYSIWYG COMMAND MAP

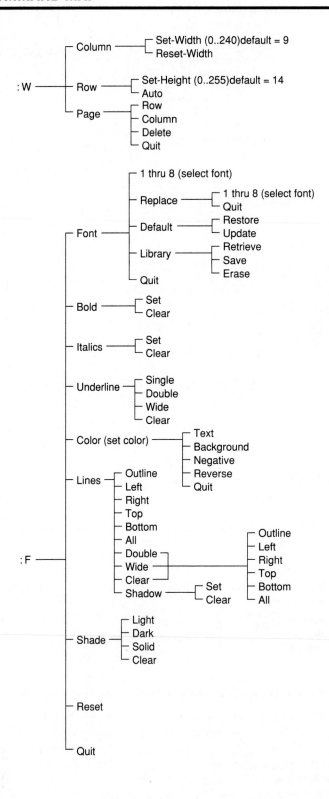

- :W
  - Column
    - Set-Width (0..240)default = 9
    - Reset-Width
  - Row
    - Set-Height (0..255)default = 14
    - Auto
  - Page
    - Row
    - Column
    - Delete
    - Quit

- :F
  - Font
    - 1 thru 8 (select font)
    - Replace
      - 1 thru 8 (select font)
      - Quit
    - Default
      - Restore
      - Update
    - Library
      - Retrieve
      - Save
      - Erase
    - Quit
  - Bold
    - Set
    - Clear
  - Italics
    - Set
    - Clear
  - Underline
    - Single
    - Double
    - Wide
    - Clear
  - Color (set color)
    - Text
    - Background
    - Negative
    - Reverse
    - Quit
  - Lines
    - Outline
    - Left
    - Right
    - Top
    - Bottom
    - All
    - Double
    - Wide
    - Clear
      - (Double, Wide, Clear:) Outline
      - Left
      - Right
      - Top
      - Bottom
      - All
    - Shadow
      - Set
      - Clear
  - Shade
    - Light
    - Dark
    - Solid
    - Clear
  - Reset
  - Quit

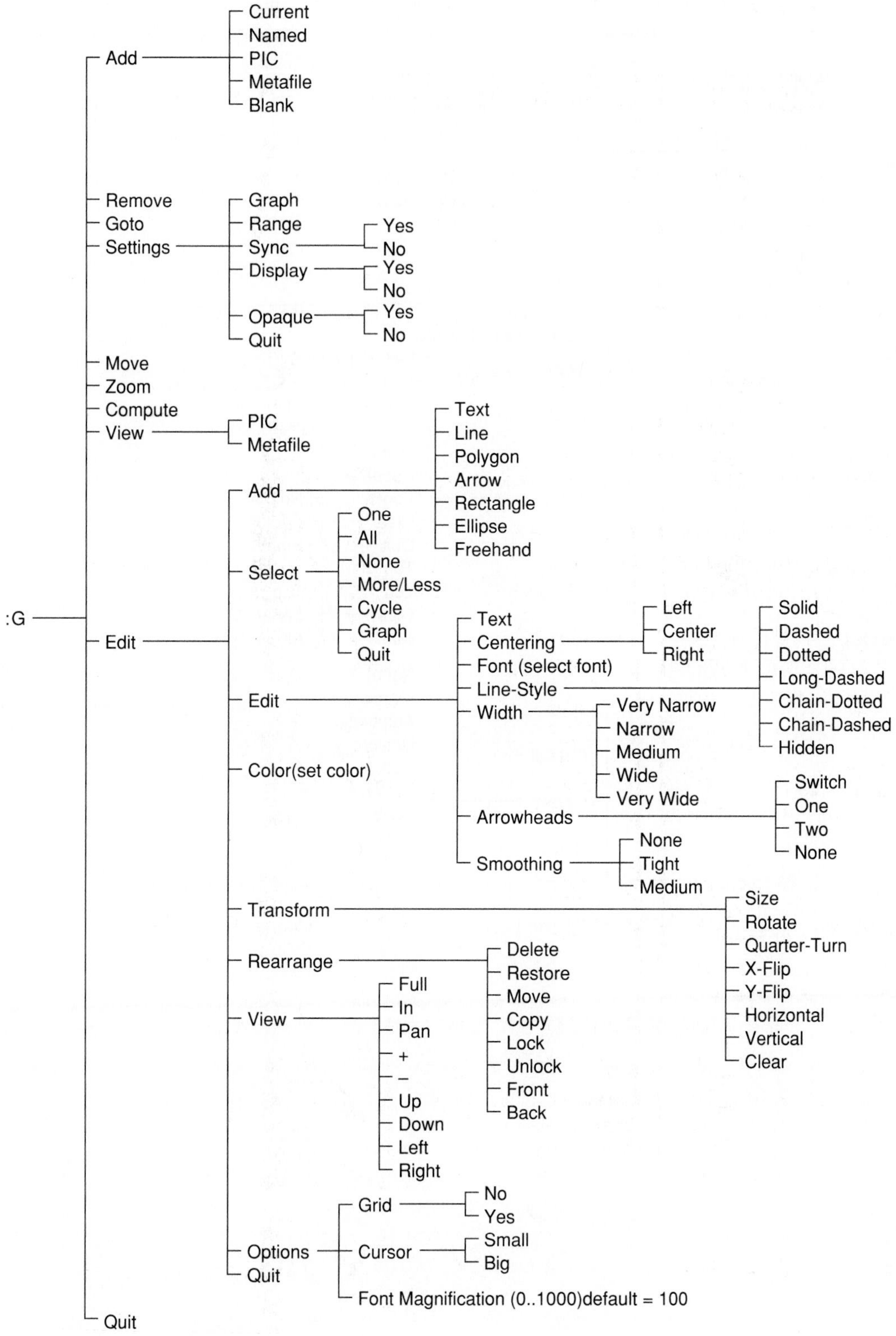
:G
Add
Current
Named
PIC
Metafile
Blank
Remove
Goto
Settings
Graph
Range
Sync
Yes
No
Display
Yes
No
Opaque
Yes
No
Quit
Move
Zoom
Compute
View
PIC
Metafile
Edit
Add
Text
Line
Polygon
Arrow
Rectangle
Ellipse
Freehand
Select
One
All
None
More/Less
Cycle
Graph
Quit
Edit
Text
Centering
Left
Center
Right
Font (select font)
Line-Style
Solid
Dashed
Dotted
Long-Dashed
Chain-Dotted
Chain-Dashed
Hidden
Width
Very Narrow
Narrow
Medium
Wide
Very Wide
Arrowheads
Switch
One
Two
None
Smoothing
None
Tight
Medium
Color(set color)
Transform
Size
Rotate
Quarter-Turn
X-Flip
Y-Flip
Horizontal
Vertical
Clear
Rearrange
Delete
Restore
Move
Copy
Lock
Unlock
Front
Back
View
Full
In
Pan
+
–
Up
Down
Left
Right
Options
Grid
No
Yes
Cursor
Small
Big
Font Magnification (0..1000)default = 100
Quit
Quit

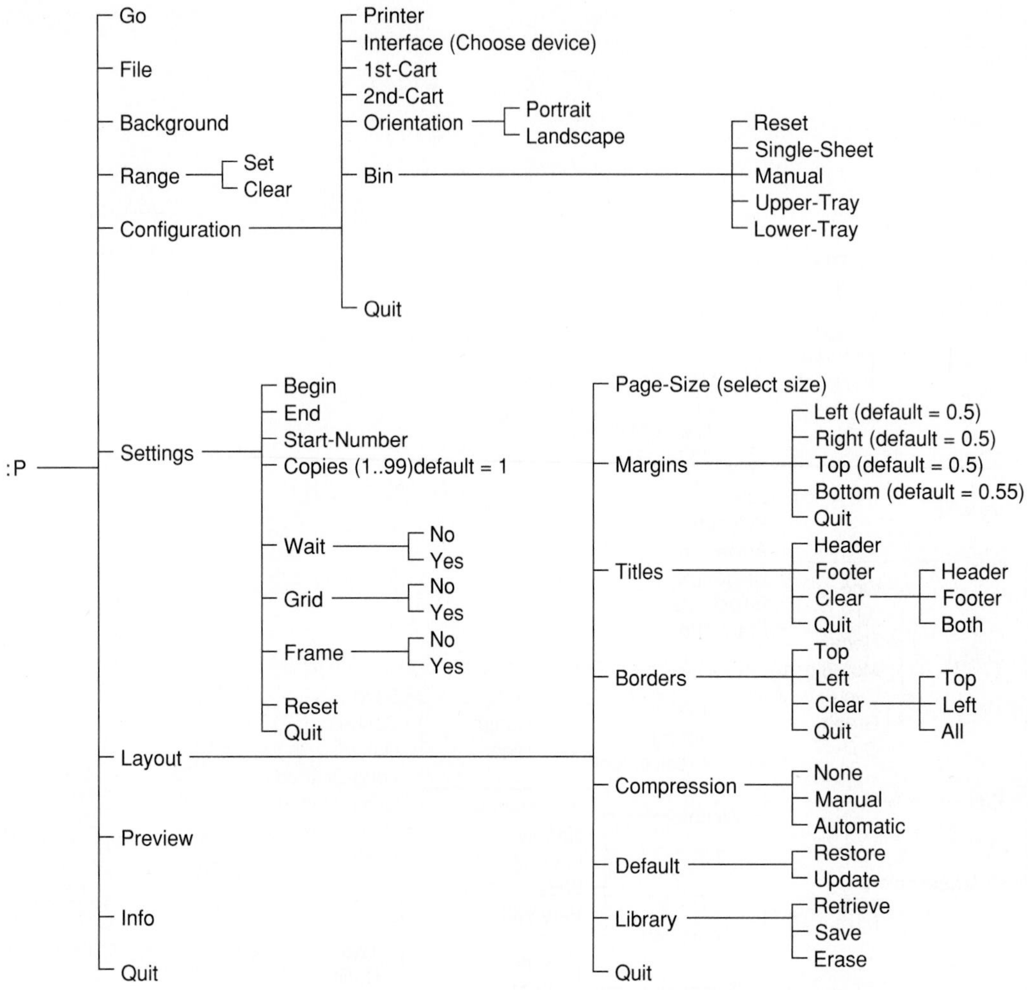
:P
Go
File
Background
Range
Set
Clear
Configuration
Printer
Interface (Choose device)
1st-Cart
2nd-Cart
Orientation
Portrait
Landscape
Bin
Reset
Single-Sheet
Manual
Upper-Tray
Lower-Tray
Quit
Settings
Begin
End
Start-Number
Copies (1..99)default = 1
Wait
No
Yes
Grid
No
Yes
Frame
No
Yes
Reset
Quit
Layout
Page-Size (select size)
Margins
Left (default = 0.5)
Right (default = 0.5)
Top (default = 0.5)
Bottom (default = 0.55)
Quit
Titles
Header
Footer
Clear
Quit
Header
Footer
Both
Borders
Top
Left
Clear
Quit
Top
Left
All
Compression
None
Manual
Automatic
Default
Restore
Update
Library
Retrieve
Save
Erase
Quit
Preview
Info
Quit

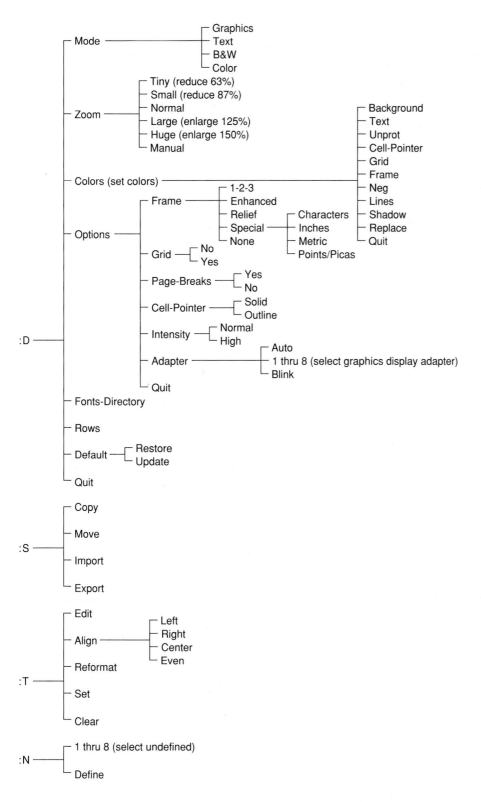

- :D
  - Mode
    - Graphics
    - Text
    - B&W
    - Color
  - Zoom
    - Tiny (reduce 63%)
    - Small (reduce 87%)
    - Normal
    - Large (enlarge 125%)
    - Huge (enlarge 150%)
    - Manual
  - Colors (set colors)
    - Background
    - Text
    - Unprot
    - Cell-Pointer
    - Grid
    - Frame
    - Neg
    - Lines
    - Shadow
    - Replace
    - Quit
  - Options
    - Frame
      - 1-2-3
      - Enhanced
      - Relief
      - Special
        - Characters
        - Inches
        - Metric
        - Points/Picas
      - None
    - Grid
      - No
      - Yes
    - Page-Breaks
      - Yes
      - No
    - Cell-Pointer
      - Solid
      - Outline
    - Intensity
      - Normal
      - High
    - Adapter
      - Auto
      - 1 thru 8 (select graphics display adapter)
      - Blink
    - Quit
  - Fonts-Directory
  - Rows
  - Default
    - Restore
    - Update
  - Quit
- :S
  - Copy
  - Move
  - Import
  - Export
- :T
  - Edit
  - Align
    - Left
    - Right
    - Center
    - Even
  - Reformat
  - Set
  - Clear
- :N
  - 1 thru 8 (select undefined)
  - Define
- :Q

Appendix B
File Transfer Among Popular Software Packages

B

B–1 INTRODUCTION

This appendix presents guidelines for importing and exporting files to and from selected software, thereby enabling you to utilize the best features of each software package. By importing files from other software you also save time and frustration because you do not duplicate the same data file. The guidelines cover file transfer among DOS, WordPerfect 5.1 and 6.0, Lotus 1-2-3, dBASE III Plus/dBASE IV, Quattro Pro, Paradox, and BASICA.

Some software applications such as Quattro Pro and Paradox provide extensive support for file transfer. Other packages such as Lotus 1-2-3 provide a translate utility that enables you to translate one file format to another. The guidelines in this appendix involve exporting and importing ASCII files. For extensive information about the availability and use of the built-in file transfer facilities of each software application, consult the package's documentation.

B–2 WHY USE FILE TRANSFER?

File transfer allows the movement of a file generated by one software application program to another. There are three good reasons for performing such a task:

1. Utilizing a capability of one software package that is not available in another. For example, you might transfer a Lotus 1-2-3 spreadsheet to a report generated by a word processing program thereby creating a factual and comprehensive report. You may also want to import dBASE data into 1-2-3 for graphing—a feature that is not available in dBASE.
2. Utilizing the enhanced power in one package for the same basic tasks that can be performed by two software applications. For example, database operations performed by 1-2-3 are much faster than those performed by dBASE; therefore, you might want to translate a dBASE file into a 1-2-3 spreadsheet for faster processing.
3. Converting data files from earlier software application programs to more recent versions. This is a common practice. Consider converting VisiCalc (the most popular spreadsheet program before 1-2-3) files into 1-2-3 files. Without data transfer facilities, you would have to enter all the data again, a very time-consuming, error-prone, and tedious task.

B–3 WHAT IS AN ASCII FILE?

Probably the easiest and most straightforward method for file transfer is to use ASCII files. ASCII (American Standard Code for Information Interchange) is a data format generated and accepted by most software application packages.

An ASCII file, or simply a "print image" file (sometimes called a DOS text file), is a file composed of standard keyboard characters. To verify whether a file is in ASCII format or not is a simple task. At the DOS prompt type *TYPE file name.extension* and press Enter, for example, *TYPE SAMPLE.TXT* (press Enter). If the file is displayed on the screen in standard keyboard characters, it is in ASCII format; otherwise it is not. In other words, you should be able to read an ASCII file. For example, 1-2-3 files generated by the /Print File command (files with the PRN extension) are ASCII files.

As mentioned earlier, different software packages include specific capabilities for file transfer. For example, 1-2-3 includes the translate utility, which is able to translate from and to several different file formats. The next few sections provide specific guidelines for file transfer among selected software applications.

B–4 FILE TRANSFER AND DOS

Files created by the COPY CON, EDLIN, and EDIT (in DOS 5 and 6) commands are automatically in ASCII format. If you are using EDLIN, enter the following command to load and edit an ASCII file:

EDLIN SAMPLE.BAT (press Enter)

In this case both EDLIN and SAMPLE.BAT are assumed to be in your default directory and drive. If they are not, you must include the drive identifier and/or the exact path. SAMPLE is the name of the file and BAT is its extension. After you have loaded the file, it is available for editing. When you save a file in EDLIN or EDIT, the file is automatically saved in ASCII file format.

B–5 FILE TRANSFER AND WORDPERFECT 5.1

B–5–1 Creating ASCII Files

To generate an ASCII file in WordPerfect press Ctrl+F5 (Text In/Out). You are presented with the following menu:

```
1 DOS Text;  2 Password;  3 Save As;  4 Comment;  5 Spreadsheet: 0
```

From this menu select option 1 (DOS Text). You are presented with the following menu:

```
1 Save;  2 Retrieve (CR/LF to [HRt]);  3 Retrieve (CR/LF to [SRt] in HZone): 0
```

From this menu select option 1 (Save). At this point WordPerfect responds with

```
Document to be saved (DOS Text):
```

Type in a name (for example, SAMPLE) and press Enter. The file extension is optional. You must also specify the drive identifier and/or the correct path if you are not saving into the default drive and directory.

It is a good idea to save your file in WordPerfect format as well. To do this use either F10 or F7. If you do save your file in WordPerfect format, be sure to use a different name; otherwise, the file created in ASCII format will be overwritten by the file with the same name in WordPerfect format!

B–5–2 Importing ASCII Files

To import an ASCII file into WordPerfect press Ctrl+F5 (Text In/Out). From this menu select option 1 (DOS Text). From this menu select either option 2, Retrieve (CR/LF to [HRt]) or option 3, Retrieve (CR/LF to [SRt] in HZone). Type the name of the file and press Enter. The file will be imported into the WordPerfect document at the cursor position.

The "CR/LF" refers to the carriage return/line feed codes in the ASCII file. These codes are used to end one line and move the cursor to the next line.

Using the CR/LF to [SRt] option enables the imported file to closely match the WordPerfect format. If you use this option, you should set the margin width of your WordPerfect document to closely match that used by the ASCII file. If you use the CR/LF [HRt] option, set the WordPerfect document margin wider than the margin of the ASCII file that is being imported.

B–6 IMPORTING FILES INTO WORDPERFECT: A SECOND METHOD

Another method of importing ASCII format files into WordPerfect is through the F5 (List Files) key. To use this method, press F5. WordPerfect responds by displaying the name of the default directory in the lower left corner of the screen. If this drive/directory path is correct, press the Enter key; otherwise, type the desired drive and directory path and press Enter. WordPerfect displays the listing of files contained in the displayed directory. To import an ASCII file from this screen, you have two options.

1. You can highlight the file that you want to import and select 1 or R (Retrieve) from the List Files menu. WordPerfect briefly displays

   ```
   Document Conversion in Progress
   ```

   in the lower-left corner of the screen as the file is being imported. The imported file is converted into standard WordPerfect format and displayed on the screen.
2. Highlight the file that you want to import, then press Ctrl+F5 (Text In/Out). WordPerfect responds by displaying

   ```
   (DOS) Retrieve [drive:\path\file name.extension]? No (Yes)
   ```

   If you press Y, WordPerfect retrieves the specified file without further prompting.

Note that using this method does not trigger the "Document Conversion in Progress" message that a normal retrieve request generates. This is so because WordPerfect does not need to convert the document into WordPerfect file format. The file is imported in its simple ASCII format with no additional format codes.

B–7 FILE TRANSFER AND WORDPERFECT 6.0

WordPerfect version 6.0 provides a powerful tool for file transfer. To convert a WordPerfect 6.0 file to another file format, follow these steps:

1. Create or retrieve your WordPerfect 6.0 file.
2. From the File menu select the Save As option.
3. Type the desired name (up to eight characters) and then choose the Format option. You can choose from a list of more than 30 file formats.

4. After highlighting the desired format, choose the OK option. At this time the WordPerfect 6.0 file is converted to the selected file format.

To import a file to WordPerfect 6.0 format, do the following steps:

1. Choose the Open option from the File menu or press the Shift+F10 key-combination.
2. Type the filename of the file you want to convert, or select it from the File Manager or QuickList, then choose OK.
3. From the provided list, highlight the current format of the file you want to open.
4. Choose the Select option.
5. Choose the Save As option from the File menu.
6. Type a filename (up to eight characters) for the converted file.

If you use the original filename, the converted file will be replaced with the file in WordPerfect 6.0 format.

You should remember the converted documents are saved in WordPerfect 6.0 format unless they are converted as ASCII files. WordPerfect 6.0 saves converted ASCII files as ASCII files by default.

B–8 FILE TRANSFER AND LOTUS 1-2-3

B–8–1 Creating ASCII Files

To create ASCII files in 1-2-3, use the /Print File command. After selecting /Print File, you must specify the desired range (press Enter), then select Align, Go, and Quit. When you print to a file, the file is saved with a PRN extension. Remember that when you generate an ASCII file from your spreadsheet, the converted file is no longer a true worksheet. To maintain this spreadsheet in its original form, you must use the /File Save command before conversion and save your file in WK1 format. However, if you forget to save in standard format first, 1-2-3 offers the /Data Parse command which enables you to convert this ASCII file back to its original form. After issuing the /Print File command you must specify the Range, then choose Align, then Go, and finally Quit. The Quit command closes the file and finalizes the file creation process.

B–8–2 Importing ASCII Files

To import an ASCII file into 1-2-3, use the /File Import command. After issuing this command specify the file name and then press Enter. You are prompted to select Formulas or Values. Select Values. The file is imported into the spreadsheet at the position of the cellpointer, and as many rows down and columns to the right as necessary are used to accommodate the entire file.

B–9 FILE TRANSFER AND dBASE

B–9–1 Creating ASCII Files

In dBASE, to create an ASCII file you use the COPY command. The syntax of this command is:

COPY TO {file name}/{scope}/FIELDS {field list}/FOR {condition}/WHILE {condition}/TYPE {file type}

The scope, FIELDS, FOR, and WHILE entries are optional. These options provide more control over the final results. The TYPE option indicates the type of file to be created. Three file types are most commonly generated by dBASE:

1. WKS (worksheet): This file extension generates spreadsheet files accepted by 1-2-3. For example, to generate a 1-2-3 WK1 file in dBASE, at the dot prompt type *COPY TO SAMPLE.WK1/TYPE WKS.* Now in 1-2-3, by using the /File Retrieve command, you can bring this file into 1-2-3 and perform any operations on it.
2. SDF (system data format ASCII file): This file type copies database fields using the same format as the fields in the database file structure. It does not contain field separators; therefore, there is no space between fields. An example is *COPY TO SAMPLE/TYPE SDF.*
3. DIF (VisiCalc worksheet): This format was originally used by VisiCalc—the first commercial spreadsheet. It now can be read by 1-2-3 also. An example is *COPY TO SAMPLE.TXT/TYPE DIF.*

B–9–2 Importing ASCII Files

To import an ASCII file into dBASE, at the dot prompt issue the APPEND FROM command. For example,

APPEND FROM SAMPLE.TXT

As usual you can use the FOR condition to append selected records. In this example, the SAMPLE.TXT file will be appended to your current file.

Export and import facilities are also available through the dBASE III Plus assist menu and dBASE IV Control Center.

B–10 FILE TRANSFER AND 1-2-3 PIC FILES

1-2-3 generates PIC files when you issue the /Graph Save command. By integrating graphs into your reports, you can significantly improve the quality of your documents. In the past, graphs were manually cut and pasted into reports. By using the procedure described below, you can electronically include any of your 1-2-3 graphs in WordPerfect 5.1 documents. Follow these steps:

1. Start with 1-2-3 and create the graph of your choice.
2. By using the /Graph Save command, save your graph. This procedure generates a file with a PIC extension.
3. Exit 1-2-3 and start WordPerfect 5.1. Press Alt+F9. This invokes the graphics menu:

```
1 Figure;  2 Table Box;  3 Text Box;  4 User Box;  5 Line;  6 Equation: 0
```

4. Press 1 or F for Figure. The following menu is displayed:

```
Figure: 1 Create;  2 Edit;  3 New Number;  4 Options: 0
```

5. Options 2, 3, and 4 are used when the graph has already been imported into the document. In our case, select 1 or C for Create. The following menu is displayed:

```
Definition: Figure
1 - Filename
2 - Contents                 Empty
3 - Caption
4 - Anchor Type              Paragraph
5 - Vertical Position        0″
6 - Horizontal Position      Right
7 - Size                     3.25″ wide x 3.25″ (high)
8 - Wrap Text Around Box     Yes
9 - Edit
```

The Filename option indicates the name of the graphics file to be imported into your WordPerfect document.

The Contents option will be modified after a file has been retrieved into the memory of the computer through the use of option 1. In our case, after loading a PIC file, Contents will be set to "Graphic."

The Caption option allows you to enter a caption to appear with your graph.

The Anchor Type option allows you to specify how the graph should appear in relation to the text that surrounds it. If you select option 4 (Anchor Type), you receive the following menu:

```
Anchor Type: 1 Paragraph;  2 Page;  Character: 0
```

If you select the Paragraph option, the graph stays with the text that surrounds it even if the surrounding text is moved to a new position in the document. If you select Page, the graphics box stays at a fixed location on the page even if the surrounding text is moved to a new position in the document. If you select the Character option, the graph is treated as part of the text.

The Vertical Position and Horizontal Position options allow you to specify where the graph will appear on the page. If you select option 5 (Vertical Position), WordPerfect responds:

```
Offset from top of paragraph: 0″
```

If you select option 6 (Horizontal Position), WordPerfect displays the following menu:

```
Horizontal Position: 1 Left;  2 Right;  3 Center;  4 Full: 0
```

It is up to you to decide the exact position of your graph.

The Size option allows you to specify the exact height and width of the graph on the page.

The Wrap Text Around Box option allows Yes or No alternatives. If you select Yes, the text wraps around the graphics box. If you select No, the text is allowed to print over the top of the graph. Usually, you should select the Yes option.

The Edit option brings the graph to the screen.

6. After selecting the Create option, select F (for File name). Enter the drive, path, name, and extension of your file (if the file is not on the default drive) and press Enter.
7. Exit this menu by pressing the space bar; then press Shift+F7 and select option 6 (View Document). Your graph is displayed on the screen. To print the graph, press the space bar and select option 1 (Full Document).

B–11 FILE TRANSFER AND QUATTRO PRO

B–11–1 Creating ASCII Files

Follow the steps outlined next to create an ASCII file using Quattro Pro. For this exercise we assume that the spreadsheet you are saving occupies the range of cells A1 through F5 (A1..F5).

1. Press the / (forward slash) key to access the main menu.
2. Press P (Print).
3. Press B (Block). Assuming that your cellpointer is located in cell A1, Quattro Pro responds with the following prompt:

```
[Enter] [Esc] The block of the spreadsheet to print: A1
```

4. Type *A1..F5* and press Enter.
5. Press D (Destination). Quattro Pro displays the Destination menu.
6. Press F (File). Quattro Pro prompts you with the following message:

```
Enter print file name:
```

7. Type a name for your file (up to eight characters) and press Enter. We typed *SALES* and pressed Enter. Quattro Pro now returns you to the main Print menu.

Quattro Pro saves the spreadsheet data, using the file name you specified, with the extension PRN.

To verify that the ASCII file was created successfully, use the left-arrow key to display the File menu, then select the Utilities option, then select the DOS Shell option. Quattro Pro responds with the following message:

```
Enter DOS Command, Press Enter for full DOS Shell
```

Press the Enter key; you will be presented with a DOS prompt. Type the following command to view the ASCII file:

TYPE SALES.PRN (press Enter)

(Note: If you entered a different file name, replace the word "SALES" with the name you specified.) The data from cells A1..F5 will be displayed on screen. Type the DOS command EXIT and press Enter to return to Quattro Pro.

B–11–2 Importing ASCII Files

Make sure you have a blank spreadsheet, then follow the steps outlined to import an ASCII file into Quattro Pro. We assume that you have generated an ASCII file using another application, in this case, 1-2-3.

1. Press the / (forward slash) key to access the main menu.
2. Press T (Tools).
3. Press I (Import).
4. Press A (ASCII Text File). Quattro Pro responds with the following prompt:

```
Enter name of file to import:
```

A listing of all files in the default directory with the extension PRN is displayed for you. You may highlight the desired file name and press Enter, or you may type the drive, path, and file name of the desired file and then press Enter. Quattro Pro imports the specified ASCII file and displays its contents on screen for you.

B–12 FILE TRANSFER AND PARADOX

B–12–1 Creating ASCII Files

Follow these steps to create an ASCII file using Paradox. We assume that you have already created a table consisting of 10 records.

1. If necessary, press the F10 key to display the main menu.
2. Press T (Tools) to select the Tools option from the main menu.
3. Press E (ExportImport) to select the ExportImport option.
4. Press E (Export) to select the Export option. Paradox responds by displaying the various output file formats that are available to you.
5. Press A (ASCII) to select the ASCII option.
6. Press D (Delimited) to select the Delimited option. Paradox prompts you to enter the name of the table that will be used to create the ASCII file.
7. Press the Enter key and Paradox responds by displaying the names of tables that are available to be selected.
8. Highlight the desired table name and press Enter, or type the name of the table from which you want to create an ASCII file and press Enter. We highlighted the table name CUSTOMER and pressed Enter. Paradox responds with a prompt requesting the name of the converted file.
9. Type a name for your output ASCII file, then press Enter. We typed CUSTLIST then pressed Enter. Paradox responds in the lower right corner with the message

```
Converting Customer to custlist.TXT . . .
```

The ASCII file is created on the default drive, in the default directory, under the file name that was specified during the ASCII file creation process.

When the message in the lower right corner of the screen stops flashing, ASCII file creation is finished.

Follow these steps to verify that the ASCII file has been successfully created:

1. If necessary, press the F10 key to display the main menu.
2. Press T (Tools).
3. Press M (More).
4. Press T (ToDOS). Paradox will clear the screen and display a DOS prompt for you.
5. Type the following command to send the contents of the ASCII file to the printer:

   TYPE CUSTLIST.TXT > LPT1

   (Note: If you used a name other than CUSTLIST for your ASCII file, specify that name instead of CUSTLIST. Also, if LPT1 is not the port you are using for printed output, specify the correct output port instead of LPT1.)

Your output will be sent to the printer. Each record in the file will be printed on a separate line with commas separating each field and quotation marks surrounding the contents of each field. View the ASCII data output to make sure that it is correct, then type *EXIT* and press Enter to return to Paradox.

B–12–2

Importing ASCII Files

Follow the steps outlined next to import an ASCII file into Paradox. We assume that you have already created a comma delimited ASCII file using another application program.

1. If necessary, press the F10 key to display the main menu.
2. Press T (Tools) to select the Tools option.
3. Press E (ExportImport) to select the ExportImport option.
4. Press I (Import) to select the Import option. Paradox responds by displaying various application program file formats that are available to you.
5. Press A (ASCII) to select the ASCII option.
6. Press D (Delimited) to select the Delimited option. Paradox prompts you to enter the name of the file to be imported.
7. Press Enter to view the names of available ASCII files from which you can select.
8. You may highlight the desired import file and press Enter, or type the name of the desired import file and press Enter. We typed SALESMAN.TXT and pressed Enter. Paradox responds by prompting you for the name of the new Paradox table that will be created as a result of the import operation.
9. Type the name of the new Paradox table that will be used to hold the incoming ASCII data and press Enter. We typed TEST and pressed Enter. Paradox imports the ASCII file data; it displays the imported data from left to right on the screen with the name of the new table in the upper left corner and Field-1, Field-2, and so forth displayed at the top of each column of data.

B–13 FILE TRANSFER AND BASICA

BASICA can generate ASCII files in several ways. The following program is one that can be used to generate a sequential ASCII file. The resulting file can easily be imported to any software that accepts ASCII files.

```
10      REM TO CREATE ASCII FILE CALLED STUREC
20      OPEN "STUREC" FOR OUTPUT AS #1
30      FOR I=1 TO 3
40              READ A$,B$,C
50              WRITE #1,A$,B$,C
60      NEXT I
70      CLOSE
80      DATA SUSAN SHAY, BUSINESS, 3.85
90      DATA KIM BROWN, COMPUTER, 2.60
100     DATA ED STRONG, MATH, 4.00
110     END
```

To see the contents of the ASCII file STUREC, type these instructions:

```
RUN (press Enter)                    (program will run)
SYSTEM (press Enter)                 (exit from BASICA to DOS prompt)
A > TYPE STUREC (press Enter)
"SUSAN SHAY","BUSINESS",3.85
"KIM BROWN","COMPUTER",2.60
"ED STRONG","MATH",4.00
```

Also, if a file is saved using the SAVE "File name",A command, the file is saved in ASCII format with the BAS extension automatically supplied.

BASICA can read an ASCII file by using the LINE INPUT #1 command. For example, you can read an ASCII file line by line into a one-dimensional array in a BASICA program. The following routine reads a 1-2-3 ASCII file (PRN file) called MYFILE.PRN into array X$(100):

```
10      DIM X$(100)
20      OPEN "MYFILE.PRN" FOR INPUT AS #1
30      J=1
40      WHILE NOT EOF(1)
50            LINE INPUT #1,X$(J)
60            J=J+1
70      WEND
80      END
```

The following routine prints the contents of array X$:

```
10          FOR I=1 TO J
20                PRINT "X$(I)=",X$(I)
30          NEXT I
40          END
```

SUMMARY

This appendix reviewed ASCII files and the advantages of file transfer among different software. Specific guidelines for file transfer using DOS, WordPerfect, Lotus 1-2-3, dBASE, Quattro Pro, Paradox, and BASICA were presented. To become familiar with this important topic, you have to practice by creating a sample file in one software package and exporting or importing it into the other packages.

REVIEW QUESTIONS

1. What is file transfer? Why should it be done in some cases?
2. What is an ASCII file?
3. How do you know if a file is in ASCII format?
4. How do you create an ASCII file using DOS?
5. How do you create an ASCII file using WordPerfect?
6. How is an ASCII file imported into WordPerfect?
7. How do you import a PIC file into WordPerfect?
8. What are the advantages of importing a PIC file into a WordPerfect document?
9. How do you create an ASCII file using 1-2-3?
10. How is an ASCII file imported into 1-2-3?
11. How do you create an ASCII file using dBASE?
12. How is an ASCII file imported into dBASE?
13. What are some of the file transfer features of Quattro Pro?
14. How is an ASCII file imported into Quattro Pro?
15. How do you create an ASCII file using Paradox?
16. How is an ASCII file imported into Paradox?
17. How do you read the contents of an ASCII file into a BASICA array?
18. How do you create an ASCII file using BASICA?

Appendix C
A Quick Trip Through Microsoft Windows

C

C–1 INTRODUCTION

This appendix presents some of the unique advantages of Microsoft Windows[1] as a graphics-based environment compared with a character-based environment such as DOS. After discussing how to get in and how to get out of Windows, we will look at the procedures for using a mouse and the keyboard in the Windows environment. Next, the help and tutorial facilities of Windows will be introduced. The appendix concludes with discussions of the different parts of a Windows screen, running applications in Windows, quitting an application, working with the Clipboard, and working with a Windows group.

C–2 WINDOWS 3.1: AN OVERVIEW

Windows 3.1 is based on a graphical user interface (GUI) environment (pronounced "gooey") that runs on top of DOS (i.e., you must have DOS to run Windows). This graphical environment has several advantages not found in the DOS character-based environment. Let us summarize some of these advantages:

1. Windows is easier to use than DOS because with Windows you do not need to memorize the strict DOS command syntax. In Windows you can perform all DOS functions and more through a series of pull-down menus.
2. All Windows applications share the same principles. When you learn one Windows application, you can easily transfer some or all of what you have learned to other Windows applications.
3. The user can work with Windows applications using a mouse, the keyboard, or shortcut keys for speed (described later in this appendix). All these options enable you to become more efficient using Windows programs.
4. Windows presents a multitasking environment. This means that using Windows you can run more than one program at the same time. Imagine that you are typing a report using WordPerfect and decide you need a spreadsheet created in Lotus 1-2-3. If you are using Windows you can easily switch to Lotus 1-2-3 and incorporate the desired spreadsheet into your report. You can even integrate a graph into your report. Perhaps you decide that you need a telephone number out of your online telephone directory. You can easily run your telephone directory software, access the correct phone number, then exit the telephone directory software without ever exiting WordPerfect.
5. Windows applications and DOS applications can be run simultaneously. You can even run multiple DOS programs and multiple Windows programs at the same time.
6. Several programs can be linked together. If you change data in one program, the same data in the other program will be changed automatically.
7. Windows allows better memory management. You are not restricted by 640 K, the traditional DOS barrier. Using Windows, you can use memory well beyond 640 K. Windows makes your hard disk an extension of your RAM. If a program does not fit into your RAM, it will simply spill over to your hard disk.
8. Accessory programs are free of charge. Windows comes with a group of accessories that are readily available to you free of charge:

[1] For a detailed discussion of Microsoft Windows, consult *Information Systems Literacy: Windows 3.1* by Hossein Bidgoli, published by Macmillan Publishing Company, 1993.

Table C–1
Unique Advantages of Windows

Ease of use.
Shared principles among Windows programs.
Use of mouse, keyboard, and shortcut keys.
Multitasking.
Ability to run Windows and DOS applications at the same time.
Linkage of several programs.
Better memory management.
Free accessories.
True WYSIWYG.

- Windows Write—a simple word processor
- Windows Paintbrush—a drawing program
- Windows Terminal—a communications program
- Windows Print Manager—a program that allows you to work and print at the same time
- Many more useful programs such as the Calculator, Calendar, Notepad, Cardfile, and the Clock
- True WYSIWYG Windows allows you to display on the screen exactly what will appear on the printed output. This is called What-You-See-Is-What-You-Get (WYSIWYG). Using this feature, you will have a pretty good idea of the output of an application before printing it.

The unique advantages of Windows are listed in Table C–1.

C–3 GETTING IN AND OUT OF WINDOWS

The first step is to install Windows on a hard disk system. Windows will not run on a floppy system. After installing Windows, switch to the drive and directory containing your Windows files by using the DOS CD command (e.g., type *CD WIN31* then press Enter); then type *WIN* and press Enter. You will be presented with a screen similar to the one shown in Figure C–1.

There are three methods that you can use to get out of Windows. The first is to move the mouse pointer to the File option at the upper left of the screen and click the left button of the mouse. You will be presented with a screen similar to the one shown in Figure C–2. Move the mouse pointer to the Exit Windows option and click the left button. The second method is to move the mouse pointer to the control-menu box at the extreme upper left of the screen and double-click the left button of the mouse. The third method is to move the mouse pointer to the control-menu box and click the left button once. You will be presented with a screen similar to the one shown in Figure C–3. Move the mouse pointer to the Close option and click the left button.

Regardless of which of these three methods you use, you will be presented with a screen similar to the one shown in Figure C–4. Move to OK and click the left button of the mouse to leave Windows. If you click while on Cancel, this indicates that you have changed your mind and you wish to stay in Windows. When you exit Windows you exit either to DOS or to your starting menu, depending on how you started Windows in the first place.

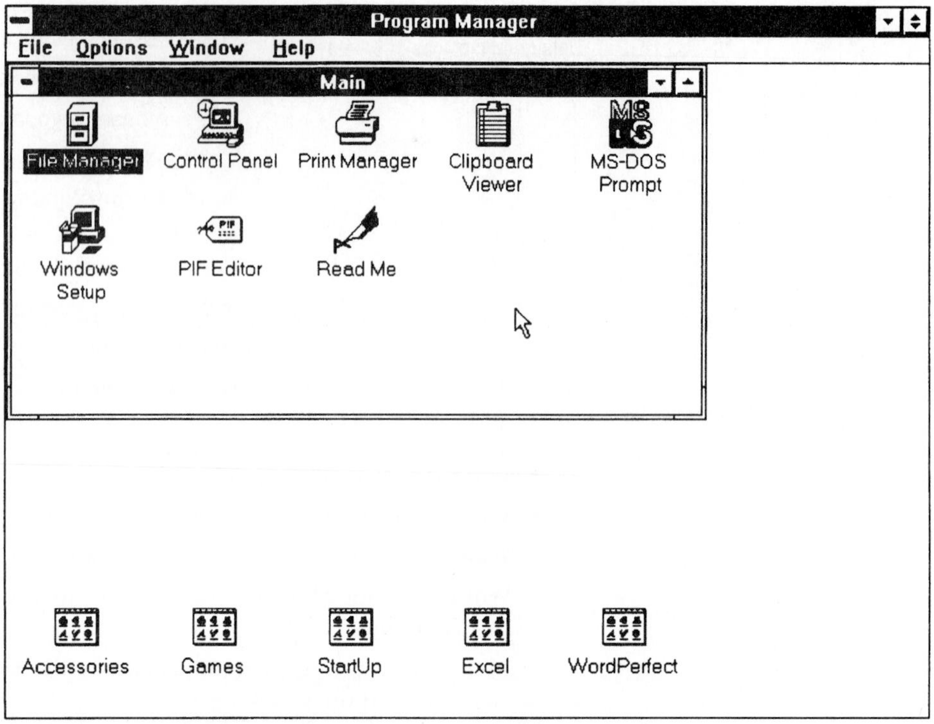

Figure C–1
Windows starting screen.

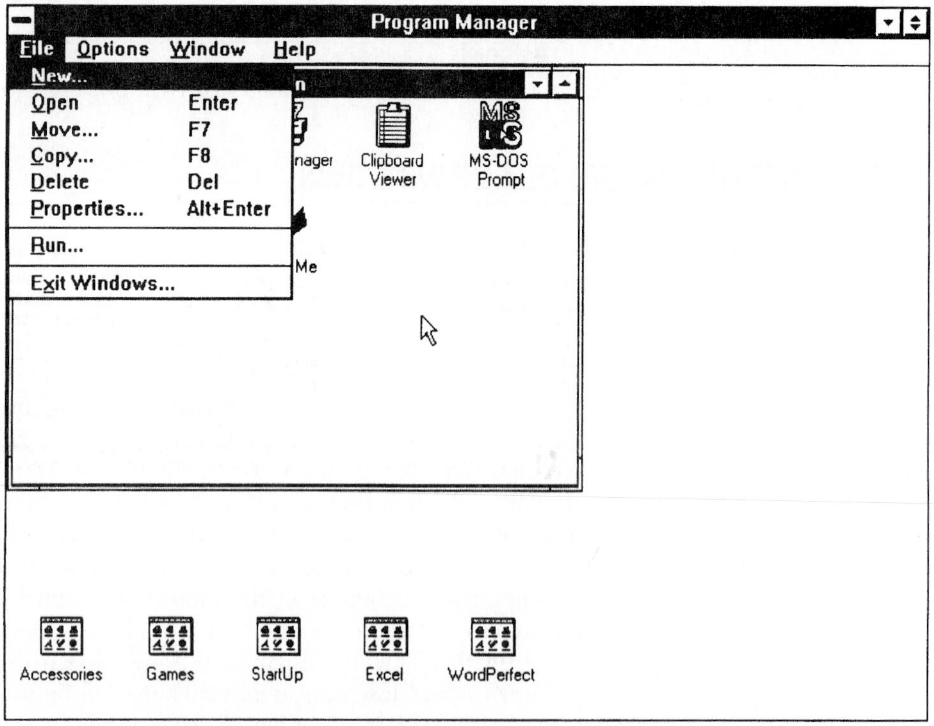

Figure C–2
File pull-down menu.

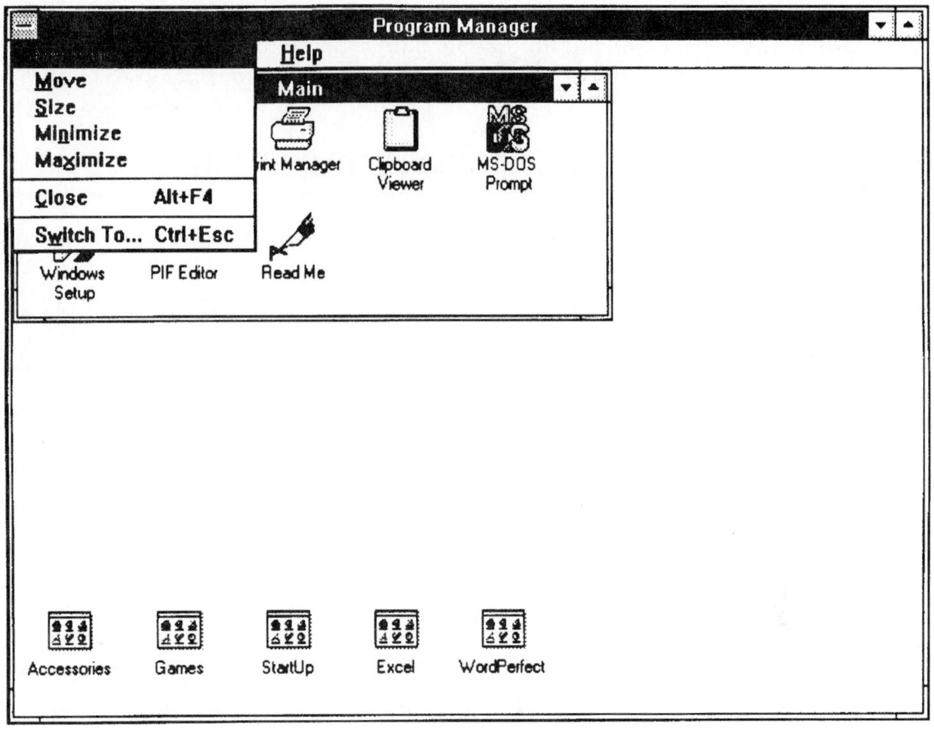

Figure C–3
Control-menu box options.

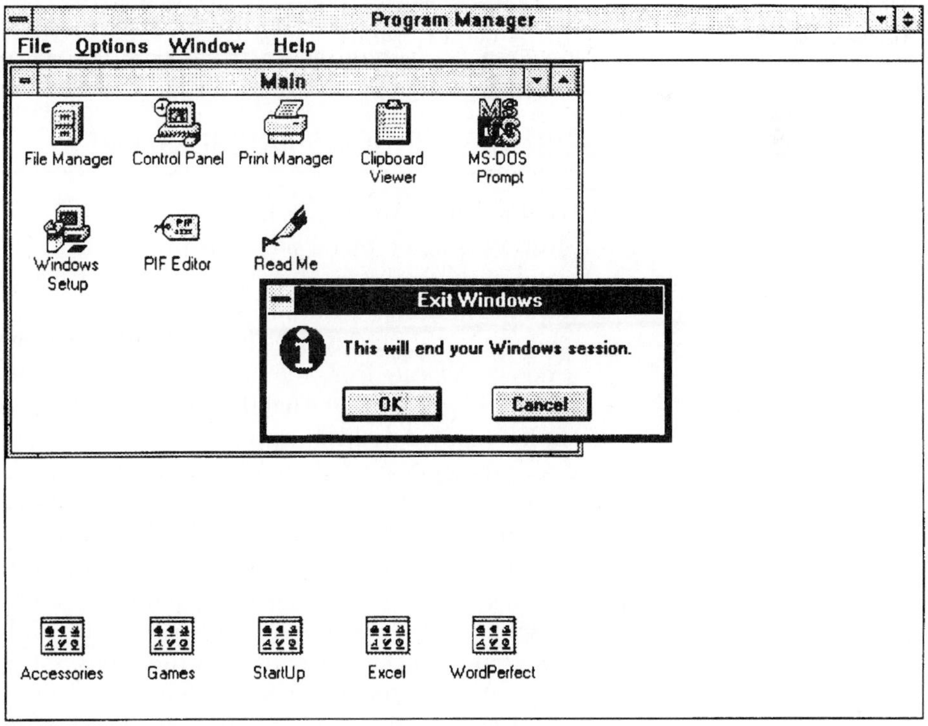

Figure C–4
Windows exit dialog box.

You can also use the keyboard to exit Windows. To do so, press Alt+F to open the File menu then either press the letter X or move the cursor to Exit Windows and press Enter. Press Enter again to exit Windows.

C–4 UNDERSTANDING WINDOWS TERMINOLOGY

Windows, just like other software, has its own terminology. Among the important terms are desktop, icon, and mouse. Let us briefly explain each.

Desktop in Windows is similar to the surface of a desk. All your Windows work takes place in the desktop. When you start Windows you start at the desktop. You can do a number of tasks from the desktop; among the most common tasks are the following:

- Fast application switching—going from one application software to another
- Icon spacing change—moving around the existing icons, deleting the unwanted ones, and so forth
- Displaying your document
- Changing colors

An icon is a graphic representation of an application or a document. You can move the mouse pointer to the desired application icon and double-click the left button of the mouse to start the application or open a document.

The mouse will be explained in detail in the next section. It is the main interface between you and Windows and Windows applications. Although you can use the keyboard or the shortcut keys, using the mouse is probably the most efficient way to accomplish most Windows tasks.

C–5 USING A MOUSE IN THE WINDOWS ENVIRONMENT

Windows offers three user interface options: keyboard, mouse, and shortcut keys. Most users agree that a mouse is preferable to a keyboard in graphical environments such as Windows because of its speed, accuracy, ease of use, and other special functions that it can provide. Using a mouse you can easily select pull-down menu options, quickly execute application programs, move and/or resize group windows, relocate icons to new locations on the screen, and much more.

If you are right handed, hold the mouse in your right hand, and if you are left handed, hold the mouse in your left hand. Place the mouse on a flat surface (preferably on the mouse pad) and rest your hand on top of it. Place your thumb on one side of the mouse and the two fingers on the opposite end of your hand on the other side. This will leave your index finger and middle finger positioned over the mouse buttons. Lightly rest your fingers on these buttons. To see how the mouse works, move the mouse in a circular motion and look on the screen for the mouse pointer. You will see that it is also moving in a circular pattern, matching the movements of the mouse. If you move the mouse to the left, the mouse pointer moves to the left side of the screen; if you move the mouse away from you, the mouse pointer moves to the top of the screen.

Now let's try selecting some menu items using the mouse. Move the mouse so that the mouse pointer is pointing to the File option at the upper left of the screen, click the left button of the mouse. If you have done this correctly, the File pull-down menu will be displayed (see Figure C–2). Move the mouse pointer

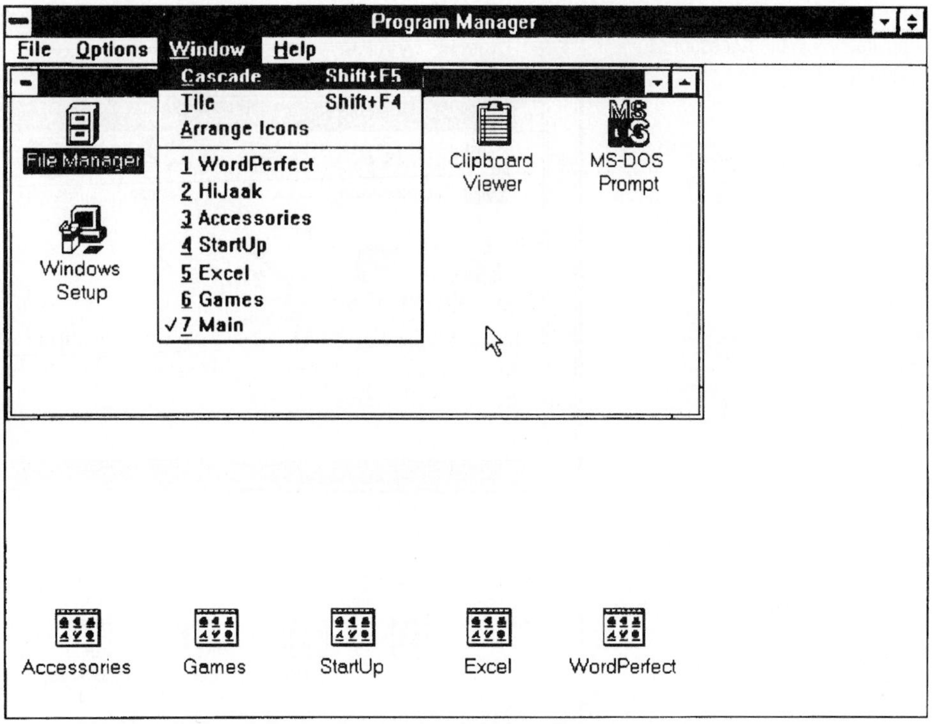

Figure C–5
Window pull-down menu.

to the Window option and click the left button again to display the Window pull-down menu (Figure C–5). Notice that positioning the mouse pointer and clicking the left button selects the desired menu item automatically. For now, move the mouse pointer back into the middle of the screen and click the left button to "deselect" any currently highlighted menu items.

Rapid double-clicking of the left button while pointing the mouse pointer onto an icon automatically executes the application that the icon represents. To see how this works, move the mouse pointer to the Accessories icon and double-click the left button. This automatically opens the Accessories window (Figure C–6). Now you can double-click on any of these options.

Let's try another example. Move the mouse pointer to the MS-DOS Prompt option in the Main group (see Figure C–1) and double-click the left button. Windows responds by displaying a DOS prompt. Type the command *EXIT* (press Enter) to return to the Windows main screen.

Finally, you can move windows, group icons, application icons, and so forth to other locations on the screen using a method called "click and drag." To try this, point the mouse pointer onto the title bar of the Main group window (see Figure C–1). Click the left button; then, while holding the button down, drag the mouse pointer to a new location on the screen. You will notice that an outline form of the Main group moves with the mouse pointer. Your window will be relocated to the position of the mouse pointer when you release the left button.

Let's try changing the size of the Main group window. Move the mouse pointer to the right edge of the Main group window. Notice that at a certain position over the edge of the window the mouse pointer becomes a double-pointing arrow. When you see this, click and drag a small distance to the right. Again notice the outline form; when you release the mouse button, your window will conform to the size you just constructed by dragging the mouse. If you change your mind before releasing the left button of the mouse, press the Esc key.

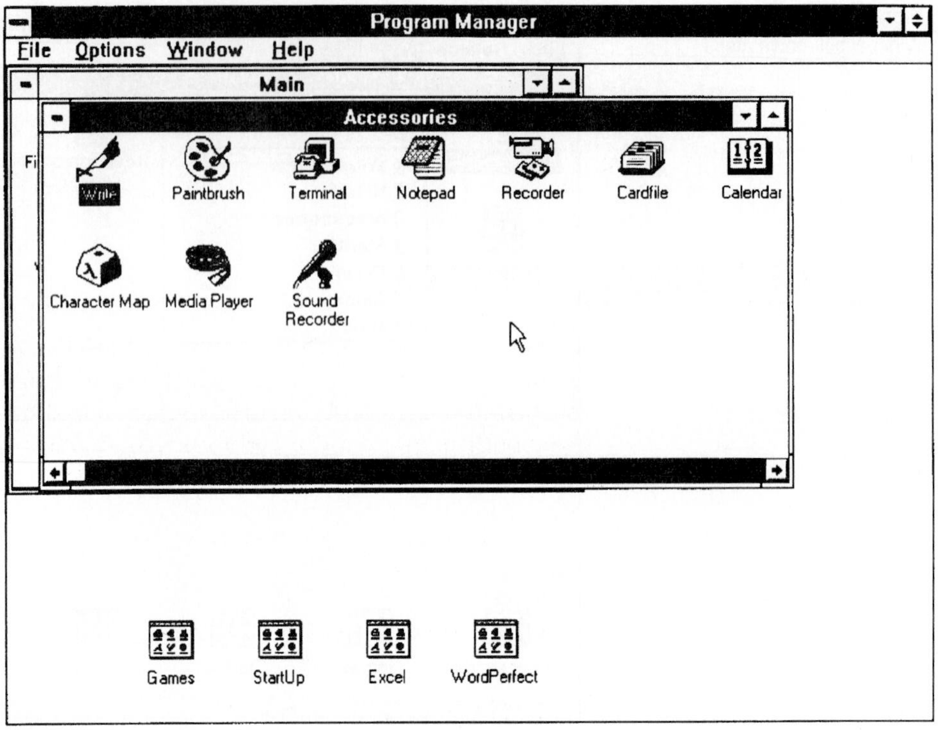

Figure C–6
Applications in the Accessories group.

As a final example of moving screen items to new locations, move the mouse pointer onto the MS-DOS Prompt option inside the Main group window. Click and drag the icon to a new location outside of the window, then release the left button of the mouse. The icon will obediently follow your command to position itself in a new location. For now, drag the icon back into the Main group window.

C–6 USING THE KEYBOARD IN A WINDOWS ENVIRONMENT

As mentioned, Windows and Windows programs allow use of the keyboard in addition to the mouse. Keyboards are comfortable for good typists, and since keyboards have been around for years, people are more familiar with them than with the mouse.

If you are working with Windows and want to use a keyboard, you may use one of the following areas of a keyboard:

- The typing keys located in the center of the keyboard. These keys are similar to the keys of a typewriter.
- The numeric and cursor movement keys located on the right side of the keyboard. Enhanced keyboards have a dedicated cursor movement pad. For standard keyboards, if you press the Num Lock key, the numeric pad serves as a 10-key machine for entering numbers. Cursor keys are used to move the cursor around.
- The function keys: F1 through F12 located across the top of the enhanced keyboard or F1 through F10 on the left side of the standard keyboard. All these keys perform different functions depending on the application program you are using.

Windows and Windows applications can also be accessed through the combination of keys called shortcut keys. The key-combination method always involves one of the following special keys—Shift, Alt, Ctrl—combined with another key. For example, Alt+F invokes the File menu. To use a key combination, first press either the Shift, Alt, or Ctrl key and hold it down; then press another key. In this appendix, the mouse is emphasized as the major Windows interface.

C–7 HELP FACILITIES OF WINDOWS

As you can see in Figure C–1, one of the options in the Program Manager is Help. The Program Manager, which is the heart of Windows, is used to start other applications and organize applications and files into groups. If you move the mouse pointer to the Help option and click the left button, you will see a screen similar to the one presented in Figure C–7. You can move the mouse pointer to any of these options and click the left button to execute the desired option. For example, if you click left on the Contents option, you will receive a screen similar to Figure C–8. As you can see in this figure, the Search option is available; it enables you to search for a particular topic. You can also select the Glossary option to generate an alphabetized listing of all the topics in Windows.

C–7–1 Tutorial Facility of Windows

If you select the Windows Tutorial option from the Help pull-down menu, you will be presented with a screen similar to Figure C–9. The tutorial provides an overview of Windows and mouse operations. If you have not used a mouse before, this tutorial is very helpful.

Figure C–7
Starting screen of the Help option.

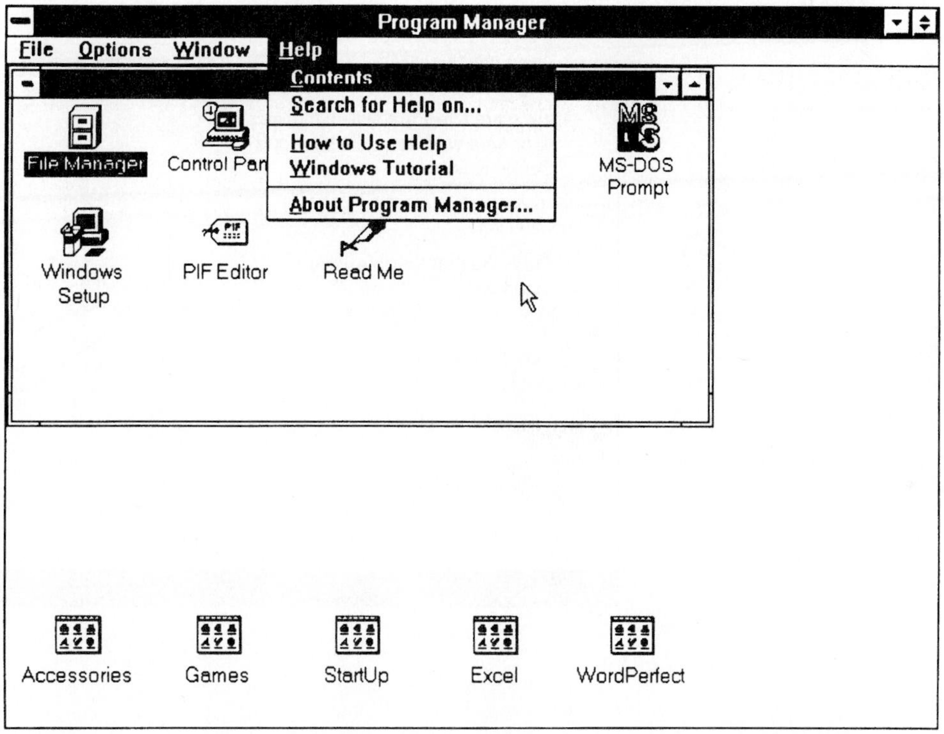

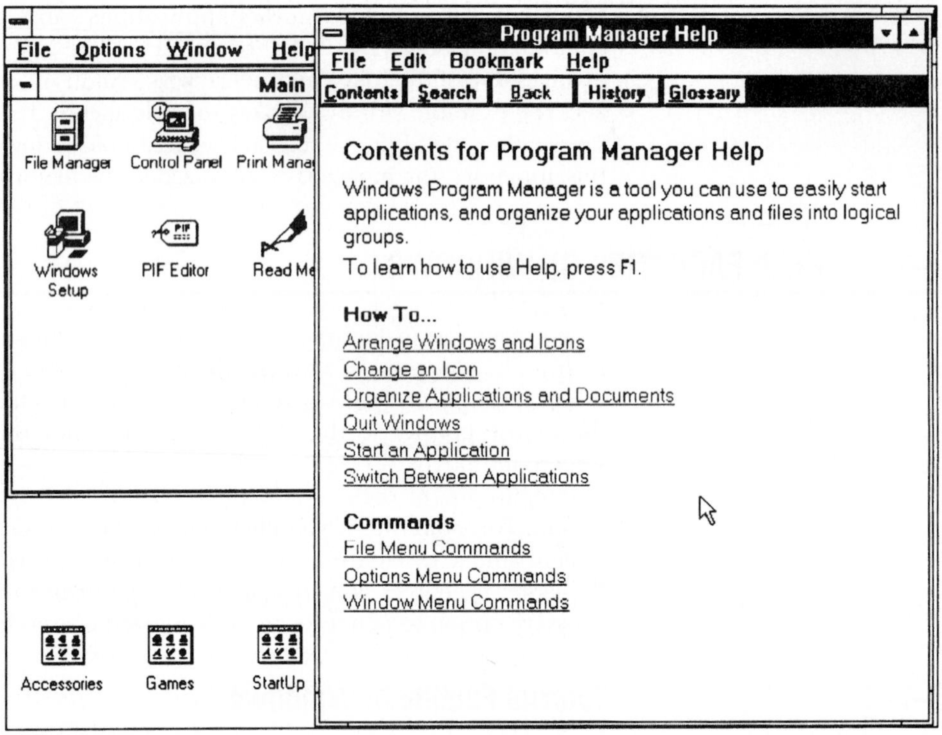

Figure C–8
Information under the Contents option of the Help menu.

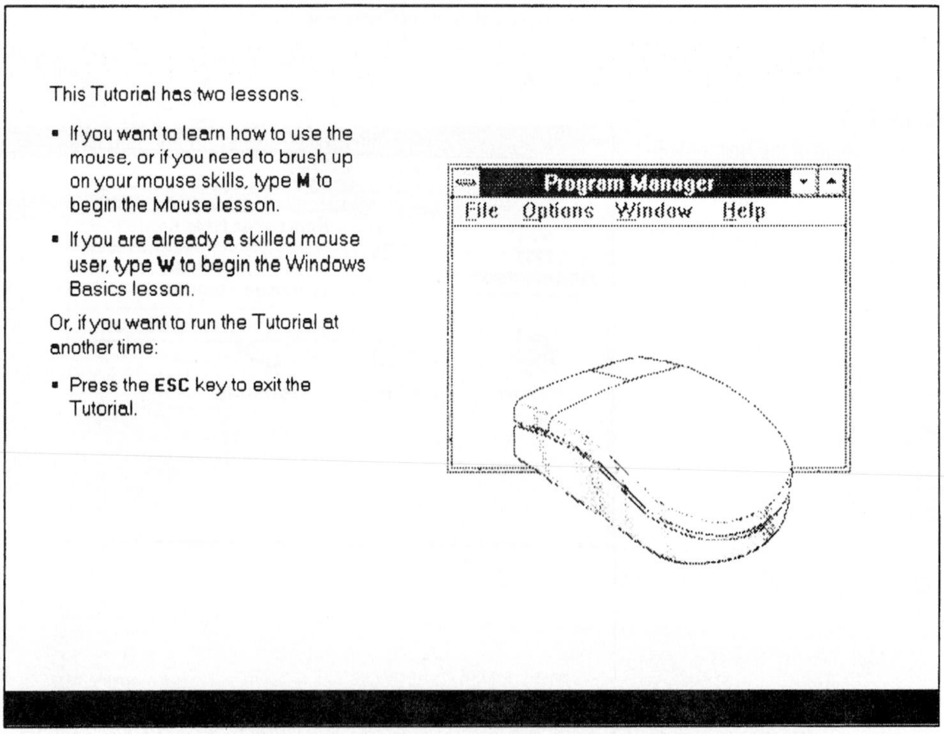

Figure C–9
Starting screen of the Windows tutorial.

C–8 DIFFERENT PARTS OF A WINDOWS SCREEN

Most Windows screens include the elements illustrated in Figure C–10. Refer to the figure as you read the following descriptions:

- The Window title (in the Title bar) is usually the name of the application, name of a document, or name of a file. In Figure C–1, the window title is Program Manager. In Figure C–10 the title is Notepad—[Untitled] because no document has been opened yet.
- The Control-menu box is at the upper left of each window. The control-menu box is very helpful if you are using the keyboard to work with Windows. By using control-menu commands, you can resize, move, maximize, minimize, close Windows, and switch to applications. If you use a mouse, you can perform all of the tasks just mentioned by clicking and dragging.
- Insertion point indicates the current position of the cursor at any given time in your document. Text and graphs will be inserted at this point. (Not shown in our figure.)
- The Menu bar lists available menu options. For example, in Figure C–1 the menu bar includes File, Options, Window, and Help. In Figure C–10, the menu bar includes File, Edit, Search, and Help.
- The Minimize button can reduce the window to an icon.
- The Maximize button can enlarge the active application window so that it fills the entire desktop. After you enlarge a window, the maximize button is

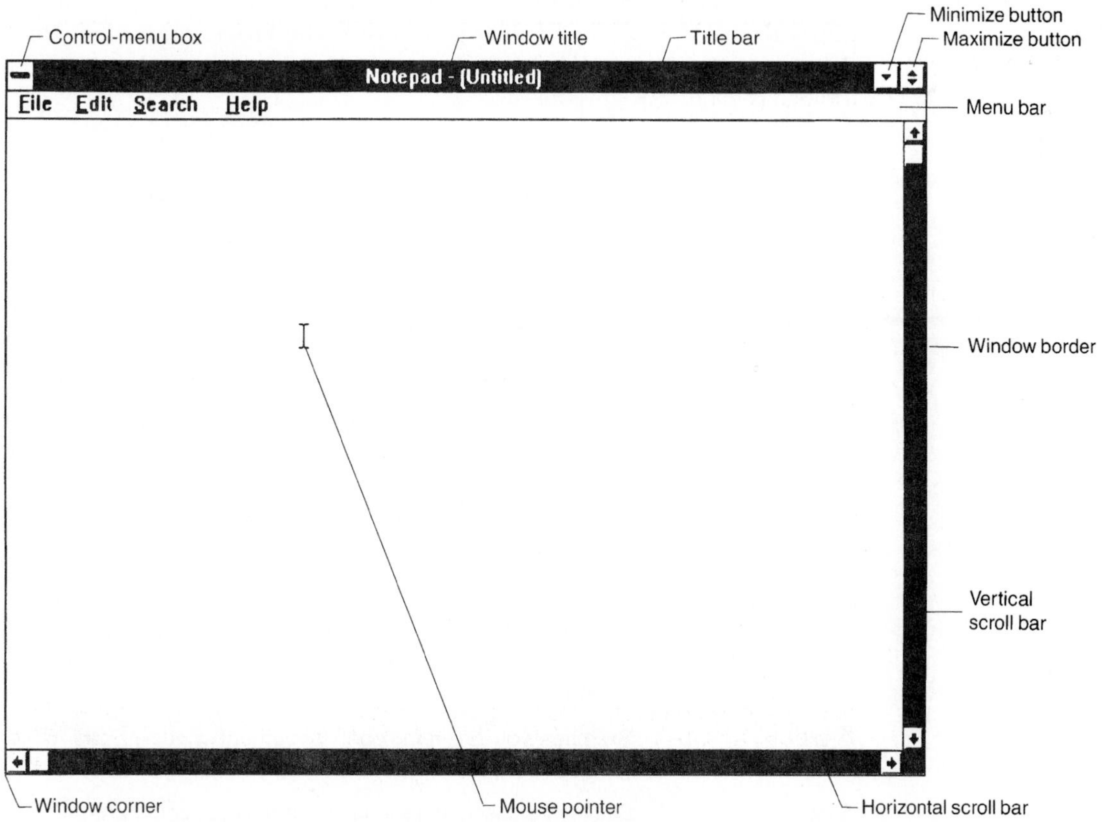

Figure C–10
Elements of the Windows screen.

replaced by the restore button. (This is the case in Figure C–10.) You can click the restore button to return a window to its previous size.

- The Window border is the outside edge of a window. You can lengthen or shorten the border on each side of a window.
- The Vertical and Horizontal scroll bars are used to view parts of a document that do not fit on the current screen.
- The Mouse pointer is a small arrow that moves on the screen corresponding to the movement of the mouse on your desktop. The mouse pointer changes to a double-pointed arrow when it is moved to the edge of a window.

C–8–1 Control Menu Commands

Table C–2 summarizes the control menu commands. Some applications do not have all of these commands. For example, Figure C–11 does not include all the commands outlined in Table C–2.

C–9 WHAT IS THE PROGRAM MANAGER?

As soon as you start Windows you start the Program Manager. The Program Manager always runs during a Windows session. As you will see later in this appendix, a variety of tasks can be performed through the Program Manager. When you run other applications, the Program Manager runs either in the background or as an icon on your desktop.

When you first start Windows the Program Manager opens on your desktop with the Main group window open inside the Program Manager window (see Figure C–12). This may be different from your system, depending upon how Windows has been configured.

Table C–2
Control Menu Commands

Command	Function
Restore	Restores the window to its former size after you have enlarged it (by using the Maximize command) or reduced it to an icon (by using the Minimize command).
Move	Uses the keyboard to move a window to another location.
Size	Uses the keyboard to change the size of a window.
Minimize	Reduces a window to an icon.
Maximize	Enlarges a window to its maximum size.
Close	Closes a window or a dialog box. You can also use this command to quit an application from an application window.
Switch To	Opens the task list. This features enables you to switch between running applications. It also arranges windows and icons on your desktop.
Next	Switches you between open document windows and icons. This is available for document windows only.
Edit	Displays a cascading menu with additional commands.

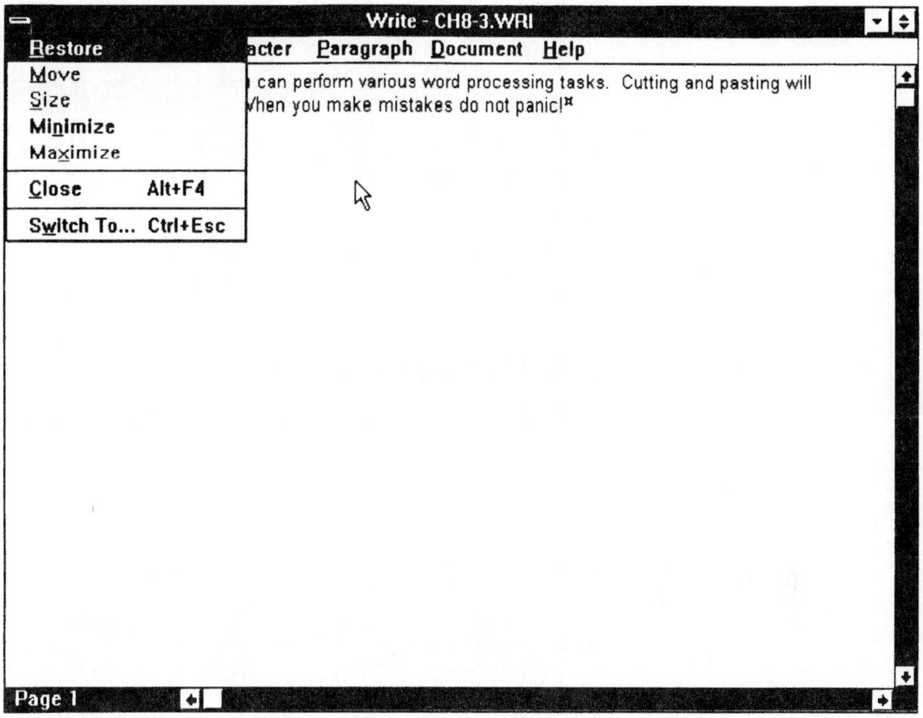

Figure C–11
Control menu options.

The Accessories group, the Games group, the StartUp group, and applications groups are represented as group icons along the lower border of the Program Manager window (see Figure C–12). Your screen might be slightly different from what is presented in Figure C–12.

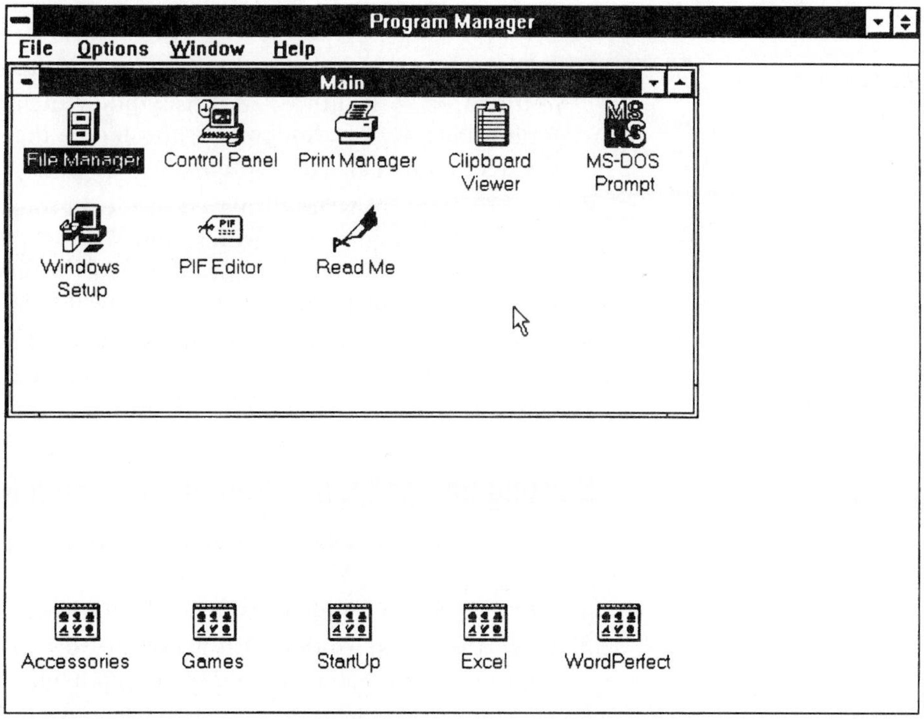

Figure C–12
Program Manager window.

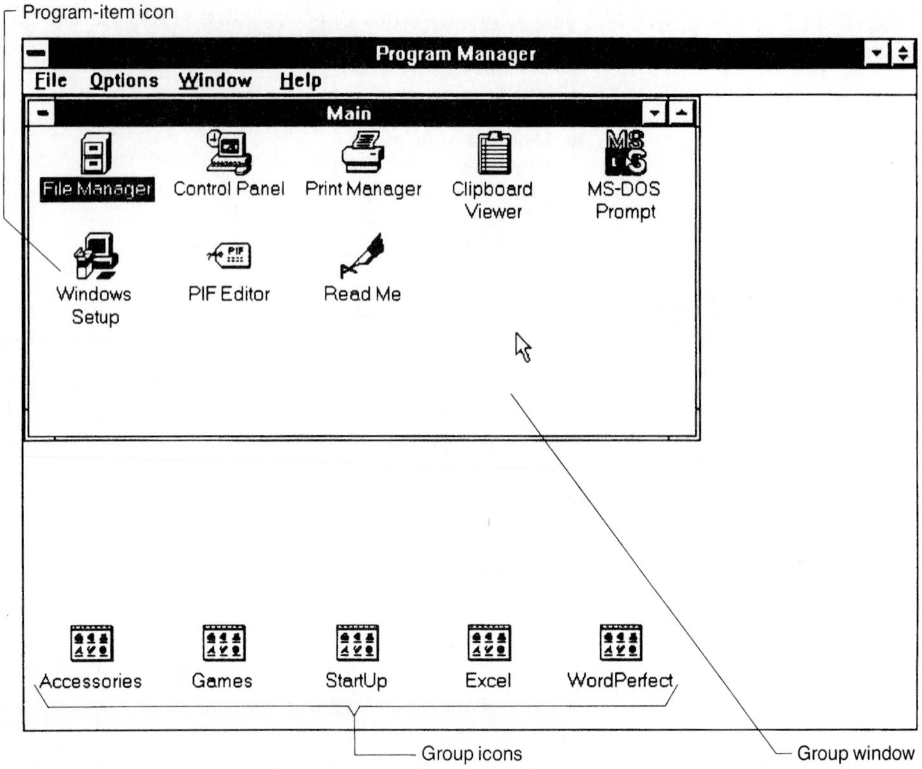

Figure C–13
Different parts of the Program Manager window.

C–9–1

Different Parts of the Program Manager Window

Refer to Figure C–13 as you read the following descriptions of the different parts of the Program Manager window:

- Group window is a separate window inside the Program Manager window. As you can see in Figure C–13, this window includes icons that start different applications. Group windows are affected by the commands from the Program Manager menu bar: File, Options, Window, and Help.
- Program-item icons are displayed inside a group window and represent applications, documents, accessories, and so forth. You can select program item icons to start particular applications. For example, you can double-click the File Manager icon to start it.
- Group icon is a minimized group window. These icons are displayed in the lower border of the Program Manager window. Figure C–13 shows five of these icons.

C–9–2

Starting an Application from the Program Manager

Use the mouse and follow these steps to start an application:

1. Open the Program Manager Window (if it is not already open).
2. Open the group window (if it is not already open) that includes your desired application by double-clicking the group icon.
3. Double-click the icon for your desired application.

C–10 RUNNING TWO OR MORE APPLICATIONS AT THE SAME TIME

Windows allows you to run more than one application at one time. When you run multiple applications at the same time, the processing speed may be slower than normal. Processing speed also depends on the type of computer that you are using. To start several applications, start them in the desired sequence using the method that we just discussed.

C–11 SWITCHING BETWEEN APPLICATIONS

When you are running more than one application at a time, the window in which you are currently working is called the active window. The active window appears in the foreground. It might overlap or completely block other application windows that are also running on your system. To make another application active, you must select its window.

To switch between applications, you can choose one of the following methods:

1. If the application is visible, click the mouse anywhere in the application's window. If the application is running as an icon, click left on its icon, then click left on the Restore option.
2. Press Alt+Esc repeatedly to navigate through all the open application windows and icons. When you see the desired one, press Enter.
3. Display Task List by pressing the Ctrl+Esc keys. You will be presented with a screen similar to the one displayed in Figure C–14. In the Task List window, double-click the name of the desired application or highlight the name of the desired application and then select Switch To from the options available in the dialog box.

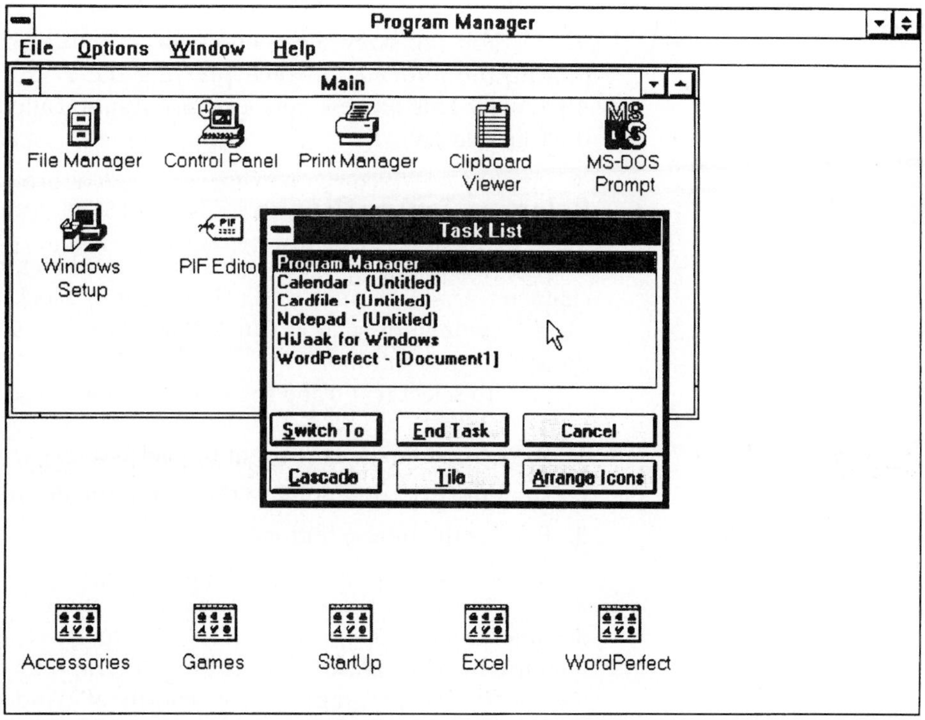

Figure C–14
Task List dialog box.

To return to the application that you last used, press Alt+Tab.

C–12 TRANSFERRING INFORMATION USING THE CLIPBOARD

The Windows Clipboard serves as a temporary location that stores information. Using the Clipboard, you can copy or move information from one application and then copy ("paste") it in another application. The information that you copy to the Clipboard stays there until you clear the contents of the Clipboard or copy other information to it.

The Clipboard can also serve as a buffer for exchanging information among several applications.

C–12–1 Moving or Copying Information to the Clipboard

How information is moved or copied to the Clipboard depends on the type of application that you are running—a Windows application or a non-Windows application. It also depends on whether your application is running as a window or a full screen.

A Windows application allows you to easily move or copy information to the Clipboard. You can also move or copy an image to the Clipboard. To copy or move information to the Clipboard, follow these steps:

1. Highlight or select the text or the information that you want to move or copy. (For highlighting text, see the next section.) You can copy or move text, graphics, or both.
2. From the application's Edit menu (e.g., the Edit menu of Lotus 1-2-3), select Cut or Copy. Cut removes the selected text from its current position to the Clipboard. Copy only takes a snapshot for the Clipboard; the existing information remains intact.

You can copy the contents of an entire screen to the Clipboard by displaying the information then pressing the Print Screen key or Shift+PrtSc or Alt+PrtSc. This process puts a snapshot (also called a bitmap) of the screen onto the Clipboard.

C–12–2 Selecting Text or Graphs

Editing commands can be performed on a block of text instead of on a single character. First you must select (highlight or block) the text. Then you can select various commands such as Cut, Copy, Bold, and so forth from the Edit menu of the application software.

To select text using the mouse, follow these steps:

1. Point to the first character of the desired text.
2. Drag the insertion point to the end of the desired text.
3. Release the mouse button.

To cancel the selection, click the mouse button again anywhere in the document. Some applications allow you to select a word by double-clicking it, a sentence by triple-clicking, an entire paragraph by quadruple-clicking, and so on.

To select a graph in the majority of Windows applications, you can click left on it.

C–12–3 Transferring Information from the Clipboard

To transfer the contents of the Clipboard to another application, follow these steps:

1. Start the desired application.
2. Position the insertion point at the place that you want the information from the Clipboard to appear.
3. From the Edit menu of the application (e.g., the Edit menu of Lotus 1-2-3), select Paste.

C–13 QUITTING AN APPLICATION

When you are done working with an application, you should exit from it. Use one of the following methods to exit a Windows application:

- Select Exit from the application's File menu.
- Select Close from the Control menu.
- Double-click the control-menu box.
- Press Alt+F4.

To quit a non-Windows application, select the application's Exit or Quit command.

C–14 WORKING WITH GROUPS

Figure C–15 shows groups containing program-item icons that represent applications, accessories, or documents. To start an application from a group, you have to select the application's icon. As you can see in Figure C–15, Windows includes several predefined groups as follows:

1. The Main group contains Windows system applications:
   - File Manager—manages your files and disk drives
   - Control Panel—allows you to change the configuration of your system
   - Print Manager—allows you to install and configure printers
   - Clipboard Viewer—allows you to view, edit, and save the contents of the Clipboard
   - MS-DOS Prompt—allows you to exit to the DOS prompt
   - Windows Setup—displays the system configuration
   - PIF Editor—is a tool for editing program information files
   - Read Me—includes basic information about Windows
2. The Accessories group includes several interesting applications such as word processing, drawing, painting, communications, and so forth.
3. The Games group includes several games that you can use for learning the basics of Windows or for fun.
4. The StartUp group contains applications that start when you start Windows. This group is empty until you add applications to it. You can add any application to the group.

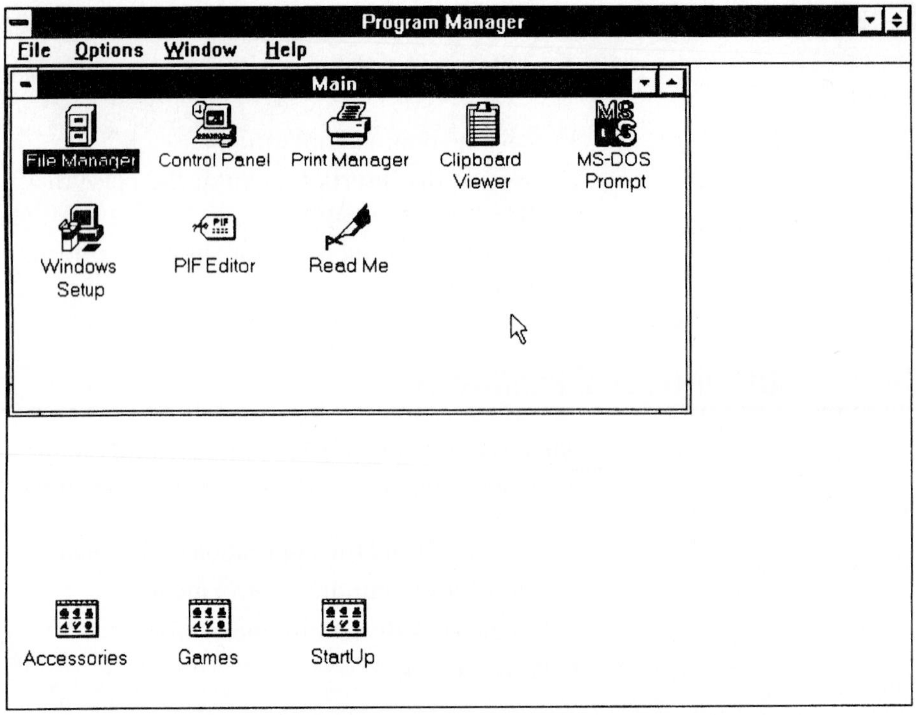

Figure C–15
Example of groups.

5. The Applications group contains applications found on the hard disk during setup. If you select the custom setup, and select not to have Windows set up applications from your hard disk, your Program Manager window will not contain an Applications group. This is the case in our example.

C–14–1 Opening a Group Window

To start an application you must first open its window then select the appropriate program-item icon. To open a group window double-click the group icon.

SUMMARY

This appendix provided an overview of Windows operating system. The advantages of Windows as a graphics-based environment were highlighted. After the process of getting in and getting out of Windows was explained, some of the basic features of Windows were discussed: using the mouse, selecting from the Windows screen, using the Program Manager, running an application, working with the Clipboard, and working with a group.

REVIEW QUESTIONS

1. What are some of the advantages of Windows?
2. How do you start Windows? How do you exit from it?
3. What is a desktop? What is an icon?
4. How do you use the mouse in Windows environment? How do you use the keyboard? Which one is easier to use?
5. How do you receive online help in Windows?
6. How do you get the tutorial facility of Windows started?

7. What is the control menu? How do you activate it?
8. What are some of the commands in the control menu?
9. What is the Program Manager?
10. How do you start an application from the Program Manager?
11. How can you run more than one application in Windows at the same time?
12. How do you switch between applications?
13. What is the Clipboard?
14. How do you transfer information from an application to the Clipboard?
15. How do you quit an application?
16. What is a group? How do you start a group?

Index

ISBN 0-02-309514-8
90000>
9 780023 095146